Death Orders

Death Orders

The Vanguard of Modern Terrorism in Revolutionary Russia

Anna Geifman

Praeger Security International

AN IMPRINT OF ABC-CLIO, LLC
Santa Barbara, California • Denver, Colorado • Oxford, England

Library of Congress Cataloging-in-Publication Data

Geifman, Anna, 1962–
Death orders : the vanguard of modern terrorism in revolutionary Russia / Anna Geifman.
p. cm.
Includes bibliographical references and index.
ISBN 978-0-275-99752-6 (alk. paper) — ISBN 978-0-275-99753-3 (ebk.)
1. Terrorism—Russia—History. 2. Political violence—Russia—History. I. Title.
HV6433.R8G45 2010
363.3250947'09041—dc22 2010006611

ISBN: 978-0-275-99752-6
EISBN: 978-0-275-99753-3

14 13 12 11 10 1 2 3 4 5

This book is also available on the World Wide Web as an eBook.

Visit www.abc-clio.com for details.

Praeger
An Imprint of ABC-CLIO, LLC

ABC-CLIO, LLC
130 Cremona Drive, P.O. Box 1911
Santa Barbara, California 93116-1911

This book is printed on acid-free paper ∞

Manufactured in the United States of America

For my son and my daughter—may they not know terror; may they choose life.

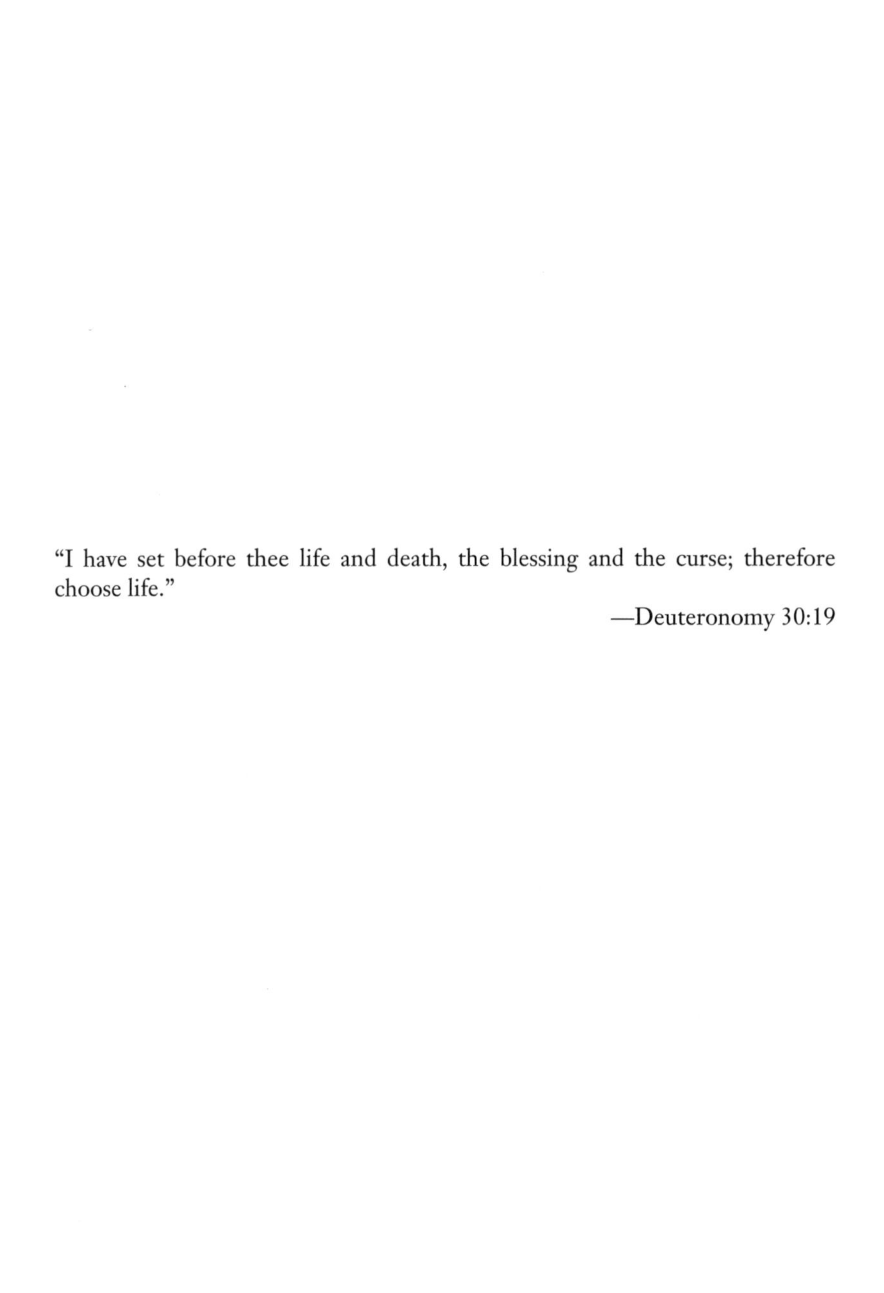

"I have set before thee life and death, the blessing and the curse; therefore choose life."

—Deuteronomy 30:19

Contents

Preface

I have written this book after having researched and published on the topic of modern terrorism for 25 years. As a student of the Russian radical tradition and the 1917 revolution, I initially focused on political violence in early 20th-century Russia and then extended my investigation into the Soviet period. Subsequently, my professional interest in psychohistorical methodologies led me to explore psychological incentives for aggressive behavior and ideologically motivated hostility, as they evinced themselves in the Russian political setting. Patterns of fundamentalist brutality for the sake of all-encompassing utopian and millennial causes gradually emerged; they appeared to transcend the framework of a specific culture, crossing the temporal, geographical, and ethnic boundaries. My research thus guided me to ask questions related to the universality of contemporary terrorist practices and to apply psychohistorical means of inquiry to modern and postmodern terrorism in various parts of the world, particularly the Middle East.

When in the mid-1980s I began working on political extremism, terrorism was an important academic matter and occasionally a sensational news item but by no means a pressing political issue or a primary topic of public debate—as difficult as that is to believe today. Over the years, the main arguments of this book took shape against the background of the escalating threat of fundamentalist violence. I have lived in areas affected by terrorism; for me, its repercussions have become part of personal experience, as it did for millions of people worldwide. My general thesis and central points of contention crystallized as I researched, published, taught, and discussed my work with colleagues, students, and friends, some of whom were also victims of terrorist brutality. With their intellect, erudition, intuition, emotional knowledge, and technical skill, they all have helped shape this book, rendering it truly a collective effort:

I am especially indebted to my friends Levi Glozman, who read drafts of the manuscript and offered most intelligent criticism, and Lilya Finkel, who edited the first version of the text. My colleagues Golda Akhiezer, Moshe Hazani, Paul Hollander, Richard Landes, Cathal Nolan, and Jeffrey Woolf have contributed useful comments for improving various chapters, as did Iosef Arbeli, Tamar Hayrikyan, Andrea Mosterman, and Helena Rimon. Amanda Scobie and Grace Hoffman were excellent research assistants.

I am grateful to my Boston University students in the Russian Revolution and Psychohistory seminars: they were eager to discuss my research, posed excellent questions, time and again giving me an opportunity to refine the arguments.

At various stages of writing, the following people supported me with their genuine concern with the subject, suggestions, and encouragement: first and foremost Julia Segal, as well as Larisa Amir, Aaron and Ruth Belostotsky, Zbysek Brezina, Vera Brofman, Michael Brook, Tim Crane; Ilan Danjoux, Cookie Diestel, Aleksey Dynkin, Haviva Eliasian; Ran Farhi, Daniel Goldenberg, Moshe Goncharok, John Haule; Moshe Hemein, Yitzchak and Talia Imas, Gene Itkis, Ariel Kogan, Alexander Kolotov, Genya Kraytsberg, Tatyana Leonova, Anna and Vladimir Lerner, Haim Levitsky, Nona Lukina, Greg Margolin, Liuba Musko, Pinchas Polonsky, Leonid Praisman, Alex Riman, Alex Rybalov, Marina Salganik, Eliezer Shargorodsky, Eleonora Shifrin, Elana Sirota, Gidalia Spinadel, Marina Suslov, David Tolioupov, Mikhail Vaiskopf, Nechama Wells, and Monika Zitkova.

The Boston University Graduate School of Arts and Sciences funded my research-related travel, for which I would like to express my gratitude. I am sincerely thankful for the financial support from the Lady Davis Fellowship at the Hebrew University. I owe a special debt to Mark Sopher, Executive Secretary of the Trust, for his generosity with advice and encouragement; his friendship and thoughtful kindness facilitated my work in Jerusalem enormously. My research in Israel was supported by the Kamea fellowship, and I gratefully acknowledge this unique opportunity.

While I was writing this book, my whole family, and especially my sister, has been there for me—patient and caring, but no one has influenced my attitude toward terror more than my father, of blessed memory. By word and personal example he taught an essential skill for upholding life—never to give in to fear.

Introduction

> History must be written of, by and for the survivors
>
> —Anonymous

> While nothing is easier than to denounce the evildoer, nothing is more difficult than to understand him.
>
> —Fedor Dostoevsky

Demolition of a structure is an elaborate task, requiring thought and effort. Razing a building or bridge entails knowledge about the complicated arrangement of its parts—ways in which components are put together and kept in place as a unified whole. A demolisher worthy of his name needs to be able to locate a focal point of the whole configuration and then obliterate connections between essential elements that uphold the edifice. Damage is not definitive if it affects the framework's peripheral building blocks rather than the hub of the construction—infinitely more so when that construction is an intricate sociocultural design and, as it happens to be, the object of demolition via state-of-the-art terrorism.

Effectively to achieve its ends, terrorism must strike at the central nerve system of the collective organism it seeks to annihilate. Conspicuously, it disrupts the proper functioning of the government and public institutions; subtly, it also impacts less perceptible aspects of the societal layout, deeply and in multifaceted fashion. The most extreme form of guided brutality, terrorism impinges on the psychological context of a culture under attack. More elusively, it targets the core ethical values and spiritual grounding, those essential, if invisible, bonds that link and maintain the colossal structure of contemporary life.

"The struggle to define terrorism is sometimes as hard as the struggle against terrorism itself," notes Israeli scholar Boaz Ganor, executive director of the International Institute for Counter-Terrorism, referring to 109 scholarly classifications of terror. In a valuable attempt to outline the terms of discussion, Ganor discards the notorious cliché, "One man's terrorist is another man's freedom fighter," which emphasizes that "all depends on the perspective and the worldview of the one doing the defining." Nor is it helpful to bracket the term "terrorism" together with such designations as "guerrilla warfare" or "revolutionary struggle." This approach obscures the issues and confounds the means of the perpetrators with their justifications. Ambiguity of terms may also serve to legitimize the terrorists' methods. Thus, Yasser Arafat's deputy Salah Khalef (Abu Iyad), a leader of Fatah (Palestinian National Liberation Movement) and Black September, responsible for numerous lethal attacks, swore that he was firmly opposed to terrorism, which, he claimed, must not be confused with *de rigueur* belligerence. Likewise, Syrian President Hafez al-Assad has repeatedly denied that his country assisted terrorist conceding that it did support armed "struggle against occupation."[1] However, ample proof incriminates Assad's regime in sponsoring terror outside the "Arab arena," most frequently in Israel and Europe.[2]

To escape "a semantic trap" laid by the extremists and their allies, Ganor defines terrorism as "the intentional use of, or threat to use violence against civilians or against civilian targets, in order to attain political aims." Non-political homicide is an example of "criminal delinquency, a felony, or … insanity," unrelated to terror. It is distinguished from other forms of organized aggression, such as civil insurrection or guerrilla warfare, because it recognizes no ethical limits while exploiting "the tremendous anxiety, and the intense media reaction evoked by attacks against civilian targets." The key word here is "intentional," as opposed to accidental injury inflicted on noncombatants. A collateral damage to nonbelligerents is not terrorism, if it is incurred while aiming at the military.[3]

A hallmark of terror, which escalated over the past century, is that its objectives have degenerated from punishment of individual adversaries and attempts to coerce the privileged to indiscriminate cruelty and carried out *en masse*. In fact, those who die are not primary targets. We can thus infer that the terrorists perpetrate their random "public symbolic violence"[4] and its devastating emotional effect on the observers, who have not been physically implicated in the episode of bloodshed—"to spread fear in a population larger than that actually affected."[5]

"Dissertations will be written about the euphemisms" the media employed to describe scores of "insurgents," "separatists," and "hostage-takers."[6] Prior to 9/11, the dominant historiographical tendency was to depict terrorists as protectors of the downtrodden and altruist combatants against economic exploitation.[7] More recently, scholars took for granted violence against foreign oppression, promoting the radical Left myth of terrorism as a response to colonization, the U.S. presence in distant lands, and other West-imposed injustices. The diluted Marxist arguments, although hardly corroborated by evidence, are often accepted blindly as soothing explications; they render terrorism "explainable," "logical," and almost "normal."[8] Yet, the labels of "freedom fighters" or "nationalist rebels" do nil to elucidate underlying drives or common traits discernable beneath the disparity of goals and creeds.

I do not aim to present an all-inclusive analysis of terror. In this book, it is defined as "violence or its threat intended as a symbolically communicative act in which the direct victims of the action are instrumentalised as a means to creating a psychological effect of intimidation ... in a target audience for a political objective."[9] I am concerned primarily with prototypes of terrorism perpetrated by the proverbial "true believers," portrayed by Eric Hoffer as representatives of *totalitarian or proto-totalitarian, fanatic movements.* These violent factions and networks differ in their doctrines, but all "appeal to the same types of mind" of a dogma-driven zealot. As outlined in Hoffer's classic book, *The True Believer*, such movements have mastered the art of "religiofication," that is, converting concrete grievances into messianic aspirations and "practical purposes into holy causes."[10] They operate within distinctive parameters of a "theology of Armageddon—a final battle between good and evil," in which at stake is no less than universal salvation.[11]

Terrorism as a variant of "totalism,"[12] whose devotees—anarchists, Marxists, or Islamists—are actively engaged in recasting their milieu in accordance with their "all-or-nothing claim to truth." The totalistic thinking is characterized by intellectual and ethical rigidity, and "simplistic once-and-for-all resolution of problems, so as to eliminate unbearable ambiguities" and to fulfill a vision of remodeling environment. In this sense, terrorists' intentions—acknowledged, as well as hidden—are of major importance.[13]

I hope to delineate the psychohistorical blueprint intrinsic to a specific variety of "adventuristic, annihilatory" terror that originated in the first decade of the 20th century.[14] It escalated and intensified over the hundred years—to emerge, by the dawn of the new millennium, as one of the greatest threats we face today. This mode of structured violence has disengaged from a particular social context and accumulated destructive energy. It transcends an impetuous rejoinder to detrimental socioeconomic circumstances or adherence to a militant doctrine. Its key facets manifest themselves globally, rather than in an isolated culture or geographical location. They emerge during far removed eras, entailing a complex mindset and collective behavior typologies of totalism or fundamentalism.

The primary setting of this book is late imperial and early Soviet Russia—a birthplace of the new type of violence. Insurrectionists had killed their adversaries long before the 1900s, of course, but the inimitable terror campaign to which I am referring was essentially different from assassinations that had occurred elsewhere. In Russia, terrorist routines revealed some foremost attributes of the modern and postmodern fanaticism. Indeed, intercontinental terrorism of the last 50 years "continued the tradition of its turn-of-the-century forebears."[15] As difficult as it may be to conjecture the full-grown monster in an embryonic form, most of its obscure, underdeveloped, yet horrid features were already there.

Having since been the focal points of violence replicated worldwide, key elements of extremism may serve as archetypes, exposing similar aspects of terror in other periods and regions. Its uncanny nature is further underlined by the fact that such diverse movements, one avowedly atheist, the other fanatically devout, share so many similarities. By bringing together history, psychology, and ethnic studies, this book adopts an intercultural and interdisciplinary methodology and highlights behavioral analogies in terrorist activity during the past decades.

"If you would understand anything, observe its beginning and its development," says Aristotle. We can gain a great deal by looking deeply to see why and how terrorism evolved. By scrutinizing the Russian precedent, the book seeks to illuminate the numerous obscure facets of fundamentalist terrorism that may be comprehended more clearly from a temporal distance.

Professional literature on terrorism is gigantic. Scholars ask theoretical questions; for instance, whether available data warrants speculations about a "terrorist personality" predisposed for aggression. There is an equally extensive scholarship on local and international terrorist trends—from militant nihilism to radical Islamism. This book incorporates a representative body of sources and relies predominantly on primary documents and secondary works that focus on salient patterns of contemporary fundamentalism.

* * *

On September 1, 2004, amid the annual festivities across Russia on the "Day of Knowledge," at least 32 heavily armed, masked terrorists had detained 1,200 children, their relatives, and their teachers inside School No. 1 in the town of Beslan in North Ossetia. Vague television reports broadcast "snapshots of horror-stricken parents waiting and praying in the schoolyard. Hours passed in fruitless negotiations." They reached a stalemate after the captors requests for hostages to receive food and medications from the outside."[16]

Within hours, a girl with diabetes passed away in her teachers' arms. Many others had begun hallucinating. The youngest fainted and had seizures. The terrorists did not allow any medical help. "Dying? Let him die. We are the terrorists, we're here to slay," the captors retorted to pleas for a drop of water for a boy who was unconscious.[17]

On September 3, several blasts shook the school. As the "security forces were making their way inside the burning building, amid smoke, screams, and confusion, cameras followed half-naked boys and girls jumping out of windows and running to safety." They ran for their lives, while terrorists methodically shot them in the back from the rooftop.[18]

On television screens frantic mothers and fathers could be seen rushing about, looking for their kids, weeping with relief or sorrow, grabbing and hugging them, alive or dead. Casualty estimates soared, multiplying with every passing hour. Altogether, at least 334 were killed, among them 186 children; over 700 were wounded.

Images of armed men shooting point-blank at boys and girls stripped of their clothes stir terror and terrible memories. Where have we previously encountered defenseless nakedness and the stunningly composed, otherworldly faces? The ash- and blood-covered bodies looked so skinny as if after a long captivity. The ruins of that school, where hundreds of prisoners suffered from unbearable heat and dozens perished in flames, were not just the site of another terrorist act; they became "a symbol of mass homicide, akin to the chimneys of Auschwitz."[19]

* * *

As a historian of political violence, I have dealt with death in all colors, shapes, and forms. Research involved reading mounds of records about "oppressors and exploiters" torn to pieces in bomb explosions. Archival photographs of faces disfigured by the sulfuric acid recount dreadful stories of extremists projecting deep hatred and punishing "despicable traitors" and designated enemies. I had been studying terrorism for 25 years and presumed to understand the rules of this deadly game until I received a letter from a friend in Moscow about the Beslan massacre—fatefully on the third anniversary of 9/11. What happened in this tiny town in North Ossetia "is horrendous and utterly incomprehensible," she wrote:

> When it all began, I started calling my folks in Vladikavkaz to find out if anyone we knew was trapped... Beslan is only 30 km away.... My brother Alan said that his friend's wife and two sons, 8 and 11, were there.... This man's wife left her 3-month-old daughter with a neighbor—just for an hour, till the next feeding—and took the boys to school...
>
> On September 3rd, when everything was over, I got in touch with Alan again; he'd called Tamik (that's the guy's name)... Both boys were O.K.: he'd found the older one, who said that his brother was safe and sound; he had just run home. Since Tamik's wife was wounded and hospitalized, he hurried to the hospital....
>
> But... when Tamik returned... he found only his older son at home. And when he started asking him where his brother was, he realized that the boy was in a state of profound shock. He was dazed and confused. What he had told his father was just wishful thinking.
>
> Tamik then rushed out to search for his younger son. No trace of him—either among the live or the dead. The anguished father checked every morgue, examined every corpse... each shred of clothing and footwear. No result... the older boy obviously started having hallucinations and does not comprehend that his brother died—probably burned to ashes during the fire. Tamik doesn't want

> to believe it. He looks as if he has become 10 years older.... Alan says that he is completely distraught and persists in his search, even though it's obvious that there is no hope.[20]

The greatest classical historian of the 19th century, Theodor Mommsen was not afraid to compromise his professionalism by asserting that "history is neither written nor made without love or hate." An overwhelming experience, for me Beslan was a turning point: terrorism was no longer an issue that I could tackle solely as an intellectual enterprise. I have written this book as an expert in my field, taking full responsibility for the validity of my sources, arguments, and conclusions; however, I must also acknowledge that I am not emotionally distanced from the topic.

Beslan is a metaphor and a prophecy. We can grasp its message, if we dare listen and are able to endure it. Like a red thread it links the not-so-distant past and the present, on which terrorism has stamped its lethal imprints. I approach it as a scholar and person with firsthand experience and emotional knowledge, indispensable for appreciating the impact of violence. Someone who has been blessed and spared from the agony of a sufferer would never fully share his pain. I have come across it only indirectly, when researching and teaching in the terror-stricken Israeli town of Sderot.

Between 2001 and 2009, approximately 12,000 Qassam rockets produced by Hamas[21] exploded in or around the residential Sderot, a western Negev town, about a mile from Gaza. Since the August 2005 Israel evacuation from the Strip, missile attacks dramatically amplified: over 7,000 missiles were fired, 3,200—the largest number per year—in 2008 alone.[22] The rockets fell as if on schedule, hundreds on some weeks. The authorities introduced the "Red Alert," official notification about every launched missile. A recorded voice would cut into the racket of the day or the stillness of the night abruptly to announce that everyone had 15 seconds to get to a shelter. I have never heard a more repulsive female voice; it is very disturbing, especially when the warning is repeated and interrupted each time by a falling missile.

A Qassam exploding every couple of months and causing moderate damage did not initially qualify as a tragedy, but it was not long before the multiplying casualties of shrapnel and flying glass stirred the citizens from their "it-will-pass" confidence. They left town in mass numbers: the Sderot population, some 19,300 people at the end of 2006, has declined by up to 25 percent, according to the 2008 figures. Amid the disrupted local economy and property incurring millions of dollars in damage from the ongoing shelling, nearly everyone who stayed suffered psychological trauma.[23]

Yehudit Bar Hai introduces herself as a Sderot resident and a volunteer at the Israeli Trauma Center for Victims of Terror and War. A rocket attack can happen anywhere at any moment, she says. You can be sitting in a coffee-shop and hear the alert: "your heart misses two beats, you check... that your head is still connected to your shoulders," and you make sure that no one else is hurt. You might be shopping, suddenly there is a warning, "and people just panic."

They do "try to run a normal life...in this nightmarish situation." It is nothing like surviving an accident: "We're talking about eight years here..."[24]

These years of unrelenting traumatization by way of terrorism accentuated its raison d'être, inbuilt in the word's root—"terror." Imprecise Qassam shelling has resulted in 13 fatalities, which were obviously not Hamas' prime targets. Violence in Sderot is blatant in exposing its core general function—always to terrorize and demoralize a community at large by inflicting widespread fear. While working there, I have had multiple occasions to witness this habitual fear on contorted faces of adults and children who dashed into the closest bomb shelter at the first sounds of a "Red Alert." Watching them, petrified, tensely staring at you without seeing, just waiting anxiously to hear the explosion, is infinitely more frightening than the blast.

I wrote this book largely from a humanistic perspective, entailing both an intellectual and ethical dilemma. In order to discover why human beings come to espouse ideology that turns them into mass murderers, a psychohistorian must relate to their points of view and consider their emotional attitudes empathetically. Yet this stipulation forfeited my conviction that terrorism was unmitigated evil. But the necessity to connect to killers on a human level compromised my sense of justice and basic values. It also seemed incompatible with sympathy for the victims, some of whom I knew personally. Their pain did not fit between the margins of an academic project.

This book describes *perpetrators of violence as its very first fatalities.* The rank-and-file, recruited for homicide and dispatched to spill blood for the sake of a subversive organization or terrorist state, are conditioned to perceive their victims as inanimate targets of annihilation. Before the terrorist is capable of slaughter, he is dehumanized into a mechanism of destruction: our most human facilities—to make a free moral choice and to have empathy—are "carved out" of him.[25] Understanding the process of recasting an individual into a live weapon does not, however, presuppose blind compassion: once engineers and managers of terror have molded draftees into instruments of death, they become an implacable enemy and must be recognized as such.

In the beginning of the book I introduce Robert Lifton's pivotal paradigm of "historical dislocation," or disintegration of ethical norms and aesthetic conventions, as a cardinal precondition for the rise of terror. In his pioneering study Michael Mazarr scrutinized terrorism as an "uprising against...modernization," an ubiquitously traumatic process that "manufactures myriad sources of social tensions."[26] I am venturing beyond the cultural and sociohistorical field to a less tangible sphere of existence, which the crisis of values and meanings also affected and infused with violence. In other words, I am presenting the advent of a new type of terrorism as a dark spiritual experience.

Since the early 1900s, terrorists assassinated men in uniform as symbolic targets and destroyed inanimate emblems of authority and traditional culture. Increasingly, however, their main adversary has become the civilians, attacked randomly: in the late-imperial and Soviet periods as "class rivals"; presently in

Israel as symbols of the insufferable "Zionist entity"; and in the West as the proponents of "godless materialism." These "scenarios are not *tactics* directed toward an immediate, earthy, or strategic goal, but *dramatic events*,"[27] staged to celebrate terrorism as a comprehensive psychological warfare and mechanism of coercion.

In modern and postmodern phases, the terrorists have developed their nonverbal, yet exceedingly effective "socializing" with open audiences, their targets being the "means of communications," rather than symbols per se. Acts of terror serve as perpetrators' ghastly messages, circulated by transnational news media and reaching millions. Eyewitnesses of violence thus find themselves in an aberrant relationship with their potential killers. This association is similar to a bond between hostages and their captors.

This study shifts attention from terrorists' doctrines to their endeavors that have previously been hidden or ignored. The analysis emphasizes a vast discrepancy between the declared creed of terrorist leaders and the practices of the rank-and-file. In various epicenters of terror, the perpetrators of violence also persistently demonstrate utter dogmatic ignorance—glaring behind the poorly assimilated slogans, socialist or Islamist catchphrases, supplied by their dispatchers. The discord between their avowed intentions and their actions suggests that what the terrorists say about their motives may not be what really drives them. Usually, their broadcast agenda is but a publicity device to legitimize violence. Instead of taking authentications at face value, it is essential to address the largely subconscious motivations behind archetypal terrorist behaviors.

The book illustrates a strong connection between the political and criminal psychologies. It also provides multiple examples of terrorism as indistinguishable from banditry. Specifically addressed is the exploitation of children for terrorist ends, erroneously believed to have become rife in the late 1990s but in fact well-known in Russia a century ago.

Suicide terrorism is not an exclusively Muslim phenomenon, as it is generally supposed. Nor is it, as holds an erroneoud opinion, Hezbollah's invention in Lebanon in the 1980s.[28] There is plenty of evidence about radicals' suicidal assaults since 1905. In our days, forging their bodies into "human bombs," they use the language of religious martyrdom just as fervently as their predecessors had validated self-destruction by the lofty ideal of social liberation. I intend to show that, all rhetoric aside, terrorists frequently die in "camouflaged suicide."

In light of 9/11 and Beslan, it is astonishing that the terrorist's image still remains habitually mystified and ennobled, his actions justified as self-defense. "Terrorist discourse" is indicative of the universality of the intellectual position of the Left with regard to terror, national discrepancies notwithstanding. This book evaluates left-liberals' attitudes towards terrorism in the early 20th-century Russian empire, Europe, the United States, and, especially, Israel—one of its epicenters. In regions afflicted by militancy, responses mirror an array of conventional attitudes, communal canons, and culture-bound assumptions. I propose to examine the psychology of terrorism in conjunction with a range of contemporary reactions to threat, acknowledged or displaced with an assortment of mental constructs and rationalizations. The purpose is to demythologize the terrorist and to divest him of the aura of an altruist "freedom fighter," acquired as part of "the worst intellectual heresy of our age: the romanticism of violence."[29]

When Lenin and his party took hold of power in 1917, for the first time in history former insurrectionists set out to implement a genocidal class-based and government-upheld utopia by methods they labeled the "Red Terror." The book compares Bolshevik policies with those of the Hamas, which had engaged in violence based on an apocalyptic ideology prior to its victory in the January 2006 elections to the Palestinian Legislation Council (PLC) and seizure of control over the Gaza Strip in July 2007. Immediately after their takeover, the Hamas began to impress the *Shari'a* laws and Islamist rites for the sake of fundamentalism with "the banner of Allah over every inch of Palestine."[30] Its "Muslim essence" and accentuated *jihad* (sacred war against enemies of faith) distinguish Hamas from secular nationalists and their terrorist tactics. It is fighting "a holy war until final victory," not only to receive from Israel the disputed territories but mainly to promote an extremist version of Islam under a proto-totalitarian administration[31]—akin to the underlying objective of the Soviets to advance their millennial world revolution. The Bolshevik–Hamas comparison yields a behavioral typology of terrorists as fundamentalist leaders.

We simply have no idea what many Muslims think of Jihad. In Ahmadinejad's Iran, to ask a citizen would be as helpful as to invite his Russian counterpart living under Stalin to comment on the Cold War. But survivors of the Nazi and the Soviet terror, those who learned the hard way, are perhaps most qualified to remind us that "history lessons are often incredibly simple and blunt, yet for all our powers of reason we . . . miss the most basic and uncomplicated of points": it does not matter what the majority want when, under the oppressive regimes, "the fanatics own them."

> We are told again and again . . . that the vast majority of Muslims just want to live in peace. Although this unqualified assertion may be true, it is entirely irrelevant. It is . . . meant to make us feel better . . . to somehow diminish the spectra of fanatics rampaging across the globe in the name of Islam. . . . It is the fanatics who bomb, behead, murder, or honor-kill. . . . The hard quantifiable fact is that the "peaceful . . . silent majority" is cowed and extraneous.[32]

Like the Bolshevik and the Nazi state-builders, today's leaders engage in construction of a specific "death culture" of dehumanization and glorification of brutality—projected from the underground terrorist cell onto a society under their control. Dehumanization of both the victim and the aggressor is a distinct characteristic in such a culture. Justifications for terror vary in accordance with the movements' concrete political agenda; yet, beneath factional rhetoric, fundamentalist violence possesses one common criterion, also its underlying driving force: preoccupation with thanatophilia—love of death.

Adherents of the totalist outlook declare dying to be their commitment and aspiration; it is also an item of veneration. To death, their secular deity, they offer quasi-religious human sacrifices. Hence, the double meaning in the title of this book: it reflects two claims—that the fundamentalist terrorists have come to resemble holy orders or cults and that it is death, their ultimate point of reference or "deity," that dictates their moves. As their supreme offering, I investigate the unprecedented, premeditated intimidation of children in designated "fear zones"—a trademark of the post-9/11 phase of terror. I hope to show that, paradoxically, this modern variant of death-worship leaves room for an optimistic prediction for terrorists' self-annihilation.

Terrorism is our shared predicament, and understanding of its causes, manifestations, and intrinsic connotations will ultimately be a result of a sustained versatile effort of specialists—security experts, culturologists, psychologists, and science professionals. A historian, I bring to this joint venture the ability to see patterns of terrorist onslaught over the last century. The first step toward freeing ourselves from anxiety—the extremists' principal medium—would be to look the danger in the eye. We would not have been so shocked by the destruction of the Twin Towers in New York, and might have even managed to prevent the attack, were it a matter of general awareness that such a tragedy had already been envisaged. In 1906, the radicals planned to utilize a "flying apparatus" to drop explosives on the imperial Winter Palace in St. Petersburg,[33] anticipating by over a hundred years the gruesome realization of terrorists' dream on 9/11.

Chapter 1

A Birthplace of Modern Terrorism

Dostoevsky's *Demons*, a provincial nightmare of the last century, one would have thought, are, before our very eyes, crawling over the whole world into countries where they were unimaginable, and by the hijacking of planes, by seizing hostages, by the bomb explosions, and by the fires of recent years signal their determination to shake civilization apart and to annihilate it!

—Aleksandr Solzhenitsyn

Every age, every culture, every custom and tradition has its own character, its own weakness and its own strength, its beauties and cruelties; it accepts certain sufferings as matters of course, puts up patiently with certain evils. Human life is reduced to real suffering, to hell, only when two ages, two cultures and religions overlap.

—Hermann Hesse

Revolutionary terrorism in Russia in the early 1900s was essentially different from erstwhile political assassinations. We can trace the history of political assassinations back to the late-11th century, when the ill-famed Assassins (from the Arabic *Hashshashin* or *Hashashiyyin*), an offshoot of the Ismaili Shi'a sect of Islam, were the first group on the fringes of the Muslim society to make systematic use of *organized, targeted murder as a political tool.* Having rebelled against the existing Sunni order and seeking to build their own state, they used small blades or daggers as weapons of choice that precluded escape and terrorized their adversaries among the ruling elites, as would their followers in various parts of the world in upcoming epochs.[1]

Every episode in this gory tradition was a sensation, given that the proponents of terror directed their efforts against carefully preselected luminaries, top figures in the establishment. True to form, terrorist activity was sporadic and numerically insignificant. Even amid the rash of anarchist bombings in western Europe and the United States in the 19th century, victims of each assault usually counted in single-digit numbers. It was "quite a busy period for European terrorists," notes historian Franklin L. Ford, referring examples of ideology-motivated vengeance applied between 1851 and 1900 against a total of about 40 prominent Europeans.[2] During the "decade of the bomb" in the 1890s, "chiefs of state, or their nearest available representatives, were struck down at the rate of nearly one per year."[3]

From the 1870s, nowhere were terrorist strikes as recurrent as they were in the Russian empire. There, during the next 25 years approximately 35 attempts by radical Populists claimed nearly 100 lives.[4] Yet, though more frequent than elsewhere, these operations were similar to isolated, few-and-far-between acts of murder committed by lone perpetrators in other parts of the world. The beginning of the 20th century was a turning point, giving birth to a new phase of terrorism with its conspicuously modern traits.

Russian extremists who came to dominate the political scene contrasted sharply with most of their predecessors, such as combatants of the legendary People's Will party (Narodnaia Volia)—the first modern terrorist organization in the world. Operating in the late 1870s and early 1880s, the party chose its targets on the basis of individual responsibility and attacked influential officials of the autocratic regime, whom the revolutionaries held responsible for reactionary policies. Their objective was both a reprisal and "propaganda by deed." As part of the group's popular mobilization tactics, assassinations were to drum up the "sleepy Russian masses" for a colossal revolt.

These efforts failed, even though the terrorists did claim remarkable successes. One after another, the revolutionaries took the lives of several prominent bureaucrats and police chiefs, instilling fear in the high government circles. Ministers and other eminent administrators sought safety in self-imposed confinement and thought twice before leaving their heavily guarded St. Petersburg mansions. Yet formidable as it was, the People's Will did not interrupt the habitual flow of life in the country—except once, on March 1, 1881. On that day, a party member tossed a handheld bomb at Alexander II's carriage, as it was passing over the capital's Catherine Canal. Shaken but unscathed, he stepped out of the bulletproof vehicle to help the gravely injured driver; then, a second terrorist detonated his homemade explosive device under the tsar's feet.

"I was deafened by the new explosion, burned, wounded and thrown to the ground," a high-ranking police officer remembered. "Suddenly, amid the smoke and snowy fog, I heard His Majesty's weak voice cry, 'Help!'... Twenty people, with wounds of varying degree, lay on the sidewalk and on the street. Some managed to stand, others to crawl, still others tried to get out from beneath bodies that had fallen on them. Through the snow, debris, and blood you could see fragments of clothing, epaulets, sabers, and bloody chunks of human flesh."[5] On the splintered flagstones, next to his injured and unconscious assassin, lay Alexander II, with blood pouring out of his shattered legs and his abdomen ripped open. He was mortally wounded and died in the Winter Palace a few hours later. The long hunt of the People's Will for the "crowned game" was finally over.[6] And the country was set off on a catastrophic course.

Sporadic extremism of the late 19th century was but a prelude to the enormous escalation of political violence in the 1900s. Gone were the days when radicals took the time to select their targets from among the high-posted dignitaries. Around 1905 a true "epidemic of combat"[7] broke out, and terrorism, writes historian Norman Naimark, became "so addictive that it was often carried out without even weighing the moral questions posed by earlier generations."[8] The new terrorist campaign "assumed gigantic proportions" indeed, acknowledged the revolutionaries.[9]

Unlike periodic attacks against rulers as punishments for specific deeds or policy—cruel, repressive, and punitive in the eyes of the insurrectionists—political murder was now systematic. Between 1905 and 1907, in various regions of the empire the terrorists came to be responsible for over 9,000 casualties among officials and private individuals.[10] Already in the early 1900s, virulent assaults thus acquired the key characteristics of modern extremism, as it revealed itself across the globe in the century to come. The regularity of mass-scale killing rendered Russia the birthplace of new terrorism.

Unprecedented anywhere in the world, pervasive terror coincided with the political turmoil of 1905–1907 and was a symptom of the country's deeper predicament—a rapid breakdown of the traditional environment following the 1861 serf emancipation. Tsar of Russia since 1894, Nicholas II confronted multiple domestic adversaries. In the countryside, peasants burned estates and killed their owners, seizing land. In the cities, impoverished proletarians organized strikes and lockouts. Those of non-Russian nationalities, who for decades had harbored antagonism toward the imperial authorities, in 1905 turned border areas into centers of open rebellion. Soldiers and sailors mutinied. University and even secondary school students protested against oppressive education. Professional revolutionaries hastily organized political parties as weapons to fight the state and the bourgeoisie. And the left-liberal intelligentsia cheered the all-out revolt. In the midst of mounting disorder terrorism served as both the result of and the catalyst for the country's crisis. A primary *modus operandi* for undermining the regime, terror created a situation that contemporaries described as "bloody anarchy" or simply "one vast madhouse."[11]

Violence reached its peak in 1907, but historians' assumption that in 1908 it brusquely declined to only several incidents over the course of the year is not accurate. In fact, terrorism continued to ravage the country, which was slowly recovering from the revolutionary storm. From the beginning of January 1908 through mid-May 1910, 3,783 people were killed and 3,851 wounded, rendering the radicals responsible for 7,634 victims across the empire.[12]

Journalists spilled much ink depicting spectacular terrorist attacks in late 1905, when, confirmed a liberal publicist, "murders flooded the periphery and the center with blood."[13] As they occurred daily, often many times a day, assassinations quickly ceased to provide sensation, and newspapers began to ignore them. Soon, acts of terror became more common than traffic accidents.[14] From April 27 to July 9, 1906, terrorists killed 177 people in 317 attempts.[15] By 1907, they claimed a rough average of 18 casualties each day, and then the editors no longer bothered to provide detailed reports on every occasion. Rather, newspapers in various regions introduced a special rubric entitled "Revolutionary Assaults." They included extended lists of "politically-motivated robberies," the so-called expropriations, or simply "exes." These were armed raids, in which proceeds were allocated for the cause of liberation—at least so the perpetrators claimed.[16]

The "exes" contributed their share of bloodshed and also wrought tremendous economic damage. In the 19th century they had been rare; almost without exception the radicals rejected this tactic with an "unconcealed feeling of disgust."[17] By 1905, however, numerous extremists had begun to justify armed raids as an excellent means to intimidate the enemy; theft of state property became part of their effort to destabilize the establishment. With confiscated funds, the expropriators sought to sustain themselves financially as full-time revolutionaries and to procure weapons and explosives. For many organizations the only source of income was robbery. Members classified expropriations as "economic terror" and deemed "entirely artificial" its separation from political terrorism.[18]

On October 14, 1906, members of a militant Maximalist faction carried out the Fonarnyi Lane "ex," one of the most breathtaking robberies in history. Armed with Browning pistols and small bombs, the combatants attacked a heavily guarded carriage on its way from the St. Petersburg customs office, transporting over 600,000 rubles in bank notes and currency to the Treasury and the State Bank. Counting on the element of surprise, the Maximalists staged their act at noon, in the teeming city center. Several revolutionaries opened fire at the convoy and hurled hand grenades. Others snatched sacks containing the money and flung them into a waiting carriage; half-hidden inside was a lady, her face concealed under a thick veil. The accomplices sped away, their flight covered by comrades' rapid fire at the police. They carried with them a fortune of around 400,000 rubles—a huge sum at a time when the purchasing power of the Russian currency allowed a modest living on less than a ruble a day.[19]

Few terrorist groups could aspire to prizes of this magnitude, but "in the capitals, in provincial cities, and in district towns, in villages, on highways, on trains, on steamboats," smaller-scale expropriations occurred daily.[20] Liquor stores were preferred targets, along with post offices, clinics, and churches. In

October 1906, 362 "exes" took place across the empire; on the single day of October 30, the police collected 15 reports about politically motivated robberies at various state institutions.[21] According to the Ministry of Finance calculations, in the period from early 1905 through mid-1906 alone, revolutionary raids cost the imperial banks more than 1,000,000 rubles, price tag of human life aside.[22]

By the most conservative approximation, the terrorist exploits yielded over 16,800 killed and wounded in the years 1905–1910. Some political assassinations occurred between 1901 and 1905. A few also took place after 1910, in the years preceding the collapse of the imperial government in 1917. All in all, in the last 17 years of Russia's imperial regime, about 17,000 individuals fell victim to the 23,000 terrorist attacks.[23]

At the turn of the 20th century, most extremists did not yet have the means or the skills to kill hundreds or even dozens of people with a calculated precision and with special effects of a slaughter. Except in well-planned assassinations of dignitaries, the terrorists typically spent little or no time preparing their assaults and compensated for frequent failures with the incredibly high rate of recurrence. The endless stream of terrorist acts thus plunged the empire into a bloodbath: "Bombs were thrown on any pretext or without one," recalls a former police official. People found them in postal packages, in coat pockets, in fruit baskets, and on church altars. "Everything that could be blown up exploded"—from liquor stores to gendarme offices and from statues of Russian generals to churches.[24]

The popular nickname given to a small bomb was "orange," which quickly became part of the vocabulary. It also appeared in many anecdotes and in widely circulating trendy satirical couplets:

> People have started getting wary
> They consider fruit quite scary.
> A friend of mine, as tough as granite,
> Is frightened of the pomegranate.
> Policeman, ready to bark and grumble,
> At the sight of an orange now trembles.[25]

The radicals never gave up attempts to smuggle explosives into the country from abroad, mainly via western and southeastern Europe, but home bomb-making turned out to be easier. Police sources confirm that "the manufacturing of bombs assumed enormous proportions, and there were such successes in this technology that now a child could make an explosive device from an empty sardine can and a handful of drugstore supplies."[26] Corroborating this testimony is a notebook of a 15-year-old schoolboy named Vasilii Kniazev, who accurately copied a recipe for homemade caramel candies next to equally precise instructions for making an explosive device: a bit of nitroglycerine, a few nails, and some bolts.[27] Countless times, such dilettante experimentations with the "infernal machines" led to accidents, injuries, and deaths, but a popular aphorism defined fate in the terrorist lingo: "Luck is like a bomb—it can strike one man today, another tomorrow."[28]

* * *

"Things fall apart; the center cannot hold." Though referring to Ireland, W. B. Yeats's line depicts precisely turn-of-the-20th-century Russia. There, the inescapable "sense of decay"[29] accompanied the disintegration of the cultural setting, undermined as it was by the emasculation of the "communal spirit" at the foundation of the society.[30] The country's swift industrialization undercut centuries-old ways of life based on cooperative land cultivation. Vigorous urbanization impeded customary interactions and routines based on the Russian Orthodox adherence to *sobornost'*, or conjoint God-worship. The "Russian idea," in all its multifaceted developments, synthesized around one central theme—the urgency to catch up with other European cultures in espousing individualism. The country was rapidly turning into a "modern society," proud of its special emphasis on the hitherto unrecognized powers and responsibilities of the individual.

Prior to the 1900s, with the strong cultural emphasis on the shared, at the expense of the individualistic, lifestyle, an ordinary Russian had comparatively low-level experience as a distinct, separate being.[31] His self-perception was closer to what Alan Roland identified the "we-self" of India and Japan, as opposed to the "I-self" of any Western society. Noting the "inadequate development of the personal factor" in his country's life, philosopher Nikolai Berdiaev emphasized that the Russian "has always loved to live in the warmth of the collective...the bosom of the mother." Historians went further and argued that in Russia an individual could not subsist outside the collective.[32] It spared him from angst-provoking conflicts, such as aspiration to control one's life through independent decision-making coexisting with desire to avoid risk and relegate responsibility; self-doubts and the quest for self-assertion; or the required privacy and simultaneous fear of isolation. No longer confined within the agricultural or religious commune, around the turn of the 20th century, for the first time in history, the Russian began to perceive himself as "I," not "we." It was the potentials of the self, as opposed to compliance with common needs, that from then on determined one's adjustment to modern life, survivability and strength.

As with other pivotal points in Russia's history, disruption of the taken-for-granted sociocultural order occurred too abruptly to allow a smooth transformation from collectivism to individualism. Scores of displaced and unsettled individuals found themselves as loners in urban environments and experienced the new situation as arduous and disheartening. Thousands severed physical and spiritual ties with their indigenous communities, but only relatively few found sufficient inner resources to face the demands that modernity—and its foremost "challenge of *pluralism*"[33]—made on their puerile and maladjusted selves, striving to function adequately outside the traditional commune.

Perhaps more consequential than miserable economic conditions—and in the early stages of the industrialization, they were miserable indeed—psychological adaptation to the new milieu and lifestyle was exceedingly slow. The dilemma of the awkward Russian individualist entailed a failure to relate organically to the new reality, "to establish an immediate bond between himself and the larger social life," without which personal "achievement hangs like a pall that shrouds dullness and vacancy."[34] Lifton called "historical dislocation" this breach "of connection men have long felt with vital and nourishing symbols of their cultural practices—symbols revolving around family, idea systems, religions, and the life cycle in general," every value, meaning, and link that binds us to life and sustains our psychological existence.[35]

The breakdown of social values led to widespread disappointment marked by depressive states of senselessness and unreality—those that R. D. Laing considered inevitable attributes of a self alien to itself, in a psychic disarray, to which Lifton refers as "death-in-life." Concomitant with alienation, "death anxiety," or the existential dread, inevitably invaded and soon dominated the lives of "the not staunch" and the "half-cracked," as writer Andrei Belyi christened the sufferers from an array of life-undermining symptoms, such as emptiness, apathy, hopelessness, and disengagement.[36] Obscure presentiment of non-being permeated the dislocated and rootless souls in which vitality had thus been subverted.[37]

The urban populace swelled from around 9 million people in the mid-19th century to about 25 million in 1913, with inhabitants of most major Russian cities increasing four- or five-fold. Resident figure in the capital roughly doubled between 1890 and 1910. The city "population remained predominately single, far more so than the average for the Empire as a whole, and among European capitals St. Petersburg had a particularly low per-capita ratio of married inhabitants."

Outside the commune, the solitary existence was disconcerting and devoid of basic security. Estranged from their new surroundings, numerous unsettled personalities sought to escape the traumatic aspects of individualization by finding substitutes for the economic and spiritual communality and the disappearing time-honored family structure. The first generation workers of the same trade united in the *artels*, interim labor cooperatives in which profits were shared by the participants. Newcomers to the city among university students of same geographical backgrounds joined the so-called *zemliachestva*, or "associations of the land." Still, these efforts to simulate comfortable familiarity were inadequate to ameliorate individuation-related tensions.[38] Fast-paced city life, "in which factories replaced cathedrals as the great monuments of a new society" and "the instruments of technology had come between humankind and God,"[39] did not offer a relief for apprehension and the feelings of helplessness to the germinating self.

Modern individualistic society requires one "to stand on his own feet, assert himself;" it provides few, if any, cultural means of relief for mental strain through self-abrogation and release from Nietzsche's *principium individuationis*, says psychologist Karen Horney. One might reduce devastating effects of individuation-related angst by abandoning himself "in something greater, by dissolving the individuality, by getting rid of the self with its doubts, conflicts, pains, limitations and isolation,"[40]

Anxiety, which is "the central core of individualized selfhood...cannot be got rid of by personal effort, but only by the ego's absorption in a cause greater than its own interests."[41] To escape the anguish associated with historical dislocation, its many victims sought salvation in rejecting the ailing "I" and dissolving their nascent selves in a new commune—the political movement. Belyi explains this metaphorically: "lonely paths amidst snow piles of misunderstanding" lead to places of refuge, in which "everyone among the misunderstood finds an asylum." There they develop "the cult of the new home"[42] and reassert the power of the traditional "we" over the painfully maladjusted "I."

In various parts of Europe in the second half of the 19th century, the extraordinary mobility and urbanization of population created "an extraordinary number of persons uprooted from ancestral soil and local allegiances. Experiencing grave economic insecurity and psychological maladjustment, these were very susceptible to demagogic propaganda, socialist or nationalist or both."[43] Less prepared for the advent of modernization, the Russians were vulnerable to an even greater degree, increasingly prone to take an opportunity to release the bottled-up rage, especially when external circumstances stimulated the expression of distress. The difficult transformation process in Europe turned into a crisis in Russia, where it surfaced suddenly around 1900 and spiraled swiftly into a political calamity. "It was as if something was in the air hovering over each and every one of us," remembered poetess Zinaida Gippius recalled: people "rushed about, never understanding why they did so, nor knowing what to do with themselves."[44] Frustration and anger accumulated almost visibly.

Revolution appeals to those who "crave to be rid of an unwanted self." The ideal potential convert to radicalism "is the individual who stands alone, who has no collective body he can blend with and lose himself in and so mask the pettiness, meaninglessness and shabbiness" of his existence. This is why the true believer clings to the cause with a fervent attachment and attributes sanctity to it: the movement attracts and holds a following because—magically—it reduces the traumatizing effect of individuation and satisfies "the passion for self-renunciation."[45] By immersing themselves into a revolutionary society, ostensibly for the sake of a great common goal, the proselytes give themselves a chance to behave "selflessly" in the strictly morphological sense of the word. Thus were thousands of Russians trapped between the requirement to activate their selves and the torturous difficulty, if not outright impossibility, of making choices, building relationships, and utilizing opportunities—in other words, of living on the level of their underdeveloped and befuddled "I." Dejected, they readily succumbed to incitement to turn against the environment that had rendered them failures.

In this period, intricacy and nuance were the highlights of the Russian Silver Age, a period of intense cultural vicissitude, intellectual turmoil, and aesthetic pursuit. Like the rest of the country, its most imaginative and cultivated minds had to confront and cope with the experience of modernization. The emotionally and spiritually strongest found the challenge invigorating and transmitted it into sources of creative energy and verve. They personified Russia's buoyancy and healthy energy, contributing to the nation's vibrant and pulsating aliveness. The early poetry of Osip Mandel'shtam allegorized the individual's vitality and spirit and reflected his autonomy on the new path of maturation.

The era's feast of refinement and effervescent intellect manifested itself in musical, artistic, philosophical, and theological masterpieces, works of insight and courage, but also in vehement rebellion against convention. The all-out revolt against the sociopolitical elites was, like the revolution in the arts, an integral feature of the Silver Age mentality: "Circumstances were ideal. The pre-war years, the boiling pot...Everything that declared itself as a protest was received with sympathy and curiosity; any scandal discharged the atmosphere and freshened stale air."[46] "In a certain sense," recalled a memoirist, "we were the revolution before the revolution—so profoundly, mercilessly, and fatally did we destroy the old tradition."[47]

The protest was intrinsically nihilistic. Though seeking to "desymbolize" age-old culture and to attack its meanings, the rebellious intellectuals did not share one program or a single set of beliefs. "We met under different banners; the banner that united us was the denial of life that had formed us and the struggle against" this life, recaptured writer Andrei Belyi.[48] Absorbed by their zeal to negate, they inadvertently enervated a prime aspect of being human—something that the Lifton paradigm emphasizes as a form of "symbolic immortality"—a compelling urge to maintain a sense of permanence and a quest for an attachment "to what has been before and what will continue after our finite individual existence." By seeking to undercut the world of which they were integral parts, the rebels contributed to the process of historical dislocation and undermined their own connectedness to life—no longer upheld by deep-rooted bonds.[49]

In the crumbling environment, people were starving for ideas that could give coherence to their fragmented world. What Lifton recognized as "ideological hunger" they sought to satiate with a feverish quest for a new system of values. Forlorn, confused, and apprehensive "self-styled Nietzschean supermen" also fostered the cult of power as compensation for deep insecurity and need for affirmation.[50] They thus espoused revolution, which provided the context, structure, and semi-religious legitimization for destruction as a way of life. Before terrorism erupted in full force, "one could already begin to sense the smell of burning, blood, and iron in the air," confirmed Russia's most renowned contemporary poet, Aleksandr Blok.[51]

Rigid policies of the autocratic government encouraged extremism as an unavoidable course. Grievous economic conditions during the early industrialization phase also seemed to validate a claim that exploitation, competition, and alienation of individuals—the most odious features of modern society—would disappear only after the overthrow of capitalism. Significantly, the sociopolitical protest was in harmony with the country's flagrantly explosive cultural atmosphere. In the capital, the incoherent yet wayward "spirit of destruction pervaded everything...the sullen rancor of the steel-plant worker, the disjointed aspirations of the fashionable poetess...The law courts were thronged with hysterical women, greedily imbibing the gory details of sensational trials....The country was being drained of its lifeblood to feed the insatiable specters haunting Petersburg," which, as always in Russia, was dictating the latest style.[52] These destructive forces shattered life outside the capital as well, as terrorism began to overshadow all other forms of rebellion. "With the fall of the hegemony of the moral and social boundaries" and amid hastened decomposition, resolve "to destroy is a highly visible and urgent theme in the writings and actions of the terrorists."[53]

How ironic it was that modern terror—with its paramount feature of murder en masse—appeared in Russia precisely at the turning point from collectivism to individualism, with its pivotal goal of cultivating the "I." At a time when, despite its multiple perils, the new power of the self inspired the nation's initial ascent on an animated spiral of modernity, the terrorists smothered the nascent individual, rejecting him for the sake of their innovative tactic of killing randomly. In accordance with its essential nihilistic intent—"we want to smash...people!"[54]—terror came to epitomize the most radical "alternative lifestyle" of the 1900s. Terrorism was aimed at the budding culture's defining theme—individualism, assailed, as it was, by the extremists' new emphasis on undifferentiated death. No longer a marginal phenomenon, from then on terrorism evolved as a particularly brutal form of counterculture.[55]

* * *

Terrorism has been on the rise again since the late 1960s, although initially records might not have appeared as particularly worrisome: by numerical comparison, political belligerence of the 1905–1907 era remained unsurpassed—until the arrival of the new millennium. Of the total of close to 25,000 terrorist episodes that took place worldwide between 1968 and 2006, nearly 10,000 happened during the initial 30-year period, and the other 15,000 (59.9%) occurred between 2000 and 2006 alone.[56] In six years starting in October 2001, terrorists killed about 11,800 worldwide and tens of thousands were maimed and crippled for life.[57] In the conflict-ridden Middle East, over the 50-year period beginning in the 1950s, 1,399 Israelis were killed by Arab terrorists. However, in the next six years the casualty figures escalated stunningly, showing 1,177 Israelis killed and 8,341 wounded between September 2001 and the end of 2007.[58]

Statistics also demonstrate the reversed ratio of assaults and victims: fewer attacks take more lives because perpetrators have learned to employ modern technology. They also benefit from experience, accumulated over the last hundred years, incorporating the know-how of suicide terrorism. Its potency was illustrated most vividly by two instances that occurred in a single month. On October 12, 2002, there took place in the tourist district of Kuta in Bali, Indonesia, a nightclub bombing by a militant South Asian organization called Jemaah Islamiyah—the bloodiest act since the destruction of the Twin Towers with it's 2,974 fatalities: it left 202 people killed and 209 wounded. Eleven days later, the Chechen combatants staged the "Nord-Ost" theater holdup in Moscow, where of the 850–900 hostages, at least 129 died, scores received serious injuries, and some were permanently disabled.

Before the mid-1970s, the sum total of casualties in a terrorist assault was usually statistically negligible, but in 1979–1989 the death toll per incident went up to 1.15, increasing in the following years to 1.8 fatal outcomes. After 1999, the average terrorist occurrence claimed 2.58 lives. Even more revealing—and prophetic, as time showed—is that in violent acts performed by faith-driven terrorists (such as Hezbollah and Hamas) in 1979–1989 the death figure was 2.9, more than twice as high as in attacks unrelated to sanctified causes.[59] In the next decade, the lethality of religious terrorism doubled, skyrocketing to 5.98 deaths per incident. Supplemented by data for mutilated and handicapped survivors, these numbers underscore a patent trend for "quality killing."[60]

From the early 1900s on, never would modern political violence be a straightforward, if extreme reaction to immediate political or socioeconomic circumstances. History has repeatedly shown that oppression or poverty does "not automatically generate discontent, nor is the intensity of discontent directly proportionate to the degree of misery."[61] Alternatively, the "milieu most favorable for the rise and propagation of mass movements is one in which a once compact corporate structure is, for one reason or another, in a state of disintegration."[62]

"Whenever modernization touches societies, it leaves instability and dissatisfaction in its wake," recapitulates Mazarr. Some cultures manage this transition relatively easily: they achieve rising living standards, increasingly legitimate institutions, and—most importantly—succeed in "defraying the psychological cost of...progress." Others do not fare as well. They are the ones who suffer from a distinctive set of conditions "and take a similar route to antimodern radicalism." In "certain strikingly uniform circumstances, even when separated by decades or continents...a deadly composite of factors create a psychological burden too intense to sustain." The anxieties of modern life, which in most places "smolder under the surface or spark nonviolent remedies," then "burn white-hot with cathartic terror."[63]

The reason for growth of Islamism is not destitution, as some observers suggest. An overwhelming expert opinion is that, on the contrary, "there is only a weak and indirect relationship between poverty and terrorism,"[64] and "the Arab world actually compares favorably to other developing regions when it comes to preventing abject want."[65] Unique may be the case of Osama bin Laden's conversion from a profligate and hedonistic offspring of a billionaire family to a visionary with messianic aspirations to "split the world into two camps—believers and infidels."[66] More often, Islamist organizers and propagandists are the neophytes of the middles classes. Still, they come from the privileged strata of the Muslim community.

They are also the beneficiaries of secular instruction and training: research shows that the university-educated individuals, including those that have studied in Western countries, may constitute up to 69 percent of the extremists.[67] The Bali bomber Imam Samudra, is a typical case: his schooling combined European technology (electronics) and the Darul Islam version of theology. Samudra's "education bore fruit," yielding a computer technician–terrorist.[68] Mohamed Atta, leader of the 9/11 hijackers, graduated with a degree in architecture from Cairo University and—to heighten the bitter irony—studied city planning in Hamburg, Germany.[69] Among the masterminds of Islamism, "the role of disaffected intellectuals, of angry educated technocrats, of spurned aspirants to a globalized middle class life, remains very prominent."[70]

Nor are the rank-and-file suicide terrorists recruited from the downtrodden or the illiterate. Nizar (Nezar) Nawwaf al-Mansur al-Hindawi, a Jordanian charged by the Syrians to destroy El Al flight 016 from London to Tel Aviv on April 17, 1986, came from an Amman establishment family; his two uncles had held cabinet posts.[71] Umar Farouk Abdulmutallab, a 23 year old aspiring "holy warrior" with alleged ties to al-Qaeda in Yemen, was the son of a prominent Nigerian banker; he had been a student in a British boarding school and then earned the engineer's diploma in London before his failed attempt to blow up a transatlantic Northwest Airlines flight to the United States on Christmas Day in 2009.[72] The Hezbollah "is an interesting organization because it is chock-full of professionals—contractors, engineers, architects, demographic experts."[73]

During the decade beginning in 1993, Palestinian Arabs attempted and carried out more than 250 suicide attacks, the majority perpetrated by Hamas, but also committed by Fatah and the Islamic Jihad, as well as the Popular Front for the Liberation of Palestine and the Forces of Palestinian Popular Resistance. "One-third of the suicide terrorists were university students or graduates, approximately 40 had a high school education." The remainder had completed primary schooling, but the overall distribution represented "a considerably higher level than the average education of the Palestinian population as a whole."[74] Islamists elsewhere in the Muslim world are also "vastly more educated than their compatriots"; a puzzling fact is that their circles are overrepresented by those trained in engineering.[75] Muslims recruited for terrorist purposes in the United States are computer literate and are increasingly enlisted online, in chat rooms, via YouTube and Facebook. In fact, Islamists or not, the majority of terrorists over the past century "were not poor or ignorant but well-off and educated."[76]

As much as Russian terrorism in its day, Islamist fundamentalism is bred by historical dislocation, or a "trauma of uprootedness."[77] "Rapid modernization in the form of high economic growth" correlates "strongly with the emergence of ideological terrorism," especially "in countries where sudden wealth (e.g., from oil) has precipitated a change from tribal to high-tech societies in one generation or less." As norms crumble or "seem irrelevant, new radical ideologies (sometimes based on religion and/or nostalgia for a glorious past) may become attractive" to the psychologically "displaced."[78] Terrorism thus "emerges from peoples' reactions to the modern, Western-shaped world" and "the anger and confusion of that reaction." Estranged from communal routines and conventions of the mainstream Islam, numerous individuals are cast into "exile."[79] Like the uprooted and the insecure Russian extremists a hundred years ago, most of whom had found themselves consigned to the periphery of the emerging modern culture, the "Western-based Islamic terrorists are... a lost generation, unmoored from traditional societies and cultures."[80] In the last decades, the Muslim world has undergone a "transformation not unlike that of Europe in the late 19th century. Large numbers of villagers and tribesmen have moved to the vast urban slums of Cairo, Algiers, and Amman, leaving behind the variegated, often preliterate Islam of the countryside. Islamism has filled the void, offering a new identity."[81]

The dislocated outcasts are challenged to come to terms with modernity, which "generates vast alienation. Old ways of life are disrupted; new ones are not yet established." The burden of pluralism, with its conflicting and confusing options, can be crippling. Religious commitment is undermined, along with familial hierarchies. Self-perception as a member in a group comes under direct threat. Beloved cultural meanings, crucial "to furnishing human beings with a stable concept of reality, are torn apart." Basic individual "needs—security, identity, dignity, belonging"—are frustrated, all contributing to a developing mindset of the enraged victim, humiliated, "besieged, thwarted, filled with real and invented grievances."[82]

Islam's encounter with the West over the so-called "Century of the Muslim Decline" is associated with pain and the sense of injustice, which must be articulated. Sufferers of historical dislocation in Russia ascribed their misery to detrimental sociopolitical conditions in their country and to its oppressive leadership. Their Muslim successors pair the sting of injured pride with most pronounced traits of modernity. "Global economic standards and capitalist social structures assault traditional Muslim approaches to interest, insurance, and community," argues Emmanuel Sivan in his excellent book *Radical Islam.* Other foes are the "scientific method," which "subverts the habits of thought essential to true faith," and the "cult of economic growth, hedonism and permissiveness." These vices undermine family—the shrine of Muslim society—and overall morality—with the help of the media, which diffuses "promiscuity and consumerism." The list of things to hate also includes more abstract notions of democratic liberalism, utilitarian individualism, globalization, conspiracy against Islam, and the general "Weststruckness" or "Westoxication," as Iranian writer Jalal Al-e Ahmad called the perceived affront on the Muslim culture.[83]

Vehemence against "Western civilization is not primarily resentment against exploitation by domineering foreigners"; rather, it is the result of a degenerating communal life.[84] It is particularly difficult for those who find themselves on the fringes of the Muslim world, away from and deprived of the customary sustenance of the collective. Beyond its boundaries, these embryonic "selves" have difficulty functioning. They feel purposeless and are "frustrated by a Western society that does not meet their expectations."[85] And all the technological advances, material comforts, and other "advantages brought by the west are ineffectual substitutes for the sheltering and soothing anonymity of a communal existence."[86]

In psychological terms, Islamism "is a psychosocial disease characterized by the bad management of internal emotions in the Arab Moslem world."[87] Among the dispirited, there are some whose personal circumstances combine with generalized disaffection to escalate it to the level of "a boiling fury." These individuals are sought after and become easy prey for recruiters. "They conspire—forming secret... cabals," and movements, and they offer the disconnected outsiders a new system of values and an ideology, "a narrative—an actual story with a logical flow from glorious past through decadent present to reglorified future," as well as prototypes of heroes (rebels) and villains (the persecuting local and global enemies).[88] They provide all key attributes of a religion. The "identity entrepreneurs" also refurbish bruised honor and proffer a way out of the devastating private quandary through a process that entails turning the accumulated amorphous rage into directed and organized hatred.

Rage is central to the terrorist mentality. "As opposed to anger, which is quite specific in terms of what provokes the feelings and who or what the subject is, rage is generalized, unfocused and often of unknown etiology." It is easily manipulated to be "expressed at abstractions," such as a bourgeois class or the West.[89]

Hatred, psychologists tell us, "dwells on the past, thinks of revenge in the future, and... in linking past and future, establishes a sense of continuity"; as such it "might contribute to a person's identity"[90] and give "purpose to an empty life. Thus people haunted by the purposelessness... try to find a new content not only by dedicating themselves to a holy cause but also by nursing a fanatical grievance. A mass movement offers them unlimited opportunities for both,"[91] providing "substitute symbols" of hate.[92]

Hannah Arendt notes that "rage and violence turn irrational only when they are directed against substitutes."[93] This happens when the malcontents bond in ideological "brotherhoods" and designate a leader, a class, or a culture as a "symbolic explanation of and a psychological substitute for the far more complicated and pluralistic sources of... distress. In this case, "passive rage may be converted into active terrorism."[94]

Ideologists of the transnational Islamism introduce "the alienated marginals to a larger *umma* (community) of believers, from Tangier to Jakarta to London," reintegrating them into a group and resurrecting their lost sense of the communal self. The displaced and aggravated outcasts join the ranks of radical movement to restore broken and much-sought-after connections, and to "become members of a vibrant, if dangerous and destructive, international" corporate body.[95] To lose themselves in its oneness is their only salvation—"in becoming an anonymous particle with no will, judgment and responsibility" of their own.[96] In these circles dispatchers seek out particularly traumatized and embittered victims of modernization to participate in terror attacks against the environment, to which they had not been able to adjust.

Islamism unites "religious symbols and rhetoric with the ideology of revolutionary action," and various terrorist groups, including al Qaeda, "owe an explicit debt to 20th-century European doctrines of the extreme Right and Left." Such "distinctively Western terms as 'revolution,' 'state,' and 'ideology'" are attached to the "adjective 'Islamic'." Specialists point to the fact that the Islamist thinking has been influenced by a variety of seditious trends. These range from Italian Fascism (unquestionable loyalty to a charismatic leader and glorification of armed force in the paramilitary "Islamofascist" organization) to Nazism (the marriage of the physical and the spiritual) to Marxism ("revolutionary vanguard" against the exploitative "selfish individual" of the liberal West *and* the archaic practices of Islam). Diluted "Leninism in an Islamist dress" is the creed partially embraced by most Jihadists.[97] They are "best understood not as a traditional movement but as a very modern one," a latest incarnation of fundamentalism.[98]

Fundamentalists' psychological maladjustment precipitates aggression against the mainstream milieu. Akin to the Russian revolutionaries, Islamists direct their destructive energy persistently, if not always overtly, against prevalent cultural values, while making use of the know-how and the conveniences modernity offers. Certainly not "atavistic Luddites"; they assail it from within, with its own tools, such as technologies and the media. They also utilize its volatility.[99] We can discern the countercultural aspect of terrorism in the West (and in other modern societies greatly impacted by Western intellectual tendencies, such as Israel) in relation to a dominant set of principles clustered under the tag of postmodernism.

The influential postmodernist worldview embodies diverse, highly complex, ambiguous, paradoxical, and often contradictory intellectual and aesthetic tenets, fragmented and loosely fused by motifs of relativism and skepticism. In its sheer form, postmodernism rejects universality of any type—in judgment, knowledge, idiom, conventions, and ethics. It repudiates the idea of any objective truth (and sometimes even fact and meaning behind phenomena), which, it is commonly claimed, is not "discovered" but "constructed." Reality is thus in the hands of fabricators of a particular culture and, as such, is subjective to its appreciation by the onlooker and the perceiver. It is variable—depending on and accessible solely to the individual level of awareness. This outlook, which reached the apogee of its popularity in the early 1990s, guards against attempts to impart any absolute certainty, tantamount to intellectual coercion. Pluralism and maximum expansion of personal experience and options are prime objectives and implications of the postmodernist viewpoint.

In the 1900s the Russian radicals revealed their militant nihilism primarily in the sociopolitical realm. Battling cultures permeated with postmodernism, their present-day successors aim deeper, striking at the level of personal consciousness. While the postmodernist mindset bestows on the man the majesty of an "actuality designer," its enemies turn increasingly large numbers of individuals into anonymous casualty figures. Nihilism insinuates that "everything is meaningless,"[100] including one's alertness to his final departure—an inimitable, profoundly private exertion and potentially a creative achievement. By sapping meaning from death, the terrorists negate life's last vital experience.

The nihilistic denial and aggressiveness with regard to mainstream cultural tenants compels the extremists to defy language as a normative mode of discourse. Spurning dialogue, on which such great emphasis has been placed in modern and postmodern epochs, the terrorists have developed their own nonverbal, yet exceptionally effective way of communicating with giant audiences. Their means of communication are their targets.

Acts of murder are perpetrators' messages to the enemy. In the words of one Hamas leader, suicide bombings in residential neighborhoods of Tel Aviv and Jerusalem are "letters to Israel."[101] These communiqués, written in blood and circulated by sensational media coverage, are countercultural by definition, if culture is to be understood through the prism of envisaged, refined, and realized forms of mutuality.

Devotees of postmoderism dismiss "all forms of absolutism from eras past, especially Judeo-Christian faith and morals," and, paradoxically, "idolize absolutely their new secular trinity of tolerance–diversity–choice."[102] Any misgiving about the supremacy of these idols is blasphemous and inimical. The terrorists, who operate within the confines of their own simple- and single-minded *totalist counterculture*, are unable to coexist with the complexities, contradictions, and ironies inbuilt in "the other" way of life. Dull and primitively belligerent, they seek to obliterate it, in all its perplexing and lively manifestations. Annihilation becomes their raison d'être.

Chapter 2

The Uniform as Symbolic Target

> I did not know what kind of person the Samara governor was and what sort of official career he had, but...this was unimportant. He would probably have been killed even if he were the best governor.
>
> —Grigorii Frolov, assassin of the governor of Samara province in July 1906

> Though this be madness, yet there is method in 't.
>
> —William Shakespeare, *Hamlet*

The administration of Nicholas II, or "Nicholas the Last," as this proverbially ineffectual ruler came to be nicknamed, apparently in the very early days of his reign, operated in accordance with the tsar's declared intent to preserve the traditional political institutions of his empire as firmly as did his late father.[1] He would do so with the help of his sizable civil bureaucracy, a well-developed police force, and in cases of mass-scale domestic insubordination, the military. Yet, the unbridled campaign of terror in the early 1900s appeared as a threat the imperial regime did not expect and did not know how to handle.

Pertinent for Russia's predicament was Alexis de Tocqueville's pronouncement in *On the State of Society in France before the Revolution of 1789* that tyrannies are in greatest danger when they begin to reform and show liberal tendencies.[2] It is at these most critical moments of transformation that the foes of a political system are especially eager to intensify their use of violence. A sad irony of Russian history was that terrorism of the early 1900s reached its apogee upon the establishment of the constitutional order, after the emperor had granted the Manifesto of October 1905. The "October Manifesto" guaranteed legislative parliamentary powers to the State Duma and fundamental civil liberties to the Russian citizens. The radicals took this concession for what it indeed was—a sign of autocracy's weakness, which only encouraged them to take steps toward further destabilization and ultimate disintegration of their "terror-friendly" environment by way of bulging militancy.

The situation may appear familiar and akin to one following Israel's effort to attain peace with its neighbors by signing the so-called Oslo Accords of 1993, otherwise known as the Declaration of Principles on Interim Self-Government Arrangements, envisaged as a milestone in the process toward a resolution of the Arab–Israeli conflict. As part of the compromise, Israel agreed to withdraw its military forces from sections of the Gaza Strip and the West Bank, areas to be incorporated into the new Palestinian Authority (PA), and recognized Arafat's Palestinian Liberation Organization (PLO) as the legitimate voice of the "self-governing Palestinian people." In return, on paper the PLO renounced terrorism against Israel—in practice causing the outburst of the worst forms of violence in its history within the next decade, as well as deterioration of living conditions in the PA.[3]

When terrorism began to take mass forms in Russia in the post-1905 era, any official became a potential target—not as a consequence of his past actions but merely by virtue of his association with the detested political system. The terrorists thus began to attack state representatives of all ranks indiscriminately—ministers, high-ranking bureaucrats, police and military, street cops, soldiers, guards, and anyone else who fell under the extremely broad category that the extremists labeled as "watchdogs of the old regime."

Initially, prominent figures of the tsar's entourage remained the terrorists' most sought-after targets and were the first to go. However, protected by the state, they were also the most difficult to kill. Top-level assassinations required serious planning, competent management, trained cadres, and substantial financial investments; terrorists could carry them out only under the patronage of a large revolutionary organization.

The Party of Socialists-Revolutionaries (PSR), formed in late 1901, was the first newly consolidated radical organization since the dissolution of the People's Will formally to incorporate terrorist tactics into its program. To carry out thoroughly planned assassinations of the country's leaders—primarily in St. Petersburg and Moscow—the PSR headquarters established a special conspiratorial group that assumed the title of the "Combat Organization" (*Boevaia Organizatsiia*).

Its debut in terror occurred on April 2, 1902. A newly recruited member, former student Stepan Balmashev, dressed in the uniform of an aide-de-camp, which misled security of the Mariinskii Palace in St. Petersburg, entered the reception room of Interior Minister Dmitrii Sipiagin. With the precise movement of a would-be military officer, Balmashev handed the executive an envelope that contained his death verdict. He waited, allowing Sipiagin a few seconds to read to the end; the letter was signed "the Combat Organization."

When the minister looked up, flabbergasted, still not fully conscious of what was going on, the terrorist filet off two dead-on shots.

Balmashev was hanged in the infamous Schlisselburg prison a month later, but his lethal theatrical performance on behalf of the Combat Organization opened its all-out terrorist campaign. On July 29, 1902, woodworker Foma Kachura fired at the governor of Khar'kov, Prince I. M. Obolenskii. The terrorist missed his target but wounded the city's police chief, who had the misfortune to be in close proximity; Kachura's bullets were doused in strychnine.[4]

On May 6, 1903, Socialist Revolutionary Egor Dulebov (alias Agapov) shot and killed N. M. Bogdanovich, governor of the Ufa province. There, like in many other regions, chief administrators would be assassinated immediately after having been appointed, sometimes even before having had a chance to meet their immediate subordinates. The SRs alone took the lives of 33 vice-governors, governors, and governors-general, and 16 city governors across the empire.[5] Black humor of this period reflected death expectancy: "Last evening, His Excellency the governor-general held a small reception at his residence when he accepted congratulations from his associates on the three-week anniversary of his successful command of the area."[6]

The assassinations continued without interruption, earning the PSR a nickname—"the party of terror"—for a whole series of startling terrorist ventures against top officials in the capitals. One of the SRs' most spectacular attacks took place on July 15, 1904. Interior Minister Viacheslav von Plehve was on his way to a regular appointment with the emperor, when terrorist Egor Sazonov ran up to his carriage and tossed a bomb. The man whom radicals and liberals alike hated as one of Russia's most notorious reactionary was torn to pieces.[7] The Interior Minister had always known that it was only a matter of time before he would fall victim to a terrorist act; yet, diehard that he was, Plehve remained capable of morose self-irony. His servant once reportedly asked if he should remove from the staircase of his house the black bunting that had been hung for Sipiagin's funeral. Plehve replied, "No, you'd better save it; you can still use it for me."[8]

Inspired by their escapade, which the SRs had considered "a question of honor for the party," the Combat Organization set out to strike against the Romanov dynasty directly. On February 4, 1905, terrorist Ivan Kaliaev cast a homemade bomb under the carriage of the tsar's uncle, Grand Duke Sergei Aleksandrovich. A proponent of arch-conservative nationalist course, responsible for repressive educational policies and the expulsion of 20,000 Jews from Moscow at the start of his tenure as the city's governor-general, Sergei Aleksandrovich was the first member of the imperial family killed since 1881. The bomb blew up with a thunder that residents heard even in remote corners of Moscow; people in the neighborhood thought that this was an earthquake. The site of the explosion near the Kremlin featured the usual attributes of a terrorist feat: a shapeless heap "of small parts of the carriage, of clothes, and a mutilated body" of the Grand Duke with no head, and with fragments of human flesh and limbs scattered across the pavement.[9] The blast was so powerful that "some of Sergei's fingers were found on a nearby roof." The police persuaded his royal relatives to stay away from the funeral: it could not guarantee their safety.[10]

In December 1905, Admiral F. V. Dubasov became Moscow's fourth governor-general since February. "Good for Dubasov, such a difficult moment, and he did not lose his head," jeered the Muscovites; "but not to worry, he will lose it yet," they smiled knowingly.[11] Sure enough, on April 23, 1906, SR Boris Vnorovskii, dressed as a naval officer, threw under Dubasov's carriage what looked like a box of candies, wrapped in gift paper and tied with a ribbon. The explosion took the life of the terrorist and the governor's aide-camp; the coachman and several bystanders received injuries. Dubasov escaped unharmed, but three days after the botched assassination attempt, a satirical journal *Octopus* came out with a timely riddle—also a warning:

Question: What is the difference between the European ministers and ours?
Answer: The European ministers get thrown out of office, and ours get blown out![12]

Dubasov left his post before the extremists would have another chance to blow him to bits, but the prevailing wisdom held that any prominent official was doomed to fall victim to the terrorists sooner rather than later. The public might have taken for granted the PSR's death sentence to Plehve given his reactionary politics, yet, revealed one party member, the "organization had decided to execute all the ministers and their deputies, beginning with those who were least guarded."[13] Under the circumstances, it made no sense to print a biography of a new appointee, sneered the wisecrackers among journalists; the editor should wait a few days and then publish the same material in the obituary section.[14]

By late 1905, a bomb tossed under the carriage of a powerful public figure was a trademark of the SR assassinations. Whether or not the bureaucrats survived, their coachmen often suffered injuries and death. The closest contemporary analogy would be bus drivers in Jerusalem, victims of bomb blasts inside their vehicles during Intifada. Similarly, coachmen of Russia's statesmen unexpectedly found themselves trapped in one of the most hazardous occupations at the time. The bomb that tore to pieces the Grand Duke Sergei Aleksandrovich also severely wounded his coachman, and within days, commoners in the capitals recited a popular poem, titled "His Excellency's Driver":

Saddened by the past examples,
A driver to a powerful lord
Tries to soften SR terrorists
With lamenting, pleading word:

"Worthy terrorists, I toast you
And wish you a speedy victory!
But I beg you to take measures

> For my personal safety.
> I'm concerned about the future,
> Fear cuts me like a knife;
> Can you find a type of bomb
> That would spare the driver's life?"[15]

The Russians, however, could hardly be expected to retain their celebrated sense of humor at the expense of the state as the avalanche of violence after 1905 quickly descended from high circles to literally anyone in the government service. The sporadic centrally located attacks of the SR Combat Organization, though still making the newspaper headlines, drowned in countless terrorist episodes staged by other groups and individuals. Some of them still sought to inflict havoc in the capitals, but the majority preferred the periphery, where they felt free to operate with exceeding impunity.

During a one-year period beginning in October 1905, 3,611 officials of various ranks lost their lives or were injured as a result of terrorism across the empire. By the end of 1907, that number had risen to nearly 4,500.[16] From early January 1908 through mid-May 1910, 732 administrators were killed and 1,022 wounded. In sum, there were approximately 6,254 casualties during 1905–1910.[17] Adding to this number political assassinations of the 1901–1905 era and a few that took place after 1910, from the turn of the 20th century to the end of the imperial regime, terrorists were responsible for at least 6,300 victims among uniform-clad individuals across the country.

From late 1905 on, most perpetrators were anarchists. By virtue of their creed that eulogized unlimited freedom from any authority, they were hostile to the idea of unifying their loosely organized scattered circles, scattered across the empire, into a centrally controlled movement. In carrying out casual terrorist assaults, the anarchists acted side by side with the so-called Maximalists, dissenters from the PSR who had found its course not radical enough and who now participated in "pogrom-like mass killings."[18] Together, the anarchists and Maximalists competed for revolutionary glory with the numerous obscure extremists, who operated under such revealing titles as "Terror," "Death for Death" (*Smert' za smert'*), the "Black Cloud" (*Chernaia tucha*) and "Black Ravens" (*Chernye vorony*). One group had a lyrical name: "League of the Red Fuse" (*Liga krasnogo shnura*)[19]

That the anarchists "competed" for combat accomplishments with the Maximalists and other revolutionaries should be taken literally. Some proposed to organize terrorist "hunting parties," arguing that in certain historical moments it is indispensable indeed to "remove from the surroundings" even most petty officials "for pedagogical purposes."[20] The extremists often challenged and "raced" one another to see who would commit the greatest number of murders, often exhibiting jealousy over others' skill.[21] Analysts describe a similar tendency of "overbidding" in the Middle East, where terrorism is carried out "in competitive spirit," and a group "initiates or escalates suicide bombings to gain an ascendancy over other organizations.... Here the target audience is not the Israeli government but the Palestinian population. The emergence of al-Fatah's Al-Aqsa martyr brigades, for instance, was a direct response to the perceived success of Hamas." Not infrequently, competing claims of responsibility for the same attack would come from several factions, rivaling for the terrorist laurels.[22] "Woodchoppers" (*drovokoly*) was the name given to their Russian predecessors by a fellow radical. By early 1906, terrorism in a very real sense had transformed into a sport, in which players regarded their random and anonymous victims as nothing more than moving targets.[23]

It became the favored entertainment for the extremists to open fire at soldiers or Cossacks and to throw bombs into the police barracks. "When the burning fuses hiss, the policemen jump out the windows"—this was a show worth seeing.[24] A terrorist would wait patiently for a chance to toss a bomb down from the balcony into the middle of a passing military detachment.[25] Another favorite game of the extremists, while out for an evening's stroll, was to throw sulfuric acid in the face of the first policeman encountered on the street.[26]

"These were days," recalls a former gendarme investigator, "when several major terrorist acts went hand-in-hand with dozens" of lower-caliber assassinations. Threatening letters did not count; there was a rare police officer who did not receive them.[27] Of the 671 employees of the Interior Ministry who were killed or wounded by terrorists between October 1905 and the end of April 1906, only 13 held top posts; the other 658 were city street policemen, coachmen, and security personnel.[28] The respectable liberal publication *Pravo* (*The Law*) reported that in June 1906, attacks on officials averaged 19.4 per week, and the fatality rate was soaring.[29] It no longer made a difference whether one was a gendarme or a traffic cop; both were fair game. In fact, more rank-and-file policemen and soldiers lost their lives than any other state servants simply because they were such an easy prey, they were visible enough to attract the attention of anyone seeking an opportunity to express anger—as were the Cossacks, guards, and prison staff.

Maximalists in St. Petersburg and Moscow busied themselves with developing breathtaking terrorist enterprises, including a plan to send a carriage full of dynamite into the courtyard of the secret police (Okhrana) building. They had prepared enough explosives to destroy entirely the massive structure of the police headquarters, hoping to maximize deaths either by fire or under the debris.[30] Since few such large-scale operations could be materialized, the radicals supplemented them with multiple, if less dramatic feats. In once such incident, a Maximalist rang the doorbell of a police-occupied apartment and then shot randomly at anyone who showed up in the hallway. He escaped, leaving at least three people dead.[31] "Every day there are several assassinations, either by bomb or revolver or knife, or various other instruments," complained an Okhrana agent; "they strike and strike anyhow and at anybody...and one is surprised that they have not yet wiped out all of us."[32]

The upsurge of assassinations flooded the border areas, such as the Caucasus, the Baltic regions, and the empire's western provinces, including Poland, where even the most conservative estimate of the extent of violence speaks for itself. In the city of Warsaw alone, 15 lower-ranking officials lost their lives on an average month in 1906.[33] During the notorious Bloody Wednesday on August 2, extremists affiliated with the Polish Socialist Party (PPS) attacked scores of police and military patrols simultaneously in various sections of the city. They killed nearly 50 and injured twice that number.[34] In the course of 1905–1906, the terrorists in Poland assassinated 790 military, gendarme, and police officers and wounded 864.[35]

Terrorist organizations benefited from widespread anti-Russian attitudes in Poland and other fringes of the empire, where separatist sentiments ran high and where from time to time private citizens proved willing to help—not because they shared the radicals' sociopolitical objectives, but solely to express their nationalist sentiments. Antagonistic to the tsar's rule nationalist sympathizers among the locals sometimes refused to provide aid to wounded civil and military appointees of St.Petersburg. Some donated money specifically for the purchase of weapons; others helped manufacture explosives. There have been a few cases when individuals not affiliated with extremist organizations attacked police convoys on the streets and liberated arrested terrorists.[36]

The situation was similar in the Caucasus, where in 1904–1905, "assassinations of representatives of the old regime occurred almost daily."[37] In various corners of the region, the extremists attacked military and police officers and inflicted unremitting violence on the Russian Orthodox church, butchering the clergy.[38] Mass-scale attacks spilled into 1906 and beyond. In 1907, the Russian viceroy Prince I. I. Vorontsov-Dashkov reported a gravely understated total of 689 terrorist acts. He did his best not to appear inert or inept in the eyes of his St. Petersburg superiors; yet his report acknowledged that 183 officials had been killed and 90 injured.[39]

Unlike the defiant Poland and Caucasus, Latvia, Lithuania, and Estonia had little prior history of open protest against the imperial order. Yet according to the governor-general's office, 1,700 assassinations and 3,076 armed assaults occurred in the Baltic region during 1905–1906.[40] We should accept these figures with caution. In the general chaos, the local authorities could not always separate political violence from common crime; yet it is certain that over a two-year period ending in January of 1906, 110 members of the police force in the city of Riga died in terrorist attacks—one of every four on staff.[41] The radicals also exterminated other local military and civil servants, many of whom belonged to the German nobility that traditionally played a dominant role in the region. United into militant bands, the extremists plundered and burned the nobles' country manors; their less heedless comrades accused them of vandalism for destroying large libraries, priceless paintings, and other works of art. In 1906–1907, extremists devastated and burned more than half of all estates in the Riga district alone, inflicting 1.5 million rubles in damage.[42] Once again, the dark humor of the day illuminates the situation better than any description: "Opening soon will be an exhibition of the revolutionary movement in the Baltic provinces," declared one anecdotal newspaper announcement; "among the exhibits are reported to be: a real live Latvian, a German castle that has not been destroyed, and a policeman who has not been shot."[43]

In their dispatches to the central administration, authorities in the particularly unstable areas recognized that they were completely powerless to control events and described their influence as "only nominal." Such was the situation in the borderlands and the so-called Pale—designated as restricted places of residence for most Russian Jews. In these rebellious localities, the police often did not even dare to show themselves on the street, where they were targets for gunfire on sight.[44]

* * *

The enormous wave of terror achieved its primary purpose as early as 1905; the authorities were confused and worn out, confessing that the omnipresent terrorists have paralyzed all their "strength and means for struggle."[45] Moscow city governor G. P. Medem—the fourth person to hold this post between January and November 1905—petitioned to be relieved of his duties since "he felt physically and morally exhausted."[46] Other servicemen of various ranks expressed a similar sense of helplessness and despair; their past experience with the People's Will's strikes against individually selected enemies was of little help in the situation of mass terror. By mid-1906, in the midst of widespread violence, top police officials in St. Petersburg were ready to set aside all other matters, including investigation of revolutionary propaganda, illegal print operations, and labor protest, in order to concentrate on their most urgent problem, the extremists' plans for terrorist acts and expropriations.

The police chiefs found themselves under enormous pressure from the Winter Palace, where the royal family and the court voluntarily submitted themselves to virtual house arrest. Other prime targets for terrorist attacks also demanded from their subordinates strong anti-terrorist measures and immediate results. Yet, although individual members of the police forces revealed outstanding personal courage and selflessness, on the whole, the initial "reaction to the mounting terrorist campaign can only be characterized as vacillating and irresolute."[47]

Lower-level security officials appeared especially ill-equipped as protectors of the tsarist regime, with their superiors lamenting that in 1905 they were in charge of "a caricature of the secret political police."[48] Many policemen thought only of personal safety and either applied for immediate retirement and fled their posts or simply failed to appear for duty to replace their assassinated predecessors.[49] The head of the St. Petersburg Okhrana faced constant noncompliance from his agents, who threatened to go on strike: they were too scared of the terrorists to proceed with their work. Street policemen, equipped with outdated rifles and sabers, also demonstrated cowardice and sometimes allowed combatants to disarm them without any resistance, begging the extremists to spare their lives. "I know what a Browning is like: just one nudge and it starts shooting all of a sudden," complained one terrified officer, who had a revolver in his pocket when the radicals attacked him.[50] Local authorities admitted that they lived in constant "terrible panic." According to one report, the incidence of nervous ailments of the gendarme corps augmented dramatically.[51]

Realizing that it could not rely on the police system, the autocracy sought to strengthen it with the help of the military. In fact, law enforcement personnel often refused to act against the extremists unless it had the support of the army in guarding banks, post and telegraph offices, railroad stations, trains, and other usual terrorist sites, including police stations. For its part, the military leadership on all levels resented the deployment of troops for security purposes—practices that impeded regular national defense training and demoralized the rank-and-file. At a time when expropriators raided financial institutions on a daily basis, photographs illustrated the administrative response better than any report: as a typical scene, at the guarded entrance to a bank or a post office, three soldiers protected each policeman from Russia's most formidable foes at the moment, its domestic enemies.[52]

The authorities' incompetence against the daring and increasingly adroit expropriators quickly became the subject of trendy satire. In one anecdote, the police officers allegedly received the following "new energetic directives" after a bank robbery:

1. Guard thoroughly those sites that have already been robbed by the malefactors;
2. Report all robbery cases no later than an hour before their occurrence;
3. Take photographs of criminals who have disappeared without a trace;
4. Send the entirety of stolen sums to police headquarters without delay as material evidence;
5. Travel around the city and ask each individual inhabitant whether it was he who stole the money from the bank.[53]

With lawlessness being the order of the day, some confused and desperate officials took justice into their own hands and turned into vigilantes. One way to combat the revolution was to adopt its tactics, they decided, and proceeded to organize small combat bands for the purpose of assassinating radical activists. Their only achievement was further anarchy.[54]

It took months before the Russian authorities began to overcome their initial paralysis for the benefit of an effective counterterrorist policy. The effort was associated primarily with the person of Petr Stolypin, appointed to the post of interior minister on the eve of the First Duma opening in April 2006. A few months later, the former governor of the Grodno, then the turbulent Saratov province, became also chair of the Council of Ministers and thus the de facto prime minister—out of term, as far as Stolypin's career was concerned, above all because no one else dared take these appointments. "Sedition, unrest and criminal attacks" had placed the empire under siege, the extremists had declared war on the government, which was forced to respond accordingly, with "rapid, firm and undeviating" measures,[55] the interior minister announced in his new hard-line policy aimed to demonstrate that terror could be stopped.

It was the Maximalists who took up the challenge to prove him wrong. On August 12, 1906, two men dressed in gendarme uniforms and one in civilian clothes entered the Stolypin's St. Petersburg mansion on Aptekarskii Island. When guards tried to stop them, the terrorists detonated their 16-pound bombs in the anteroom, instantly killing themselves along with 27 innocent petitioners—the poor, women, and the elderly—all awaiting appointment with the interior minister during his visiting hours. The Maximalists missed their main target: by chance Stolypin's office was the single room that suffered relatively little harm; only an ink well was thrown from his desk by the force of the explosion and stained his face and clothes. However, along with dozens of others casualties, the terrorists wounded the minister's four-year-old son, crippled his teenage daughter, and caused enormous property damage: "The whole house was shrouded in heavy smoke," a witness reported, "The entire façade was destroyed. All around lay fragments of the balcony and the roof. Under the debris—the broken carriage and writhing wounded horses. Moans were heard all around. There were pieces of human flesh and blood everywhere."[56]

On Stolypin, who as governor had been terrorists' target in the past, the viciousness of this suicide attack had an effect contrary to the intended fear. "You will not intimidate us,"[57] he declared from the Duma floor, and on August 19, 2006, initiated a system of field courts-martial for civilians in regions proclaimed to be under either martial law or "extraordinary security." Appointed by local military commanders, five officer-judges in these courts would issue rulings against individuals whose implication in extremist practices—such as terrorist attacks, robberies, as well as fabricating, concealing, or utilizing explosive devices—were obvious enough not to require prolonged investigation. Defendants were allowed to call on witness, but they had no access to legal advice during the closed hearings, which convened within 24 hours of the arrest and reached verdicts in 48 hours. The verdicts could not be appealed and would be implemented no later than 24 hours after pronouncement.[58]

Stolypin's measures were aimed to address earlier leniency, with which law enforcement personnel and the judicial system as a whole had handled multiplying terrorist cases. Its inability to protect the country from raging violence triggered discouragement and paralysis among police officials in charge of establishing security. One police department officer described the general mood:

> The latest verdicts in political trials are truly horrifying, for after several months, all those convicted, having pent their terms in confinement, return to the path

> of revolutionary activity with redoubled energy. In reading such verdicts one really loses heart... What is the use of wasting money on the investigation and detainment of people who will be locked in prison for several months at best and then let loose with an opportunity to go back to their previous work.[59]

Memories of "complete freedom" in prisons prior to 1907 were carried by many radicals after liberation from confinement.[60] "Discipline and supervision were often shockingly lax;" intimidated guards often closed their eyes to or "resisted halfheartedly" political inmates' escape attempts[61]—an option that many extremists bypassed: to remain in incarceration, they admitted to have "consented... voluntarily" knowing "that they would surely soon become free" legally and thus avoid the life of a wandering fugitive.[62] Prison terms were relatively short; the terrorists could usually count on the interference of liberal lawyers and judges to rescue them from severe punishments, fear of which generally did not serve as serious deterrent from partaking in terror. Under the circumstances, with terrorism holding "the country in its bloody grip... no government in the world could have remained passive."[63]

In the century to come, another attempt at mass-scale ideological violence, this time in Peru, perhaps most closely resembled the Russian situation in the early 1900s. Maoist Shining Path (Sendero Luminoso) and the Cuban-inspired Marxist-Leninist Tupac Amaru Revolutionary Movement (Movimiento Revolucionario Túpac Amaru—MRTA) were the two main rebel groups that operated in Peruvian provinces and the capital of Lima in the 1980s and 1990s. "They terrorized Peru," recapped former U.S. ambassador to Venezuela Alvin Adams, the State Department's associate coordinator for counterterrorism between 1987 and 1989.[64] The human and economic toll was devastating: civil rights groups estimate that more than 30,000 people became victims of indiscriminate bombings, assassinations and kidnappings of officials, bank robberies, and attacks on Western embassies and businesses; the extremists also blew up electrical transmission towers, generating city-wide blackouts, and set off explosives inside the ruling party's headquarters. The regime of Alberto Fujimori succeeded in its vicious anti-terrorism crusade that continued over a decade and claimed approximately as many lives as had taken the terrorists. The 21st-century resurgence of Shining Path's activity, notably a bomb explosion that killed 9 and wounded 30 outside of the U.S. embassy a few days before President G. W. Bush's expected visit to Lima in March 2002, followed in 2003–2009 by sporadic, yet recurrent grenade and dynamite attacks against the Peruvian police and army officers, suggests that the struggle may not be over.[65]

Under Stolypin's leadership, the "most sustained, brutal and... controversial repressive campaign[66] lasted for eight months when military jurisprudence resembled legality only vaguely. A typical sentence handed down by the field courts was hard labor—up to 15 years for manufacture and possession of explosives, and death—almost without exception as a reprisal for being involved in terrorist acts and armed robberies.[67] As a result, by the time the extra-judicial system expired in April 1907, between 950 and 1,100 extremists had been shot or hanged by the military execution squads.[68] Simultaneously, the government took urgent steps to improve domestic security, especially police investigative methods, as well as to toughen the detention system. Probably the most talented minister since the death of the great 19th-century administrative genius Alexander Speransky, Stolypin envisaged a series of imperative domestic reforms, infeasible before he had harnessed radicalism—the challenge he took on as a hard-liner and a commanding "master of the situation."[69]

Fury erupted against the "Bloody Nicholas" and his extra-legal procedures to suppress the extremists. The liberal left cursed Stolypin; world-famous novelist Leo Tolstoy, the "voice of consciousness" of the nation, announced that state violence was far worse than terrorism from below. The establishment suffered from an overwhelmingly negative public image in Europe as well: "virtually all leaders of society and most of the press vehemently denounced" Russian despotism.[70] The extremists hated the prime minister more than the inert Nicholas II and considered Stolypin their number one enemy, whose elimination was "even more important than the removal of the Tsar himself."[71]

As long as "bombs are used as an argument, ruthless retribution is certainly a natural response," the prime minister countered in response to overwhelming criticism.[72] When an overconfident deputy publicly labeled his policies "Stolypin's neckties," the handsome aristocrat stepped down from his ministerial seat in the Duma and challenged his offender to a duel, forcing him to apologize. "Our prime minister is noted for his terrible manner of knotting ties round people's necks,"[73] intended puns and anecdotes still reflected his image, concocted as the personification of oppression.

Stolypin remained the exception among high-ranking statesmen, vacillating and anxious not to antagonize the radicals still further or to appear as semi-Asiatic barbarians in the eyes of their country's Western allies. Penitent defenders of the old regime felt guilty for being on the "reactionary side"; some sympathized with the "unfortunate politicals" and occasionally even helped their declared enemies—contributing to their perception of the autocracy's fading strength.[74]

To be sure, the courts-marshal and other counterterrorist measures did deter many extremists: having reached its peak in August 1906, the wave of attacks against state officials slowly began to wane. Reduced violence coincided with the general weakening of the revolutionary storm—attributable in equal measure to Stolypin's relentless effort against the radicals and to his impressive socioeconomic reforms, aimed primarily at enhancing citizens' responsibility for the adherence to common and property laws.

Even so, terrorism had "succeeded in breaking the spine of Russian bureaucracy; wounding it both physically and in spirit."[75] It never fully recovered from the traumatizing experience of the 1905–1907 era, as became evident already in the next decade. Fatefully, Stolypin had fallen victim to the last major terrorist incident in the prerevolutionary period. When a new surge of antigovernment activity broke out in early 1917, there became apparent on the political scene a glaring absence of a statesman sufficiently committed and equipped with enough fortitude to overcome the crisis. As it was, men called on to defend the imperial order succumbed to intimidation of what they came to perceive as a recurrence of the prior devastating experience. A déjà vu, it caused a paralysis of will, this time fatal to the autocracy.

better to have maintained it?

* * *

Indiscriminate and symbolic killings of officials intensified the extremists' onslaught against modern culture by undermining the "individual," modernity's focal point and showpiece. For the first time in history, the extremists acted as if their target had effectively relinquished his humanity once he had associated himself in any way with the enemy camp. From that moment, in the eyes of the radicals, he no longer merited treatment as anything other than a fragment in the state organism. As far as they were concerned, that tiny particle had no separate self or existence apart from the larger entity, hideous and liable for obliteration.

Striving primarily to uproot the establishment by eliminating its nameless representatives en masse, as opposed to punishing them for particular deeds, terrorism dehumanized them via an outright denial of personal responsibility. Random murder rendered victims' choices invalid and empty. Deeper than their immediate and apparent political aims, the radicals strove to shatter the core of the contemporary culture, which extolled a vision of the maximum self-realization and individual rather than collective, decision-making. Emblematic violence thus came to pose as a nihilistic, countercultural rejoinder to the epoch's quintessential ideal.

Any object, invested with meaning, could denote a loathed reality; symbol was in the eye of the extremist beholder. A Russian citizen wearing a badge after 1905 would be attacked as a live emblem of the establishment. Figurative enemies—anonymous state and public employees, whose jobs required that they follow a dress code—found themselves at risk. Guards became Russia's endangered species, as did essentially any daredevil audacious enough to show himself publicly in a uniform.[76]

Human beings perished, and so did inanimate representations of the traditional sociocultural environment, caving in under the terrorists' blows. The extremists detonated explosives next to historic buildings, monuments, and statues of national heroes—emblems of the imperial grandeur. To add weight to their campaign against religion ("opium for the people"), which the radicals believed endorsed and substantiated oppression, they razed churches, shrines, and monasteries. They also made attempts to demolish ritual objects held sacred by the Russian Orthodox believers, such as the revered Icon of the Virgin of Kursk[77]—similar to blazing churches in today's Pakistan and synagogues in Istanbul and Karakas. Gestures of unmitigated contempt for centuries-old values, these have also been potent practical steps by militant nihilists to obliterate life's symbolic foundations, as in the barbaric destruction of the 1,500-year-old statues of Buddha, hewn out of a cliff in the valley of Bamiyan, northwest of Kabul. In the eyes of the Islamists, the United States is a representation of reviled modernity, and their ultimate accomplishment in emblematic annihilation to date was the 110-story World Trade twin towers, "an icon of American enterprise," and "the Pentagon, the symbol of American military supremacy.[78]

The perpetrators of political violence integrate underlying contemporary values impressionistically and express their attitudes in sweeping strokes. They draw on the environment, as they did in St. Petersburg, whose regal architectural ensemble served a stage for "street theater of performance violence,"[79] and its arrow-like, strictly parallel avenues as the would-be broadsheet lines to convey the terrorists' intimidating messages to the public at large. The choice of targets is vital for issuing statements replete with symbolic associations, as affirmed in the notebook of Osama bin Laden's devotee El Sayyid Nosair: "We have to thoroughly demoralize the enemies of God.... by means of destroying and blowing up the towers that constitute the pillars of their civilization, such as the tourist attractions and the high buildings of which they are so proud."[80]

The 1972 Summer Olympics in Munich boasted a motto: "the Happy Games." This was the second such event after the 1936 Games in Berlin, the capital of the dark Nazi power about to plunge the world into a bloodbath. Now the world was to witness a spectacular sporting event, symbolizing optimism and international friendship in the restored democracy. This was precisely the moment chosen by the "Black September," a covert special-operations unit of Arafat's al-Fatah, to break into the Olympic Village, take hostage, and eventually murder 11 Israeli team members and coaches, "striking at a target of inestimable value (in this case a country's star athletes) in a setting calculated to provide the terrorists with unparalleled exposure and publicity."[81] The massacre denoted extremists' eagerness to kill the athletes, who represented the state of Israeli with their blue-and-white sport outfits with the Magen David insignia. The terrorist act was equally emblematic in its undisguised negation of the ancient cultural tradition, perceived by millions as integral to Western civilization. With hindsight, the slaughter revealed itself as yet another symbol—of the ongoing acceleration of terrorist violence directed primarily against civilians.

CHAPTER 3

Civilians under Fire

A man in white gloves... [is] an enemy who deserves death.

—Russian anarchist

"I want to do evil, and it has nothing to do with illness."
"Why do evil?"
"So that everything might be destroyed. Ah, how nice it would be if everything were destroyed."

—Fyodor Dostoevsky, *The Brothers Karamazov*

Russian terrorism evolved in such as way that the line between state and society "was completely obliterated." Miller cogently elucidates the patterns of the 20th-century political violence: "Behind this expanding zone of battle was the desire to annihilate the implicit social contract... Former distinctions between tyrants and the oppressed were no longer operative. The entire relation between citizens and authorities became politicized. Although everyone might not have been guilty, no one was innocent."[1]

According to terrorist statistics encompassing the period from 1905 through the end of 1907, 2,180 private individuals had lost their lives, and 2,530 had been injured in attacks across the empire—the total of 4,710 being just above the figures concerning victims among government officials. Of the 7,634 terrorist casualties in the subsequent years, however, at least 5,880 were civilians and only 1,754 state employees.[2] By that time, violence had clearly lost the overwhelmingly anti-bureaucratic overtones of the earlier era. While killing government servants of various ranks indiscriminately, the extremists broadened the category of their enemies to include individuals whose work and social status had nothing to do with the autocratic regime. It was as if the new wave of terrorist acts has turned from a means into a self-serving end—in Russia and, in the century to come, elsewhere; it was also "as if these acts were designed to maximize the savage nature of their violence."[3]

For the anarchists, Maximalists, and members of many obscure extremist gangs, the political goal to overthrow the government of Nicholas II was only a partial objective. Their "program maximum" included the demolition of the contemporary order entirely—with all its laws and institutions, its religion and customs, and its traditions and relationships. They therefore disagreed with the official policy of other radicals, such as the SRs, regarding the use of contained terror: it was not enough, the extremists insisted, to win concessions from the state via violent action; terrorism should continue until the final hour of the bourgeois establishment. Their hostility thus extended to the bourgeoisie, against whom they wished to take direct action "without entering into any compromises" and "without putting forth any concrete demands."[4] By "direct action" these radicals meant terrorist assaults on their class enemies' lives and property.

The largest and most active anarchist organization in Russia was a federation of scattered groups known as the "Black Banner" (*Chernoe znamia*). Its members cheered casual, reckless, and boundless violence. In their opinion, the existing state oppression and economic enslavement were sufficient motives "for direct attack, collective or individual, on the oppressors and exploiters, requiring no justification."[5] These activists recognized the arbitrary nature of the terrorism they promoted and even gave it a special name: "motiveless terror."

The "Black Banner" ideology, which emphasized the anarchists' struggle against private property, legitimized their strikes at each and every industrialist, entrepreneur, or property owner—not for a particular offense against the downtrodden, but because he represented the capitalist world. An exploiter he was, if only because of his social position. Thus, any attack against property holders, however random and senseless it might have appeared to the general public, was in the anarchists' eyes a step toward the liberation of the people.

Other groups bolstered the notion of motiveless violence. The Anarchists-Communists endorsed it because in comparison with antigovernment terrorism, "economic (antibourgeois) terror was a better means of propaganda" of revolutionary ideas. With this in mind, the group leaders urged their followers to cast aside all scruples when throwing bombs into restaurants and theaters because these places of entertainment existed exclusively for the amusement of the rich. "The death of the bourgeoisie is life for the workers," the extremists insisted.[6] Anyone who was not a dispossessed proletarian deserved to be killed along with other enemies of the revolution—members of monarchist clubs, associates of patriotic or reactionary publications, conservative intellectuals, judges, and the clergy. In the true spirit of motiveless terror, anarchists who belonged to the group called "Without Authority"

(Beznachalie) carried out haphazard acts of violence under the far-reaching slogan "Death to the bourgeoisie!" And finally, the Anarchists-Individualists announced that they considered themselves free to kill anyone at all, even if the only aim behind the murder was personal gratification. The way they saw it, any terrorist act, without distinction, contributed to the destruction of the oppressive environment.[7]

It is small wonder that in the midst of bloodletting, human life was cheapened and quickly lost all value. Terrorists' victims soon included individuals from every social stratum, most being by no means exploiters of the poor; some were not even property owners. Yet as far as the revolutionaries were concerned, the range of their class enemies was very wide: from bankers, factory directors, and wealthy merchants to petty retail dealers and supervisors in shoemakers' shops who refused to go along with a strike or who hired strikebreakers during a work stoppage.[8]

The anarchists often directed their attacks not only against owners and administrators of a particular industrial or commercial enterprise (and occasionally their family members) but also against its managers, technicians, engineers, and other specialists. They were part of the oppressors' camp by virtue of their education, employment, and even appearance. In fact, a well-dressed person out on the streets of some provincial town took a chance with his life; a trigger for extremists' aggression could simply be that he did not look like a typical worker and perhaps wore glasses. It was enough for someone to possess a watch to be labeled a bourgeois who deserved a bullet.[9]

Hailing class revenge, extremists tossed hand grenades into first-class railway compartments full of apparently prosperous passengers. On November 14, 1905, a group of Anarchists-Communists threw two bombs, packed with nails and bullets, into a large family café in the Hotel Bristol, where more than two hundred customers were present. The terrorists' only aim, as stated in a post factum leaflet, was "to see how the foul bourgeois would squirm in death agony."[10] A month later, newspaper headlines screamed of motiveless violence again: on December 17, 1905, the anarchists exploded bombs in the Libman Café in the terror-ravaged Odessa. They intended this attack to be a sensational social protest statement, but the ruined coffee shop, as it turned out, was not an elite restaurant for the well-to-do, but a second-class establishment, a favorite hangout for students and intellectuals.[11]

Not that the perpetrators thought of such acts as faux pas. Motiveless terror was effective regardless of the social status of its victims, and the extremists went on hurling hand grenades into local grocery shops for no better reason than "protest against private property."[12] They tossed bombs into streetcars because passengers could, presumably, afford the fare.[13]

Writing this, I remember one of my visits to Jerusalem in 2002, at the height of terror. Fresh in everyone's memory was the August 9, 2001 blast that razed pizzeria "Sbarro" in a busy pedestrian crossing; 15 people, 7 of them children, were killed and 130 wounded. On March 9, 2002, another terrorist exploded inside a popular coffee shop "Moment" killing 11 and injuring 54. On July 31, the Hebrew University student cafeteria was gutted by a bomb detonated during lunch time; 9 Israeli and foreign citizens were killed and 85 wounded. A colleague of mine met me at the downtown café Rimon. We sat at a table, and, casting an inquisitive look at the door, he noted as a matter of fact: "If a suicide bomber walked in now, he would kill two specialists on terrorism in one blow."

* * *

On March 20, 1995, members of the Shoko Asahara–led cult Aum Shinrikyo ("Supreme Truth") released a deadly sarin nerve gas on several subway lines at the peak of the Monday-morning rush hour in Tokyo, a site of one of the busiest commuter systems in the world. The purpose of the act was an "apocalyptic statement" about the imminent universal cataclysm or "Armageddon," which it certainly was for hundreds of passengers writhing on the floor, convulsing, gasping for air, vomit and blood gushing from their noses and mouths. As part of this "theatrical display of... deliberately exaggerated violence," the Aum Shinrikyo experts had considered adding a floral scent to sarin "to encourage more people to inhale it." If the gas had not been diluted to 30 percent of its full strength so as to protect the cult members transporting it, thousands subway patrons would have perished. As it was, the Aum Shinrikyo assault was responsible for 12 deaths, over 5,500 injuries, and an upsurge of panic among the users of public transportation in Japan and elsewhere.[14] In botched efforts of "science supported mass murder," cult members established chemical factories, staged at least nine biological attacks, and had sprayed microbes and germ toxins from rooftops and convoys of tracks to fight "dark conspiracies" of Jews and Americans (the U.S. "Beast," as in the *Book of Revelation*), and in preparation for world revolution. Avid to bring about the Day of Judgment, terrorists, in the 1900s or in the 1990s, do not discriminate between state officials and private citizens.

We are unable to estimate even roughly how many civilians have been killed and wounded since the 1991 outbreak of the Chechen war of independence from Russian control. Death figures range from 100,000 to more than 200,000, and the lack of precise data testifies to the genocide. The rebels blame it on the federal forces. Independent sources confirm that the Russian military and anti-terrorist units have indeed been engaged in aerial bombardments, "mopping operations," and torture and abuse of inmates in the so-called filtration camps; they are responsible for gross violations of basic humanitarian norms and the law in the war-ravaged territory of Chechnya.[15] To supplement criminal behavior of the enemy, the would-be indigenous "protectors of the national rights and honor" have committed their share of atrocities in this grisly conflict, exposing the civilians to daily robberies, extortion, assaults, rape, and murder. Armed gangs led by self-appointed commanders have divided the area into spheres of influence, ravaged by competition among the profit-making warlords—supported and exploited by third parties, fundamentalists of various orientations concerned with promoting conflict and militancy rather than specific Chechen national interests. The trademark of these rebels has been enslavement and kidnappings for ransom—a form of expropriation to finance terrorist activities: in 2003 alone the combat groups abducted more than 330 people; in 2004 that number soared to 500.

Violence quickly spread to territories adjacent to Chechnya, such as North Ossetia, culminating in the Beslan school massacre, for which terrorist commander Shamil Basaev claimed responsibility. "Whatever horrors the Russians have perpetrated upon the Chechens," recaps journalist David Brooks, in discussing the meaning of the carnage, "it wasn't Russian authorities who stuffed basketball nets with explosives and shot children in the back as they tried to run away."[16] The group of hostage-takers included Chechens but also Russians and, according to uncorroborated reports, citizens of up to 10 Arab countries.[17] This "terrorist international" had nothing personal against children, their parents, their teachers, or the Ossetins generally, who were neutral in the lingering Russo–Chechen conflict and certainly in no position to influence its outcome. Nor, under any circumstances, could the organizers of the school holdup expect the crisis to cause Putin's government to succumb to their pointless demand—evacuation of Russian troops from Chechnya.

The act of hostage-taking and the brutalities that followed were but a means to achieve a psychological effect on the public by staging a show of meaningless suffering in the North Caucasus. A would-be scene of the national liberation struggle, said to have been fought "to exact retribution for the sake of honor."[18] In truth, the region turned into a playground for adherents of Vahabism and other forms of Islamic extremism.[19] Western media have reported on the local combatants being integrated into the al-Qaeda network, with its representatives from Saudi Arabia, Jordan, Morocco, Algeria, and Egypt operating side by side with the Chechens and some Georgians, including those involved in gun contraband and drug trade.[20] According to intelligence sources, until his death in 2006, al-Qaeda's main liaison in Iraq, "Prince of Jihad" Abu Musab al Zarqawi, trained terrorists in the Caucasus, as did Abu Khabab, the group's chemical and biological weapons specialist. Some security experts have warned that the region, only three hours by plane from Europe, might replace Afghanistan as an "al-Qaeda zone." Chechnya could become "an aircraft carrier" from which Islamic terrorists would launch attacks against major European cities.[21] Bin Laden must have had good reason for contributing $25 million to local criminal business model of jihad.[22]

Authorities may dispute the validity of these threats but not the fact that the ambitions of Caucasian terrorist chiefs surpass the avowed goal of Chechen independence. Basaev "talked of taking the fight beyond the borders of Chechnya to establish a pan-Islamic state across the northern Caucasus."[23] His lieutenant Amir Ramzan boasted in an interview with the Chechen propaganda web site Kavkaz Center: we form "militant sabotage groups locally. We are joined by a lot of Kabardinians, Dagestanis, Karachaevans, Ingushetians and even Ossetians" of Muslim faith. The interviewer then asked, "That means that those in Russia who say that you want to create a caliphate in the Caucasus from [the Caspian] sea to [the Black] sea, are right?" "Yes, it is so," confirmed Ramzan, "I swear by Allah, this is only the beginning."[24]

One can go on and on, describing deadly incidents in various parts of the world that the perpetrators classify as "military operations against civilians." From the beginning of the so-called second or al-Aqsa Intifada, which broke out in September 2000, through January 1, 2005, 1,030 Israelis lost their lives as a result of terrorist acts; 717 of them were killed in attacks directed specifically against civilians. Between 2001 and 2007, among the 8,341 wounded, 5,676 were civilian victims.[25] Palestinian terrorist acts against civilian targets in Israel accounted for 88 percent of suicide missions and for 75.4 percent of conventional attacks.[26]

"Allah willing, this unjust state will be erased" from the face of the earth, the Palestinian religious leaders announce during public prayers, one of those leaders being Sheikh Ibrahim Madhi of Gaza. "The time will come, by Allah's will, when their property will be destroyed and their children will be exterminated, and no Jew or Zionist will be left on the face of this earth," proclaims another cleric, Ziad Abu Alhaj, on public television.[27] The extremists have repeatedly declared any and all Israeli citizens to be legitimate targets because they *represent* (even if not necessarily espouse) Zionism, the mortal enemy.

Terrorists strike at defenseless citizens because they anticipate a greater rate of success than if they were to attack well-protected military targets. Perhaps more importantly, the psychological effect of arbitrary civilian death is much stronger than the impact of casualties among the enemy in uniform. Osama bin Laden obviously acted on this assumption when in February 1998 he issued a *fatwa* (religious ruling), underscoring the urgency to target particularly the American civilians.[28]

* * *

In the early stages of the Russian crisis, terrorists found occasional understanding of and, in rare cases, assistance from the lower strata of society, especially workers, impressed by the radicals' proclaimed effort to help the toilers. The owner of a small tin shop refused to take payment for his services: "I am soldering bombs free of charge," he said to the revolutionaries who came to pick up the "infernal machines."[29] But as the rapidly intensifying violence became an all-pervasive experience of daily life sympathy for the terrorists and their cause waned quickly, and many of their former supporters began to collaborate with the authorities. They turned revolutionaries in and assisted the police in making arrests at the scene of a crime. People were so enraged by unbridled brutality that occasionally the officers could not prevent violent beatings of the apprehended bombists. Some fearless priests and rabbis castigated the combatants in their sermons, despite great risk of revolutionary vengeance.

Time and again Russian extremists set off explosions in churches and threw bombs into synagogues. Jewish anarchists made a sport of taking over these houses of worship just before Sabbath—to insult the congregation. Maximalists, as well as members of the Jewish "Bund," also offended their predominantly religious communities by occupying and using temples as strategic sites for gun battles and bombings. For their part, many Jewish families observed the traditional week of mourning (*shivah*) when a son or daughter joined the radicals. "Wish the ministers...would hang all these rotten guys, who only know how to throw bombs," ranted a devout Jew. Frightened by their aggressive outbursts, the rabbis and elders in the *shtetl* settlements sometimes called for the Cossacks.[30]

If the Jews solicited protection from their traditional enemies, the proverbially anti-Semitic Cossacks, the extremists' abuse of coreligionists must have been critical indeed. Yet informed as the public was about the pogroms and other instances of mob violence against the Pale Jews, it was largely unaware of the tragic irony of the more complex situation involving the radicals. The Jewish anarchists would take over a synagogue, forcing the shtetl elders to appeal to the authorities for help. A shootout between the revolutionaries and the Cossacks would follow, and the next day, liberal newspapers would publish angry articles, condemning the "storming of the house of worship"—allegedly yet another atrocious violation of fundamental human rights on the part of the official anti-Semites.[31]

Whereas the unfortunate students who happened to be customers in the Libman Café at the time of the 1905 anarchist explosion were accidental victims of motiveless terror, civilians, including people of modest means and the needy, became its direct targets if they opposed the extremists. When a worker or peasant dared to testify as a court witness against a revolutionary defendant, his comrades would take blood vengeance on the "informer and spy." Coachmen who hesitated to provide their services to terrorists fleeing the scene of an act also paid with their lives. The radicals punished strikebreakers and workers who resisted the agitators' efforts to mobilize the proletarians for strikes, lockouts, and other forms of "class protest." Unprivileged socioeconomic status no longer safeguarded against the extremists' wrath; it fell upon even the poorest of the poor.

Terrorism brought chaos to the remote and border areas of the empire. Within the Baltic region, violence was most widespread in Latvia, where the radicals terrorized the citizens of urban centers, subjecting entire areas to their control. The so-called Federal Committee of Riga, which united various extremist groups, took over the city administration: it arbitrarily levied taxes, prohibited merchants from trading, and conducted hastily prepared but tightly controlled trials of their opponents. The tribunals handed out death sentences occasionally for such offenses as "insulting the revolutionary regime." Taking advantage of their position as judges, the radicals frequently settled accounts with personal enemies, executing them as alleged supporters of the old administration.[32]

In fact, no one was safe. People lived in the atmosphere of all-out fear and simply hoped to survive the terrible times. In localities particularly affected by revolutionary chaos, such as Riga, where gunfire was regularly heard on the city streets, a man leaving his house did not know whether he would come back. Nor could he be sure that upon his return he would find his family alive.[33] When extremists tossed bombs and shot indiscriminately at the police and the military, more and more women, children, and other innocent bystanders turned into victims of the relentless bloodshed. "Everyone was seized by panic":[34] the population was terrorized to such an extent that in some areas undertakers refused to provide their services for the victims of revolutionary violence. Close relatives were too frightened to show up at their funerals, as were many priests, who did not dare to say the last prayer for the killed.[35]

Latvian extremists also assaulted private residences, conducted searches, and confiscated money and private possessions. They became notorious for swift and bloody looting raids targeting country estates of the wealthy landowners, whom they robbed and murdered. They also ransacked farms and villages, forcing the resident peasants to provide them with food, money, and shelter. For the bourgeoisie—that is, the relatively well-to-do farmers—the attackers introduced taxes ranging from 50 to 100 rubles. In other Baltic provinces the terrorists did their best to surpass their Latvian comrades; they destroyed the nobles' estates, inflicting over 7.8 million rubles in damages.[36]

Anyone who offered resistance was executed, as were pastors, clerks, teachers, and intellectuals opposing the revolt. The radicals labeled them spies and "flunkeys of the counterrevolution." A former revolutionary recalled that his comrades "literally terrorized police informers and traitors"; when in humorous spirits, the extremists shot through their pillows at night from behind the windows "as a joke."[37]

The Armenian Revolutionary Party—"Dashnaktsutiun," or "Union"—was the Caucasian analogue of the PSR in Russia. Operating under the motto "Freedom or Death," it was responsible for the overwhelming majority of terrorist acts in the region. The Dashnaki, as it members called themselves, were mostly Armenian refugees from Turkey—young, homeless, dispossessed vagabonds with no family ties. Hardened by their struggles with the Turks and the Tatars (as the Azerbaijanis were called at the time), they were not trained in any trade and knew only how to use their knives.

Like their counterparts in Latvia, the Dashnaki terrorized whole localities in the Caucasus by forcing wealthy citizens to pay predetermined taxes—as much as 80,000 rubles annually—for the benefit of the party. Their comrades in other extremist groups, like the "Red Hundreds," imposed dues on entire villages. Those who resisted were killed immediately—lest others follow their example.

Of the 3,060 terrorist attacks that the Interior Ministry reported for the Caucasus in 1907, 1,732 were classified as robberies, which left 1,239 people dead and 1,253 wounded. These uncorroborated numbers might have included acts of non-revolutionary banditry, but even the most conservative appraisal of political violence in the Caucasus speaks for itself, as do the available local figures. In the single month of April 1907, the terrorists in the industrial center of Armavir killed—often in broad daylight—some 50 businessmen. Presumably, these industrialists and entrepreneurs had refused to donate money for the revolutionary cause, unlike some of their more compliant colleagues: by that time, the Armavir radicals' total gain from extortion was nearly 500,000 rubles.[38]

Everywhere across the empire, amid ubiquitous attacks on state and private banks in 1905–1907, people were reluctant to invest their money in any financial institutions. As usual in Russia, popular humor mirrored the gravity of the situation. Consider a definition of "bank" included in the make-belief *Newest Encyclopedia Dictionary* was "a place where in the old days one would safeguard money."[39]

Whereas the wave of political assassinations began to subside in late 1907, expropriations continued. In a span of two weeks from February 15 to March 1, 1908, the radicals' raids yielded nearly 448,000 rubles.[40] Russian citizens might have been unaware of precise statistics, but it was no secret for anyone that altogether revolutionaries confiscated hundreds of thousands of rubles directly from private individuals. Although it was risky to deposit savings in the bank, to keep large sums of money at home was not wise either—because of the constant threat of expropriations and extortion. Not only the bourgeoisie but also civil servants, artisans, and intellectuals "installed double and triple bolts on their doors, made secret peepholes to check every visitor, and even in the daytime let strangers in only after hesitation and substantial interrogation," reported a witness; "everyone was seized by panic; everyone expected raids."[41]

The daily expropriations obliterated all boundaries between political and economic terror. As undiscerning as other revolutionary assaults, the "ex" hit the poor very hard—for example, when the Donbass anarchists staged holdups at the Russian Red Cross and confiscated money intended as aid for the peasants.[42] Likewise, anarchists in St. Petersburg stole payroll funds from factory cashiers—salaries that were supposed to be paid to the blue-color employees.[43]

The average daily wage of a skilled worker in St. Petersburg in 1905 was roughly one-and-a-half rubles. An ordinary unskilled worker received 87 kopeks a day. As a rule, peasants earned even less. An expropriation of a few hundred rubles was devastating for dozens of dispossessed individuals, as it was when the extremists "confiscated" cash from various cooperative associations of workers and artisans. These *artels*, formed to facilitate temporary work, sometimes accumulated several thousand rubles by the end of a project and therefore were particularly attractive for the expropriators, who robbed and murdered the very people they claimed to represent.[44]

It is impossible to venture even a rough estimate of the total funds radicals stole from private citizens. Few if any of the autonomous anarchist groups engaged in "exes" troubled themselves to keep records of incoming resources or expenditures. The SRs, operating on the periphery, although officially part of the larger organization, rarely informed the central leadership about planned assaults. They also failed to report acts that had already taken place, frequently perpetrating "exes" on their own initiative and at their own risk, without the sanction of even their local leaders, victimizing and occasionally murdering the poor.[45] Having invalidated private property as quintessentially evil, fewer and fewer revolutionaries had scruples about daily assaults against it.

The expropriators "take sums in tens of thousands, but also do not shy away from single rubles," a contemporary remembered.[46] Over the course of a single year beginning in October 1905, the radicals confiscated a total of roughly 7,000,000 rubles—overwhelmingly from private individuals.[47] People's homes and businesses were less heavily guarded than state commercial enterprises and monetary depots, and the risk of apprehension was proportionately smaller. More often than not, the extremists went for the easy spoils.

The revolutionaries routinely robbed merchants and store owners—some of them were people of considerable wealth, but others barely made ends meet by operating their tiny bakeries and grocery shops The radicals stole money and possessions from parish priests and petty officials. They raided people's homes and forced owners, Browning pistols held at their temples, to hand over cash.[48] Some expropriators killed for trifling rewards: one of the victims in the anarchist campaign against street vendors was an old woman selling lemons in the outskirts of Odessa.[49]

This is not to suggest that the revolutionaries passed over chances to get their hands on the easy money by raiding large private businesses. One such enterprise was a sugar factory in the province of Kiev from which they stole 10,000 rubles in cash. In an incident less fortunate for the raiders, they tried but failed to confiscate large sums on board a commercial ship. Revolutionaries also broke into churches to requisition gold, silver, and other valuables. Still, because they usually chose more modest targets, the extremists preferred to compensate for the relatively small size of the take with the sheer frequency of their assaults. They ran out of funds quickly and sought new sources of instantaneous profits.

Extortion and blackmail were the most common methods of fund-raising for the anarchists and members of obscure extremist groups; some even incorporated this tactic into their names, such as the Odessa-based "Black Falcon Anarchists-Blackmailers" (*Anarkhisty-shantazhisty-Chernyi Sokol*). In 1906 its members collected or invented compromising information about selected individuals and then informed them in writing that unless prompt payments were made, the incriminating evidence would be made public. But usually the radicals did not even bother to produce extortion letters; instead, they appeared in person at someone's door and yelled the habitual "Your money or your life!" If they were not happy with the proceeds of the ad hoc visit, they stated their demands—ranging from as little as 25 to as much as 25,000 rubles—and set up a return appointment. The "exploiter," stated a carelessly written note bearing the party seal, was to contribute the specified sum to the revolutionary cause by a certain date or face death.[50] Most targets of extortion chose to comply, yet occasional refusals led to reprisals: typically, a bomb would be tossed into the home or office of an obstinate merchant or store owner, as a punishment to him and a warning to others.

From time to time, people did make attempts to resist. In communities in the remote regions of Siberia, the Far East, the Jewish Pale, the borderlands, and other unstable areas, where extremist groups had virtually invalidated the administrative machinery, potential victims of terror sought organized means of establishing minimal security and looked for ways to fight back. Occasionally, they acted on advice from the authorities: a governor would call for a meeting with merchant representatives; admit that in the situation of widespread lawlessness, he was helpless to ensure order; and advise them to employ their own guard to protect their property because neither the police nor the military officers were up to the task.[51] In the tiny industrial town of Krinki, in January 1906, factory owners formed a union to defend themselves from the incessant anarchist terror. In the Baltics, the local nobility and particularly the German barons sought to protect their honor, as well as their lives and possessions, and organized armed self-defense units, so as to resist the radicals' intimidation. In Riga, where citizens found it was useless to appeal to the authorities for assistance against the extremists, citizens united in groups such as "Self-Defense" and the "Society for Neighborly Help." Some 1,500 members joined and together were able partially to deflect the revolutionary assaults by armed retaliation.[52] The archpriest in Kazan employed personal bodyguards; monks in a nearby monastery filed a petition to be allowed to carry revolvers.[53]

In the Caucasus, where anarchist and semi-criminal revolutionary gangs terrorized individuals, villages, towns, and entire provinces for months, the locals occasionally resisted "the bandits"—radicals not affiliated with any party who simply called themselves "freedom fighters" or, in one case, the "Non-Party Union of Terrorists" (*Bespartiinyi soiuz terroristov*).[54] Merchants and entrepreneurs organized their employees into self-defense groups to defend their possessions from the expropriators. In Baku, property owners sought to protect themselves financially: at one point, they covered up to two-thirds of the total expenses for maintenance of the local police force.[55]

A story upon a story, the endless chain of episodes of assaults, break-ins, and theft...A bunch of Anarchists-Communists kidnapped a merchant from whom they had already extorted 1,500 rubles. Now they demanded more, but this time, he refused to cooperate. Frustrated, the radicals tortured him: they cut off his ear; they also flayed and scalded him. The merchant did not budge. The only way out of the situation, so embarrassing for revolutionary honor, was to kill him—which they did.[56]

The anarchists extorted money from intellectuals and professionals, including doctors and medical aids, despite the fact that some of them held liberal views and were sometimes willing to assist the revolutionaries in various ways. One dentist in Ekaterinoslav made his apartment available as a hideout for the radicals. Little did they know that his residence would turn out to be far from secure—and not because of police intrusion. Soon after the conspirators had gathered to discuss their agenda, a few extremists from another group tossed a bomb through a window as a reprisal for the dentist's previous refusal to comply with their demands for "a donation."[57]

In Kiev, on June 14, 1908, a man and a woman walked into a shoe store, pointed a pistol at the owner, and presented him with a threat letter from the anarchists. They categorically demanded a total of three pairs of boots. Relieved, the store owner thought just a second and decided not to resist.[58]

* * *

In April 2004, the Palestinian Human Rights Monitoring Group in east Jerusalem, directed by activist Basem 'Eid, published a report on the "Intrafada," as inhabitants of Gaza, Ramallah, Jenin, and other cities call the state of near-anarchy prevailing in the Palestinian Authority. Militant bands employ readily available firearms to enhance their arbitrary rule, the way their predecessors did in Russia a century ago. Seeking to strengthen their own position, officials encourage domestic conflicts and often side with gangs and militias that terrorize and abuse the peaceful Arab populace in the PA territories on a daily basis. The town of Nablus is said to have been at one point "ruled by two armed illiterate thugs." People on the PA payroll perpetrate 90 percent of gangland lawlessness, and from 1993 to 2003, combatants were the cause of 16 percent of all civilian deaths among Palestinian Arabs, according to the report.[59]

Arab militants intimidate the civilian population under their control by "show trials" of alleged Israeli "spies and collaborators," who are summarily executed by hanging or by firing squad, as they have been on numerous occasions in the Palestinian Authority.[60] Aside from those sentences to death by three-judge "military courts," many are lynched while in detention, on their way to or even during trial.[61] Private video footage, shot on site, obviously at great risk for amateur filmmakers, has exposed the humiliation of half-naked prisoners escorted through the streets of Palestinian cities.[62] Photographs show terrorists dragging mutilated bodies of would-be collaborators across the pavement, and the reaction of passersby, "or lack thereof, indicates that this is a common scene."[63] Citizens have seen worse—grisly scenes, such as a young man displaying a bloody heart he had ripped from a body of a dead compatriot, to a crowd of supporters dancing and cheering in approval.[64]

Statistics of political violence within the PA are sparse and difficult to verify. Approximately one-third of all Palestinian Arabs who lost their lives in the year 1989 were killed in the "Intrafada." In 1991, 238 Palestinians died—by stabbing, hacking with axes, and shooting—at the hands of their extremists Arab brethren, more than triple the number who suffered in clashes with Israelis, according to the *Near East Report.* From time to time, Western media gets a glimpse of the mutilations, the cutting off of ears and limbs and the pouring of acid on victims' faces, as *The New Republic* described on November 23, 1992. Not surprisingly, many locals are relieved to find an Israeli soldier rather than a masked Palestinian combatant knocking at their door late at night, the *New York Times* reported on June 12, 1991.

Brutality inflicted upon civilians by the extremists intensified in 2007 when the Hamas wrested control of Gaza from the forces of PA President Mahmoud Abbas of al-Fatah, the largest constituent element of the PLO. "The use of torture is dramatically up," according to one U.S.-based Human Rights Watch. Arab defenders of civil liberties have decried widespread mistreatment and torture in Palestinian jails since 2008—an issue that assumed new urgency with a flare-up of Hamas–Fatah violence in the Gaza Strip. "The security forces in both the West Bank and Gaza have carried out large-scale, arbitrary arrests of political opponents," a Palestinian human rights group, Al Haq, warned in an 85-page report. Among hundreds of real and alleged supporters of the rivaling factions detained by each side, an estimated 20 to 30 percent suffered torture and severe beatings with sticks. Victims were tied up for days in painful positions and forced to kneel on broken glass. A 33-year-old construction worker from Nablus reported that he was hospitalized after an interrogator rammed a screwdriver into his back. Al Haq described the mistreatment as systematic.[65]

"If you were to read the local Palestinian newspapers you would be appalled by dark headlines," confirmed Basem 'Eid in 2007: "killing, kidnapping, arson, shooting, revenge." It is the gunmen who "threaten and spread fear among the Palestinians," admits this Muslim human rights activist, also an opponent of Israel.[66] The conclusion of the 2004 Palestinian Human Rights Monitoring Group "Intrafada" report thus remains accurate: it is a mistake to attribute incessant violence in the region and the Arab plight exclusively, or perhaps even primarily, to the Israeli–Palestinian conflict. It is an error to take at face value terrorists' rhetoric, which holds foreign oppression responsible for the habitual bloodshed and routine victimization of the PA civilians, who suffer as a result of the extremists' effort to dominate politics.

The terrorists claim to pursue the "people's revolution": for the common benefit fighters allegedly carry out inexhaustible carnage. All ostentatious declarations notwithstanding, however, it is the ordinary Russians, Chechens, and Arabs who are the principal victims of terrorism. This is so for the average person in various parts of the world where extremists are in a position to impose bloodshed as a lifestyle. In the apparent al-Qaeda suicide missions in Riyadh, Saudi Arabia, and Casablanca, Morocco, in May 2003, most victims were Muslims.[67] When on November 15 of the same year, al-Qaeda-trained suicide bombers from the Turkish Great Eastern Islamic Raiders Front (IBDA-C) targeted two synagogues in Istanbul, they killed 6 Jews and 23 Muslims who happened to be nearby; over 250 were wounded, primarily the terrorists' "brothers in Islam." In a telephone call, an individual claiming to be from this organization is reported to have said, "The reason [for the attacks] is to stop the oppression of the Muslims... Our acts will continue."[68]

* * *

Despite their penchant for bemoaning the suffering masses, Russian radicals in the early 20th century persistently exhibited the mentality summarized by a trendy motto: "the worse, the better" (*chem khuzhe, tem luchshe*). The revolutionaries clung to "the millennial promise" of a foreseeable socialist or anarchist redemption, already thought to be looming on the horizon. For the "apocalyptic moment," only yet another step toward the abyss was needed. Things must simply be allowed, or pushed, to become bad enough; such was the concept behind the "*politique du pire*."[69] In practical terms, the notion presupposed that further deterioration of the country's domestic situation would contribute to the growing instability of the regime and thus benefit the radical cause. The closest contemporary analogy is revealed in patterns of suicide terrorism, when periodically "an extremist organization with maximalist goals launches a wave" of deadly missions "to break up ongoing negotiations between the Israeli government and a moderate grouping," sabotaging all prospects of a potential peace. Some analysts present such "spoiler strategy" as a fixed model of development in the region,[70] as well as worldwide: terrorists "thrive on festering conflicts such as those in the Middle East, Indonesia, Afghanistan and Kashmir."[71]

It is highly revealing that the first organized conspiracies against the Russian imperial regime emerged in the year 1861, immediately after "tsar-liberator" Alexander II had freed millions of peasant serfs and initiated the Great Reforms of the 1860s and 1870s. The 1881 assassination of the only liberal on the Russian throne was perhaps the most glaring example and symbol of "the worse, the better" tactic and its consequences. When the tsar walked out of his palace to die on the fateful day of March 1, he had left on his desk a completed proposal for a limited form of elective parliamentary representation—a project entailing a gigantic step in the steady course of the country's liberalization. Subversion would have been rendered meaningless, and the extremists' position as self-proclaimed defenders of the common good would have become unjustifiable, had the liberal line been implemented. As it was, Alexander III, the disheartened son and successor of the assassinated reformer, promptly reversed this broadminded policy for the sake of "tightening the system." The Duma would not come into fruition until a quarter-century later, as an indisposed concession from Alexander II's grandson to heavy pressure from the radicals, when the rebellion was already in full swing. The ongoing violence spared the extremists from dreaded irrelevance.

Assuming that people's proclivity for protest was directly proportionate to the degree of hardship, the radicals sabotaged and condemned any financial aid or volunteer initiative aimed at alleviating suffering. Such charities deviously helped the government to deal with general impoverishment and only strengthened the "sickly regime," they believed.[72] As one optimistic revolutionary wrote in a private letter, "If, God willing, we have a bad harvest this year, you'll see what a game will begin."[73]

A freedom fighter had to be at ease with paradoxical logic: he "must further with all his power the evils that will exhaust the people's patience," because any damage to their welfare was propitious for the revolution.[74] Therefore, "in a lively, uplifted mood," radicals abroad celebrated the news from St. Petersburg: hundreds were dead and wounded after the army opened fire at a workers' demonstration on January 9, 1905. A revolutionary explained: the "Bloody Sunday" would surely "be the signal for a victorious struggle."[75]

"You thought that my inner voices scream: 'bread!' and plead: come and save? You are doing me much honor, undeservingly. I know about the hunger...and all the horrors, but I am not sorry and won't go save anyone. The last thing I would do, go to the cohort of the dying," confessed an embittered young woman, Vladimir Zhabotinsky's acquaintance from Odessa. She was about to join a cause that the extremists almost never unveiled—"the legion of destroyers...the cohort of the scorchers."[76]

Such is the mentality that drives terrorists at times of conflict to set up their rocket-launching sites in or near kindergartens and schools—to maximize inadvertent civilian casualties and use them to portray the enemy as "baby killers." During the 2009 fighting in Gaza, the use of children as human shields became a trademark of the Hamas operations—a fact that its leaders flaunt.[77] The terrorists have also incorporated other uninvolved civilians into their network, having built an extensive militant infrastructure in resident and industrial areas. Booby traps have been installed in homes, hospitals, educational institutions, and mosques; Hamas also has placed snipers between buildings in which people were hiding to evade the Israelis during exchanges of fire.[78] A combatant planting an explosive device and then running to hide inside a building full of civilians waving a white flag has turned into a symbol of Hamas terror strategy.[79]

Very similar are the practices of the Taliban, which "are also putting more civilians in harm's way." Since 2008, the UN data show that the Afghan Islamists have shifted away from the frontal attacks on security forces they had favored early in the conflict. The terrorists' new weapon of choice is the improvised explosive devices (IEDs). The very nature of IEDs makes random "civilian casualties inevitable, but in some cases civilians appear to be specific targets"—as when the Taliban planted 16 IEDs in girls' schools.[80]

Contrary to the perpetrators' claim to fight on behalf of the weak, "Islamic terrorism does not have its origins below, in the misery and longings of the masses...The terrorists are mentally detached from the people (although they may believe to be, and give themselves the appearance of, representing them)...they don't know the real poor and their needs...They are...totally obedient to, indeed obsessed by, certain *ideas*."[81] Compassion for their brothers' plight has hardly been a primary stimulus for the extremists' behavior, substantiates the February 2009 UNRWA (UN Relief and Works Agency) public announcement: UNRWA announced its suspension of truckloads of humanitarian aid deliveries to the Gaza Strip after the Hamas militants had stolen twice in a single week hundreds of tons of supplies, including flour, food packages, blankets, and other goods, which the relief organization had transported to the Palestinian territory to help the refugees civilians. It was the "policemen" who expropriated the goods, complained the UNRWA operations director in Gaza; his staff tried to resist, but the armed activists "took over" the supplies at gunpoint.[82]

The UNRWA announcement constituted a UN acknowledgement that Hamas was using the Palestinian population in Gaza "cruelly and cynically" for its own purposes and thus held direct responsibility for its hardships.[83] Such statements, however, are atypical. The UNRWA depends on the terrorists' goodwill for a chance to ameliorate the humanitarian crisis in the region. Sometimes the UN relief workers choose simply not to report incidents of civilian aid theft, lest they antagonize the new rulers of Gaza.[84]

That Hamas had seized warehouses storing humanitarian provisions was no news for Israel, which nonetheless transferred close to 80 trucks a day to the Gaza Strip, even as over 2,700 rockets and mortars were being fired at Israeli civilians in the year 2008 alone. Aid shipments continued—absurdly, many believed—during the ensuing counterterrorist Operation Cast Lead in January 2009. At that time, Hamas used medicine bottles, which Israel had transported to Gaza for the manufacturing of small grenades to be employed against the Israeli Defense Forces (IDF). The Islamists filled with explosives and installed fuses in bottles originally containing a vitamin supplement called "Super-Vit" and a drug called "Equetro," taken by sufferers from bipolar episodes.[85]

When they do dispense subsidies coming in from the West and Israel, the militants take credit—and score political points, posing as providers for the poverty-stricken Gazans. At the same time, according to a UNSCO report, the first year of the Al-Aqsa Intifada cost the PA between $2.4 and $3.2 billion, resulting in the drop of real income by an average of 37 percent and a twofold increase of citizens living below the poverty line—to the soaring 46 percent.[86] Under these conditions, a large cut of the PA budget was appropriated for personal use of its chiefs, who made private fortunes through the channels of their offices—also lucrative illicit businesses. In the words of a Jordanian official, "The PLO isn't a revolution. It's a corporation."[87] Scandalous disclosures of Arafat's fortune merely hint at the extent of corruption: at the time of his death in 2004, his shady funds, hidden in multiple banks, were estimated to be $300 million to $3 billion.[88]

But perhaps "the worse, the better" tactic validates thievery amid shattering destitution. While enriching themselves, PA leaders persistently count on hardship as an effective propaganda device, to blame the enemy and validate violence in the eyes of the afflicted Gaza residents. Suffering—amplified when opportunity allows—thus turns into another means to promote the cause.

Chapter 4

Ideology Abused

> A faith is something you die for, a doctrine is something you kill for.
>
> —Anthony Neil Wedgwood Benn

> Red death is much better than black life.
>
> —Ayatullah Ruhollah Khomeini

Unlike in the People's Will era, when planners of terrorist acts were also the executioners, those who coordinated assaults since the early 20th century rarely took part in them. Terrorism now presupposed a division of labor. In the late 1890s, after a period of relative (and deceptive) tranquility, when the imperial government managed to keep the radicals disunited, Russian revolutionary leaders ventured abroad to set up in several major European cities the headquarters of their newly-formed political parties—away from the watchful eye of the Okhrana. From then on, they typically limited their role to general management of violence, leaving it to their subordinates to do the dirty work. Some strategists remained with the terrorists throughout preparatory activities prior to an assassination, but they seldom implicated themselves in the actual killing.

One benefit of this policy became obvious immediately: whereas the practitioners of terror frequently fell into the hands of the security police, the leaders were apprehended very rarely. After 1905, the masterminds of terror easily found candidates for recruitment and, at least on the local level, sacrificed the rank-and-file just as easily, as dispensable and disposable contraptions. Success in premeditated combat operations was not a given, however; against well-guarded targets in the capitals and provincial centers, terror entailed painstaking organization, in which the essential feature was forging the perpetrator as a well-functioning gadget in a complicated mechanism of destruction.

The first stage in the process of "constructing violence" was conscription of suitable cadres among the disenchanted and the dislocated by the country's sociocultural breakdown. As it turned out, the task required substantial psychological acumen, which the architect of all early PSR terrorist ventures, Grigorii Gershuni, demonstrated perhaps more than any other "soul hunter." An "artist of terror" in the eyes of the Okhrana, and the "tiger of the Revolution" in the radicals' view,[1] Gershuni was "clever and cunning"; his fellow revolutionaries likened him to an awe-inspiring Mephistopheles, with "eyes that penetrated one's soul and...an ironical smile on his face."[2] Personally, he never resorted to arms but had "the power of influencing people almost to the point of hypnotism."[3] He "possessed an incredible gift to take hold" of inexperienced, easily-carried-away young men and women. Almost everyone he "worked on" to recruit for the Combat Organization "would soon totally submit to his will and become an unquestioning executor of his orders," recalled former police officials. Still, he did not trust new conscripts to act on their own, so he typically stayed with a terrorist until the time of the attack. There was no escape from his constant urging, testified worker Foma Kachura, who trembled before Gershuni, could not resist his coercion, and reluctantly shot the Khar'kov governor Obolenskii. In prison, Kachura began to testify against Gershuni only when he saw a picture of his chief in a prisoner's robe and handcuffs. There was "something satanic in this pressure and influence of Gershuni on his victims," recalled an Okhrana officer who had come to know him well.[4]

In contrast to the People's Will era, when terrorism was the tool of a tightly knit conspiracy of educated, theory-oriented dissenters from the privileged milieu and intelligentsia circles, by the early 20th century, intellectual principles in general and socialist ideology in particular largely had lost their relevance as primary motivation for violent action. Some ideologues of subversion recognized a malicious syndrome that had infected the antigovernment camp and caused "the degeneration of the revolutionary spirit." A salient symptom of the "terrible disease"[5] was the loss of dogmatic awareness.

Ideological decline concurred with—and to a great extent resulted from—the democratization of the radicals' ranks. Whereas there were no more than 100 extremists in the early 1860s, and some 500 adherents of the People's Will in late 1870s, by 1907 the PSR counted 45,000 members. These numbers do not include sympathizers—1,000 or so for the radicals of the 1860s, 4,000–5,000 for the People's Will, and roughly 300,000 for the SRs. The Russian "underground acquired a new physiognomy, molded by the social and cultural background of people alien to the world of the linen napkin-and-silverware revolutionary intellectuals" of the 19th century.[6] After 1905, the collective portrait of the revolutionary movement became as socially "complex as the social structure of Imperial Russia itself."[7]

In the tremulous turn-of-the-century environment, the newly developing industrial proletariat was unsettled and restless. Still less than 3 percent of the country's population, it yielded the majority of post-1905 militant activists. Caught in the country's turbulent urbanization were young, usually single men from impoverished peasant families. They had migrated from the countryside in search of employment and swarmed the fast-growing cities as first-generation unskilled workers. Amid poverty, drunkenness, and diseases in the slums, typical of early phases of the industrialization, legions of blue-color laborers became most susceptible to radical indoctrination. Workers carried out some 70 percent of SR terrorist acts. The percentage of proletarian-terrorists in other radical groups might have been even higher.[8]

The extremists from the labor milieu could not compare with their predecessors in intellectual and ideological awareness—if only because of the overwhelming illiteracy among them in the post-1900 era. More often than not, they had received minimal schooling. Many were semiliterate boys and girls, "green youths, absolute babes in the political sense," lamented an older comrade.[9] Some peasant-turned-working-class terrorists had not even had elementary education and did not know how to read.

Along with the first-generation workers, numerous non-Russian perpetrators of antigovernment violence contributed a great deal to the waning away of earlier elitism, as well as intellectual and ideological discernment in the extremist ranks. Terrorist Semen Ter-Petrosian, better known as "Kamo, the Caucasus Brigand," was thrown out of school at the age of 14. Of humble social background, the young man apparently paid little attention to his studies even prior to his expulsion, judging from the fact that he mastered basic Russian grammar and the four elementary arithmetic operations only when he halfheartedly abandoned his main area of expertise—large-scale expropriations in his native Georgia—after the 1917 revolution.[10]

Numerous recruits among Jewish workers were semiliterate in Yiddish and barely able to read simple Russian texts; they could not be expected to understand theoretical writings and certainly not the fine points of revolutionary doctrine. Many active anarchists who operated in the Pale did not know a word of Russian.[11] Even in their mother tongues the terrorists often could not express themselves coherently, let alone formulate their reasons for involvement in the revolutionary struggle. They had great trouble verbalizing, much less defending, their "extremely obscure perception of the revolution" and were unaware of the basic differences among party programs, confessed a fellow radical.[12]

Memoirs and stenographic records of court hearings involving cases of post-1900 extremists reveal how genuinely confused many of them have been about socialist theory. But that's not to say that their ignorance deterred them from violent feats. Convoluted postulates were no longer essential guidelines for the terrorists. When asked why he had attempted or committed murder, the defendant often seized the chance to propagate his revolutionary convictions from the court floor, either of his own will or, more typically, in accordance with prior instruction from his dispatchers.

He would open his fiery speech with a diatribe against oppression. His goal was to end subjugation of the toilers, and this was why he attacked their abusers, on behalf of his party. The difficulty was that he could not think of the party's name. Unperturbed, the terrorist might try to impress the court by his affiliation with an awe-inspiring, if fictitious, group, such as the "Social Revolutionary Anarchist-Communists." Naively, combatants would sometimes declare themselves to be "from the party of revolutionaries," as did members of one haphazardly formed gang of expropriators in the village of Khutora, who had raided the home of a local priest and escaped with a treasure of 25 rubles.[13] Often, the terrorists could only justify their exploits with half-literate and clumsy street language, consisting of a mixture of clichés and curses. They called for revenge against the "scoundrels" and the "jerks." "Long live revolution! To hell with everything else!" was their battle cry and the last word in court before the verdict.[14]

A look at the membership of the SR Combat Organization suggests that it was not an ideology that united the combatants. Fedor Nazarov adhered to views of a convinced anarchist; Abram Gots declared himself a follower of Immanuel Kant; Boris Savinkov, indifferent to socialist dogma and "the people's cause," joined the revolutionary ranks and coordinated terrorist missions as a "thrill-seeking adventurer," confirmed his comrades in the PSR.

The leaders' attitude toward their sanguinary business is vivid in Savinkov's novel *Pale Horse* (*Kon' blendnyi*), originally published under his nom de plume V. Ropshin in 1909. Seeking to analyze the mentality of the assassin, the book reveals that whatever meager altruism once might have existed among the radicals has drowned in a sea of cynicism, negativity, moral corruption, and pure criminality. Savinkov's protagonist, a leader of the terrorist band, is a crippled soul and a loner, with an invariably skeptical approach to all ideas and ideals. He admits that he himself does not know why he participates in terror. He has no long-term goals. Profoundly egotistical, he is alienated not only from the "toilers," eulogized in revolutionary rhetoric, but also from his own comrades—by the impenetrable inner wall that conceals the blankness of his insecure and ailing self. His shield against perceived threat in everyone is indifference and disdain towards enemies and fellow-terrorists alike; entrapped in his own conflicts, he "spits on the whole world."[15] His defensive contempt and inability to empathize with others are boundless. Merciless and corrupted by bloodshed, he finally commits a murder for strictly personal reasons.

The novel's autobiographical character[16] reveals that even in his own eyes, the author—a member of the SR Central Committee and a renowned head of the Combat Organization, second only to Gershuni—appeared to be none other than the embodiment of a certain Nikolai Stavrogin from Dostoevsky's *Devils*. The archetypal creator of new terrorism was restless, anxious, prone to apocalyptic thinking, and death-driven. He was also "the highly specialized technician of revolution,"[17] as was his latter-day incarnation Ali Hassan

Salameh (alias Abu Hassan), nicknamed the "Red Prince," the notorious commander of Force 17, Arafat's personal elite security squad and prominent member of Black September. Germany-educated, wealthy, ambitious, the flamboyant son of an upper-class Muslim family, and married to Lebanese celebrity Georgina Rizk, the 1971 Miss Universe, Salameh had been trained in guerrilla tactics in Egypt and the Soviet Union. He directed the assassination of Jordan Prime Minister Wasfi Tel (Wasfi al-Tal) and, among his other exploits, was behind the 1972 hijacking of Sabena Flight 572 from Vienna to Lod, Israel.[18]

For a terrorist leader, the most sought-after recruit was someone with few—and preferably no—emotional ties and symbolic meanings. A 20-year-old Leiba Sikorskii was an ideal candidate as a typical "dislocated person" who joined the Savinkov's terrorist crew three days before its intended attack against Plehve. He had left his parents in the Jewish Pale and, penniless, come to St. Petersburg. He spoke poor Russian and felt anxious and lost in the huge city. The only person he knew in the capital was an SR combatant, who recommended him to Savinkov. The terrorists' chef gave him a hundred rubles—a sum Sikorskii had never seen before—and appointed him to be a reserve bomb-thrower. Savinkov could not care less about the neophyte's political credo.[19] As unconcerned with subtleties of faith seemed to have been the handsome Palestinian "Red Prince," who electrified an entourage of youthful fans with his revolutionary fervor as much as with "young skirt chasing," his impressive sport cars, and his penchant for Islam-prohibited whiskey drinking.

The new breed of terrorists regarded party "conferences, meetings, and congresses with badly concealed disdain" and "believed in terror alone," if we are to listen to their own words. They "could not stand polemics"—a mere excuse for not fighting. Though prepared to spill blood and die for the revolution, they discarded theoretical issues with contempt. Some of them did not have enough rudimentary knowledge of class theory to be called socialists.[20] "Apparently rudimentary" was also Mohamed Atta's "mastery of Islamic texts," but this did not stop him from swearing to die as a martyr or from piloting American Airlines flight No. 11 into the North Tower of the World Trade Center.[21]

The assassin of Samara governor Frolov had initially met "true revolutionaries" in prison, while serving a term for a common crime; he soon became involved in the PSR combat activities merely "to find out what kind of party it was."[22] Other self-proclaimed liberators of the people were not curious and preferred not to be bothered with programmatic questions and theoretical complexities. SR terrorist N. D. Shishmarev, who killed the chief of the Tobol'sk hard-labor prison, believed that his ignorance of the party program actually contributed to the radical cause; activists who became overly preoccupied with dogmatic issues ran the risk of losing their determination, he argued. Like the anarchists, for whom a true freedom fighter must first and foremost have "combat in his blood,"[23] most SRs agreed that in revolutionary times, "militant temperament and enthusiasm" for combat were more important than any theory.[24]

"I have not read a single book, but in my heart I am an anarchist," an extremist would repeat with pride.[25] Others, however, lamented their political illiteracy: "We are weak in theories and incapable of carrying out party work. We are of no use, except for obtaining money by means of 'exes.'"[26]

In the fund-raising business, fortune always seemed to smile on Kamo and his gang of outlaws, a bunch of highway robbers who had no concept of the ideology but whom he brought under discipline and inspired with revolutionary spirit. The band staged a series of expropriations, of which the most notorious was the "Tiflis 'ex.'" On June 12, 1907, the terrorists exploded bombs in a central square of the Georgian capital and then assaulted two stagecoaches loaded with banknotes, coins, and currency from the Tiflis State Bank. Leaving dozens of bystanders dead and injured, Kamo and his men escaped the scene of the crime firing revolvers and carrying with them 250,000 rubles. The money was destined for the so-called Bolshevik Center (B. C.) abroad—a clandestine circle of Lenin's supporters within the predominantly Menshevik Central Committee of the Russian Social Democratic Workers Party (RSDRP).

Mastermind of most profitable expropriations, the Bolshevik Center was under constant attack from the less opportunistic, yet jealous Mensheviks, who demanded their portion of the loot. Unable to force the Bolsheviks to share, they satisfied themselves with a bitter epigram aimed at "Lenin and Co."—the "swindlers":

> "How do you like those 'exes'?" B. C. was questioned once.
> "I love them," B. C. answered. "They're lucrative for us.[27]

"Behind the raging debates on the philosophies of Marxist materialism and empirical criticism lay the politics of another kind of material: money," affirms an expert on Bolshevik shady machinations; in reality, the ideological squabbles among RSDRP leaders were over control of the party treasury.[28] Outraged by what Leon Trotsky subsequently labeled the Bolshevik methods of "expropriation within the Party," the Menshevik majority sought to expel the "bandits, counterfeiters, and thieves" from its ranks.[29] Yet because the Mensheviks had evidently nothing against expropriations per se and resented only the Bolshevik refusal to share the proceeds, the party, argued one Social Democrat, "would be forced to expel the entire Central Committee."[30]

The "exes" caused a deep controversy within the Social Democratic (SD) forces, specifically among the Menshevik, Bolshevik, and Bund factions. In theory, the party disallowed expropriations along with other forms of terrorism, incompatible, the SD leaders insisted, with the Marxist canons. "Using bombs for individual terrorist acts was out of the question since the party rejected individual terror"—so ran a typical statement affirming the RSDRP's official viewpoint.[31] A weapon for "a handful of heroes," terrorism "will not harm autocracy," which can be defeated only by way of a mass participation of the working class. Terror was "inexpedient, and therefore *harmful*" for the people's cause, the SD publications stressed.[32]

Practice, however, was very different. Although much less frequently than the SRs and the anarchists, the SDs resorted to terrorist tactics. In fact, members of every faction of the RSDRP implicated themselves in political assassinations and in numerous confiscations of government and private property, despite token declarations that terror was "unscientific" from the Marxist viewpoint. The perpetrators violated their party's ideological position because, for the most part, they were eager for action and could not care less about "empty theory" and the "well-known Social Democratic nonsense."[33]

On January 27, 1906, a Bolshevik combat detachment in St. Petersburg attacked the tavern Tver, a meeting place for factory workers in the shipbuilding industry, who belonged to the monarchist "Union of the Russian People." Some 30 patrons were present when the terrorist exploded three bombs inside the tavern. The workers tried to flee the building, but the Bolsheviks waiting outside fired revolvers at them at close range. Two people were killed and some 20 wounded, and the terrorists, who might have expected more impressive results from the staged carnage, escaped unscathed.[34]

Similar episodes occurred throughout the country.[35] By 1907, the Marxists were often indistinguishable from any other extremists, when "militant youth lost control and began to deviate toward anarchism," killing guards, city policemen, and gendarmes. "They were infected" with the terrorist spirit; all they wanted was to act, to spread violence for violence's sake, their chiefs conceded.[36] The perpetrators were utterly indifferent to whether terrorism was compatible with their group's ideology.

Sometimes the leaders exploited their subordinates' aggressive tendencies for fund-raising purposes, making sure, however, that "on paper" they would formally resign from the organization, so as not to compromise it by "unscientific methods of struggle." "The Mensheviks would chew us up" if members of Kamo's band did not leave the party—only for the record—Lenin allegedly said to Stalin, the man responsible for all Bolshevik operations in the Caucasus.[37] Marxist theory aside, Lenin endorsed terrorist acts in 1916 to enhance the country's destabilization during World War I, demanding strict secrecy from his associates in Petrograd, lest it be discovered that the Bolshevik leadership was behind the attacks.[38]

Even the Mensheviks, the least extremist and most theory-conscious among the SDs, were sometimes "surprisingly close to the anarchists," according to a party activist.[39] The rough Mensheviks of the Caucasus assassinated their enemies far more often than their colleagues in any other part of the country. Due to the Menshevik efforts, in Georgia life turned into a "bloody nightmare," testified one survivor.[40] "Revenge, revenge, revenge... these were the words that came from the hearts of our comrades," remembered a revolutionary; "Social Democrats who reject terror in principle now must turn to it as the only means of struggle."[41]

And so they did, repudiating all Marxist allegations that political murder, unlike the class struggle, was useless for revolutionary purposes. The SDs assassinated government officials, military personnel, wealthy industrialists, factory administrators, merchants, and aristocrats. They terrorized police officers and killed them "like gamebirds."[42] For the rank-and-file Mensheviks, the official party rhetoric against terror was an empty sound.

The Bund's sphere of influence was the Pale, in or near the Jewish settlements. In places like Gomel', Bobruisk, Vil'na, and other centers of Jewish life, the Bundists were active perpetrators of terrorist violence, although they had a hard time competing with the daily terrorist feats carried out under the black banner of anarchism. On the other hand, the Bund's combat activities in Odessa were more successful than those of the SRs, their chief local rivals for revolutionary glory.[43] Like other rank-and-file SDs, the Bundists knew next to nothing about Marxism and cared as little about the party ideology; nor did they see its prohibition of terror as an obstacle to their campaign.

Radical Marxists in Latvia and some independent SDs in Lithuania contributed to the overwhelming anarchy in the Baltics. Like most of their Russian, Caucasian, and Jewish comrades, they recruited new members primarily from the lower social strata. These heedless novices in the revolutionary camp did not exhibit even minimal curiosity about the class theory; nor did they have patience for theoretical controversies. One "immediately became a combatant, if only he had a revolver in his pocket," affirmed a former activist.[44]

Rarely deterred from joining forces due to conflicting philosophies, the militants initiated a united front—across-the-board collaborations among the practitioners of terror from various political circles. Their leaders in Paris, Geneva, and other centers of émigré politics insisted on strict separation along the ideological party lines, yet the rank-and-file activists in Russia considered programmatic discrepancies immaterial for the daily operations. The resulting doctrinal flexibility—or, more accurately, indifference toward theory—allowed the terrorists to work in partnership as a single extremist bloc.

"All supporters of political terror should feel like members of a single family," notwithstanding specific creeds, urged Vladimir Burtsev, independent revolutionary and an early proponent of terrorism in Russia.[45] As long as their mutual goal was to uproot the establishment, the rank-and-file radicals were comrades in spirit, he insisted, disregarding the ongoing conflicts, intrigues, and acrimony among leaders of rivaling parties, who sought to control the revolutionary cadres and funds.

"Why can't we work together?" Savinkov appealed to foremost Maximalist dissident Mikhail Sokolov, a persona non grata in the eyes of the PSR leadership. "As far as I am concerned, there are no obstacles. It makes no difference to me whether you are a Maximalist, an anarchist, or a Socialist-Revolutionary. We are both terrorists. Let's combine our organizations in the interest of terror," urged the SR chief. But "you have declared war on us," replied Sokolov, who also believed that programmatic disagreements should not stand in the way of combat work. "Not we, but the Party of Socialists-Revolutionaries," rejoined Savinkov, drawing a sharp distinction between the official line of the PSR and the benefits of the terrorists.[46]

Away from the capitals, the SRs collaborated with the Maximalists, with the anarchists, and with members of various SD groups. In preparing assassinations and expropriations, they joined into mixed and multi-faction mergers, permanent or temporary, created solely for the purpose of a specific terrorist enterprise. The Social Democrats of different leanings were happy to cooperate not only with other RSDRP members but also with the party's political rivals, independent extremists whom the SD leadership called bandits. Sometimes revolutionaries set up larger gangs, such as the one led by Aleksandr Lbov, nicknamed "Terror of the Urals" (Groza Urala) for the panic his SD and Maximalist associates inflicted on the region with incessant "exes" and assassinations of so-called exploiters among factory directors and shop managers.[47]

The Maximalist and anarchist groups accepted assistance no matter where it came from. They collaborated among themselves and with anyone else willing to contribute to their motiveless terror, defined simply: "Where it is not enough to remove one person, it is necessary to eliminate them by the dozen; where dozens are not enough, they must be gotten rid of in hundreds."[48] Ideological nuances were the last thing on the mind of the Maximalists who on August 12, 1906, blew themselves up in Stolypin's house with the cry "Long live freedom, long live *anarchy!*"[49] The explosives, which caused approximately 60 casualties, were manufactured in an SD bomb laboratory operated by Leonid Krasin, the Bolsheviks' chief terrorism expert. He also supervised the production of hand grenades Maximalists would utilize in the sensational October 14, 1906, Fonarnyi Lane expropriation.[50]

Group memberships changed constantly as dissenters from the SR and SD organizations formed smaller and more autonomous groups to escape central control—or whatever remained of it in the periphery. Unrestricted even by minimal ideological guidelines, these nonconformists ignored orders from their party leaders and obeyed only their local elected chiefs. As "courageous and daring" as a typical combatant would be, "and as much as he scorned death, he was still extremely reckless and undisciplined," acknowledged a Latvian SD.[51]

Unbridled extremists "discredited the party by their banditry," protested their forsaken leaders, who expelled the wayward members from the RSDRP.[52] The drifters then found new comrades among the anarchists and the terrorists in obscure groups with no definite programs or ideology. Having joined these semi-criminal gangs, they were free to pursue violence unrestrained by ideological formalities.

Acute "identity confusion" was no bigger worry for a bunch of Lithuanian SDs who proudly called themselves anarchists[53] than it was for the Maximalist perpetrators of Stolypin's house explosion, who hailed the anarchy before blowing themselves up. The way to deal with such irrelevant technicalities was to ignore them and worry not about ideological intricacies. Kamo, the "idealistic robber" who worshipped Lenin, but had less than rudimentary understanding of class theory, found the most original solution to programmatic controversies. Kamo happened to be present at a heated debate on an agrarian issue but quickly became bored and impatient. "What are you arguing with him for?" he asked his Bolshevik friend. Pointing at a dumbfounded Menshevik, Kamo suggested, just "let me cut his throat."[54]

* * *

Intimate familiarity with the revolutionary milieu confers a sense of its artificiality. The extremists may act as though they are disconnected from the bona fide reality and themselves are not fully valid—living as if play-acting in an ersatz, simulated existence or, rather, its replica. Often, they seem to be partaking in a prearranged, well-staged theatrical dramatization or spectacular "performance violence,"[55] in accordance with primed scripts and rehearsed scenarios rather than reactions to authentic circumstances.

The black mask of the perpetrator, while serving a practical purpose to conceal appearance, at once becomes a symbol of the countercultural nature of modern terrorism. "These masks are the uniforms of the new armies of the 21st century and the new kind of violence" that "no longer distinguishes between war against the stranger and war against members of your own society. . . It doesn't have boundaries" that demarcate threat. The mask is a countercultural emblem also because "this new violence doesn't have a front, it doesn't have a face."[56] The camouflage renders the terrorist anonymous, identical to other representatives of the murderous force; the disguise deprives him of the individual identity he denies his victim.

Masqueraded, the extremists act as though they memorized their lines in strict obedience to party orthodoxy, having repeated and mastered their every step, lest they depart from the prescribed recital on the revolutionary stage. Thus, the behavior of Amrozi bin Haji Nurhasyim, a bomber responsible for the October 12, 2002, Bali nightclub bombing, was permeated with theatrics. Journalists have noted that Amrozi spoke "as if he had learned the response by rote and was just itching for a podium, from which to preach that "the West"—"Americans, Jews and their allies"—has "brought terrorism on itself" by "secularism, democracy, human rights, the free market, and opposition to terrorism, and drugs."[57]

The extremist often perceives his experience as a "very interesting game"[58] or a play. Inevitably, he projects the "as if" outlook onto his environment, which is rendered illusive. In the terrorist's pseudo-actuality, nothing is compelling and irreversible. Murder too loses much of its gravity: "it is only when we see ourselves as actors in a staged (and therefore unreal) performance that death loses its frightfulness and finality and becomes an act of make-believe and a theatrical gesture."[59] Annihilation of life becomes simple, ritualized, and almost trivial because the perpetrator's awareness falls short of integrating living as genuine. Pretending and role-playing, on the contrary, acquires validity within the framework of the grandiose political spectacle, in which eager acting-out is a thing to do.

Many extremists behave as if they identify with heroes of the myths and legends in their national traditions.[60] Others play divine beings, as did Mikhail Bakunin, who, prior to his conversion to anarchism, had given himself "over to religious passions that slid easily into messianic grandeur, in which he saw himself as another Jesus": "My proud and inflexible will... my high destiny. I am a man. I will be God."[61] Bakunin exhibited conflicted, insecure, and authoritarian personality, which combined fixations on sexual incapacities and probably impotence with a "messiah complex... megalomaniac belief in his own power... hatred of this world" and fascination with Satan, "the eternal rebel, the first freethinker" and liberator. "I suffer because I am a man and want to be God,"[62] Bakunin confessed. So would, in years to come, many other true believers, such as cult leader Shoko Asahara, who imitated Armageddon and promised the creation of "a new and transcendent human world" because he "wanted to be like Christ."[63]

"There is no striving for glory without a vivid awareness of an audience,"[64] and as is often the case with antisocial and narcissistic personalities, the goal of these political performers is to act out their self-imposed roles for the sake of anyone willing to see them play. Occasionally, they verbalize their intent to acquire publicity as a result of a major terrorist success, whose boldness "must amaze the entire world."[65] In our urbane society that has banished dying from public life,[66] transmuting death into a spectacle is an astounding countercultural endeavor indeed. A classic act, forever to remain in the annals of modern political drama, took place in Cairo on November 28, 1971: after a Black September commando gunned down the prime minister of Jordan in the foyer of the Sheraton Hotel, a fellow assassin, Momzer Khalifa, knelt and lapped with his tongue the victim's blood as it flowed from Tel's chest wounds across the marble floor.[67]

"I am proud! Finally I have done it," Khalifa proclaimed after the assassination. "We have taken our revenge on a traitor," he said, referring to Tel's role in the September 1970 expulsion of Arafat's insurrectionists from Jordan. "We wanted to have him for breakfast, but we had him for lunch instead."[68] Black September sought not revenge alone; more than anything, Arafat craved publicity for the Palestinian cause, even negative if it had to be so in the initial stage of a prolonged political game. The ghastly scene in the Cairo Sheraton, reported in major newspapers, achieved its purpose by creating the image of a frenzied zealot—soon to be amended to a symbol of the "Palestinian liberation struggle," an uncompromising freedom fighter.

Histrionic effect is consistently present in the radicals' manifested welcoming of anguish, as in a famous 1903 episode during Gershuni's arrest, which he elevated into a show of revolutionary martyrdom—quite in line with both his predilection for melodrama and the ability "to calculate literally every step."[69] As soon as the police officers had chained his legs, the SR terrorist chief bent down, lifted the irons, and kissed them, as if they were a sacred object.[70] This theatrical and patently symbolic gesture greatly amplified Gershuni's status in the antigovernment community, raising his prestige to that of a cult guru: the apocalyptic political culture demands from the builders of social paradise, as a response to every disappointment and failure, that they be willing to receive pain and, at least figuratively, "to seek still *more self-mutilation* in order to *earn the millennium*."[71]

The extremists' resounding statements by way of gunshots and bomb explosions are made for the sake of the "spectators"—sensational acts of killing being a preferred form of discourse with the survivors and witnesses, also prospective fatalities. These are the terrorists' audience, locked within the framework of an aberrant and potentially deadly affiliation dictated by the extremists. According to the unwritten rule of the game, spectators today may turn tomorrow into targets, or a new medium for the terrorists' self-expression.

On October 23, 2002, 42 heavily armed, camouflage-clad Chechen terrorists, among them many women, the so-called Black Widows, entered the main hall of the Dubrovka theater in Moscow and, firing assault rifles in the air, took approximately 850–900 hostages during the performance of the "Nord-Ost" musical. The gunmen's leader, Movsar Barayev, declared that unless the federal authorities withdrew Russian troops from Chechnya within the following week, the rebels would kill their captors, the performers and the spectators, including foreign nationals and children. Surrounded by terrorists carrying hand grenades and explosive devices strapped to their bodies, with mines deployed throughout the theater, the hostages—some calm, others hysterical—awaited their fate. While Russia's political and cultural representatives negotiated with the militants, the FSB Alpha and Vympel units prepared for an assault. In the early morning of October 26, rescue operatives pumped a mysterious toxic gas into the building through the air conditioning system, and as both the hostage-holders and their victims began to succumb to its lethal effect, the "special purpose" squads raided the theater.[72] The as-if quality of terrorism had reached the point of refined dramatization: the audience was forced to play a part in the real-life performance, in which it was being killed by both the terrorists and the state.

* * *

Without downplaying the role of religious factors, "it will not do simply to call Osama bin Laden an Islamic fundamentalist" since "the Islamism of which he is a symbol and a spokesman is not a movement aimed at restoring some archaic or pristine form of Islamic practice." Furthermore, for all their professed fidelity to the Qur'an, Islamist leaders today are quite prepared to breach ideological tenets while waging their all-out war against the West and Israel:

> Osama bin Laden's famous 1998 *fatwa*, in which he declared jihad on the United States and any American fair game for his followers, is a case in point...bin

> Laden has no credentials as a religious authority and no right, under traditional Islamic practice, to issue a *fatwa*. It is a bit like Hitler issuing a papal encyclical...The mere fact that bin Laden was willing to cross this line shows the extent to which Islamism has undermined traditional Islamic legal authority.[73]

Affected piety within the intercontinental cohort of jihadists is not a sole or a principal inspiration for aggression against common "enemies of the Qur'an." The creed is "hijacked" and exploited as a tool for destructive purposes, rather than served, by the organizers of violence, according to Jessica Stern's vivid explication.[74] A renowned European intellectual, von Hans Magnus Enzensberger argues in his recent tour de force that Islamist terror has nothing to do with religion.[75] Faith is reduced to a radical brand of "political idolatry" and used "as a way to mobilize support."[76] "This is simply politics" given a "retroactive Islamic legal basis, even if a wholly fabricated one"[77] for the systematic use of violence; from a Muslim point of view it is "blasphemy when those who perpetrate such crimes claim to be doing so in the name of God."[78] Doctrine is the extremists' mouthpiece to validate a purpose; it is not the purpose; it is a means, not the end; "ideologies are crutches, not the true motivation."[79]

As hundred years ago, much of today's terrorism results "not in any particular grievance that can be treated, but in the Intrigues, power struggles, jealousies, and machinations" of extremist players, whose cloak of religious zeal sanctifies atrocity. In "the web of international relations,"[80] routine requirements of the murderous trade, rather than conjoint worship, are behind the effort of a transnational Islamist network to ensure steady shipments of funds from Tehran for the Palestinian Islamic Jihad to its headquarters in Damask. As per agreement with Iran, the Jihadists receive a pecuniary bonus for each attack against Israel.[81]

The rank-and-file militants champion Mohammed's creed, of course, but their proclivity to engage in violence is not dictated by an integrated understanding of the doctrine, nor is it a consequence of a profound concern with, and insight into, theological complexities. In this sense, Muslim combatants in various corners of the world differ little from their unsophisticated counterparts in the turn-of-the-20th-century Russia. There, as enthusiastic as self-avowed Marxists might have been about the call to "expropriate the expropriators," many would have easily believed that *Das Kapital* was someone's first and family names.

In the 1970s and 1980s, involvement in radicalism preceded indoctrination in the case of the West Germany–based militant left-wing Red Army Faction (*Rote Armee Fraktion*), or RAF; it had descended from the Marxist-Leninist cum anarchist Baader-Meinhof Gang but "many of the captured terrorists started reading Marx only in prison."[82] In the same way, the overwhelming majority of "fighters for Islam" relate only to the most primitive interpretations of the Qur'an. The analysis is supplied by their leaders, who typically offer out-of-context citations à propos the expediency of jihad—originally a broad, at least partially spiritual concept emphasizing "striving in the way of Allah" (*al-jihad fi sabil Allah*). Islamist ideologists do not elucidate but label. The United States is reviled as a driving force of an iniquitous civilization, not an adversary Christian state, even if its citizens are branded as "crusaders"; the World Trade Center for the Islamists was a symbol of "Big Satan's" national pride, not Christianity. Nor are "the Zionists" hated as observant Jews, whom "soldiers of the Qur'an" must forcibly convert. The Islamists regard the Americans and the Israelis as enemy national groups and representatives of hated cultures.

For the purposes of recruitment and deployment of combat cadres, the extent to which terrorist leaders are able to validate dogmatically their slogans or sermons, colored with abhorrence of "the infidels," is largely immaterial; in fact, research among imprisoned jihadists consistently shows them as "rather poor Islamic scholars." Some do not even appear as particularly devout Muslims in the eyes of the conscripted, nor are they overly preoccupied with the level of religious devotion of those they send to die for Allah.[83] A well-drilled axiom is often sufficient to legitimate a follower's generalized hostility and proclivity for violent action. The 2002 Bali massacre perpetrators had expected the targeted nightclub to be full of Americans, but when they learned that among the citizens of 20 countries they had killed were many Australians, a Jemaah Islamiyah combatant quipped: "Australians, Americans, whatever... they are all white people." His comrade vowed: "There will be more bombs until the Westerners are finished... we are going to destroy your countries all round the world." Designated foreign symbols are part of the idiom of enmity. Another Jemaah Islamiyah terrorist identified those that offended him the most: "the U.S., George W. Bush, George Soros, Zionists, Rotary and Lions clubs, and supermarket chains."[84]

Analogous to the poorly articulated hatred for their milieu on the part of the dislocated Russian extremists, Muslim combatants have in their arsenal a concoction of preapproved claims. These include love for Allah, devotion to the nation, vengeance, and desire to end one's life as *shahid* (martyr). Repeated time and time again, these are clichés reiterated mechanically.

"A mechanical militancy," anarchist Iuda Grossman called the process in which a person, once a terrorist, begins to act automatically, hardly conscious of his reasons for inflicting death. The Russian radicals murdered "as if infatuated" with the terrorist "art for art's sake."[85] The requirements of a daily routine take over the combatants' lives, and before long they proceed to act in robot-like fashion. They rarely reflect and concentrate exclusively on the pressing task at hand—execution of the terrorist act as an essential goal and an *idée fixe*.

In line with the general tendency, for the Russian extremists violence "became the focal point, their raison d'être. The ultimate political and social goals were overshadowed by the immediacy of the terrorist campaign."[86] So, too, militants today are driven not by a final ideological aspiration but by the struggle itself, which renders the radical's existence meaningful, at least in his own eyes. The combatant lives for the sake of his ongoing and all-out battle—a defining factor of his identity as an enemy of that environment which the radical ideologists have assigned to demolition. And his identity is constantly affirmed by relentless effort at subversion. "Communism is on the horizon," Russian Marxist propagandists tirelessly repeated, for the ideal served its purpose best as an imminent, yet forever-distant apocalyptic prospect. Not unique to Russia, over time the extremist is known to become less and less in touch with obscure inner motives and to dissociate even from feelings related to violence. Whether a Russian anarchist or a Muslim fundamentalist, the modern terrorist *exists*—not lives but rather functions solely as an instrument of annihilation.

Allegedly idealistic movements "transform themselves into profit-driven organized criminals, or form alliances with groups that have ideologies different from their own, forcing both to adapt." Of course, the reverse may also happen: the Islamic Movement of Uzbekistan (IMU) originally took upon itself a narrowly defined "mission to topple Uzbekistan's corrupt and repressive post-Soviet dictator, Islam Karimov." However, once the IMU made a partnership with the Taliban's leader, Mullah Omar, it began promoting the agenda of global jihad.[87] Terrorists of the Turkish Great Eastern Islamic Raiders Front advocate a programmatic potpourri of Islamic rule based on the *Shari'a* laws and leftist economic ideology.[88]

From the early 1900s on, terrorists all over the world tended either to discount ideological tenets, or adopt them to practical requirements of the radical united front. Official Soviet insolence with regard to matters of faith was of little relevance for result-oriented Islamists already in the 1950s. Never mind persistent persecution of their coreligionists in the USSR. One Syrian fundamentalist leader swore that he and his followers would bind themselves to Russia "were she the very devil."[89]

"Other Middle East states export dates, rugs, or oil; Syria exports trouble," observed an American ambassador to the country that Assad had made "virtually a member of the Soviet bloc." In return, the Soviets have provided "a variety of assistance to Syrian-backed terrorism," including weapons and training in their use. While building his "special apparatuses for terrorism," Assad sanctioned Syrian Arab Airline crews to bring explosives, guns, and drugs into the United Kingdom; his operatives staged bombings in West Germany; together with the Ba'th Party of Lebanon and the Lebanese Communist Party, they carried out suicide attacks against Israeli and South Lebanon Army troops. Lebanon's president stated in 1988 that the Iranians would not have dared to take foreign hostages in his country without Syrian approval. East German and Bulgarian "security advisors" worked in Syrian camps; combatants also went to the Soviet Union and eastern Europe for specialized instruction, learning Russian or other East bloc languages along with the surreptitious features of the terrorist trade.[90]

After the collapse of the Soviet Union, there appeared in the post-Communist Russia numerous publications declassifying the formerly top-secret information about terrorist training schools and camps on Soviet territory, as well as in Cuba, Bulgaria, Czechoslovakia, Hungary, and East Germany. One such institution was the "Learning Center for preparation of foreign militants No. 165" in the Crimea. In the period between 1965 and 1990, this base alone graduated around 18,000 "combatants from various national-liberation movements in the countries of Asia, Africa, and the Middle East." Aside from terrorist training, "students" were indoctrinated in the basics of the class struggle: "First it is necessary to teach at whom to shoot, then how to shoot," their instructors would say.[91] "Moscow ran a virtual terrorist academy," hosting thousands of third world revolutionaries in the guise of full-scholarship students at the Patrice Lumumba University.[92] At the time of perestroika, progressive rhetoric emphasizing emancipation of the toilers no longer brought rewards of weapons and money,[93] and groups such as the PLO were quick to abandon their Marxist-Leninist orientation. So too did the Popular Front for the Liberation of Palestine (PFLP), which since 2001 "shifted its emphasis" and adopted the language and the tactics of jihad "to attract a greater constituency."[94]

Alliances based on common destructive goals surpass all ideological and national barriers and render them irrelevant. The early-20th-century Russian extremists shared expertise with fellow anarchists from Bulgaria and Italy on how to make explosives and smuggle them to the United States; just as readily, they extended collaboration to radical nationalists in India and Persia.[95] After the British had appointed Hajj Ali al Amin al Husseini as Mufti of Jerusalem in 1921, he organized the so-called *fedayeen* squads to terrorize Jewish residents. Twenty years later, during a rendezvous with Hitler on November 28, 1941, "the most authoritative spokesman for the Arab world" in the Fuhrer's eyes received firm assurances that "Germany stood for uncompromising war against the Jews" and "would furnish positive and practical aid to the Arabs involved in the same struggle."[96] In our days, a Swiss neo-Nazi named Albert Huber, on the board of directors of the Bank al Taqwa, accused of being a major donor to al-Qaeda, is a proponent for joining forces with the Islamists.[97]

Since World War II, there has not been one large ethno-terrorist group that has lacked organizational or financial ties crossing national lines and yielding most improbable hybrids. In May 1972, Kozo Okamoto and two other members of the Japanese Red Army machine-gunned mostly Puerto Rican pilgrims and other passengers at Lod airport near Tel Aviv. The group's immediate objective was to overthrow Japan's government and monarchy, its long-term goal was world revolution. However, in the Lod operation, where they killed and wounded over 100 people, the Japanese terrorists acted on orders from the PFLP. Likewise, the Baader-Meinhof Gang participated in combat training of various terrorist groups in Palestinian camps in Lebanon and Jordan,[98] along with as many as 40 other extremists groups, whom the PLO "sometimes charged between $5,000 and $10,000 for a six-week program of instruction." The Japanese and the German terrorists could afford the cost of training: they were part of the conglomerate of some 73 Muslim and non-Muslim parties supported by the Syrian government.[99] In this multinational network, personal identity is beside the point: Egyptian recruits may be trained in Pakistan and Kosovo and then dispatched to make terror in the Philippines and Kashmir. In the mid-1990s, about 20,000 people from 47 countries passed through al-Qaeda jihad bases in Afghanistan.[100]

The propensity to serve as agents of destruction is the single criterion that brings worldwide killers of various, sometimes conflicting, ideologies to the global united front. Universally, subversion is the goal that overshadows and bypasses individual organizations' specific dogmatic and political claims. A French counterespionage officer employed a useful analogy to explain the collaboration between terrorist factions: "they resemble the firms making the same produce which normally compete but sometimes band together as members of a trade association to cooperate."[101] Their "primary product is political violence," confirms a recent study of 381 militant groups operating worldwide between 1968 and 2008.[102]

The unruly "triborder" South American region, joining Paraguay, Brazil, and Argentina, which has emerged as "the world's new Libya." This is a region "where terrorists with widely disparate ideologies—Marxist Colombian rebels, American white supremacists, Hamas, Hezbollah, and others—meet to swap tradecraft." They mix and match capabilities, train, and use joint facilities, a modus operandi that has "become the hallmark of professional terrorists today."[103]

Chapter 5

Terrorists as Common Criminals

> It is impossible to guess where a comrade anarchist ends and where a bandit begins.
>
> —Georgii Plekhanov

> Morality is everything which contributes to the triumph of the revolution. Immoral and criminal is everything that stands in its way.
>
> —"Catechism of a Revolutionary"

No longer bound to or by a compelling set of philosophical principles, the extremist mindset manifested a proclivity to unfetter itself also "from all moral restraints," complained both the critics and the supporters of radical politics.[1] "Everybody knows," of course, affirmed a former oppositionist, that "the so called 'liberation movement' of 1905 and 1906" drew in the broad masses and with them "inevitably absorbed an undesirable element who did not have anything in common with the Revolution, and who discredited it."[2] Contemporaries gave these extremists a collective name: the "seamy side" (*iznanka*) of the insurgency.[3] Petr Struve characterized the epitome of such a radical as "a merger of revolutionary and bandit."[4]

A professional thief named Movsha Shpindler from the town of Grodno was also known as Moishe Grodner. He enjoyed great respect in the robber milieu for his dexterity, boasting his nickname the "Golden hand." Shpindler knew no other trade, but when at some point in his career, he joined a group of local anarchists, his criminal activities acquired a conspicuously idealistic tint. He "was not familiar with the fine points" of the anarchist program, yet his reputation as an accomplished burglar followed him to the radical circles; Shpindler was "one of the most devoted" participants "in the entire Russian movement," his comrades agreed, if only because his terrorist career was "marked by incredible diversity." He procured weapons and took part in expropriations, as well as in numerous other daring feats. He liberated a jailed comrade, wounding several convoy soldiers. He threw a bomb into the carriage of the governor-general of Belostok and, although wanted by the city authorities and always on the run, killed a spy on his every return to his native Grodno. Shpindler's death reflected the destiny of a true believer: he shot himself with his last bullet after a bloody confrontation with the police during a house search.[5]

Dostoevsky noted the initial signs of criminalization already among the 19th-century radicals, who served as prototypes for his *Devils*. Among these rare pathological personalities, first place in disrepute went to an unscrupulous, self-seeking schemer named Sergei Nechaev, upon whom the novelist had based his sinister Petr Verkhovesnkii. Nechaev effectively combined "his own variety of charisma with astute psychological manipulation, fraud, intimidation, and blackmail... to rule a frail network of conspiratorial cells."[6] He acquired notoriety in 1869 for instigating the murder of a comrade: to enhance his authority as leader of the radical "People's Retribution" group, he falsely accused a rival of collaborating with the police. Nechaev's concurrent aim was to solidify his following by binding its student-members with the jointly spilled blood. His main contribution to the insurrection cause, however, was the coauthorship, with anarchist maharishi Bakunin, of the "Catechism of a Revolutionary"—a compilation of guiding principles for conduct of a professional radical.

An ideal member of a conspiratorial cell is an instrument of the revolution; he exists solely for its purposes, states the document, destined to become seminal in the subversive tradition. The devotee has to break "all the bonds which tie him to the social order... with all its laws, moralities, and customs, and with all its generally accepted conventions." He must be ready to kill pitilessly; "he should not hesitate to destroy any position, any place, or any man in this world." Indeed, "day and night he must have but one thought, one aim—merciless destruction" of the entire corrupt civilization. Of his environment he is an "implacable enemy"; he lives for the sole purpose of obliterating it speedily.[7]

"Terrorism was given its specific modern forms" when, stimulated by the "Catechism," scores of Russians converted to conspiracy."[8] Even though Nechaev-the-man was a black sheep of the revolutionary family, adherents to radical subculture found "Nechaevism" attractive.[9] And what had been an aberration became the norm after 1900, with Nechaev turning into the spiritual father of a mass-scale extremist movement. "The new type" or "the new breed" of radical, as it was branded by contemporaries, at the height of the 1905 crisis in Russia came to dominate the antigovernment camp numerically and in spirit.[10]

Extremists of the new type, who operated alongside the idealists and by the early 1900s outnumbered them, showed ambivalence bordering on cynicism with regard to utopianism and social altruism. Unlike the romantics among their predecessors, some of them declared that it was plainly foolish to sacrifice their lives for a future, even that in an envisaged social paradise.[11] Ambiguous about their purposes for partaking in acts of violence, they justified it in ways that betrayed a confused mindset—a brew of criminality and primitive radicalism. Andreas Baader, the ill-famed leader of the Baader-Meinhof Gang, would be a Western analogue of the new breed of extremists. A juvenile delinquent, Baader had stolen motorbikes, wrecked cars, and taken part in pub brawls before he came to lead a band in the 1970s that sought to free the oppressed by robbing banks, setting fire to department stores, and bombing German supermarkets, as a sure way to ignite world revolution.

Lithuanian SD Ivan Lidzhus killed about 30 "enemies of the revolution," among them a personal rival; in Nechaev-like fashion the terrorist had designated him a police informer. The radical took part in "exes" in the name of his organization but also did not refrain from misappropriating money for his own needs. A fellow expropriator reached a balanced ethical compromise, as far as the robberies were concerned: to use half of the loot from an armed assault to help the downtrodden proletarians and the other half to treat himself to a private estate on the Geneva Lake. As much as this extremist sympathized with the socialists, their hope for a just social order seemed to him totally unrealizable, and as much as he hated the bourgeoisie, in point of fact, he "could not help but envy it."[12]

The process of transformation from a romantic into a common criminal was usually a short one. A small SR or SD combat unit originally formed to acquire means for the party would begin to "act independently"—a euphemism for members' procuring quick cash "for their own upkeep, through assaults and threats." When unable to obtain the official expropriation mandates from their organizations, the extremists would sometimes give their "targets" counterfeit credentials—with sloppily forged party seals.[13] More and more often, they would use money solely for themselves and soon break ties with their mother SR or SD organizations. Although they might call themselves anarchists, in reality they acted like gangster bands, occupied primarily with robbery, extortion, and looting for personal profit.[14]

"The Worker's Organization of the Party of Socialists-Revolutionaries in Belostok requires you to contribute immediately...seventy-five rubles....The Organization warns you that if you fail to give the above-stated sum, it will resort to severe measures against you, transferring your case to the Combat Detachment."[15] Multiple make-believe factions of the PSR, such "Beetles of Kazan" (*Kazanskie zhuchki*), existed only on the letterhead—used by imaginative extremists in need of money for writing extortion notes.[16] In 1906–1907, the Anarchist-Communist "Karma" and other groups that operated under the black flag "deteriorated into semicriminal gangs...looting for personal profit."[17] They adhered to no particular ideological outlook, yet employed anarchist rhetoric to justify pure banditry, confirmed St. Petersburg Okhrana chief A. V. Gerasimov.[18]

Members of one anarchist crew active in the Moscow area matched Gerasimov's description perfectly and contrasted sharply with the traditionally accepted image of the selfless idealist. The band's chief was a navy deserter, who claimed responsibility for 11 murders yet had no interest in the anarchist program and failed to grasp its meaning until his arrest. He yearned only for action and the resulting material profits, he admitted. His girlfriend, a registered prostitute, also belonged to the gang, as did his comrades from similar shady backgrounds. Among them was another fugitive sailor, who had been sentenced to hard labor for taking part in killing a priest and robbing a church, and that convict's mistress, a thief with a police record.[19]

When a self-proclaimed freedom fighter had a lengthy history of contact with the police and the courts, it was nearly impossible to separate his involvement in political extremism from other forms of antisocial behavior. One I. Domogatskii, an anarchist from Baku, admitted to having killed 16 people and wounded 8—all by himself, he boasted—not to mention his involvement with comrades in the deaths of another 50 men, mostly low-ranking police officers, in addition to committing 14 robberies. He committed these heroic acts for the sake of liberating mankind after having served time in prison for common murder.[20] Countless radicals had similar records, and it is small wonder that the pubic could no longer distinguish a political extremist from a common criminal. "How does a murderer become a revolutionary?" ran a popular riddle. "When, Browning in hand, he robs a bank. How does a revolutionary become a murderer, then? In the same way!"[21]

An archetypal radical of the new type might be apprehended for felonious conduct initially, then return to prison several years later for having participated in an assassination attempt, and eventually end up in court again on rape charges.[22] A blood-spattered saga, violent acts interchanging variously, the criminal-terrorist pattern has repeated time and again until the present day. Some survivors among the Beslan hostages name as particularly vicious and terrifying one of their captors, Vladimir Khodov, aka "Abdullah," who had been arrested for a sexual assault before becoming second in charge among the extremists implicated in the school massacre.[23] In a recent study of over 400 members of violent Islamist groups, dozens of extremists in a compiled sample "had a criminal record prior to the terrorist related offence."[24] Some researchers claim that figure to be approximately 50 percent.[25]

As many as nine-tenths of all expropriations were acts of banditry, lamented Gershuni;[26] other party chiefs were not sure whether to classify these robberies as terrorism or as common crimes. The Bolsheviks who attacked a mail train at the Miass station and took 60,000 rubles in paper money and 24 kilograms of gold referred to themselves as bandits. Robbery was now synonymous with expropriation even in the radical lexicon because so many assailants—the majority, in fact—came to perceive expropriation as a lucrative, if risky, profession, "a trade."[27]

"Exes" were the raison d'être for most quasi-revolutionary groups, and even many local organizations that retained ties to centralized parties operated mainly on budgets from expropriations.[28] All other activities, the extremists carried out occasionally, between raids, if time permitted, or abandoned altogether. More than 60 percent of all anarchists convicted by the tsarist courts received their sentences for armed assaults.[29] In the Caucasus and the Urals, the Bolsheviks staged expropriations even when they did not need the money, admittedly "to stay in practice."[30]

The militants' vacillation between radical versus criminal identity manifested itself especially clearly when they failed to deliver the proceeds of many "exes" to the party treasury and instead divided the money among themselves. All factions within the Russian revolutionary movement shared this problem; yet their leaders refused to acknowledge that validation of attacks on private property led to theft of party funds. Outraged, they set up courts of honor, or tribunals, which expelled offenders from the ranks of their organizations. Among other extremists, the anarchists and the Maximalists, contemptuous as they were of the bourgeois legal process, were especially prone to issuing death sentences on the slightest suspicion that money had "stuck to the hands" of an expropriator. Despite their spur-of-the-moment vengeance, embezzlement continued and by 1907 had assumed gigantic proportions—in tandem with innumerable expropriations.

The central Maximalist organizations lived in "a grand style" on misappropriated money. Within six months of the Merchant Bank of Moscow's expropriation on March 7, 1906, when the Maximalist took 800,000 rubles, the assailants were nearly out of funds.[31] After the Fonarnyi Lane expropriation, only 60,000 of the 400,000 stolen rubles were accounted for because the Maximalists used the money "without any control" and "for whatever purposes," their leader admitted; two members of the group might have escaped with 25,000 each[32]—a giant sum of money at the time, an amount that could support an average Russian for nearly a lifetime.

Shady machinations disguising themselves as acts of political violence under a veneer of idealistic rhetoric, while characterizing the revolutionary movement of the new type, did not, obviously, qualify every extremist as a self-seeking bandit. Numerous "anarchist-fanatics and ascetics," evinced unqualified devotion to their cause and determination to live in accordance with its declared ideals: they "dressed in rags, ate only enough to avoid starvation, and forbade themselves any pleasure or entertainment bearing even a trace of luxury," remembered one impressed police captain, who could not be accused of radical sympathies.[33] Even though the total sum acquired by Kamo's group as a result of expropriations was between 325,000 and 350,000 rubles,[34] far from wasting party funds for private needs, he survived on 50 kopecks a day. Other members of his gang of seven, who inhabited a two-room apartment, were allowed no more. Two of the combatants were once forced to stay in bed all day because their comrade had borrowed their only pair of trousers. Mobsters as they might have been, they were also idealists.[35]

When fortunes did disappear from party treasuries, revolutionaries accused one another of pocketing the money. One would try to blackmail another for cash, threatening to report him to comrades as a police spy if he refused to comply. They bickered and fought over the loot like common thieves and often broke up their cells. Then, off each went his way with a bit of the take.[36]

Despite routine collaboration and migration of the rank-and-file extremists from group to group, relationships among combatants within the united terrorist front were not always idyllic. Their partnership was undermined by inter-faction rivalries—usually over expropriation spoils. Former collaborators would engage in violent exchanges of verbal abuse and threats. Unable to settle conflicts peacefully, they would also get into physical fights and steal money and weapons from one another. Terrorists even used arms against one another, as an argument all of them understood best[37]—and in a pattern that their numerous followers would repeat over the following century, members of the Shining Path were involved in violent clashes with their rivals from the Tupac Amaru Revolutionary Movement, among many others. Maksim Litvinov, Lenin's trusted associate after 1905, once sent two Georgian terrorists to the RSRDP headquarters to demand 40,000 expropriated rubles that the Menshevik Central Committee had gone ahead to spend; the Georgians would "bump off" one of its members, Litvinov threatened, if the money were not returned to the Bolsheviks.[38]

Ironically, these enemies of private property sometimes used stolen cash to buy a small store or start another business of their own, even though they knew that their former comrades would be after them. From time to time, the radicals succeeded in tracking the renegades down, as when they paid a surprise visit to the home of an ex-revolutionary who lived in Paris as a private shop owner. When threatened with death, the expropriator-turned-*marchand* started to negotiate. His newly acquired entrepreneurial skills came in handy; in the end, he managed to convince his former colleagues to accept only half of what he had stolen.[39]

Other embezzlers were even more fortunate. Having acquired thousands as a result of expropriations in the Caucasus, the local SDs lived lavish lives and "spent money without restraint." After the expropriation of 315,000 rubles from the Dushet Treasury in April 1906, a large portion of the loot remained in the hands of a man named Kereselidze who had orchestrated the raid, as a member of the Revolutionary Party of Georgian Socialists-Federalists. He immediately gave up his glamorous career as a radical for the sake of tranquil life in Geneva. There he enjoyed deluxe lodgings and the extravagance of a private automobile. He could satisfy his expensive tastes only because of his luck in Georgia, he bragged to fellow émigrés.[40]

Accustomed to easily available fortunes, the extremists squandered tens of thousands of rubles on luxuries, prostitutes, and alcohol and submerged themselves in a bacchanalia of debauchery. Heavy drinking is a usual resort for habitual killers, apparently not an unusual problem even among those who are ready to die the Qur'an.[41] A Russian Maximalist depicts in his memoirs a revealing episode: 15 extremists spent an entire day carousing and in the process lost one of their comrades, who died, probably of alcohol poisoning. The doctor arrived to witness an ugly scene: next to the corpse one man lay unconscious, while his inebriated pal tried to force their dead companion to drink one more round. The others paid no attention and continued with their orgy.[42] Modern-days terrorists have cultivated much better manners and are usually more temperate, but when extremist colleagues from different corners of the globe get a chance to socialize in the hospitable Damascus, the lobby of their favorite Sheraton hotel "acquires the atmosphere of a gangland meeting."[43]

Russian radical activists called their wayward associates "the scum of the revolution," sometimes expelled them from the parties' ranks, and on occasion even condemned them to death for especially abhorrent, "revolting expropriations."[44] Publicly, leaders denounced banditry, yet it was better to tolerate the "thoughtless and harmful acts" of the expropriators than to paralyze their "spontaneous activity," declared world-famous anarchist Petr Kropotkin in a private letter.[45] Its corrupting effect on the rank-and-file aside, criminal behavior was the revolutionaries' ally; it destabilized the autocratic regime as much as did political activism.

Nowhere did the political extremist merge so fully with the thug as in prisons and hard convicted bandits. There, many ex-terrorists and expropriators preferred the company of convicted bandits. In conflicts between regular and political prisoners, they chose to side with their new pals, even if it meant taking physical action against fellow politicals. Whether they were unaffiliated militants or formal members of the SD, SR, or anarchist organizations, they staged expropriations within prison walls in accordance with "all the rules of the art."[46] The local raids turned into knife fights, and this is why the inmates often admitted that they "feared their own comrades more than the jailers."[47] Unlike previous generations of revolutionaries, who despised and refused to have anything to do with their prison officers, many convicted new-type militants were "buddies" with their guards and, along with non-political detainees, begged them for cigarette butts, cash, and other petty favors. From time to time, however, a conflict would break out, replete with the filthy and abusive language of street thugs: a guard was "a bitch" and ought to be "blown away," the so-called freedom fighter would swear to tell his comrades outside the jail.[48]

In prisons, the radicals also used the opportunity to recruit into their ranks a wide variety of shady individuals, hooligans, and riffraff from the "lower depths" of the Russian society. "Brigands...are the only genuine revolutionaries in Russia," Nechaev had said,[49] and his followers among the new extremists welcomed to the radical camp professional thieves and other hardcore criminals. The anarchists were particularly skillful in these efforts, but the SRs and the SDs claimed success as well. "They scream: Down with the expropriators, the robbers, the criminals...But the rebellion will come, and they will be with us. On the barricades, a hardened burglar will be more useful than Plekhanov," Bolshevik Aleksandr Bogdanov endorsed Nechaev's suggestion to unite with the bandits' "adventurous tribes."[50]

A revolutionary should not take part in capitalist production, the anarchists of the "Without Authority" group explained to inmates sentenced to prison terms for burglary and assaults. He "must not, by his work in a factory or in a shop, strengthen and enhance the position of the same bourgeoisie that is subject to merciless extermination." A freedom fighter "ought to satisfy his material needs by means of robberies and the theft of possessions from the wealthy."[51] In the past, the burglar had done exactly that, and the anarchists encouraged him to be proud of his "advanced class consciousness." Thievery was merely a product of the existing political order and therefore "not a crime," the local anarchists comforted thugs from the Odessa underworld.[52] Felony, be it murder or robbery, in fact contributed to the destabilization of the hated regime. Understandably, former bandits, now accepted as full-fledged members of the extremist community, appreciated hearing from the agitators that banditry was "socially progressive."[53]

To cater to the criminals' "eternal gripe against those around, the infantile desire to relocate responsibility from oneself to whoever," the revolution offers a special ethical system, "in which all their actions, deeds and their motives are excused. They are always victims. Even most malicious acts they are simply forced to perform under the pressure of circumstances."[54]

Demagoguery of a lofty cause allows for "a false sense of well-being. . . . To free oneself from the pressure of one's own conscience *and* thereby achieve the acceptance of and belonging to others." This happens "when the group adheres to a new ideology which transcends the individual for the good of all."[55] Hence, the mores and the whole "subculture of the criminal milieu, their vile essence notwithstanding, were not exempt from a recognizable attraction, a romantic halo." Murder entailed "something of a consecrated ritual" and "a sacred act."[56]

As part of their recruitment techniques, the radicals provided their criminal protégés with convenient justifications for the lifestyle they had already chosen as their own. The felons did not need to alter their behavior; they would continue doing what they did best—rob and kill—but now under the antigovernment banner. "Confiscation of private capital—this is what the revolution is," Maximalist leader Vladimir Mazurin stated clearly and simply.[57]

Their self-esteem enhanced, the brigand society readily adopted and followed the crude logic in "stealing what had been stolen" or "expropriating the expropriators." It is difficult to gauge to what extent lofty slogans incited the criminals to further violence. On the other hand, their presence in the antigovernment movement influenced it tremendously. It also produced an altered collective image—a mishmash of the extremist and the bandit that no one could tell apart. When not engaged in shady enterprises with pseudo-revolutionary objectives, these militants accepted commissions from anyone who wanted to use their combat experience—for anything from kidnapping to murder for hire. "A landowner for twenty rubles," said the radicals in advertising their cheap skilled labor.[58]

Violence corrupts, and sometimes individuals and groups altered their priorities, vacillating between self-protection and aggression. Such was the case with the "Green Hundred," an organization formed in August 1907 by Armenian entrepreneurs, who eventually themselves became involved in evidently contagious quasi-anarchist activities in Baku. In that city, well-to-do industrialists employed the services of armed bodyguards, whom they had recruited from the local underworld of thugs and daredevils. These bodyguards, known as *kochi*, were prepared to risk their lives protecting their employers against the extremists, but they also commonly took part in various crimes and violent acts for personal benefits.[59]

Trapped in anarchy, some enterprising citizens sought to extract profits from it. Wishing to settle scores with private enemies, they offered the expropriators their rivals' names and financial information, so as to enjoy secret revenge over these candidates for blackmail at no risk to themselves.[60] Lawbreakers of all shades did not remain behind events either: in the Baltics, they occasionally approached people on the streets and offered their services as paid assassins.[61]

"A prosecution officer costs this much, a police officer—this much, an army personnel—that much." stated the July 3, 2009, Interfax report; referring to prices in the U.S. dollars listed in a notepad that belonged to a combatant killed by Russian troops in the North Caucasus. The Investigation Department of the Federal Prosecution Office confirms that some terrorist acts in this violence-ravaged area were carried out by "remunerated volunteers." Among them, Russian officials claimed, were citizens of foreign countries, "Arab and Azerbaijani paid-for-hire."[62] Recruitment of revolutionary cadres in return for direct financial compensation by now has turned into a century-long tradition.[63]

In the early 1900s, a draftee would get an advance, sometimes as small as 15 rubles, along with a handful of bullets, followed by a promise for additional remuneration after he has proven himself in action. Some killers-for-hire received regular salaries,[64] but at other times, a few drinks were enough to finalize recruitment.[65] A rookie did not always know whether the individual who conscripted him for an assassination represented a particular antigovernment organization or was merely using him as an instrument for personal vengeance. Over time, the cost of a commissioned murder dropped abruptly, proportionate to escalating violence: when prices reached rock bottom, the services of a private killer were available for less than three rubles per head.[66]

* * *

Perhaps nothing was as tragic as the victimization of children in this brutality-ravaged environment, where they became pawns in the terrorists' games—for the first, though not last, time in history. For the most part, the radicals conscripted adolescent terrorists from among the troubled youth, who had alienated themselves from their peers through deviant conduct that also had deprived them of opportunities in any normal walks of life. Accustomed to violence in the adult world, the ostracized troublemakers and dropouts found release for their frustrations in brutal acts of revenge against anyone they felt had treated them unfairly—not the political regime per se, or even the educational system as a whole, but personal enemies, such as school principals and teachers.[67] A juvenile Arab convict in Israeli prison presented an identical account of his delinquent, pre-terrorist past, punctuated by smashed windows and torched cars.[68]

By painting the teenage antisocial behavior with the colors of political protest, extremists found easy prey among the young felons—some shaken by their crimes and desperate to find *post factum* idealistic explanation for them. Recruiters also profited from the usual adolescent wish to take active part in the events that affected the lives of the adults around them and to define their own identity by incorporating the meaningful values of others. As a result of recruiters' efforts, nearly 22 percent of all SR terrorists were between the ages of 15 and 19.[69] In 1905, the SRs formed a combat unit in Belostok that consisted entirely of schoolchildren.[70] Among the anarchists and the Maximalists there were even more minors, some as young as 14 years of age.[71]

Incited to violence by older terrorists, the juveniles perceived their new life as underground freedom fighters as an intoxicating game, full of secrecy, mystery, danger, and idealistic rhetoric. Realizing that the teenagers had a better chance of success in dangerous enterprises than older perpetrators, if only because the police were less likely to suspect them of criminal intentions, the adults dispatched them to attack police headquarters and individual officers, plant bombs, or carry out expropriations—so much the better if the adolescents treated these activities as an amusing play. As part of this performance, teenagers devoted a great deal of energy to developing secret codes and passwords, as sophisticated, as they were unnecessary. One boy carved a Browning pistol out of soap, painted it black, and used the toy weapon to confiscate six real ones. The young actors enthusiastically learned their new roles that required them to change their appearances with makeup, fake beards, and—of course—masks.[72] The disguise helped them feel grown-up and "made it easier to break the law"—the way face concealment would facilitate the enactment of violence by adult extremists, as well as burglars and rapists. The mask was a statement: "I don't play by the rules. Be afraid, be very afraid."[73]

On occasion, the adolescents had genuine personal grievances against authorities, as did a 13-year-old girl in Rostov-on-Don who threw carbolic acid in the face of a police officer to avenge her brother's arrest.[74] More often, however, they were driven by adolescent disdain for authority and hoped "to do something outstanding, having to do with danger... something that might draw general attention."[75] They then made themselves available to eager adult supervisors, who sacrificed the expendable child-cadres when they did not want to risk the arrest of more experienced militants—for example, while transporting or carrying explosives to the site of a terrorist act.

Among the young delinquents, alcohol was often an important factor in making the decision to engage in hazardous operations, acknowledged one former child-extremist[76]—not dissimilar to someone like the 16-year-old drug user and distributer Anwar Ahmed Abd El Khalek Hamed, recruited in 2001 by the Palestinian terrorists.[77] Others "loved money, simple as that";[78] it was no secret that radical organizations in the periphery occasionally seduced impoverished 15- and 16-year-olds into terrorist activities, sometimes paying them as little as 50 kopeks.[79] A tenth-grader Jalal received 100 shekels for a promise to become a shahid; this money was part of a larger sum paid by adult jihadists to his recruiter—a classmate.[80]

In the same way, since the 1980s children "as young as 8 years old [have been] used to fight, guard hostages, transport arms and place bombs" by terrorist organizations, such as a military wing of the Columbian Communist party, the Revolutionary Armed Forces of Colombia (Fuerzas Armadas Revolucionarios de Columbia—FARC). Of its combatants, 20 to 30 percent are poverty-stricken children under 18 years of age: many of them "join up for food or physical protection, to escape domestic violence, or because of promises of money" and "are often ordered to participate in summary executions, torture, murder, kidnapping and attacks on civilians."[81] FARC not only recruits Colombian child-terrorists "but also pays parents for their children in Venezuela, Bolivia, Ecuador and Panama."[82] Everywhere, prices for suicide missions are very low indeed: in 2004 a 14-year-old was captured at the Hawara Check Point, near Nablus, wearing an eight-kilogram explosive belt under his shirt. The boy explained to the Israeli soldiers that he had gotten 100 shekels (approximately 27 dollars) to blow himself up.[83] They were probably not surprised: an 11 year old had agreed to do the same for five shekels.[84] To a six-year-old Afghani boy in Ghazni whom the Taliban militants gave a suicide vest to explode among the U.S. troops in June 2007, they might have offered ice cream.[85]

Regardless of the draftee's age, the recruiter in the early 1900s frequently employed a gawky jumble of arguments aimed to arouse plain avarice sugar-coated with lofty sentiments: "Proceed with your work, comrade, and you will have watches and money, and Poland will be grateful to you forever," a PPS instructor encouraged a trainee, noticing that the young man was admiring his expensive gold watch. After the novice reported having personally killed seven policemen and taken part in three expropriations, he received 18 rubles—"for now."[86] One headhunter managed to conscript a volunteer for an armed robbery by promising him a new coat.[87] Today, sufficient for recruitment of youngsters is an enticing pledge for "a better place in Paradise."[88]

As facile for recruitment the extremists of the new type might have been, they were equally unreliable: when in need of money, many offered their services as paid Okhrana informers. Some reported on their comrades out of self-interest, whereas others pretended to do the same for altruistic reasons, which they defended with a bewildering logic. An SR named Metal'nikov confessed to having accepted police employment in order to earn 6,000—a sum required for financing an expropriation, which, in turn, would supply the terrorists with funds for a major political assassination.[89] The authorities considered such informers duplicitous and unreliable yet exploited them nevertheless, sometimes for a few rubles a month. There was never a shortage of traitors: in the SR Combat Organization in 1909, among 10 to 12 active members, 3 happened to be police spies.[90]

Maximalist Solomon Ryss (alias Mortimer) fled abroad from his native Rostov, where he was wanted for forging high school diplomas. In Europe he proceeded steadfastly along the path of enlightenment, stealing and selling rare library books. Upon his return to Russia in 1906, he was arrested in Kiev during an attempted robbery of a workers' cooperative, at which time he offered his services to the police. For several months he supplied the authorities with a potpourri of facts and lies regarding the affairs of the Maximalists, whom he assured at the same time that he was feeding the Okhrana false information—a game to which some of his comrades attributed great value. His double-dealing did not last long, and police suspicions forced Ryss to flee once again. He was finally apprehended in 1907, charged with a motley of violent exploits, and, having failed to bribe the investigation officer with 50,000 rubles, was sentenced to death and hanged.[91]

From the 19th century, the revolutionaries had only one verdict for the informants—death. More often than not, great fear of betrayal drove them to issue their sentences without taking the time to investigate the alleged police connections. In a shocking episode in 1876, mere suspicion that a certain N. E. Gorinovich could be a traitor led his maddened comrades to attack him and pour sulfuric acid over his face, leaving him blind and permanently disfigured.[92] In the atmosphere of routine cruelty in the early 1900s, this story would not shock anyone. The extremists tortured suspected spies to death, slashing throats, cutting off ears and noses, and decapitating their enemies; they evinced unrestrained habitual brutality and sadism, excising their tongues as a "symbolic gesture."[93]

Here again Lenin's Caucasian aide Kamo deserved top prize, for the most original solution for cleansing the party of all real and potential police informers. He and several other combatants would dress in gendarme uniforms and stage a fake arrest of leading party activists, he proposed in 1911. "We will come, arrest you, torture you, run a stake through you. If you start talking, it'll be clear what you're worth."[94] Kamo wished to implement his plan immediately, but the Bolshevik leaders tabled it discreetly—so as not to frustrate the restless highway robber, whom celebrated writer Maksim Gor'kii titled "artist of the revolution."[95]

* * *

Modern communication technology creates new possibilities to color criminal activities with pseudo-extremist shades, essentially of the type that plagued Russia a hundred years ago. Globalization impacts aficionados of the criminal subculture; marginals, they are not immune from influences of their broader environmental context. Like the rest of the society, they are affected by characteristic parameters of their cultural milieu, including contemporary sociopolitical concerns, such as those regarding terrorism, as well as the language in which the anxieties are expressed.

"This is a message from the Ishmael Ghost Islamic Group. We are confirmed Islamic Hired killers and Suicide aids. We have been sent to assassinate you and members of your family." So begins an e-mail letter dated June 10, 2009. It was sent to multiple recipients, with this message:

> We decided that you provide the total sum of 800 USD to transport some of our expatriates out of the USA.... If you do not follow these requirements, I am sorry you shall not live to see the next three weeks, even if you see the next three weeks, a member of your family shall pay for it and another shall pay for every other week you stay alive until you are dead. To provide this money, kindly send the money via western union or money gram to a receiver in the UK.

Below this message are the particulars of the receiver, one Steven Gibbs, allegedly residing in London. "You have been given 72 hrs to send this money or else you shall pay with your life. Note: we have all your movement and the movement of members of your family monitored. Do not let them pay for your greed." The letter ends, "If anything happens to any member of our gang...your family story shall be a disaster." It is signed electronically by the "Group Treasury Officer," who politely wishes its numerous recipients to "Have a nice life."[96] This email from the "Ishmael Ghost Islamic Group" is identical in content, style, and even syntax to a typical handwritten epistolary masterpiece produced by the previously mentioned "Worker's Organization of the Party of Socialists-Revolutionaries in Belostok," "Karma," and other Russian bands bearing equally impressive names, such as the "Black Falcon anarchists-blackmailers" (*anarchisty-shantazhisty-Chernyi Sokol*).[97] The only difference is that presently "liberators of mankind" prefer their loot in hard currency.

For all the local cultural nuances, terrorist recruiters in various parts of the globe appreciate the revolutionary potential of the criminal underworld, as they did in turn-of-the 20th-century Russia. An offshoot of the Italian "Red Brigades" (*Brigate Rossi*), the anarchist Armed Proletarian Units, or NAP (*Nuclei Armati Proletari*), which operated in Italy in the late 1970s, adhered to Nechaev's view on common delinquent, "politically conditioned" in prison, as society's most progressive element. Workers' Autonomy (*Autonomia Operaia—AO*), another Italian left-militant organization, shared NAP's justification of common crime as a manifestation of the class struggle and a progressive tendency for "income redistribution." These extremists staged bank holdups, armed raids on supermarkets, and kidnappings for ransom, along with occasional attacks on the Carabinieri barracks and the Ministry of Justine personnel—side by side with a motley of ex-convicts, who were said to have developed a "political conscience."[98] Also in the 1970s, the Symbionese Liberation Army (SLA), an ideologically inspired criminal gang in California, recruited some of its cadres from the prison population to "reappropriate" money from "rich oppressors." Saudi charities fund organizations that preach radical Islam in American prisons, where recent Muslim converts among the inmates are "natural recruits for Islamist organizations."[99] Ukrainian-born sexual assailant Khodov, who distinguished himself by cruelty toward the Beslan schoolchildren, had converted to radical Islam in prison or, according to some accounts, under the influence of his brother, who had become a Muslim while serving his own eight-year sentence for murder. Upon graduating from a *medrese* (Islamic school), Khodov joined a Vahabist terrorist group.[100]

Terrorists—from leftist guerrillas in South America to the al-Qaeda network—have close ties with common criminals; more than a dozen of the large terrorist organizations are funded by illicit drugs operations, and some have transformed themselves into "profit-driven organized criminals."[101] FARC, for instance, has implicated itself in crimes from kidnappings for profit and bank robberies to "exportation of cocaine, one of the main sources of revenue for the guerrillas."[102] The Peruvian Shining Path, while "professing to be a Maoist insurgency as heart...is now in the business of protecting drug smugglers, extorting taxes from farmers and operating its own cocaine laboratories." The guerrillas "operate with the efficiency and deadliness of an elite drug trafficking organization," according to a security analyst in Lima, Peru; he "estimates that the Shining Path employs about 500 laborers in the cocaine trade, in addition to about 350 armed combatants."[103]

It is public knowledge that from Afghanistan comes about 70 percent of the intercontinental supply of opium. Revenues from its production have helped finance the al-Qaeda terrorist network.[104] The annual proceeds of the Afghan Golden Crescent drug trade, estimated to be between 100 and 200 billion dollars, represent approximately one-third of the transnational annual turnover of narcotics. Equally known is Hezbollah's drug trafficking, already in the mid-1980s sanctioned by an official fatwa (religious edict): "We are making these drugs for Satan America and the Jews. If we cannot kill them with guns, so we will kill them with drugs."[105] A less familiar fact is that among the militants in Tajikistan, "most take drugs supplied by their commanders."[106] According to the deputy prosecutor general of Russia's southern federal district, blood tests on corpses "had shown that 22 of the 32 hostage-takers were on hard drugs and had regularly injected substances such as heroin and morphine while the other 10 had been using softer drugs," during the siege of Beslan School No. 1.[107]

"We received information about a suicide bomber in an area known for local support of the anti-American insurgency," testifies a former U.S. intelligence operative who served in the Wasit province of Iraq in 2003–2004:

> An Iraqi man had strapped an anti-tank mine to his body; he threatened to detonate the explosive device and kill himself along with everyone present in the house. The IPs (Iraqi police) who detained the individual referred to him as "suicide bomber" in the report forwarded to the coalition forces. We arrived to interrogate the detainee, and he said that he wanted to force his relatives to return some plastic furniture they had taken from him.

More than an amusing wartime anecdote, the account is indicative and sheds new light on the so-called terrorist incidents that the 1,121 suicide bombers carried out in Iraq by 2008.[108] A huge percentage of these attacks may rather be acts of common crime and banditry, which have assumed astonishing proportions.

> The road-side explosive device targeted a newly constructed building. It ripped through a passing minivan, killing three students on the way home. The bombing was ordered by a contractor who failed to win the bid and hoped for a do-over by demolishing the completed project. The incident was classified as an act of violence against the coalition effort to rebuild the country.[109]

All across Iraq, thugs whose sole objective is robbery ambush and kill automobile drivers and passengers in alleged "sectarian violence." Opportunities to make money as paid assassins—political or not—are easier to find than regular jobs, especially in violence-stricken areas. Even those who are employed during the day are moved by the economic uncertainty of tomorrow, rather than a political allegiance, and do not shy away from minimal pay-offs for planting explosives at night. "It is very difficult to tell a terrorist from a common bandit"[110] when, both evincing felonious mentality, they use interchangeably the same means, similar cliché-sprinkled ideological jargon and gangster vocabulary.

Chapter 6

Camouflaged Suicide

We shall die! Oh, how gloriously we shall die!
—Prince E. P. Obolenskii on the day of the December 14, 1825, uprising in St. Petersburg

I will take my soul into my hands and hurl it into the abyss of death.
—"Shahid's Song" From a sixth-grade Palestinian textbook, *Our Beautiful Language*

A 21-year-old woman makes her entry into the police headquarters. Strapped to her body are 13 pounds of nitroglycerin and a detonating device. Before she has a chance to blow up the entire building and perish along with everyone present, she is apprehended by the security forces.

The incident did not happen in Lebanon, where the Hezbollah terrorists used human beings as ticking bombs in the 1980s. This act was not organized in Jennin, "the capital of suicide terrorism," where a quarter of all explosions in Israel are conceived.[1] Nor was the young woman a member of the Sri Lanka's Tamil Tigers, notorious for suicide bombings—some 200 since the late 1980s. The perpetrator of this mission was PSR member Evstiliia Rogozinnikova, who on October 15, 1907, planned to blow up the offices of the St. Petersburg Prison Department.

The process of historical dislocation in Russia engendered a condition that Erik Erikson called "identity diffusion," or, to stick with Lifton's terminology, "the Protean style" of conduct. The metaphor accentuated a Greek mythological figure of Proteus, who could effortlessly change his shape but found it difficult "to commit himself to a single form, a form most his own." The Protean behavior in the early 1900s entailed extravagant and sometimes compulsive trialing of "the new"—from the hitherto unthinkable "uninhibited sexuality" to toying with superficial components of exotic cultures to acts of political extremism, including suicide terror. Passionate and often hysterical as these explorations were, the source and the paramount unifying feature of the Protean search was the need to find a fresh source of vitality, a pure faith to fill the gaping spiritual void people felt after having discarded traditional values.

A "nocturnal existence," wild, sleepless, sated with "frenzied exhibitions of fantasy," described writer Mikhail Prishvin the bacchanalia of the Silver Age self-indulgence. Great was enticement for life as an endless chain of possibilities: "This was a whirlwind and readiness for all sorts of experimentations,"[2] which comprised a long list of deviations—addictions, pornography and blatantly perverse sexual acting-out, dabbing in brutality, murder, and suicide. The *decadents* sought to test the limits of individuality, challenging every old prohibition with the trendy "and why not?"[3] Perpetually in search of uncharted intense experiences, scores of them drowned the taboo in alcohol, in opium, or in cocaine-induced nirvana:

> We went insane from living indulgently.
> Wine before noon, by evening a heavy head.
> How can we sustain your feverish red
> O drunken plague, and your vain revelry?[4]

Literature of this period—from Mikhail Artsybashev's low-grade *Sanin* to Belyi's phenomenal *Petersburg*—illustrates a hodgepodge of fads that varied at whim in kaleidoscopic fashion. Fiction "turned sexual, in some cases taking on themes of incest and sadism," with protagonists indulging their "urges without restraint or regret." Historians describe "free sex" as "the norm among urban lower classes," as much as among the educated—so that "every kind of illegal liaison flourished in all ranks of society."[5] By 1906, Russia reached a "sexual crisis."[6]

For some time, *le dernier cri* in the capital was the "yellow style" in clothes and décor, a sign of cursory infatuation with the budding power of the Orient.[7] The wind would change direction easily, and soon the intelligentsia, influenced by the Symbolist representatives of the "dominant aesthetic of the Silver Age," cultivated dark apocalyptic ideation and flirted with the occult and quasi-spirituality, sometimes expressed as blood rites, satanism, and death-worship.[8]

As part of a cycle of emotional investments and disappointments in an assortment of Protean diversions, the confused and frantic "superfluous people," engaged as they were in "alternative lifestyles," would sooner or later stumble on political extremism as a modern variant of "subversive individualism."[9] In essence, it was analogous to narcotics or perhaps cheap-thrill entertainment—encompassing as outward attributes exaggerated gestures, flamboyant colors and noises, and gripping, if garish, excitement. Some admitted that participation in terrorist operations was a means to escape from apathy and debilitating boredom.[10] "I cannot live peacefully," declared an activist; "I like danger, so as to feel the thrill."[11] It was the "enterprises and adventures," others stated bluntly, that enticed and spurred them on along the revolutionary path.[12]

The thrill of subversive action had one essential advantage over all other forms of marginal behaviors. Unlike individuals engaged in diversions requiring them to cope with cheerless nadirs between peaks of excitement, the revolutionary retained the exhilaration as part of the perpetual pursuit of his visionary ideals. The forever-distant dream substantiated his otherwise erratic life and gave it a quality of transcendence, analogous to what Freud called an "oceanic feeling." For those emotionally and physically exhausted and depleted by experimentations with various more-or-less addictive fads, participation in extremist politics provided a new meaning and fierce energy to go on. "How many self-destroyers are there in Russia who fanatically direct their extraordinary capacities against themselves!" writer Aleksei Remizov exclaimed in astonishment. His famous partner in trade Maksim Gorkii went a step further: "nowhere do people wreck themselves with such headlong, senseless speed, as in our Russia."[13] The SR leader Victor Chernov acknowledged that "revolution was becoming the fashion."[14] As a craze, the Russian insurgency is hardly unique: elsewhere, over time terrorism turned out to be "a career as much as a passion." Infused with a dark spirit, Jihad, too "becomes addictive."[15]

In their new roles, the radical enthusiasts continued their engagement in self-destructive behavior, of which some seemed to be semiconscious. Their expressed goal was

> to look for the ultimate courage in the ultimate despair; to finish with all the old in order to begin from the beginning, as if there is not and has not been in the world anyone other than us. Even we do not seem to be, but we will, we will...If Russia today is a dry forest, ready for fire, then the Russian decadents are the driest top branches of these woods; when the lightening will strike, they will ignite first, setting fire to the whole forest.[16]

The new culture yielded its own archetype to be admired and emulated. The "beau ideal" was a veritable Protean man—a complicated individual, burdened by inner contradictions, of which the youth was proud, "as if these were war wounds." Everyone wished to present himself in accordance with a preferred image of "the split, bizarre type," remembered Belyi about the tendency among "the most nervous and sensitive young people."[17] They held melancholy and neurasthenia as "an attribute of refinement" and even "invented vices and perversions for themselves"—anything rather than be regarded as banal.[18] Many self-proclaimed neurasthenics cited their invented condition to demonstrate that "they [didn't] belong to the vulgar...self-satisfied masses."[19]

The "border generation" applauded everything "abnormal," "odd," or "sick" and also expressed itself antisocially.[20] Its wild festival honoring the infinite potential of liberated individual was, in fact, a parody, reiterating variations on a nihilistic punch line of exceeding belligerence. "These were the days when love and all sane and kindly emotions were regarded as commonplace and old-fashioned." On the other hand, "destructiveness was considered a sign of good taste"[21] and sought venues to realize itself as action: "Some different higher principle is needed. Since there is none, rebellion and violence of all sorts take its place...unspectacular open self-destruction—debauch, drinking, all the forms of suicide."[22] As part of the disintegrating setting, the concept of death became a new fad.

The situation in Russia was not dissimilar to the cultural climate in turn-of-the-century Vienna,[23] where "deviance increased, and society was pervaded by interpersonal and intergroup tensions, mistrust, and hostility.... Artists, who Ezra Pound calls 'the antennae of the world,' sensed the atmosphere of death and dissolution and depicted it in their works."[24] Death-wishing permeated the decadent environment and inherited its distinct features. The Russian new-age aesthetes were fascinated with a symbiosis of artistic ecstasy and destructive energy. They looked for and found "poetry in death."[25] Symbolizing the "noblest instincts" of her generation, the heroine of a famous story by Leonid Andreev, the Girl in Black, offered the only answer to hopelessness—"to meet death dancing."[26] Those among the intelligentsia who showed a predilection for "the dark side" flirted with the mysticism of death and obsessively dwelled on the concept of the "nonbeing."[27]

"In the everyday kingdom of mere things," in his meaningless existence, one "gazed into the abyss of sorrow and despair" and "saw nothing but confusion, madness, death."[28] Such was the conventional outlook of the lonely man, who "meets throughout a profound dismay at the disjunction between words and actions, ideals and reality," perceiving life as a poor performance of a vulgar play: "The entire world seems to me like some kind of masquerade," complained one victim of the modernization crisis, in which despondency was a mainstream attitude:

> All around move living beings, perhaps nice ones (friends and family), but each of them, each without exception is in a mask, loathsomely whining in another's voice, loathsomely gesticulating with another's hands, loathsomely responding with another's soul—(they all) rush about with mouths stuffed with beautiful words about right, good and truth, beauty and justice.... And when one sees this, when one feels (the monotony), one wants to run and run.

Only there is no salvation: everyone "celebrates the eternal banal masquerade."[29] Finding no escape from pointlessness, people asked themselves whether it was "honorable to live in such dark conditions...or at once to end (it all)."[30] Many found their pseudo-existence not worth dragging out.

Self-inflicted death showed catastrophic increase after 1905, reaching the figure of 370 per one million.[31] Independent sources revealed "a massive rise in suicides and attempted suicides from 557 in 1906 to a peak of 3,975 in 1910 followed by a modest decline to 3,248 in 1911."[32] Physicians and journalists declared a real epidemic of self-caused death in St. Petersburg, in which the "clash between... tradition and modernity has produced a mixture of creativity and anxiety."[33] Amidst the city's contradictory magnificence and restlessness, citizens developed "a sense of impending Apocalypse"[34] and perceived Russia's northern capital as an urbanistic monster "in the grip of nervous expectation, cataclysmic foreboding and a fatal urge to destruction."[35] Its "spirit was ruinous,"[36] aimed at self-annihilation; the rate of suicide tripled in half-a-decade: from 500 cases per million residents to a colossal 1,640 in 1910, to fall only slightly to 1,550 in 1911—"easily the highest rate in Europe."[37] Although grueling economic conditions in the early phases of Russia's industrialization were likely the main reason in the lower strata of the population, numerous acts of suicidal homicide were not at all related to deprivation. Most people who chose to kill themselves blamed not the economic poverty but the "poverty of values" or "life" as a whole, which they decided was "not worth it to live."[38]

In vogue after 1905, this attitude rendered suicide a new sociocultural trend, distinct from isolated instances when individuals took their own lives as a result of strictly personal suffering or private dramas. True to the ethos of the Silver Age, the revolutionary extremists, along with their apolitical contemporaries, submitted themselves to the "suicidal urge."[39] To a great extent, self-destructive tendencies had to do with their inability to tolerate life even after they had made their desperate attempt to ameliorate the tensions of individuation via self-repudiation in the revolutionary milieu.

The radical, dictates "Catechism of a Revolutionary," must suppress "all the gentle and enervating sentiments of kinship, love, friendship, gratitude, and even honor" for the sake of "only one pleasure, one consolation, one reward, one satisfaction—the success of the revolution." For its victory, a genuine adherent has to sacrifice all his possessions, all his social and family ties, and if need be, his life. He must have "no personal interests, no business affairs, no emotions, no attachments, no property, and no name... All the worse for him if he has any relations with parents, friends, or lovers; *he is no longer a revolutionary if he is swayed by these relationships.*" Essentially, a true believer is required to repudiate all ties with its own humanity: the revolutionary, "Catechism" declares, "is a doomed man."[40]

The sought-after refuge and self-abandonment in a revolutionary conspiracy was tantamount to "the life of a hunted wolf," recapped Lev Tikhomirov, once a member of a terrorist conspiracy. Quite as Nechaev had predicted, for a person who "must be prepared to perish not just today or tomorrow, but any second," an attachment of any seriousness was "a genuine misfortune.... Apart from five to ten like-minded persons, one must deceive from morning to night literally everyone; one must hide from everyone, suspect in everyone an enemy."[41]

Folie à duex was a term coined in 1897 by Lasègue and Farlet "to describe the occurrence of shared delusions in two or more people... relatively isolated from the outside world and its influences," who endorsed the vision of the "inducer" or "principal."[42] An aberrant psychological condition akin to *folie à duex* (or, more accurately, *folie à plusieurs*) prevalent in the self-imposed radical exile was that of ultimate desocialization and disharmony with the rest of the humanity. It simply "did not exist for me," terrorist Mariia Shkol'nik put in a nutshell.[43] SR bomb-maker Dora Brilliant severed all connections not only with society at large, but also with the rest of the party: "her entire world was confined to the Combat Organization."[44]

Rare individuals, such as "renegade Tikhomirov," found sufficient inner strength to seek a breakaway from the vicious circle of dependence on collective affirmation, but when they did, group pressure against the desperate effort to restore the power of the "I" was enormous, revealing deep insecurity within the movement. "For when the cause is less than the highest, the sense of fear... is transferred from the self to the cause—as when heroic self-sacrifice... is accompanied by anxiety in regard to that for which the sacrifice is made."[45] To allow a member to find life outside the revolutionary circle would endorse that life—something which was incompatible with the "us"-versus-"them" totalist thinking.

Following Nechaev, the group leaders classified any attempt to find meaning outside the revolution as apostasy, and tragically, most would-be-dissenters conformed. One young man confessed in his suicide note "that his inability to become a true revolutionary, his internal repulsion for that activity and unconquerable wish for an ordinary, peaceful life had tormented him." We "sentenced this completely innocent young human soul to death by our moral coercion to [adopt] a revolutionary way of thinking," lamented his friend, a future renowned philosopher; we "tyrannically violated his soul with our merciless demand for revolutionary service."[46]

Often the "revolutionaries hated the bourgeoisie as much as they hated one another," a writer close to the extremist milieu said, dispelling the myth about a radical brotherhood.[47] Terrorists found within the severely dysfunctional "revolutionary family" a sanctuary from the pressures of individuation.[48] To maintain cohesiveness, in spite of the inner discord among conflict-prone, bellicose personalities, the leaders sought to amplify fear of the outside world among the rank-and-file, keeping them in a constant state of apprehension of a haunted game.

The deleterious underground routine thus whittled away at what little was left of the vulnerable, fragmented Protean type's inner verve, draining and consigning him to the state of "death-in-life." The revolutionaries were entangled in the "as if" existence of the terrorist sect—a predicament much more perilous than the angst-permeated life they had sought to flee, eating away at one's sense of reality and aliveness. A beautiful woman in her twenties, Brilliant "spent her days in silence," in "concentrated suffering," in inner torment that filled "her saddened soul." Gloomy, "she did not know the joy of life."[49] Dejected by the futility of their runaway experience, the radicals welcomed the culturally commended "nonbeing" as their only chance to elude the intolerable distress, now exacerbated by chronic fear of extinction within the cell. Unaware of the paradox, they rationalized death-wishing with the rhetoric of revolutionary martyrdom.

Nearly a third of the SR Combat Organization, women came to make up approximately one quarter of all Russian terrorists in the 1900s,[50] and were particularly susceptible to suicidal behavior. Their idol was Sof'ia Perovskaia: from an aristocratic family, the daughter of a governor, she had become a leader of the People's Will and was the first woman in Russia to be hanged for a political crime. Beginning in the early 1880s, as a result of rapid changes in family relations and the spread of literacy, an increasing number of girls and young women from the lower strata marginalized themselves by refusing the conventionally prescribed female role: "From my earliest years I felt confined at home... I first raised revolution against my parents, against my family, then against everyone," remembered Ekaterina Breshko-Breshkovskaia, a founding member of the SR Combat Organization.[51]

The Russian government's rigid policies with regard to higher education and career opportunities drove women into the radical camp, where terrorist recruiters welcomed them into the milieu of other outcasts. The male party leaders gave them ample opportunity to assert themselves through participation in dangerous underground work and to validate their lives through extreme fanaticism. Historian Daniel Field designates them "more steadfast and more selfless than men... better revolutionaries." Likewise, a hundred years later, Ramzan Kadyrov, vice premier of the Russian-backed Chechen government, described the Black Widows as "the most dangerous for national security because they have carried out the most risky operations" against the federal authorities.[52]

In the environment conducive to hostility, an acrid brew of sociopolitical and personal motives drove many to violence. "My soul was restless and in pain," complained Breshkovskaia: "the monotony of my purposeless life became unbearable."[53] SR Lidiia Ezerskaia despised herself for triviality; her confession letter relates that she was distraught by lack of a particular talent to distinguish her among her comrades. Doubtlessly a victim of death anxiety, she agonized that at the age of 38, "time was slipping away." Her murder of Mogilev governor Klingenberg was a desperate last chance to give purpose to an otherwise empty life.[54]

For Fruma Frumkina, terrorist motives likewise "stemmed from a deep feeling of inadequacy and a desire to confirm her own importance as an individual." Here a strong impetus for self-devaluation was that Frumkina was exceptionally unattractive, to the point of being physically deformed. "I have longed, and still long" only for terror; "I have thought, and still think only of that... I cannot control myself," she raged, and, according to her comrades, she flung herself against literally every jailer at her hard-labor prison.[55] Her behavior invited reciprocal brutality, as if she wished to be hurt or, better yet, killed.[56]

Nineteen-year-old Mariia Spiridonova wrote from prison, "I want them to kill me; I cannot imagine the grief that will be in my heart if they do not kill me...My death now will have a tremendous revolutionary significance....It would be a brilliant act of agitation." In January 1906 she had assassinated chief advisor to the governor of Tambov Gavrila Luzhenovskii, allegedly for his cruelty toward the peasants.[57] Her act was suicidal; she could not hope—and did not try—to escape from the site of the terrorist attack. Hysterical and impulsive, she was emotionally undeveloped to the point that even a decade later, already a leader of the Left SR Party, she would have "the mental attitude of a high-school girl."[58] Clinging to the appealing image of a revolutionary martyr, Spiridonova savored carnivorous fables published profusely in liberal and left-wing press that claimed the Cossack officers sexually molested her after the arrest. These tales, untrue as they were, nourished her morbid ideation and simultaneously helped fabricate a monstrous image of the government. She repudiated them in a private letters only.[59]

For his devotion to Islam, a shahid is promised, aside from a place in heaven for himself and his 70 relatives, a questionable advantage in possessing a party of 72 enthusiastic virgins in Paradise.[60] And what is a woman's reward, if she happens to be the mother of a 3-year-old boy and an 18-month old girl, such as Rim Riashi from Gaza, a star of Palestinian violence who killed herself and four Israelis in a suicide bombing on January 14, 2004? Or a married mother of four, such as 26-year-old Kahira Sa'adi from Al-Ram, who on March 21, 2002, led the suicide bomber to the attack site—the central King George Street in Jerusalem—where three Israelis were killed and dozens wounded?[61] Or a 57-year-old grandmother Fatma Najar, who on November 23, 2006, set a new age record for suicide bombers?[62] Like their Russian counterparts, female suicide bombers wish to elevate the habitually degrading status of a woman in the Arab milieu as "a weeping, wailing creature always crying for help." They become ideal candidates for exploitation amid organized public festivities in honor of female martyrs for Islam and broadcasted musical montages depicting the transformation of a weakling into a warrior.[63]

The Arab media markets "the image of female suicide terrorists around the world" as "independent and determined women with strongly held opinions, who decided to take their fate into their hands...like a modern version of Joan of Arc." They are portrayed as having "special, noble personal qualities, and are also used to motivate men to follow their example." The image "fades away when sincere personal conversations are held with them," say Israeli researchers who have interviewed the survivors of many abortive suicide attacks.[64]

Killing oneself is categorically proscribed by Islam as a major sin and a cause for "eternal damnation,"[65] but dispatchers circumvent this difficulty by calling executors of suicidal acts martyrs. Their incentives vary from the desire to avenge a personal loss to ideology-inspired outrage at perceived injustice,[66] although more often recruiters select their cadres from among the "damaged goods": the seduced, raped, unmarried girls at a relatively advanced age, or divorced women. They can be barren—and stigmatized in the Muslim society: it is probably not an accident that the two Chechen suicide terrorists who brought down Russian jets in August 2004 were unable to have children.[67] A promising candidate may also be one who has been discovered to have had an affair or children out of wedlock.

"Muslim societies are shame societies," and should "a girl become pregnant outside marriage, or a wife commit adultery, or a daughter refuse an arranged marriage or even be seen outdoors with an unrelated boy, it becomes the inescapable duty of her father, husband, brothers, or cousins to kill her in order to restore the family's honor in the eyes of the local community. According to UNICEF, in 1999 more than two-thirds of all murders in the Gaza Strip and the West Bank were 'honor' killings." For a *sharmouta* (whore), the only way to remove the disgrace from herself, as well as from her family, is *istishhad* (dying as a martyr) for Allah, which cancels all sins.[68]

The same is true about women "belonging to families that carry with them the stain of collaboration," as in the sensational case of 18-year-old Ayat al-Akhras from Dehaisha, who in March 2002 was dispatched by a Fatah cell to commit suicide in a Jerusalem supermarket and killed two Israelis, including a girl her age. Akhras's father had been accused of treason because of his work with Israelis and threatened with lynching. "There was only one chance to save her family from disgrace" and violence, explained Akhras's friend, and that was for her to become a martyr.[69] The first four female Palestinian suicide bombers faced similar alternatives.[70]

An emblematic female candidate to *Shahada* (martyrdom) is a denigrated social outcast, depressed and dead-in-life indeed. The dispatchers offer the "the defective," the "not whole," dehumanized woman, a chance to gain personal meaning by becoming "a flag bearer for the Palestinian and Islamic national struggle against the Zionist enemy." They encourage, push, threaten, and coerce their confused victim to carry out the violent act as the only opportunity to uphold her worthless existence outside the community through the essentially forced martyrdom. "They used me," one of the failed suicide terrorists admitted.[71]

Because it was "more secure" to use a female, Nizar Nawwaf al-Mansur al-Hindawi sent his pregnant girlfriend, Ann-Marie Doreen Murphy, to a trip to "the Holy Land," where he promised to meet her for their honeymoon. The "simple, unsophisticated Irish lass and a Catholic" had no way of knowing that her suitcase had "a false bottom containing a half-inch thick sheet of Semtex, the powerful Czechoslovak-made plastic explosive." Hindawi set the detonator to go off when the El Al flight 016 would have been 39,000 feet over Austria. Giving the pregnant woman a kiss, he left her to board the plane with a casual "see you later."[72]

"It was always my wish to turn my body into deadly shrapnel...and to knock on Heaven's doors with the skulls of Zionists,"[73] declared Rim Riashi. In truth, she had volunteered to be a Hamas martyr only after her illicit love affair had become a known matter.[74] Still, terrorists' farewell statements may be quite poetic, probably written by party publicity experts, as they had been in Syria and in the prerevolutionary Russia.[75]

For numerous early-20th-century Russian terrorists, anxiety with regard to the world outside the underground collective quickly turned into a catalyst for self-destructive acts. Some killed themselves rather than risk falling into the hands of the police and living through the process of an investigation, trial, and imprisonment. Suicide episodes during arrests were numerous: one anarchist would explode a hand grenade under his own feet; another would place dynamite in his mouth and blow himself up.[76] SR Evgenii Kudriavtsev shot himself immediately after he had killed the St. Petersburg city governor von der Launits. "What if we fail?" pondered Kaliaev before, bomb in hand, he walked out to kill the Grand Duke Sergei; "then I think we should do it the Japanese way.... the hara-kiri." "Against all my efforts, I did not die" in the explosion on February 4, 1905, he lamented in a follow-up letter to comrades. "Happy to hear" that you have issued the death verdict, he replied to his judges, who had sentenced him to hanging.[77]

Until 1907, when conditions in most penal institutions noticeably toughened, political prisoners rarely complained of cruel and abusive treatment; life behind the bars was "merrier than any wedding," some remembered.[78] For many others, however, confinement in prisons and hard-labor colonies proved psychologically onerous to such a degree that scores of political inmates suffered breakdowns, ended their lives in mental asylums, or killed themselves. "The regime in hard labor was...very liberal" in 1906, remembered Spiridonova, who spent nearly 10 years in tsarist penal servitude; a place of incarceration resembled a club, permeated with an atmosphere of intellectual fulfilment,[79] or "an informal, but effective, school of higher learning for revolutionaries."[80] Still, numerous memoirs relate stories of prison suicide, underscoring terrorists' urgency to die: a female extremist managed to strangle herself with her long braid; another set herself on fire in her cell. Occasionally the radicals even succeeded in giving the long-awaited death political significance: Sazonov, who "wished to avoid captivity by suicide," failed to kill himself right after he had assassinated Plehve but subsequently did away with his life via another act of guaranteed symbolic immortality—suicide in protest against penal repressions in his hard-labor prison.[81]

More than a half-century later, Ulrike Meinhof, who had joined Andreas Baader and other radicals of the Red Army Faction, hanged herself in the Stammheim prison, near Stuttgart, Germany, in May 1976, "tormented by a sense of failure." Baader and two other fellow members of RAF, who had bullied Meinhof for weakness, also killed themselves in their cell in October 1977, after a failed attempt on the part of their Palestinian comrades to secure their release by hijacking a Lufthansa jet. They might have wished to use their collective suicide as an implicit murder accusation issued to the authorities; to this day, some members of the ultra-left in Germany are convinced that members of the Meinhof-Baader Gang were killed in prison.[82]

To find oneself outside the underground framework entailed an encounter with inner fragmentation and meaninglessness, often more threatening than death. The two suicide attempts Kamo made in custody were consistent with his recurrent compulsion to kill himself at other times of forced passivity, such as after the Bolshevik victory, which paradoxically plunged him into depression.[83] A radical who developed a serious heart problem, disqualifying him as "either a terrorist, or a rebel," yet was "unable to live without the cause," took his life, devoid of an alternative to violence.[84] Likewise, the unbearable normalcy of life in emigration, away from the extremist setting, drove ex-terrorists to suicide—the fate of SR Rashel' Lur'e, who killed herself at the age of 24.[85]

In the high-flown language of the proselytes, the terrorists typically explained their desire to destroy themselves by the need to atone for the spilled blood of their enemies. "I *must die*," Brilliant repeated, begging to be appointed as a bomb-thrower. Dying to redress murder was a testament of "moral sensibilities of a very high order," later thought students of political violence, who took the extremists' words for granted.[86] "For them . . . murder was equivalent to suicide. One life appeared as payment for another, and both these sacrifices served as a token of some future values," wrote Albert Camus in the *Rebel*.[87] Yet, the fact that numerous radicals had contemplated suicide and had made one or more attempts on their own lives prior to their involvement in terrorism renders irrelevant any rationalizations of their search for death.[88] In Chechnya, women who had been "raped and ordinarily killed themselves (to avoid bringing shame on the family) are now being funneled into the Black Widows."[89] "I didn't tell him (the suicide bomber) to kill himself. He wanted to and I helped him," explained one Palestinian terrorist dispatcher; confessing that he was specifically looking for "guys who were desperate and sad."[90]

Dareen Abu Aisha, a good-looking university student, threatened that unless she was assigned a task to "become a *shahida*, she would buy a knife, go kill [Israeli] soldiers at a roadblock, and die that way."[91] The primacy of terrorists' desire to destroy themselves overshadows their ethical or ideological justification of suicide, as does their proclivity to discount the "distinction between the victimizer and the victim." Their attitude today, as it was hundred years ago, is "marked by extra- as well as intra-punitiveness,"[92] evident in terrorists' testimonies. Black sheep of her family, Thouria Khamour (Teoria Hamori), from the Jenin areas, was arrested on May 19, 2002, one day before she planned to carry out a suicide terrorist attack in Jerusalem. She expressed the shame and hopelessness behind the decision to take her life into her hands: "I was 25 years old, unmarried, and my situation at home wasn't good. At age seventeen, I already tried to harm myself twice, but they stopped me."[93] "In any case my life wasn't worth anything and my father wouldn't let me marry the boy I wanted," said another failed suicide terrorist, "so, I found a Fatah operative in Jenin and volunteered, to get back at my father."[94]

Even while subjecting their lives to risk in terrorist operations, the radicals sought indirect ways of doing away with themselves—slowly, usually by undermining their own health and mental agility. Savinkov, for example, sought to "alleviate his tension by increasing consumption of alcohol and opiates. When opium failed to provide him with sufficient sedation, he began injecting morphine."[95] The night before a planned assassination, he would not leave out of sight one of his subordinates in the Combat Organization, Aleksei Pokotilov, a heavy drinker. A tense and jittery type, nervous, pale, and with "feverishly dilated pupils," Pokotilov gave the air of someone in a constant state of agitation. "For me, the entire revolution is in terror," he said and insisted on "the honor" of blowing to pieces designated terrorist targets. Eager for every chance to provoke a violent encounter with the police, he played with death constantly.[96]

"Suicidal tendencies were part of terrorist mentality, for a terrorist act was often a suicide mission."[97] When Russian anarchists blew themselves up with dynamite inside police headquarters, they chose "the means of political assassination in order to end their lives," explained a contemporary psychologist.[98] If presented with an opportunity for a suicide terrorism mission, many young men and women "would enthusiastically go for a heroic deed, rather than end their lives by suicide," acknowledged revolutionaries as early as 1901.[99] SR Lidiia Sture liked to repeat that if she had not been able to enter a terrorist group, she would have killed herself.[100] PSR leader Mikhail Gots sought to persuade a student in a late stage of tuberculosis to die the beautiful death of a political assassin;[101] on June 16, 2002, recruiters dispatched a young man infected with the HIV virus to detonate among the Israeli police officers.[102] The head-hunters did not consider these recruitment methods cynical: they acted on the assumption that suicide cloaked under the rhetoric of political altruism was preferable to "commonplace dying."

Lombroso might have been hasty in his opinion of the Russian radicals as "odd homicides" who did not have the courage to kill themselves directly,[103] notes Moshe Hazani. He argued that these "suicides indirects" did not fear death; rather, they courted it—"only on condition that it be in an appropriate value-driven context."[104] Other specialists confirm that suicide terrorists throughout the world not only are prepared to die but also desire death.[105] "I am terribly fed up with my life"[106] is probably the most open and honest explanation one ever offered as his motives for joining a terrorist group. How much more preferable it was not to disappear into the hollow nothingness of suicide resulting from hopelessness; how much more meaningful it was to sacrifice—and forever append—oneself to a great cause.

"I am in a situation where i do not have a friend, i have no one to speak too, no one to consult, no one to support me and i feel depressed and lonely. i do not know what to do." Internet user "Farouk 1986" was probably no other than Umar Farouk Abdulmutallab, whose desperate postings leave no doubt why his al-Qaeda recruiters considered him to be a suitable candidate to accomplish the Christmas-day plane disaster.[107]

The leaders claimed the combatants' lives and—literally—death, and the terrorists readily relinquished their troublesome aliveness. In exchange, they received a set of group values and the vocabulary to delineate them.[108] In their unique lexicon, "honor" translated as murder, "love" as collective dependence, "life" as conscious self-destruction. Armed with new definitions, the self-free terrorists turned into mechanical projectors of their inner ruin.

Laing emphasized the effect of being estranged from one's own body; theirs—used to impel death—were simultaneously the tools of annihilation and the instruments for earning symbolic immortality.

Employing paramilitary language, the leaders insisted that the rank-and-file terrorists were soldiers engaged in a war against "the forces of reaction." To leave the group meant to desert; to surrender was not an option either. Each fighter was to submit his personal needs to those of his "combat detachment." In exchange, he gained "symbolic empowerment" as partaker in a historic battle, a "cosmic war."[109] The "generals" and "recruitment officers" sanctioned killing as justice and conferred upon the terrorists the designation of heroes, as opposed to murderers.

"I am my own party" was the political credo of a 24-year-old anarchist-individualist named Dmitrii Bogrov. He despised both the conventional and the revolutionary ethics, and when in need of money to support his passion for gambling, he offered his services as a secret informer to the Kiev Okhrana in 1907. By 1911, his anarchist comrades, convinced of his police ties, made Bogrov a proposition quite common among the extremists of a new type: he would either commit a terrorist act against one of his superiors or face the shameful death of a traitor. His third choice was to try to escape, but the "depressed, bored and lonely" Bogrov, the "internally dismal and autumnal" cynic, who perceived life as "nothing but an endless number of meat cutlets," chose the subliminal death of a "revolutionary martyr" instead.[110] During the intermission of Rimski-Korsakov's *Tale of Tsar Saltan* on September 1, 1911, he fired two lethal shots at Prime Minister Stolypin. The assassin had to shoot from very close range because of his poor eyesight; he left himself no chance to get away from the crowded Kiev opera.

Prior to his act of meandering suicide, Bogrov approached a prominent member of the SR party, Egor Lazarev, to request that the PSR claim responsibility for Stolypin's assassination. "Do you clearly understand that in making this offer to us you are condemning yourself to death?" Lazarev asked. "If I did not understand that, I would not have come to you," Bogrov replied. "I want to make sure that after my death there will be people and an entire party who will interpret my behavior correctly, explaining it by social and not personal motives."[111] No other terrorist better elucidated the quest for symbolic immortality.

Fascination with terrorism as veiled suicide was particularly widespread among the young—a phenomenon consistent with Hazani's findings about intensified problematic behavior among adolescents at times of historical dislocation.[112] In Russia, where party leaders "created a cult of dynamite and the revolver, and crowned the terrorist with a halo... murder and the scaffold acquired a magnetic charm and attraction for the youth," remembered Vera Figner, in her youth a prominent member of the People's Will.[113] The influence of the extremist ethos was so profound that familiar teenage rebellion against parental—and generally adult—authority often took most radical, and fatal, forms. Ample opportunities for heroic self-sacrifice provided the youngsters with a lofty and socially justifiable outlet for their mundane, age-related drives.

Recklessness and adolescent adventurism, supported by boundless energy, drove them to take part in life-threatening enterprises alongside adult extremists. Like them, the minors "talked with enthusiasm about dying," while simultaneously demonstrating faith in their own immortality, common among the youth. Others, conversely, showed strong self-destructive tendencies, coupled with a yearning to prove themselves "in action." The idea to die while carrying out any "heroic deed" meant more to them than obscure revolutionary ideals—their elder comrades knew this well.[114] Some adolescents were also quick to get the hang of the adult vernacular properly to justify suicidal behavior by asserting that the true beauty of life was in "death for death's sake."[115]

Sixteen-year-old Leibish Rapoport, outraged by his mother's unfriendly treatment of his girlfriend, stole a small amount of his parents' money and in the spring of 1906 ran away from home in Ekaterinoslav. He initially considered suicide but then changed his mind in favor of a "political act." First, he wrote a threat letter:

> Mother,
>
> Keep in mind that I am presently a member of a combat organization of revolutionary terrorists, and in accordance with the committee's sanctions, must go... to various Russian cities to stage terrorist acts. But I won't hesitate to stay here and take pleasure in shooting a bullet through the head of an old biddy like you. I will report you at the committee's meeting, and I am quite certain that my comrades will not begrudge the bullets for your murder.

"Wishing to die to show that his mother was guilty of his death," the young man then claimed responsibility for the recent assassination of governor-general Zheltonovskii. He expected to be executed in two or three days after his arrest. Instead, Leibish spent many months under investigation and strict psychiatric observation before a military court sentenced him in 1909 to a 12-year prison term, of which he served only three years—thanks to his mother's tireless efforts to prove her son's innocence and a public campaign on his behalf.[116]

In other cases, children were initiated into terrorism as a "family affair." Sometimes they were victims of glaring child abuse, as when the extremists enlisted for combat purposes a 13-year-old girl whose mother had fallen in love with a member of their group and become "literally his slave," unable to protect herself and her daughter.[117] On the other hand, "Comrade Natasha" (E. F. Drabkina), a Bolshevik combatant, used her daughter for conspiratorial cover when transporting explosive mercury fulminate on her body. Thanks to her mother, the three- or four-year-old Liza became the youngest terrorist in Russia.[118]

Elsewhere, parents and relatives have followed suit: Sharin Abu Ravia, a 15-year-old girl from Bethlehem, was apprehended on June 13, 2002, at an Israeli checkpoint before she managed to put on an explosive belt and complete a suicide mission. She said that she really did want to live but had agreed to "end up in pieces in the black garbage bag" because her uncle had convinced her do to so, as the youngest of 15 children and—as a girl—a throwaway.[119] A picture of an Arab baby, wearing full terrorist attire, including a headband with a slogan of dedication to Allah and a suicide bomber belt, circulated the Internet in June 2002.[120] Unlike little Liza and the would-be six-year-old suicide bomber from Ghazni, Afghanistan, this boy was not a "real terrorist" but a live message about the totality of envisaged sacrifice—a powerful symbol in the context of the postmodern virtual reality.

* * *

Death-wishing, justified ideologically and realized via extremist acts, is not limited to a particular cultural or national origin. "However different the holy causes people die for, they perhaps die basically for the same thing."[121] Modern political martyrdom is certainly not an exclusive trademark of Islam, as many, including Muslim fundamentalists, would have us believe. It is a byproduct of a crippled vitality, longing to be inspired and revived by any available substitute with a veneer of spirituality, rather than of a specific doctrine. Ironically, ideology often serves to rationalize self-annihilating drives as a desperate effort at self-preservation.

A sense of victimization and ensuing justification of violence as self-defense are pivotal components of political extremism.[122] Engaged in unmitigated belligerence, the terrorists experience themselves as the persecuted, "the cohort of the perishing." Most would endorse the words of Eugen Leviné, leader of a doomed-to-failure Munich revolution in 1919: "we are all dead men on leave."[123]

Russian revolutionaries considered themselves victims, suffering from attacks by multiple enemies in the hostile milieu—a reflection of their own tormented, conflictive, "barren, paranoiac" psychological landscape.[124] "If you only knew how they sneered at me and how my self-esteem suffered," one embittered radical complained; "I am thirsty for... terror out of personal vengeance."[125] Sometimes a mere reprimand, fine, or minor administrative action spurred random acting-out, barely disguised under revolutionary rhetoric—as when a fired worker attacked an army general, who happened to be the first available outlet for his aggravation.[126] As a rejoinder to perceived oppression, expelled university student Petr Karpovich killed Minister of Education N. P. Bogolepov on February 14, 1901, in the first assassination committed in 20th-century Russia.

Unconscious of a projection, the camouflaged suicides sought "to tear the mask of hypocrisy from the face of the enemy, to unmask him," that is, to convert the enemy into the attacker and "provoke action even at the risk of annihilation so that the truth may come out."[127] The extremists therefore classified as aggression every attempt on the part of the government to retaliate against violence: it is impossible "to allow them to spill our blood like water."

Having "endured enough," the injured were *forced* to *respond* with aggression, a measure of the last resort, they claimed.[128]

Today, Islamists opt for the same arguments in validating brutality against the United States, its European allies, and Israel. The extremist reaction to the crumbling traditional culture is "the message of the apocalyptic," which Sivan depicted as an avowedly defensive response or a desperate final "effort before a catastrophe."[129] The Japanese Aum Shinrikyo cult relied on its members' siege mentality and fear that outside forces were intent on destroying their group. Yet, although suicide terrorists—or, rather, their dispatcher—"portray themselves as fanatic, and irrational," theirs "is rarely the last ditch attempt in the face of certain defeat." Extremist leaders who exhibit hopelessness as a trigger for violence "have adopted suicide bombings as a strategic choice... not out of desperation."[130]

The radicals strive to relocate a sense of self-estrangement, worthlessness, and resultant self-contempt to the outside, to a hated other, in line with Vamik Volkan's elucidation of "the need to have enemies."[131] Notwithstanding the degree of their objective responsibility for detrimental conditions, or those perceived as such, these are often scapegoats "to blame and attack" for assailants' inner depletion translated into externalized hostility.[132] If the enemy does commit atrocities, it confirms the paranoid projection."[133] The ideological movement provides the self-loathing and self-punishing personalities with a script for staging a gruesome show, and they are eager to begin rehearsing their roles as reluctant desperados—to satisfy their integral enmity, which demands expression via suicidal homicide.[134]

* * *

On February 7, 1908, the police surrounded SR Vsevolod Lebedintsev (Mario Kal'vino) on his way to kill Minister of Justice I. G. Shcheglovitov. "Be careful. I am wrapped around with dynamite. If I blow up, the entire street will be destroyed," he shouted before the officers took him and his accomplices into custody. Seven terrorists were sentenced to death. "How these people died," recalled a police witness—"no sighs, no remorse, no pleas, no signs of weakness... a smile on their faces."[135] SR Zinaida Konopliannikova's death sentence following her assassination of Major General Min was also a ticket to immortality; according to an observer witnessing the last moments of her life, she "went to her execution as one would go to a holiday festivity."[136] For her part, Brilliant wept upon hearing that the PSR would discontinue terrorist operations after the promulgation of the October Manifesto; the decision of the party leadership deprived her of a much-sought-after meaningful demise.

Every time a suicide terrorist act takes place anywhere in the world, we are staggered by the apparent ease with which the perpetrator repudiates his existence. It is inconceivable that a pulsating, breathing life that is about to be torn into bits of bloody flesh does not rebel against self-destruction—abnormal, if only from a biological viewpoint. The terrorist, however, is an individual emotionally drained to the point of being barely able to sustain his agonizing existence. He is already dead-in-life at the moment when he physically puts an end to his anguish. He is eager indeed to terminate the agony within, and this may explain the elation of a "trance-like state," a "kind of serene joy, often coupled with an other-worldly smile...sometimes visible on the faces of suicidal homicides prior to their deadly deeds."[137] The act of camouflaged suicide is just the final point—a definitive statement, affirming death.

When a suicide bomber walks into a bus or a café and is about to explode, he is wearing the mask of a live human being. Terrorists are happy and relieved to die; it is exhausting constantly to pretend to be, when they are not. Blok expressed this poetically: "so grueling for a corpse among the people to act as if alive and animated."[138]

Chapter 7

A Fatal Attraction

It is no accident...that many Russian liberals...wholeheartedly support terror and presently try to bolster the rise of a terrorist mood.

—Vladimir Lenin

The trouble with our liberal friends is not that they're ignorant; it's just that they know so much that isn't so.

—Ronald Reagan

The environment of condoned political violence contributed to the mounting tendency for eulogizing and even deifying it. While advocating more "cultured methods of struggle" against the autocracy, numerous "fans of terror...privately applauded every terrorist act," which undermined the government and enhanced the revolutionary fervor.[1] As time went on, the barely concealed support for extremism became more open and more widespread.

Pity for the criminal is customary in Russia. It is grounded in the religious tradition, which emphasizes atonement for a misdeed, a prerequisite for spiritual ascent. Empathy for the offender is also related to habitual tension and ill-feeling in the complicated liaison between the state and society. Regardless of the nature of transgression, as a matter of course the lawbreakers are perceived as the persecuted—denoting the relationship of conflict rather than cooperation. "If I were not a poet, I would have probably been a crook and a thief," confessed Sergei Esenin, a fashionable lyricist of the 1900s, who envisaged his own death after "a saloon brawl, a Finnish knife under heart." Esenin's verse reflected the general attitude in a milieu where bourgeois values were anathema and where dogmatic nonconformists sympathized and identified with the archetypal "poor, unfortunate" convict, chained and on his way to Siberia.[2]

Empathy for the villain may be an exaggerated variant of a Western attitude toward Robin Hood, a highway robber romanticized as a medieval hero and an emblem of primitive social justice. His modern equivalent was Grigorii Kotovskii, scion from a noble family turned ataman of a smash-and-grab gang of "merry men," who considered himself "an ideological thief." He chose not to limit his freedom by a formal affiliation with any organization. Indulging his love of luxuries and crude entertainment, he expropriated everything he could get his hands on—from money in city banks to Persian carpets in private homes—but also boasted to have distributed some of his loot among the poor. Kotovskii was widely popular in the early 1900s: if in the era of the French Revolution, wives of businessmen, "devastated with boredom... restlessly... applauded innovators,"[3] in Russia ladies from the highest social spheres, fascinated with the legendary rogue, sent him gifts and admiring notes during his imprisonment.[4] He was not alone in enjoying such celebrity after the freedom-fighter emerged as a trendy hero, and the terrorist received a magnificent halo and a place of honor in the pantheon of favored idols in progressive circles.

In January 1878, Vera Zasulich shot and wounded the governor-general of St. Petersburg to avenge mistreatment of an imprisoned comrade. By that time, the unbridgeable gap between the westernized intelligentsia and the tsarist regime that had been deepening steadily throughout the 19th century was already an integral part of mentality. Zasulich was acquitted by a liberal jury court—the decision unleashing euphoria in the educated circles—and became an instant star. Turgenev honored the vigilante in his famous poem-in-prose "The Threshold,"[5] It extolled self-sacrifice of the young woman, "a saint," and "might justify the actions of a suicide bomber today."[6]

Except perhaps in the single case when society at large mourned the death of Alexander II, in the following decades, the intellectuals abided by the romanticized image of the ideal-driven outlaw. By 1905, as insurgence exacerbated, the response from the left-liberal activists became more proactive. The idea to extract tangible benefits from the insurrection developed after the Constitutional Democratic (Kadet) party was born in October of that year.

The organization counted among its members "the flower of the Russian intelligentsia" and an exceptionally large number of "brilliant talents and prominent public figures."[7] Its many writers, journalists, lawyers, and other educated professionals personally had no taste for subversion and claimed to stand for peaceful opposition and restraint. Yet, lacking a large constituency,[8] builders of this elitist movement found it tactically beneficent to rally with the radicals because of a shared immediate goal—to overthrow the current administration.

Radicalization of domestic life was clearly to their advantage with; *post factum*, the Constitutional Democrats admitted to have calculated: rampant terror was bound to "force the authorities to make concessions."[9] The "situation was too serious to permit moral scruples," confirmed the head of the Kadets, Moscow University history professor Pavel Miliukov.[10] "As long as the stronghold of autocracy has not been destroyed, anyone who is fighting against it represents... a great blessing."[11]

In solidarity with their allies in the revolutionary camp, the Kadets repeatedly refused to proclaim moral condemnation of extremist tactics in the press or from the floor of the new Russian parliament.[12] Evading an unequivocal denunciation of terrorism was a well-considered, if undeclared policy.[13] The tactic was pursued, explained its opponents on the right, for the sake of "indulging and instigating" radicalism—liberals' "roots" and "nourishment."[14] The rightists had a strong case for indictment: even after the most gruesome terrorist episodes involving civilian casualties, the Kadets went no further than all-purpose statements about the horrors of bloodshed, always accentuating the official accountability for it.[15]

The Constitutional Democrats berated sanctions against "the poor terrorists and expropriators... led to the gallows like cattle to the slaughterhouse."[16] They filled pages of their newspapers with passionate protests against three widely publicized cases of the "senseless, blind, useless... insane... shameful... wild and barbarous... treacherous... infamous... villainous murders" carried out by right-wing extremists.[17] Lest it appeared as if the Kadets rallied behind the state, the party "never allowed itself to berate the terrorists" on the left, responsible for an avalanche of killings, especially as compared to isolated incidents of terrorism from the right. This would be the Kadets' "moral destruction," explained Central Committee member I. I. Petrunkevich.[18] The leadership apparently "feared offending its radical constituency," just as much as it "needed the threat of violence to hold over the government."[19] The moral equivalency was therefore adopted as tactic.

Though not partaking in acts of blood spilling, the Constitutional Democrats were prepared to invest financially in the common "urgency to uproot" the establishment.[20] They helped the radicals procure funds for terrorist enterprises, for example, by sponsoring fund-raiser events specifically for the benefit of the SR Combat Organization.[21] The Kadets pledged to make financial contributions to the PSR[22] and even took their fund-raising activities in the name of terror abroad. In Paris and Geneva, they clamored for escalation of the Russian struggle and glorified the SR heroes Gershuni, Sazonov, and Kaliaev.[23]

Most pro-terrorist campaigning, however, the Kadets did at home. From the parliamentary floor, party deputies acknowledged a debt of the opposition to the terrorists, who "did not spare their lives" and "played such an enormous, outstanding role" in obtaining the newly won freedoms.[24] The political spring "owed everything to the bomb that killed Plehve," they maintained[25] and commended the assassin as an example worthy of followers.[26] They did not have to hint twice: so many sought to emulate the celebrated exploit that terrorist groups "did not know what to do with them."[27]

The Kadet press and speeches habitually depicted extremists as altruists, reluctant warriors, and sufferers for the truth who were greatly "troubled by the injustice reigning in society" and could not "separate their words and emotions from their deeds."[28] The establishment, not the terrorists, was the guilty party, the Kadets insisted, and bombs were a logical response from the innocent victims of tyranny and lawlessness promoted by the bureaucratic "murderers."[29] "Filled with indignation at the impunity of various administrative oppressors," the pure souls had been provoked to commit violent acts because they had "no means of peaceful influence on these monsters."[30] Terror in fact therefore comprised "a certain social advisability."[31]

If one were to consider the terrorists' "individual qualities, as they were drawn by their biographers and their prison comrades, then it would turn out that these political outlaws are not at all villains by nature," asserted a Kadet Duma deputy. "In their personality, these are individuals of a special moral delicacy, of a sensitivity greater than that of ordinary people," the servile and apathetic characters who overlook or merely talk about obvious social evils.[32] Such rhetoric often reduced itself to sheer demagoguery, as when a liberal spokesman compared the perpetrators of terror among the anarchists to that passionate advocate of nonresistance "the greatest anarchist—Count Lev Nikolaevich Tolstoi."[33] "Remember that Christ, too, was declared to be a lawbreaker and subjected to a shameful execution on the cross," argued another Kadet parliamentary delegate; "the years passed, and this desperado—Christ—had conquered the whole world and became a model of virtue. The attitude toward political criminals is a similar act of violence on the part of the authorities."[34]

"I see familiar traits…in this young woman," a Kadet speaker said, referring to the immortalized image of a girl-martyr in Turgenev's "Threshold," and then listed the names of several convicted female terrorists.[35] Among the designated sacrificial victims was "Marusia" (affectionate diminutive of Mariia) Spiridonova, turned into a live icon with the magic pen of a liberal columnist. At the peak of a heart-rending narrative crescendo toward the girl's heroic feat against Luzhenovskii, the journalist eulogized, Mariia's "life ended; began *zhitie*," employing a set phrase used only in reference to a saint.[36]

Time and again over the next 100 years liberals reverted to sanctification of killers for a ideological cause. "Martyrs, not murderers," chanted participants of the April 2002 anti-globalization march in Washington, D.C., turning it into a Palestinian terrorist solidarity rally. Its message that the killers are heroes "typified a hundred other events all over the United States and even more in Europe, not to mention Latin America and other places."[37]

In Russia, where literature has traditionally been a barometer of national cultural swings, it was also a medium to construct the image of a humane terrorist. The country's foremost writer was Leonid Andreev, and his widely read stories, full of admiration for "the martyrs," produced a new fad—sympathy for the bombist. Andreev was "the mood of Russia,"[38] perhaps the way Camus would be in France in the second half of the century. Despite Camus's insight into the terrorists' "moral relativism and the subordination of human feelings to a higher good," he praised murder for a "justified specific cause...carried out after deep moral searching, with great reluctance, within carefully controlled limits, and with self-sacrifice." But whereas "Camus was himself troubled by the murderous inclinations of rebels and publically condemned the violence of the far left and the far right,"[39] Andreev had turned his summer house into a refuge for the terrorists. Gor'kii too converted his Moscow apartment into a bomb laboratory and a hiding place for the SR and Bolshevik combatants and donated large sums to them.[40]

Following the writers' example, scores of liberal-minded citizens considered it an ethical and social obligation to provide the radicals with money, proper documents, and shelter and to offer their houses for the concealment of weapons and explosives.[41] University professors, teachers, doctors, and lawyers came to regard assistance to the extremists as a "sign of good manners."[42] The liberal intelligentsia thus promoted a culture in which, under the impact of fabricated reverence for terror, common people came to venerate terrorists' portraits, as if they were icons. Spiridonova "is a saint, I pray to her," confessed a sailor.[43]

Young men were victims of such cultural brainwashing, sometimes with tragic results. A 16-year-old schoolboy from Kiev followed closely the lurid press campaign in defense of Spiridonova. Like her numerous other fans, he was shaken by vivid, often naturalistic descriptions of her suffering at the hands of authorities and imagined that he "madly, endlessly loved her." When the newly canonized martyr was sentenced to prison, the boy drowned himself. He explained in a suicide note to his friend:

> I prayed at her portrait, breathed the idea of her always, and thought that when they would pardon her, I would fall at her knees and tell her everything. But there is no amnesty and it seems that there will never be any for my dear Mariia who is dying out there in the Pugachev's tower and will not survive her sentence. Therefore I leave this world earlier to go where there is no Pugachev's tower—I will soon see her there.[44]

What 16-year-old does not want to be a star, admired by all her peers, and what was she to do if in the early 1900s her young friends fell in love with stars of the revolution? Girls "who had not the slightest idea about it [were] now involved in it in one way or another."[45] They emulated female terrorists "surrounded by the aura" of martyrdom.[46] Simultaneously, they developed the ideal image of a "revolutionary prince" worthy of their love.

"All school girls adored the bombists. Imagine how romantic this was: they gave their lives for their convictions! Outside the radical camp there were no ideals; everything was so mercantile, so trite, but the combatants....Just think of it!" remembered Sara El'kind, born in 1893, a half-century later. In 1907 she was a student in a woman's gymnasium in the Crimea, where she and her girlfriends sought ways to assist terrorists: when parents were away, they gave the radicals shelter and, pretending to be their fiancées, smuggled packages into prisons. "Routine life at home was *boring*, but outside...! The secrets, the mystery of the underground life were so attractive... Girls were infatuated with and dreamt of the Garibaldis."[47] And there was no shortage of young men eager to turn into Garibaldis, or Kaliaevs, on demand.

Radicalism entailed irresistible appeal. Amid the calamity of rejected meanings, totalist ideology offered a new value system, the way a religion would. Individuals hungry for substance fell for its imitation.

Popular culture reflected a vicious press campaign against two fashionable pariahs, police officers Zhdanov and Abramov, who had purportedly mistreated Spiridonova:

Schoolteacher: Dear children, what do you know about Abramov?

Children: Teacher, we haven't studied wild animals yet.[48]

The notoriety of the "savage beasts" predetermined their fate: both men were killed by terrorists in 1906.[49] The same destiny awaited Chief Military Prosecutor Pavlov, who appeared in the Duma to respond to an interpellation about his counterterrorist measures. The Kadets, along with the rest of the parliamentary Left, did not let him utter a word: "Get out! Executioner! Murderer! You have blood on your hands!" they shouted, forcing him to leave the floor. Several days later, Pavlov was assassinated.[50]

A moral condemnation of terror from the reputable Kadet party which the moderates expected in vain "could have sobered many who helped the revolutionaries without giving it much thought," years later recognized a member of its Central Committee.[51] Instead, the liberals' surreptitious endorsement of terrorism contributed to the radical cause[52] and encouraged further violence against the setting that nourished extremism. "A as rule... terrorists tend to be particularly successful if, in an already unstable society, they are able to master a small degree of actual, and a large degree of potential support."[53] The cultural milieu that supplied the terrorists with a distinguished title of freedom fighters undermined itself and after 1905 disintegrated almost visibly. The ongoing disintegration was but a gradual suicide.

* * *

From the late 19th century, nihilism inspired sympathetic writers from England to Japan to immortalize the brave avenger: Oscar Wilde in his play *Vera*, Tajima Shoji in *Stories from Europe about Women with a Purpose in Life*, and Somada Sakutaro in the *Strange News from Russia about the Criminal Case of a Heroine*.[54] "Chinese fiction canonized Sophia Perovskaiaya," and a section of *Fiction Monthly* was for a time dedicated to stories about her comrades—all "with little knowledge of the subject and with a Buddhist slant":

> Nihilists, Nihilists! I love you, I worship you. Your undertakings are brilliant and glorious. You never fail to startle heaven and earth with your ability to kill

> those emperors (the damned bastards), to rescue the multitudes of your suffering brothers and sisters.... beautiful women in disguise, young boys, and the most unusual stalwart men—but all are Bodhisattva redeemers.[55]

From the early 1900s, the intelligentsia in Europe and elsewhere openly endorsed violence. Among the luminaries, Jean-Paul Sartre, a Maoist and "lifelong apologist for Bakunin-like revolt," considered it to have "a regenerative effect on humanity,"[56] quite in line with the radicals' obsession with purification by fire. Franz Fanon, spiritual leader of the American Black Panthers and a theorist of violent anticolonial struggle, encouraged cooperation between extremists and the gangland, so that a disruptive "*victim of the bourgeois society*," would be transformed into a vital "component of the revolutionary process."[57]

Antonio Negri, professor at the University of Padua, was indicted of murdering Italy's former prime minister Aldo Moro in 1978 and of being "il grande vecchio—the grand old man—behind the Red Brigades." Italian President Francesco Cossiga accused him of poisoning "the minds of an entire generation of Italy's youth." Meanwhile, Michel Foucault famously said that Negri was imprisoned in 1979 "for being an intellectual." That he certainly was, coauthoring "an anti-globalization bible," *Empire*. Yet, although found not guilty of masterminding Moro's assassination due to lack of evidence, he could not recant association with, and possibly the headship of, a terrorist web, which included Workers' Autonomy. Like his Peruvian colleague Abimael Guzman, philosophy professor and the Shining Path chief, Negri persevered along the dazzling war path for social justice. "Every action of destruction and sabotage seems to me a manifestation of class solidarity,"[58] he wrote, apparently motivated by the logic that also led Norman Finkelstein from DePaul University to "express solidarity" with Hezbollah.[59] To "change, fundamentally, the political dynamics" in the United States, Berkeley professor of Islamic law Palestinian-American Hatem Bazian instigated: "it's about time that we have an intifada in this country."[60]

The list of professional intellectuals directly engaged in violence is short in comparison with their numerous left-of-the-center colleagues who circuitously justify terrorists. The extremists strive to demolish the "bourgeois culture," the intelligentsia's habitat, with which it is in conflict. The literati share the pains of the Protean predicament. Many come from the orthodox- or neo-Marxist background and continue along the warpath against materialism or consumerism. It is "making us all into idiots," deplores novelist Amos Oz.[61]

Terrorism is "the expression of that part of Western culture" which "has moved beyond the paradigm of progress," argues Miller. It has dominated our thinking since the Enlightenment, which assumes that social dilemmas can be solved through the application of reason and law. The radicals "have ceased to function within the framework of this central tenet," seeking instead the wholesale destruction of the social order, where the notion of advancement is at the center. "The threatening or murderous deed thus becomes a

Nietzschean or Sorelian assertion of will, to inspire meaning and purpose into a world that appears devoid of this raison d'être." Paradoxically, destructiveness then turns into the mechanism of rebirth, and terrorism metamorphoses into regenerative "progress as nihilism."[62] Its allure for the "idolaters of progress"[63] is akin to the magnetism of militant nihilism of the early 1900s.

Against the background of the contemporary spiritual crisis, the primary threat comes from Muslim fanatics, hostile to any way of life outside the confines of the *Shari'a*. Their primary target is the United States, the quintessence of iniquity: "Oh Americans...The time has come for Allah to declare war on you, oh usurers!"[64] But the fundamentalist enmity goes beyond specified hatred for the "Big Satan" and "Death to America" slogan. "We say to this West: By Allah, you will be defeated;" to regain universal control "the Arab and Islamic nation is rising."[65] This is a generic message, with minor variation communicated routinely: "Rome will be conquered, just like Constantinople was"; the conquests "will spread through Europe in its entirety and then will turn to the two Americas, and even Eastern Europe."[66]

Just as consistently, the liberals make-believe that the militant language is directed at Israel alone. And, elucidates Paul Berman, for every violent word, Israel is to blame:

> Each new act of murder and suicide testified on how oppressive were the Israelis. Palestinian terror...was the measure of Israeli guilt. The more grotesque the terror, the deeper the guilt. And, if unfathomable motives appeared to drive the suicide bombers forward, the oppressiveness of Israel was likewise deemed to be, by logical inference unfathomable—a bottomless oppression, which had given rise to the maximum of violence, which is suicide murder. The commuter buses, the pizza parlors, the discos, the hotel dining rooms, the bustling sidewalks—these exploded into random carnage. And, with every new atrocity, the search was on to find ever larger accusation to place at Israel's feet.

At the outset it "spun variations on a single theme": Zionism. It was alleged not to be an initiative for self-rule but "racism—a program of hatred and contempt....And with this idea established, a declension of tropes and images marched steadily forward" in the arguments designed to clarify reasons behind terrorism.[67]

First came the comparison between Israel and the Republic of South Africa in the days of apartheid: Zionists were but racist colonizers, according to those who knew nothing about the multifaceted metaphor of the Holy Land, embedded in the ancient faith and sustaining spiritual unity of the dispersed wanderers for over two thousand years.[68] Reducing the traditional dream of a homecoming to a colonization enterprise typified a projection of the European not-so-distant past, bigoted and antagonistic, as ignorance inescapably is.

The analogy then "yielded to a grimmer and angrier trope, which was Nazism. Israel became, in the rhetoric of its accusers, a Nazi entity—a state so utterly devoted to evil...as to make suicide murder a comprehensible reaction on the part of its victims." They "have nothing else to defend themselves with except their skins. Hence the human bombs," asserted South African–Parisian writer Breyten Breytenbach in an open letter to Ariel Sharon, published in *Le Monde*. Some opponents ultimately traced Israel's policies to Judaism, insinuating, as did Breytenbach, that "the chosen people" behaved like *Herrenvolk*—the Nazi term for the "master race." The siege of Arafat in his compound at the height of Intifada was "a crime comparable to Auschwitz," echoed Portuguese Nobel Prize laureate for literature José Saramago.[69] He all but outshined the Kadet parliamentary delegate, equating counterterrorist measures to the crucifixion of Jesus.

When the Third Congress of the Kadet party was in session in April 1906, news arrived regarding a terrorist attempt on the life of the Moscow governor-general Dubasov. Unable to hold back their excitement, some delegates applauded in approval.[70] The crowd of hundreds of progressive academics and politicians from the United States, Europe, and Latin America at the New York Socialist Scholars Conference in 2002 "burst into applause" upon hearing an Egyptian novelist defend a Palestinian woman who had just accomplished a suicide mission.[71] "There is a sense that terrorism is the weapon of the weak,"[72] insists one American scholar, replicating the cultivated sentiment of the assailants, who perceive and project themselves as the injured. Incidentally, "Jewish Nazism" is their formula too, rebound in the Hamas Charter.[73]

Israel being a hub and a victim of terrorism today, it is striking that Jewish, and particularly Israeli apologists, for extremist practices are among the loudest. Their attitude is a generic left-liberal response to radicalism, manifest in the Israeli media, artist and literary circles. This is not to suggest that writer David Grossman, whose son was killed in combat with the Hezbollah, endorses brutality or that there are no voices of dissent against "the colonial analogy."[74] Yet, like elsewhere, the intellectuals in Israel behave as if cultural preeminence is tantamount to ethical and spiritual guardianship. In accordance with their implicit claim to be the conscience of the nation, they act rather like its prophets. Their message heralds a mélange of philosophical ideas and personal aspirations—a preconceived vision of "the correct" political life in Israel. When reality is at variance with the model, prophets' fury erupts against the profligate brainchild.

Rather than a Kadet-like political strategy, for many a literati, tolerance for extremism can have more to do with the issue of identity, split as theirs seems to be. The conflict is between their Jewishness and their craving to maintain a place in the mainstream intellectual community, especially outside Israel. There they aspire for approval by the high priests in a temple of "the cult of Culture"[75] or, more precisely, multiculturalism, with its headquarters on university campuses.

The endorsement has been increasingly out of stock for the Israeli academics. They pursue professional relationships abroad and wish to publish in reputable foreign presses while in Europe, Britain, and North America colleagues blacklist them, impose sanctions against conferences in Israel, and organize campaigns to boycott its academe.[76] As I am writing these lines, the sixth international "Israeli Apartheid Weeks" (IAW) is taking place on dozens of campuses, including my own in Boston.[77]

Israeli scholars are swayed to dissociate from the new South Africa,"and—the reader might well have guessed—Nazi Germany."[78] Self-condemnation is heightened in their effort. In Israel, "we wanted to be a colonialist occupier, and yet to come across as moral," confesses the guilt-ridden Ilan Pappe, formerly a historian from the Haifa University.[79] This "rogue colonialist regional power" incites Arab violence to "create the desired atmosphere of suspicion, fear, and hatred that fascism always needs in order to flourish," explains Dr. Ran HaCohen of the literature department at the University of Tel Aviv.[80] The Muslim means of communication promptly reverberate for their propaganda purposes claims that Jews sought to conceal "mass deportations, massacres and rapes."[81] Some so-called New Historians allow their graduate students to fabricate stories of atrocities against Arab villagers and award them excellent marks for capturing "a higher truth of Palestinian victimhood."[82] They supervise prize-winning theses to demonstrate that Israeli soldiers do not rape Arab women because these enemy civilians have been "dehumanized" and desexualized.[83] Academic publications emphasize that Jewish settlers in disputed territories provoke Palestinian children to blow themselves up. As a glaring double standard, although not new for anyone familiar with the Kadet rhetoric, the "New Historians" underscore the stifled "Palestinian identity" and deny it to Jews.[84]

The Zionists are the living reminders that the identity choice may have been different for those alienated intellectuals who go so far as to argue that "there is no such thing as a Jewish people or Jewish nation." The entire premise of Zionism, as representing the aspirations for a home, therefore "is based on a lie," "invented" to legitimize colonization.[85] In a BBC radio interview, Tel Aviv University history professor Shlomo Sand compares the birth of Israel to "an act of rape." In his eyes, the solution to the country's conflict with the Arabs neighbors is the abolition of the Jewish state.[86]

Zionist "fanatics" and "marginal extremists" are the alleged source of all Israel's troubles. Professor of history at the Hebrew University Moshe Zimmermann likens the settlers' younger generation to "the *Hitlerjugend* [Hitler Youth]."[87] They are "my enemy," confirms his colleague, member of the Israeli Communist Party, Yuri Pines[88]—not the Islamists who proclaim, "Killing a single Jew is the same as killing 30 million Jews... our blood vengeance against them will only subside with their annihilation," which "is one of the most splendid blessings for Palestine."[89]

"Israel will be annihilated, Allah willing... kill them all, down to the last one," urges Sheik Ahmad Bahr, Acting Speaker at the Palestinian Legislative Council.[90] Still, says Pines, "I believe that the renewed Palestinian uprising is morally and politically just, and I wish it a success."[91] "Had the Palestinians possessed a little wisdom, they would focus their struggle on the settlements," Professor Ze'ev Sternhell suggested; alternatively, he recommended that the settlers' "fascistic current" be destroyed with the Israeli tanks.[92]

On March 6, 2008, an Arab gunman walked into the Mercaz HaRav, a religious school in Jerusalem, and opened fire at young men studying in the library. Gideon Levy, a leading *Haaretz* columnist, responded by calling the killing "a criminal act" but reminded his audience that the Zionist yeshiva was a "fascist institution" and its graduates "the mongers of hate."[93] A prominent Jewish theologian and polemicist, Professor Yeshayahu Leibowitz, the inventor of the "Judeo-Nazi" concept, has labeled the settlers "murderers on the other side of the Green Line," which demarcates disputed territories in the West Bank of the Jordan River. He has appealed directly to the Arabs: "I call on you to get guns...against them before they put you into concentration camps like leprous dogs."[94]

Historian Sander Gilman speaks of "self-loathing," the phenomenon psychologists underpin to explain why progressive Jewish intellectuals turn against the environment which sustains them, while they undermine it from within.[95] The inwardly directed ambivalence (in many cases heightened to flagrant negativity) and concomitant anxiety may account for the exaggerated attempt to demonstrate that one's identity does not count and to deny the "retrograde" ties to their history, tradition, and faith as "the tyranny of the dead."[96] This form of self-hatred is all but novel.[97] It is glaring when during his book-promotion trip in the United States, Professor Sand beseeched the Americans "to save" his people from themselves.[98]

New is the argument advanced by historian and Harvard psychiatrist Kenneth Levin that this self-destructive tendency is a corollary of "Stockholm syndrome." It has been diagnosed in terrorized individuals—hostages, who become loyal to and apologetic for their captors, responding to utmost danger, against which they develop "defense mechanisms," such as identification with the aggressor.[99] A related reaction might have caused the Hebrew University chemistry professor Israel Shahak, an ex-prisoner in the Warsaw ghetto and the Bergen-Belsen concentration camp, to absorb Goebbels-style oration, accusing Jews of sins ranging from a conspiracy to turn Arabs into slaves to ritual Satan-worship.[100] "[I] can't imagine why Israel's apologists would be offended by a comparison with the Gestapo," muses Professor Finkelstein, son of the Holocaust survivors.[101] According to Levin, the Stockholm syndrome can be injurious to large groups, or society as a whole, and may be extended from the Israeli to other academic and cultural sites.

Terrorist attacks intentionally defy predictability and logic, inflicting death on the enormous metropolis of New York as well as, and no less ferociously, on the tiny, strategically and symbolically irrelevant Beslan. "Those who witness violence—even at a distance via the news media—are...a part of what occurs,"[102] and in this sense, we are all hostages. Our experience of personal security, basic to modern perception of civilized living, is dented. Faced with potential atrocity, a Stockholm syndrome victim may seek to assuage impotent apprehension by yielding to a "fatal attraction" of identification with the enemy: "I can say there is a type of mutual trust. To a very great degree I do trust [Arafat]."[103]

Worse is the symptom of redirecting liability from the architects of organized brutality to sufferers, as in Princeton international law professor Richard Falk's case for terrorism, based on the argument that "Palestinian resistance to occupation is a legally protected right."[104] Jews on faculty at the University of California, Santa Cruz recommend to students unreferenced gossip about Israel's "genocide and ethnic cleansing"—stories of massacres "accompanied by sexual assault, particularly of pregnant women"[105] And the attack on the Twin Towers was but a retort of the Third World to centuries of American oppression, according to MIT Professor Noam Chomsky's message in his *9/11*, a best seller in the immediate aftermath of the tragedy. If it did not feel good, the United States itself was at fault,[106] argues this sage of the rabble-rousing "public intellectuals," to refer to Richard Posner's famous work by that title. We should rather call him "an intellectual crook," as Arthur Schlesinger did sagaciously already in 1969: inspired by "his ideological fanaticism," Chomsky constantly "bends references, quotations and facts."[107] More than anything else, such mental equilibrianism brings utter unawareness of any personal motive behind blaming the victim.

Blameworthiness empowers the vulnerable. Under maximum threat, it functions as fear-substitute and gives the helpless person an illusion of control. It also allows the intellectual to reject responsibility for the ethical problem of "dirty hands" entailed in the necessity to defend anything worth defending.[108] Finding fault in oneself alleviates apprehension in the sufferer of Stockholm syndrome because it absolves the attacker and turns him into an innocent party, perhaps even a friend. A longtime friend of the terrorists has been the executive director of the Bertrand Russell Peace Foundation, Ralph Schoenman, whose *Hidden History of Zionism* opens with a cry "Thawra Hatta al Nasr (Revolution until Victory)" and proceeds to catalog fact-free allegations against the Nazi-like Israelis, said to have broken limbs of Palestinian children, buried people alive, burned and tortured them to death, and gassed entire communities. Since its publication, the trumped-up tale has made its way into scholarship and the intellectual discourse, purportedly making evident "why terrorism."[109]

Guilt-ridden lamentations—"what have *we* done to them to cause their hate"—reduce the irrationality of terror that many intellectuals cannot suffer, anxious as they tend to be when faced with anything incomprehensible. Self-imposed and rationalized liability creates a fantasy that with a change in behavior or policy, terrorists could be persuaded to act "nicer." A declared war to the end against "the Zionist entity,"[110] within *any* borders, and a way of life, as represented by the "satanic America"—is ignored for assured self-defense.

In the 1900s and once again in the 2000s, the intellectuals define cultural parameters and the acceptable modes of discourse with regards to terrorism. Thus the politically correct self-defeatist vernacular makes its way into newspapers and university classrooms. In other words, the Stockholm syndrome enters the public sphere. It was unambiguous in a recent incident when several Israeli soldiers were not allowed entrance into a Tel-Aviv nightclub, as per order of its owners: the IDF uniform is an emblem of "suppression and genocide in our eyes," the club employees explained; the army hostility is "the reason for violence in the country."[111]

Never in history have we been more reluctant to call evil by its name, except when it has already cast away all disguises and, like Nazism, is defeated. Short of that, as a Yale professor declared in his lecture "On Evil" before a large student audience, the label is but a means for men invested with power to manipulate opinion by invoking anxiety. The implication of such arguments is comforting indeed: if evil is bogus, terrorism, one of its contemporary variants, is equally spurious—an illusion rather than a terrifying reality.

Focusing on security, our culture of postulated tolerance is not conducive to dealing with terrorization head-on. It compensates with unrivaled ingenuity in the use of mental and verbal aerobics aimed at devaluating terror in consciousness. This is the realm of "ivory tower" academics. They intellectualize the problem by wrestling with the 109 definitions of terrorism—an open-ended project and as constructive as would be a challenge for a historian of the French Revolution to delineate precisely what he meant by the "history" and by the "revolution." In a subliminal effort to present terror as a convoluted legal or scientific matter, they turn it into a "problem of description" as part of a "scholarly discourse." Here, language plays a primary role in rendering issues barely comprehensible, buried beneath a mound of professional terminology.[112]

A useful gimmick to diminish anxiety is to equate terrorism with more familiar types of brutality, if we have already encountered, managed to handle, and successfully integrated them as our past. The comparison of Russian anarchists or Muslim terrorists to the Ku Klux Klan and other white supremacist groups seems to suggest the dismissive "seen that" attitude. A mental defense stratagem, trivialization of the terrorist threat can run amok in conjecturing it to be, like murder, almost inherent to the human condition. "Terrorism is as old as human history," some scholars claim.[113] Specifically, suicide terrorism is relegated to the category of old news: a parallel with 9/11 must be evident, states an *Arab Studies Quarterly* article examining biblical Samson's "suicide mission."[114]

The reverse technique of "dissecting the beast" is equally rewarding as self-help against the fear of aggression. A gruesome image that hovers over the ruins of the New York towers, a monster that stares at us from the shattered windows of a European café and consumes the black carcass of a smoldering bus in Jerusalem, must not be seen as a specter of a worldwide predicament. It is soothing to dismiss a terrorist episode as a local affair in a troubled country. Purportedly for the sake of scholarly exactitude, we are comforted by overstressing the most trivial specifics, dissected bits and pieces of a general concept, each twisted and turned around and inside out—to the point where meaningful connections are no longer discernable, and it is impossible to recognize what it is that is being discussed. The intellectuals have developed this dismemberment technique to the point of genuine refinement; we prefer not to integrate or synthesize and obsessively search for peculiarities, fixating on disjoint details, lest we be able to see parallels or analogies, grasp the frightening whole, and develop insight into the magnitude of a universal phenomenon.

In the deconstructed "detached analysis" of unrelated details, that which had seemed monstrous no longer appears authentic; all we see at a given moment are isolated fragments, which do not alarm anyone. We have thus successfully played out a highbrow gambit that illustrates Orwell's absurdity "Ignorance is strength." Any intellectual must appreciate the paradox.

If we do not invoke its name, the terrifying ghoul might disappear, and so the trend is to frown upon the very word "terrorism." The ploy has made its way into the White House, which recently sanctioned a new proper expression—"man-caused disasters," apparently to dissociate from George W. Bush's "politics of fear."[115] To eradicate the "doubleplusungood" matter from the lexicon is a sure way to resolve it, Orwell reveals in his anti-utopia.

The terrorists use the conventional idiom of their larger environment to strike at it—where it hurts the most. Thus, for all its devotion to the Qur'an, Islamism is, to a large degree, a product of a fashionable Western outlook—incorporating, as needed, the post-Marxist anti-colonialist vernacular. The language of struggle is "constructed," to employ the beloved term of its inventors.[116] Of them, the most preeminent and tremendously influential has been Columbia University's Edward Said, renowned author of *Orientalism*, who called the first PLO Intifada "one of the great anti-colonial insurrections of the modern period" and resigned from the Palestine National Council after the signing of the Oslo Accords to protest that Arafat had capitulated and agreed to give up "not terrorism but the Palestinian right to resist."[117] Said and a wide variety of writers who followed him shaped the "post-colonialist discourse," which the ideology fabricators modify and adopt to incite violent action against the occupiers. In the 1998–1999 Palestinian academic year, all 150 new schoolbooks used in the PA classified Israel as the "Zionist enemy" and "equated Zionism with Nazism."[118]

To propagate their cause, designers of Muslim radicalism rely on and extract benefits from the popular "perceptive pluralism" and relativism, above all, with regard to convictions and ideas. Postmodernist devaluation of credo as illusory, ironically, yields an accurate assessment of an totalism, whose dogmatic nuances have secondary relevance. Equally ironic, however, is that this line of thinking contributes to a construction of another illusion—that the peril of terrorism, like other aspects of ersatz reality, is a chimera. Subjectivist mentality allows for a blasé stance with regard to violence-permeated rhetoric: there is no need to be troubled if, after all, the battle against modernity is as illusive as is any phenomenon within our "constructed experience."

Not infrequently, adherents of this view take a step further and excuse political extremism by pronouncing it irrelevant. This is especially noteworthy after 9/11, sometimes classified as one of many "false-flag terror operations...authored by U.S. rulers and their intelligence agencies:"[119] The EU is also faulted for its treatment of fundamentalism as a serious danger, whereas

> there is no factual base to consider terrorism as a real threat in Europe...While these crimes severely affected the lives and well-being of its direct victims and their relatives, they did not disrupt or undermine the operation of public institutions, economic life, defense capacity, the social fabric, or the well-being of the population. To state that terrorism constitutes a "significant threat to the security of Europe" is a monumental and most probably wilful (sic.) misrepresentation...Some would call this a plain lie....the figleaf behind which wars of aggression and various military interventions are hidden.[120]

In their day, the Kadets compiled and published downplayed statistics, demonstrating the triviality of terrorist activity in contrast to raging repressions.[121] We too try to calm ourselves by irrelevant comparisons of traffic accident data with those of terror-related casualties, which speak for themselves: from an monthly average of 109 lives claimed by terrorists before the attacks of September 11, "the global death rate rose to about 158 people killed per month in the six years following, an increase of 45 percent," not counting "fatalities resulting from terrorist attacks in the active combat in Iraq and Afghanistan."[122] To which we reply with Norman Mailer, "There is a tolerable level to terror."[123] True to form, it is not terrorism that is a legitimate concern, requiring high-priority attention, but the alleged governmental oppression and abuse of consciousness—prime anxiety of the postmodernist intellectual.[124]

"Plehve ought to be killed....It is time for Plehve to be killed," Prince Dmitrii Shakhovskoi had insisted,[125] joining the Kadet leadership soon after Sazonov's bomb blew the hated Interior Minister to pieces. The entire progressive society celebrated their dream-come-true in July 1904 and greeted one another with the Japanese victory cry of "Banzai!"[126] Striking as an example of inverse typology was the enormous shock of November 4, 1995, when Israeli Prime Minister Yitzhak Rabin was killed. Even among opponents of the Oslo Accords, empathy for Rabin mutated into sympathy for his policy—immediately, if temporarily, until the ensuing surge of Islamist violence turned the majority towards "great misgivings" about concessions to terrorist "peace partners." Still, across the political spectrum, the dominant reaction to Rabin's assassination was revulsion.[127]

In 2002, Adel Hadmi, member of a terrorist cell and medical chemistry doctoral student at the Hebrew University, was convicted of stealing from his lab 160 liters of acetone—to manufacture the common explosive acetone peroxide for suicide attacks against Israelis. Upon his release from prison six years later, Hadmi wished to complete his doctorate in the same laboratory. Its director, Professor Amiram Goldblum, readmitted the terrorist. One of the founders of the leftist group Peace Now, Goldblum is considered a radical even among his peacenik colleagues because he justified Saddam Hussein's Scud attacks and threats to annihilate Israel for its "failure to make concessions to the Palestinians." Concerning Hadmi's right to obtain his degree, he said that the university had no grounds for refusal; the promising scholar had already served his sentence.[128]

Defenders of extremism may be as self-hating as they are self-destructive—an eerie insight that perhaps explains why they "understand" and identify with the terrorist cause and why they are determined to make it logical to others. This line of thinking warrants a question as to whether psychologically they also relate to suicidal inclinations.[129] Understated, yet consequential self-negation may engender rationalization of extremism, highlighted by suicide terrorism—nihilism par excellence. Its first fruits the liberal intelligentsia came to taste in a place no other than Russia, where terrorists seized power in 1917.

CHAPTER 8

When Terrorists Become State Leaders

We must execute not only the guilty.
Execution of the innocent will impress the masses even more.
—Bolshevik Commissar of Justice Nikolai Krylenko

Execute mercilessly

—Lev Trotsky's telegram to comrades
in Astrakhan, March 1919

For the first time in history, the extremists of the new type acquired state control in Russia, the country where modern terrorism had taken root. Of course it was not Lenin, but Robespierre, leader of the Committee of Public Safety during the French Revolution, who had first coined the term "La Terreur" and glorified it as "an emanation of virtue."[1] Robespierre and other members of the Jacobin Club had not, however, engaged in violence prior to the fall of the monarchy and instead unleashed their Reign of Terror against "enemies of the revolution" in 1793, over four years after its onset. Russia was thus the first country ever to live under a totalist ideology upheld by men with extensive terrorist backgrounds and experience.

A similar situation developed next in Afghanistan, where the Sunni Islamist Taliban held power from 1996 to 2001, until sent into hiding as a result of NATO military involvement. Not only did it survive but, with amazing resilience, eight years later "the Taliban has re-established itself in most provinces of Afghanistan and in the neighboring regions of Pakistan." Radical Shiite Hezbollah, backed with generous financial and military support by Iran and

Syria, has become "a sort of alternative government" in Lebanon.[2] Presently, Hamas has taken up the experiment of consolidating Islamist rule in Gaza. Scholars have thus come to understand that state and non-state terrorism are "eminently comparable" and, "linked, and in some real-world cases, they feed off each other in violent cycles."[3]

In a fateful twist of transitory politics that followed the collapse of the imperial regime, the Bolsheviks usurped power as a result of a coup that toppled the ineffectual Provisional Government in November 1917. The takeover precluded a democratic course because a cardinal feature of the newly established Soviet rule was its dependence on unremitting state-sponsored political violence, inherent in the regime's origins. Terror from above manifested itself already in the first frantic weeks following the takeover and escalated into the sanguinary years of the Russian Civil War of 1918–1921.

Lenin and his associates relied on the pre-1917 terrorist mentality and practices to uphold the process of building their "Communist paradise." Aside from defending expropriations as legitimate methods of revolutionary fund-raising, prior to the Bolshevik takeover, Lenin's party "never rejected terror on principle," nor could it do so.[4] In 1905 he had urged his followers to establish armed units, identical to the SR combat detachments, for the purpose of killing the gendarmes and Cossacks and blowing up their headquarters; he also advocated the use of explosives, boiling water, and acid against soldiers, police, and supporters of the tsarist regime.[5] Throughout the empire the Bolsheviks took part in terrorist activities, including those of major political significance, such as the 1907 murder of celebrated poet and social reformer Count Il'ia Chavchavadze, arguably the most popular national figure in turn-of-the-century Georgia.[6]

Having taken over the Russian administration, Lenin and Trotsky labeled opponents of violence "eunuchs and pharisees"[7] and proceeded to implement government-sponsored machinery of state terror—projecting the conspiratorial and semi-criminal nature of the Bolshevik faction onto the new dictatorial regime. The Bolsheviks endorsed a policy they called the "Red Terror"—an instrument of repression in the hands of the revolutionary government—as a precondition for success in a seemingly visionary endeavor by a handful of political extremists to establish control over Russia's population. For this purpose, the Bolsheviks must "put an end once and for all of the papist-Quaker babble about the sanctity of human life," Trotsky proclaimed.[8]

In their rhetoric, Lenin's followers presented the Jacobin policies as a model for their own version of La Terreur and themselves as descendents of the French radicals. "Each Social Democrat must be a terrorist à la Robespierre," Plekhanov was heard saying, and for once Lenin was in full agreement with the Mensheviks' plan: "We will not shoot at the tsar and his servants now as the Socialists-Revolutionaries do, but after the victory we will erect a guillotine in Kazanskii Square for them and many others."[9] In the Bolshevik view, terrorization from above was also an expedient tool in restructuring the traditional society in accordance with the Marxist doctrine.

Building on the notion of "motiveless terror" of the 1905 era, the Bolsheviks launched their campaign of state-sponsored coercion against groups of individuals designated as "class enemies" of the proletarian dictatorship, with extermination now being "class based." In one of the first references to their new course, on December 2, 1917, Trotsky declared before a revolutionary gathering, "There is nothing immoral in the proletariat finishing off the dying class. This is its right. You are indignant...at the petty terror which we direct against our class opponents. But be put on notice that in one month at most this terror will assume more frightful forms, on the model of the great revolutionaries of France."[10]

The Bolsheviks justified terror as an ideological weapon and rejoinder to a wide range of anti-Soviet activity allegedly perpetrated by a myriad of their internal and foreign enemies—Russian reactionaries, foreign interventionists, and counterrevolutionaries of various leanings—all supposedly out to destroy the communist regime. The "accusation of terrorism...falls not on us but on the bourgeoisie. It forced terror on us," Lenin claimed the exigency for killing in self-defense, echoing the paranoid defensiveness of the terrorists during the underground period.[11] In reality, he had planned mass repressions a decade before he had a chance to introduce them as a state policy, dreaming as early as 1908 of "real, nation-wide terror, which reinvigorates the country."[12]

The Bolsheviks established their notorious political police, the Cheka (Extraordinary Commission for Combating Counterrevolution and Sabotage), months before any organized opposition to the Soviets had had a chance to develop.[13] The Cheka began its operations formally, if secretly, almost immediately after the Bolshevik takeover—on December 7, 1917, and soon became a primary instrument of the Red Terror, in accordance with Lenin's pronouncement in the following month: "if we are guilty of anything, it is of having been too humane, too benevolent, towards the representatives of the bourgeois-imperialist order."[14] By the first half of 1918, after the Cheka had already had its debut in repression, "counterrevolutionary organizations...as such were not observed," acknowledged its deputy director, Iakov Peters, known as "Peters, the Terrorist."[15] At the same period, in June 1918, the first Cheka head, "Iron Feliks" Dzerzhinskii, declared that terror was "an absolute necessity" and that the repressive measures must go on in the name of the revolution, "even if its sword does ... sometimes fall upon the heads of the innocent."[16]

Originally, the Bolsheviks had envisaged the Cheka as an investigative rather than repressive agency; its primary function was to gather intelligence and prevent offenses against the state. Having no official judiciary powers, the Cheka was legally required to leave prosecution, indictment, and final sentencing of political offenders to the new Soviet courts, the so-called revolutionary tribunals, introduced in late November 1917.[17] But the tribunals' tendency to linger on proprieties threatened the efficiency of Lenin's envisaged rule "unrestricted by any laws." As a solution, the Bolshevik leadership extended the Cheka's original mandate. Whereas its central offices in Petrograd and Moscow temporarily abstained from executing political nonconformists, on February 23, 1918, Dzerzhinskii urged provincial and district cadres to set up local Cheka bureaus, arrest counterrevolutionaries, and "execute them wherever apprehended." Enemies of the revolution would be "mercilessly liquidated on the spot," the authorities announced publicly.[18]

Accordingly, the Cheka bureaus in the periphery began to resort routinely to summary judiciary procedures. Unlimited by even the most cursory legal norms, they meted out arbitrary, often impetuous and unwarranted punishments, including death sentences.[19] Their primary focus at the moment was on combating such economic crimes as "speculation," which "encompassed practically any independent commercial activity," and "sabotage"—for example, refusal of technical experts and professionals to offer their services to the Bolshevik-controlled economy.[20]

In July 1918 the Bolsheviks massacred the Russian imperial family—a dramatic episode of primarily psychological significance, which took place six weeks before Red Terror was inaugurated as an official policy. The Soviets relegated responsibility for the decision to murder the Romanov family in Ekaterinburg to local revolutionary activists. In truth, the secret order to execute former tsar Nicholas II, his wife Alexandra, their five children, and a valet, cook, parlor maid, and family doctor was issued in the Bolshevik headquarters in Moscow and carried out by a special Cheka squad. It was not for nothing that Lenin was a great admirer of Nechaev, the expert in bonding a subversive group with the accountability for a collective crime. Lenin, too, understood that when his party was in danger of being abandoned by many vacillating supporters, it needed blood to "cement its deserting following." Trotsky supported Lenin's decision as "not only expedient but necessary:" The ruthlessness of this measure "showed everyone that we would continue to fight on mercilessly, stopping at nothing. The execution of the Tsar's family was needed not only to frighten, horrify, and instill a sense of hopelessness in the enemy but also to shake up our own ranks, to show that there was no retreating, that ahead lay either total victory or total doom."[21] From then on, the extremists had to sustain the policy of murder; otherwise, in their own eyes, past bloodletting would be meaningless and deplorable.

On August 30, 1918, Moisei Uritskii was assassinated as the head of the Cheka in Petrograd. As a questionable coincidence, on the same day government sources issued a statement about an attempt on Lenin's life in Moscow. The Bolsheviks interpreted these attacks as a coordinated action of a large-scale conspiracy—an unfounded assumption that elicited their instantaneous and inundating fear. Panic-stricken, Lenin's followers mitigated their apprehension by unleashing a mass campaign of violence. The Red Terror did not start but dramatically magnified at this time, encompassing retaliation and revenge, marked by infinite cruelty—against real, alleged, and potential adversaries: "Without mercy, without sparing, we will kill our enemies by the scores of hundreds, let them be thousands, let them drown themselves in their own blood. For the blood of Lenin and Uritskii... let there be floods of blood of the bourgeoisie—more blood, as much as possible."[22]

Under such pretext, after August 30, 1918, the Bolsheviks no longer bothered to conceal brutality. The Cheka arrested civilians randomly and executed them arbitrarily in a sweeping effort to liquidate class enemies—a loosely defined category that the Bolsheviks continuously expanded. A prominent Cheka officer, Martyn Latsis, made a newspaper declaration: "Do not look in the file of incriminating evidence to see whether or not the accused rose up against the Soviets with arms or words. Ask him instead to which class he belongs, what is his background, his education, his profession. These are the questions that will determine the fate of the accused. That is the meaning and essence of the Red Terror."[23] Soon, the Soviets developed a favorite "counter-counterrevolutionary measure"—hostage-taking.

The radicals' attitude toward the use of hostages shifted from the People's Will's explicit denial of any intention to punish their enemies by kidnapping their family members to lonely voices advocating as early as 1903 the capturing of government officials and representatives of the bourgeoisie for the purpose of using them as bargaining chips in later negotiations with the authorities.[24] After 1905, revolutionaries in the Baltics did seize civilian hostages,[25] and prominent Bolshevik Vladimir Bonch-Bruevich proposed that the St. Petersburg Committee grab "a couple or so grand dukes" to blackmail the authorities.[26] The extremists would occasionally turn against and hurt family members to threaten their enemies; in a notable incident, the terrorists murdered the father of a police informer to use his funeral as an opportunity to assassinate the son, their real target.[27]

In September 1918, as an initial step of the intensifying Red Terror, the Bolsheviks shot "in reprisal" 512 hostages, most of them "high notables" of the old regime. Simultaneously, the government decreed: in order to intimidate and punish the opposition, class enemies *and their relatives* would be sent to concentration camps.[28] By 1919 the number of inmates increased dramatically, prison camps serving as trial models for the Gulag.

The practice of hostage-taking became routine. Used as slave labor, imprisoned families of counterrevolutionary suspects were also potential "execution material." The Cheka firing squads shot these civilians regularly as a collective punishment,[29] occasionally "emptying" entire prisons of inmates.[30] Sometimes the Chekists did not even bother to waste the bullets, as in the Kholmogory camp, where bound prisoners were drowned in the nearby river. Alternatively, Lenin recommended public hanging—for a visual effect.[31] In June 1918 the authorities announced that in case of a single shot at the Bolshevik supporters in Astrakhan, "bourgeois hostages" would be executed "in 24 minutes."[32]

Faced with a wave of starving workers' strikes and peasant uprisings, the government directed its wrath against the very groups whose alleged, if more than questionable, backing had served as an argument for the Bolsheviks' political legitimacy. In two months of terror, between 10,000 and 15,000 summary executions took place, marking "a radical break with the practices of the

Tsarist regime." In almost 100 years, between 1825 and 1917, the imperial courts issued 6,321 politics-related death sentences, not all of which were carried out.[33] As we have seen, before the revolution, the terrorists came to be responsible for exactly as many casualties among state officials in a single decade, invalidating a claim that "violence, alas, was reciprocal."[34]

Alienation and anxiety, so prominent in the clandestine milieu, seem to have been even more pronounced when the extremists usurped power in Russia. Escalating brutality of the extremist clique that came to exercise tenuous control over the enormous country bore a concomitant—and mounting—dread of criminals before imminent retribution. Few if any among the Bolshevik leadership believed that their regime would outlast the two-month revolutionary experience of the Paris Commune; yet all were determined to hold on to power at any cost—for as long as possible, until they would surely be overthrown and again forced into a position of haunted runaways.[35] Psychologically, they had not changed from the underground days when, perceiving themselves as the persecuted, liable for annihilation, the radicals propelled onto the enemy their fear and belligerence. In fact, as their "power increased, so did the Bolshevik sense of danger," perception of a looming catastrophe, and urgency to harm. "We have never made a secret of the fact that our revolution is only the beginning, that its victorious end will only come when we have lit up the whole world with these same flames," said Trotsky, anticipating the millennial cataclysm—from Hungary to India. Having declared ruthless war on the international bourgeoisie, Lenin avowed that the wounded "wild beast" is bursting with "fierce hate... and ready to throw itself at Soviet Russia any minute to strangle it."[36] And if in the 1905 era the extremists did not shun from victimizing people they were allegedly liberating; as government, they did so with redoubled intensity.

Horney described the tendency to dominate "disguised in humanistic forms," as well as the quest for power, as a protection. It is "born out of anxiety" associated with feelings of inferiority, weakness, and helplessness—glaring among the extremists. It has an additional benefit "as a channel through which repressed hostility can be discharged."[37] Finally, it "strengthens group identity, since the hated other can be collectively shared and collectively destroyed." The group then "comes to see itself as exclusive, possessing a boundary the hated other may never pass or threaten... the border separates the pure from the impure... the polluted from the good," the saints from the villains.[38] The dualistic, black-and-white formula that all goodness is within, and all badness is outside inevitably had to translate into violence, in accordance with Lenin's challenge: "each man must choose between joining our side or the other side."[39] Like other variants of totalism, Bolshevism presumed the impossibility of a "third path" or neutrality:[40] "one who does not sing along with us today is against us," declared first official Soviet poet Vladimir Maiakovskii, eulogizing Bolshevik reprisals.

Repressions against other political parties began as early as November 28, 1917, with the ban of the Kadets. Still supporting a parliamentary democracy, and still not realizing that the dream was over, they were the first among the liberal public intellectuals to pay for their collaboration with the extremists, who now declared them enemies of the people. From then on, Kadet publications were closed and supporters arrested. Lenin's excuse—which he offered to simulate at least a minimal legitimacy—was that the Constitutional Democrats were not socialists.

In June 1918 the Bolshevik barred the SRs and the Mensheviks from the political process for alleged counterrevolutionary activities, and by late summer Lenin was already applying terror against former socialist comrades, many of whom were apprehended and incarcerated. Of course they were not counterrevolutionaries, Lenin frankly admitted to Swiss socialist Fritz Platten, "but that's exactly why they are dangerous—just because they are honest revolutionists."[41] Long before the Soviets legalized the ongoing practice in their Penal Code, persecution extended from renowned figures of the socialist opposition to members of their families, including children. The youngest daughter of Chernov, leader of the now-outlawed SR party, was 11 years old when she spent weeks of semi-starvation in an icy cell of the infamous Lubianka prison.[42]

In the first months after the Bolshevik takeover, Lenin had no choice but to put aside his dream of a single-party regime and grudgingly acknowledge the necessity to allot fractional authority to radical dissenters from the PSR—Left Socialists-Revolutionaries (Left SRs). The Bolsheviks invited them to join the coalition government, in which the Left SR received four Commissar positions. They also held high posts within the Soviet repressive organs, including the Cheka, where a Left SR representative served as its deputy director. In their effort to eradicate "counterrevolution," the Left SR were no less extreme than their comrades, the Bolsheviks.

On July 6, 1918, two Cheka functionaries, Left SRs Iakov Blumkin and Nikolai Andreev, assassinated the German ambassador in Moscow, Count Wilhelm von Mirbach. Lenin immediately proclaimed the terrorist act to be not only an attempt to drag the Soviet Republic into a new war with Germany, but also a motion for a full-fledged "counterrevolutionary uprising." He proceeded to arrest approximately 450 members of the Left SR faction on charges of conspiracy and treacherous violation of the two-party alliance. Most likely, the Left SR leadership, although yielding none to the Bolsheviks in extremism, had no intention of rebelling against the coalition, but Mirbach's assassination did give Lenin an opportunity to provoke the exchange of fire between former partners and to fulfill his underlying purpose of establishing the Bolshevik dictatorship.[43]

At the other end of the world, nearly a century later, the extremists are following similar patterns of eliminating political rivals. On July 25, 2008, an explosive device detonated in Gaza outside the Hilal Café, frequented by leading Hamas activists. The explosion occurred next to a vehicle belonging to the militants' commander, Nihad Masbah. Along with him, the blast killed four of his comrades and a four-year-old girl; over 20 others were wounded.

Against all expectations, the Hamas leadership did not blame Israel and instead assigned responsibility for the attack to Muhammad Dahlan, former PA Authority National Security Advisor under Mahmoud Abbas, chairman of the Fatah party. Following the explosion, Hamas Prime Minister Ismail Haniyah vowed to "seek justice" and punish all guilty. Abbas repeatedly denied the allegation that Fatah was behind the terrorist act in Gaza and proposed to initiate an independent inquiry to investigate the bombing—an offer Hamas promptly rejected.

Instead, the Hamas combatants immediately began to make arrests throughout the city, apprehending 160 people aligned with al Fatah. The arrests set off a wave of fighting between Hamas and Fatah factions. Over the next two days, Hamas continued its repressive operations in Gaza, arresting in total almost 200 Fatah activists. Fatah retaliated: *The Jerusalem Post* reported that its forces rounded up dozens of pro-Hamas politicians and sympathizers across the West Bank, including 54 people in Nablus. On July 28, Hamas banned the distribution of three Fatah-affiliated newspapers and arrested some journalists.

It was not the first or the only time Hamas combatants set out against the Fatah membership. On June 17, 2009, Fatah TV marked the second anniversary of the Hamas military takeover of Gaza by issuing a graphic video, featuring a screaming Fatah activist, dragged along the ground and beaten by Hamas fighters with a bone-crushing bat, incited by their comrades' screams of "Allahu Akbar" (Allah is Great).[44] It would be fair to state—which the video did not—that in areas controlled by Fatah, its militants have treated the Hamas rivals in similar ways.[45] For the Fatah leaders "nemeses were neither the Jews nor their Zionist benefactors" but "brother Palestinians," men who repudiated allegiance to the faction that claimed the right to Arafat's political legacy.[46]

None of this is new: in 1905, Russian extremist groups, helped by thugs, protected Bolsheviks from Mensheviks and the SRs, and vice versa,[47] their major concern being the control over party treasures. After 1917, terrorists in power finally got a chance to settle old scores. With Israel as common enemy, extremists contest political control in the not-yet-established Palestinian state and fight for its meager economic resources. To suggest that the July 2008 situation in Gaza is similar to that in Moscow in July 1918 is to emphasize the point: the terrorists in the PA demonstrate the relentless determination to establish a dictatorship, to which the Bolsheviks aspired in the past—and with great success.

By the fall and winter of 1918–19, Bolshevik terror had achieved "a level of indiscriminate slaughter never before seen."[48] Persecutions were directed at virtually anyone representing the old regime's upper classes, the bourgeoisie, and the intelligentsia. A vicious atheistic campaign to obliterate the Russian Orthodox church and religion in general brought about unremitting aggression vis-à-vis the clergy and the devout adherents of all persuasions.[49] Instigated by their perpetual dread of military conspiracies, the Bolsheviks made special effort to locate and apprehend former imperial army and navy officers; thousands were executed without a trial.[50] With a revealing ballpark figure of victims ranging between 50,000 and 140,000, violence "served the Bolsheviks...as a surrogate for the popular support which eluded them. The more their popularity eroded, the more they resorted to terror."[51]

Among perpetrators of state-sponsored terrorism, fanatics relied on "revolutionary conscience" to justify their urge to annihilate "class enemies," but operating side by side with the visionaries were the extremists of a new type—a wide variety of hooligans, criminals, and the "scum of the society." The "revolutionary riffraff" readily joined the developing Soviet *nomenklatura* and the Cheka to render a genuine new "social prototype."[52] Among them were individuals who in the post-1905 period had "entered the realm of political dissent after a squabble with the authorities, a boss, or a commanding officer. Still others turned their quixotic ideals of 'revolutionary' justice into sheer criminal acts. Finally, there were those for whom the Revolution meant money in their pockets, a lucrative business venture." Having served sentences for various crimes, these "thieves and ordinary swindlers" walked out of prison posing as political convicts in 1917 and "reintegrated into post-revolutionary Russian society quite swiftly thanks to their bogus revolutionary credentials"—reaping benefits under the auspices of the Bolshevik environment.[53] Soviet authorities were well aware that the very nature of repressive activities attracted "corrupt and outright criminal elements," and Dzerzhinskii bluntly complained, "Only saints and scoundrels" offer their services to the Cheka, but "the saints are running away from me, and I am left with the scoundrels."[54]

As in 1905, recruiters provided the lofty slogans of freedom fighters to justify felonious acts now carried out in the interest of the state.[55] It was especially difficult to differentiate between revolutionary and criminal practices in the periphery, where mass murder, robbery, blackmail, rape, beatings, torture, and startling sadism assumed astounding proportions—the "Red banditry," accompanied by incessant drinking and drug use by members of the Cheka and the tribunals.[56] Few regional or district Cheka officials were held accountable for their actions, and the only criteria for appointment to the revolutionary tribunals were undivided loyalty to the new regime and the ability to read and write. Consequently, 60 percent of the "proletarian judges" were individuals with incomplete secondary schooling; many used their positions "to pursue personal vendettas" and to extort bribes from families of the accused. People were executed "by accident": a person would be shot because his family name was confused with a similar one. In some cases namesakes were killed together purposely; the Chekists did not wish to waste time on lengthy investigation.[57] What "now goes on in the provinces is not Red Terror at all, but crime, from beginning to end," prominent Bolshevik Mikhail Olminskii protested in 1919.[58]

We obviously cannot reduce mass ideologically justified violence to psychopathology of individual participants. Yet it would also be erroneous to ignore rampant, irrational, and frequently uncontrolled brutality that permeated the Bolshevik Terror. The behavior of its numerous practitioners suggests psychological instability as a possible catalyst for viciousness. In the prevailing circumstances of a political crisis, mental aberrancy and perversions, including sadism, assumed revolutionary form—as they had had a decade earlier. As then, emotionally damaged individuals gravitated toward extremism and confirmed a strong connection between psychological imbalance and aggressive impulses, of which medical professionals had been aware for decades.

Psychosis might have been as exceptional among the extremists as it was outside the revolutionary milieu, but terrorists of the pre-revolutionary epoch suffered from a variety of other mental illnesses, including acute paranoia, severe depression, and recurrent manic episodes. Some, like Dora Brilliant, exhibited a tendency toward hysteria and experienced emotional breakdowns.[59] Others would not miss a chance for an aggressive act.[60] Quite a number of combatants periodically found themselves in psychiatric hospitals. Particularly widespread was serious pathological behavior among teenage terrorists, some of whom received treatment for psychiatric disorders.[61]

"Unbalanced," "turbulent, "completely abnormal," "mentally deranged," and "crazy," the revolutionaries called their psychologically deviant comrades; one referred to them as "cannibals."[62] Sometimes precisely because of their evident aberrancy and proclivity for aggression, recruiters were eager to enlist them for terrorist acts. Thus, Lenin treasured Kamo, recognizing that his loyal "Caucasian bandit" suffered from a mental illness and required clinical treatment; the Bolsheviks counted on his wild temperament to provide constant inflow of expropriated cash.[63] Not entirely original then would seem the idea to employ for terrorist purposes two Iraqi women with Down syndrome: the "crazy ladies" were strapped with remote-control explosives and dispatched to detonate them in crowded Baghdad markets on the morning of February 8, 2008, killing at least 99.[64]

Relatively few qualified as mentally deranged, let alone insane, but their attitude toward brutality did blur the boundaries between normalcy and pathology. Tat'iana Leont'eva, daughter of the vice-governor of Iakutsk and terrorist-fanatic of more than questionable emotional stability, murdered an elderly man, in her confused mental state mistaking him for Minister of the Interior Durnovo. Having been informed of her error, she expressed regrets but added, "In these difficult times it does not matter if there is one person more or less in the world."[65]

Dzerzhinskii, who personified the Bolshevik Red Terror, before the revolution had been diagnosed with and reportedly treated for a mental illness then referred to as "circular psychosis" (bipolar affective disorder).[66] Several of his chief lieutenants after 1918, including the notoriously vicious investigator Romanovskii, were drug addicts and unquestionable sadists.[67] The inmates in the "Death Boat," as they called the central Cheka prison in Moscow, found themselves in the hands of a former criminal-turned-Bolshevik-hero, a raging "terror of the jail," nicknamed the "Commissar of Death."[68]

"Only a truly ill patient in a state of madness behaves this way," confirmed medical experts in Germany after a thorough evaluation of Kamo following his imprisonment in 1907. He "easily loses mental equilibrium and then enters a state of obvious insanity.... We are dealing with a type of mental disorder that most accurately is attributable to a form of hysteria," was the doctors' verdict.[69] In the prerevolutionary years, Kamo was obsessed with a scheme of testing the loyalty of rank-and-file combatants by fear and torture—until he finally had a chance to put it into practice amid the anarchy of the Russian civil war. During a training exercise in 1919, the Red fighters under his leadership were attacked and captured by "the Whites"—in reality Kamo's lieutenants wearing enemy epaulets. The make-belief captors flogged their prisoners and staged mock hangings. Some Bolsheviks broke under torture, and Kamo was ecstatic: his method of separating the "real Communists" from the cowards had worked marvelously.[70]

Those predisposed to sadism craved it in amplified doses after they had begun to take part in routine bloodshed manifest during the Red Terror. They "contracted the execution habit" and became addicted to gore as if to narcotics; killing had "become necessary to them," as if it were morphine. They could not sleep unless they had shot someone dead and "volunteer[ed] for the service," revealed a contemporary reporter. Some were clinically mad; others, including aberrant juveniles as young as 14, were "half-idiots."[71]

Local Cheka committees became notorious for specific forms of torture, which they claimed as their expertise, such as scalping prisoners in Khar'kov or burying them alive in Kremenchug. In Ekaterinoslav, the Cheka officers specialized in crucifixions, and in Kiev they liked the joke of putting a captive in a closed coffin with a decaying body. "Throughout the country, without investigation or trial, the Chekists... tortured old men and raped schoolgirls and killed parents before the eyes of their children. They impaled people, beat them with an iron glove, put wet leather 'crowns' on their heads, buried them alive," and "locked them in cells where the floor was covered with corpses."[72]

"Homicide rates increase dramatically following all wars, the same for victor or loser nations,"[73] and so they did in Russia after years of bloodshed during World War I. Lenin's policies contributed further to dramatic devaluation of human life. Still, no matter how much people were conditioned to cruelty, it was apparently not a trivial matter for the Bolsheviks to find enough volunteers to jail, guard, interrogate, torture, and execute. To maintain "purity of the cause," the idealists occasionally refused to follow orders—for example, to examine 19 cases of alleged counterrevolutionaries and shoot them all, regardless of the outcome of the investigation.[74] People were too "sentimental," complained Peters, when charged with recruitment of the rank-and-file Cheka cadres.

There is a great deal of evidence that genes play a significant role in aggressiveness. Animal breeding studies have shown that it is possible to select for violent behavioral traits, and family studies have confirmed that hostility is highly heritable. Some genetic mechanisms responsible for aggression have been revealed by molecular genetics; however, the importance of environmental factors has also been highlighted by researchers.[75] The Bolsheviks were at work on forging the environment conducive to murder from their earliest days in power.

The escalating terror called for constant expansion of "manpower of the Cheka...from some 2,000 men in the mid-1918 to over 35,000 six months later."[76] The Bolsheviks partly solved their problem of filling the staff vacancies by recruiting aggravated national minorities—Armenians, Jews, and Latvians—many of whom had previously been involved in the struggle against Russian imperial domination. Lenin favored them strongly as "more brutal and less susceptible to bribery" than "soft Russians."[77] He also sought the expertise of "professionals"—the jobless Okhrana employees. Ironically, some of them excelled in their Cheka work side by side with their former prisoners—the ex-terrorists.

For professional terrorists whose primary occupation before 1917 was bloodletting, the revolution presented an opportunity to return from their places of imprisonment or foreign exile and apply themselves once again to what they did best. Most of them did not know any other trade; they were experts in serving prison terms and, once out, in killing—quite in the spirit of Nechaev's dictum: a true revolutionary "knows only one science: the science of destruction."[78] After the Bolshevik takeover, they joined and often led the provincial and district bureaus of the Cheka, worked in the revolutionary tribunals, and after 1922,served in the repressive organs of the GPU (State Political Administration).[79] Dzerzhinskii and his two Moscow Cheka associates, Latsis and Mikhail Kedrov had been involved in extremist practices against tsarist authorities and the bourgeoisie.[80] In the periphery, especially in the Urals, where they had carried out expropriations, the Bolsheviks were most successful in reassembling their old bandit-like cadres. After 1917 Lenin trusted them with terror-related tasks of special importance, including the execution of the imperial family and murder of Grand Duke Mikhail Aleksandrovich Romanov.[81]

Former SRs, Maximalists, anarchists, and other terrorists also volunteered as perpetrators of the Red Terror. Despite rife harassment of fellow radicals, they held on to a vanishing hope to preserve a united revolutionary front by proving their loyalty to Lenin's regime. Alongside with the Bolsheviks, they built the Soviet machinery of repression—soon to become the instrument of their demise.[82]

The Bolsheviks were not alone to blame for raging brutality in Russia after their takeover and especially during the ensuing civil war; the Red Terror may be compared with an array of atrocities perpetrated by the Whites. Yet, the differences between the Red and the White forces was as essential as it was between the tsarist state and the terrorists: an army does not come to fulfill a need for a new way of life; it is not a road to salvation. It "is an instrument for bolstering, protecting and expanding the present," whereas the ideological movement comes to destroy it. "Its preoccupation is with the future":[83] in the

Bolshevik case, with Communist apocalypse and deliverance. To overlook the familiar trap of moral equivalency would be to disregard that, pursuing the millennial prophesy,

> Lenin's government used terror as a method of social engineering. The Whites had never cherished a goal of recasting Russian society.... The Communist terror on the other hand was part of a grand design to eliminate entire social groups of the population by violence, as obstacles to what the Communists called socialism.... The Red Terror... established and routinized the practice of "processing" entire social strata of people without regard to personal guilt or lack thereof.[84]

Lenin's repressions were ideology-based and theory-justified, applied to entire groups that the party in power labeled ideologically impure. "Proletarian repression in all its forms, beginning with executions... is a method of molding the communist man from the human material of the capitalist epoch," elucidated Bolshevik leader Nikolai Bukharin.[85] And according to Left SR Isaac Steinberg, Commissar of Justice already during the initial months of the Soviet rule, terror was an all-encompassing "*system*... a legalized plan of the regime for the purpose of mass intimidation, mass compulsion, mass extermination.... The concept keeps on enlarging until... it comes to embrace the entire land, the entire population,"[86] because any person or "group not controlled by the Party is, actually or potentially, an enemy."[87]

Whereas we commonly assume that fear became a dominant factor of Russian life only during Stalin's reign of terror, contemporaries remembered otherwise: "the new regime mowed people right and left without discriminating much" between the guilty and the innocent, and already during the early months of the Soviet rule, people lived in terror of random house searches, arrests, and imprisonment, affirmed writer Mikhail Osorgin.[88] "There is no such sphere of life in which the Cheka would not be required to have its penetrating eye," a high-posted Bolshevik official explained.[89] The apparent absurdity of repression was, in fact, an important element in Lenin's effort to create an atmosphere of total intimidation; "the more irrational the terror, the more effective it was, because it made the very process of rational calculation irrelevant, reducing people to the status of a cowed herd." The frightened people in power thus sought to undermine the humanity of those under their control and to intimidate them "in order to reassure themselves of the legitimacy, strength, and longevity of their regime."[90]

The more invested revolutionaries are in the realization of an all-encompassing vision, the less is the cost of life, notes Camus; "in an extreme case, it is not worth a penny."[91] Consumed by the totality of their project, Lenin's associates did not feel the need to embellish their actions or conceal the extent of repressive policies. "We must carry along with us 90 million out of the 100 million of Soviet Russia's population," declared Grigorii Zinov'ev in mid-September 1918. "As for the rest, we have nothing to say to them. They must be annihilated."[92]

The Red Terror did not end with the Bolshevik victory in the civil war—as it must have had it been a reluctantly adopted weapon of self-defense and not a quintessential component of the coercive regime. A Communist writer called terror "a costume," which, like a mask, could be stored away "to be taken out again in case of need."[93] Although the Bolsheviks did put a stop to "the indiscriminate massacres of 1918–19, they made certain to leave intact the laws and institutions which had made them possible." Indeed, already by 1920, "Soviet Russia had become a police state in the sense that the security police, virtually a state within the state, spread its tentacles to all Soviet institutions." In addition to a growing staff of investigators, interrogation officers, guards, and other prison personnel, the secret police relied on the Armies of the Internal Security of the Republic, which by the middle of 1920 consisted of nearly a quarter-million men. Aside from its other duties, this internal army guarded concentration and forced labor camps, of which by the end of that year there were 84, with approximately 50,000 prisoners. Only three years later, the number of camps increased to 315 with 70,000 inmates. When Stalin—former chief of the Bolshevik combatants in the Caucasus—emerged as undisputed master of Soviet Russia in the late 1920s, "all the instruments which he required to resume the terror on an incomparably vaster scale lay at hand."[94]

Perhaps even more significantly, masses of people were accustomed to violence: "We are no longer frightened by the mysterious and the once unfathomable Death, for it has become our second life. We are not moved by the pungent smell of human blood, for its vapors saturate the air that we breathe. We are already not shuddered by the endless rows marching to the execution, for we have seen the last tremors of children shot in the streets; we saw mountains of mutilated and frozen victims of terrorist madness... We are accustomed... This is why, facing the triumphant Death, the country is silent... Its poisoned soul is incarcerated by Death.[95] Then, as the state itself became the instrument of Stalin's Great Terror, nothing stopped it from inflicting death for death's sake.

* * *

Many Western intellectuals, including such notables as George Bernard Shaw, Theodore Dreiser, Bertolt Brecht, and Louis Aragon, were mesmerized by Communist Russia in its darkest hour of Stalin's terror to the point of not noticing millions of his victims—imprisoned, purposely starved, exploited, and remolded into automatons to satisfy the needs of triumphant tyranny. These great skeptics, who took no idea for granted, extolled the Soviet paradise and fell short of discerning the Big Lie for lack of powers other than mental, despite Lenin allegedly dubbing them "useful idiots of the West." Conversely, they used their intellect with utmost dexterity—as a shield—not to allow into consciousness and not to "admit to themselves or anyone else that the millennial experiment in which they had invested so much (intellectual) energy could have failed."[96]

After his visit to Moscow in 1937—the date still a Russian euphemism for oppression and terror—Lion Feuchtwanger said that in the East he had "seen the magnificent" and witnessed true justice.[97] What is it that united him with other "political pilgrims," writers and journalists, followers in the footsteps of a Stalin apologist, *New York Times*'s Walter Duranty, who had nothing but praise for state terrorism in Cuba, Albania, North Korea, Vietnam, and China? Chomsky, while calling for the "denazification" of the United States, insisted that the people in Cambodia probably did not regard "the austere standard of hard manual labor" as "an onerous imposition" of the Khmer Rouge regime, which in 1975–1978 claimed 1,650,000 lives—one of five citizens. We should consider whether to treat this figure as "extensive fabrication of evidence"[98] or as evidence of intellectual hypocrisy to defend a "lofty cause."

Fascination with oppressive regimes in faraway lands serves as "the foil" for the intellectuals' frustration with "the existential meaninglessness" of their world, concomitant self-hating guilt and variants of the Stockholm syndrome. Disappointed with the liberal path to salvation, the political pilgrims succumb to their self-destructive longing to identify with Sartre's aggressive visionary "supermen," who allegedly "exercise a veritable dictatorship over their own needs" and "roll back the limits of the possible."[99] In their travelogues of Soviet Russia, they did "record a kind of pilgrimage to the Mecca of revolution."[100] Today they are awestruck with the power of radical Islam that collides with every value sacred to humanism, yet holds another millennial promise of deliverance. The prophecy is encapsulated in Foucault's endorsement of Iranian fundamentalism, in which he saw the potential for "political spirituality."[101] Overwhelmingly secular, postmodern Protean seekers are attracted to any higher cause that highlights redemption and the holy "unity of mankind, irrelevant under which banner—red or green."[102]

* * *

The fatal attraction of Communism—"the opium of the intellectuals"[103]—was that it was messianic. Its atheism notwithstanding, it contained an enormous potential of an avowedly scientific prediction championed as faith and venerated.[104] Concealed beneath a veneer of orthodox Marxism, discernable was the revolutionaries' deeper goal that lay in the realm of the existential: to find the ultimate answer to a pivotal quandary of being—its transience and finality—to overcome the inevitability of demise. Nathan Leites considers the extremist mindset in the context of a distinctively "Russian horror of death against which Bolshevism reacts."[105] Broader than a specifically national rejoinder to the dread of extinction, we are dealing with the communist secular metaphysics and its response to mortality. It was to be overpowered via a brilliant paradox, entailing the elimination of the individual—the source of the predicament.

"Alone—free—the human being is always defeated. It must be so, because every human being is doomed to die, which is the greatest of all failures." But, Orwell writes, outlining the totalitarian alternative in *1984*, if the man "can make complete, utter submission...if he can merge himself in the Party so that he is the Party," then "the death of the individual is not death." The notion is only tenuously related to mysticism, insinuated and popularized in the famous line from the musical *Jesus Christ Superstar*: "To conquer death, you only have to die." Yet, the momentous nihilist invention repudiated the age-old spiritual path of personal deliverance to uphold collective eternity—at the dire price for the individual. The issue of mortality would simply be extraneous as one's identity ceased to exist, his corporeal "I" fused with "a common destiny" and dissolved in the eternal "group mind."[106]

The Bolshevik conspiracy in power sought to expand infinitely the concept of "a group" to encompass millions of "others," transforming each into a selfless cell in a gigantic and everlasting state organism. "I am happy to be a particle of this power," acknowledged Maiakovskii. He obsessed about dying all his life, displaced anxiety by "numberless murders in his poetry," espoused the communist non-being, and "old by the age of thirty," surrendered to death by suicide.[107]

For Bolshevik leader Bogdanov, "collectivism was a religion, and even promised a triumph over death," necessarily surrogate, with the individual living "on through the memory of the collective." He was fascinated with blood and founded the Moscow Institute of Blood Transfusion, whose purposes were to exceed just medical: "for Bogdanov, blood is the very substance which should be exchanged between comrades and thus comradeship will flow directly into the bodies of the proletarians." "Almost mystical" was Bogdanov's reverence for the Communist commune, in which "workers will lose their sense of an individual 'I' in favor of an all-encompassing 'we' that will some day triumph over nature and achieve collective immortality."[108] His party colleague Martin Liadov envisaged that in the future communist society each person "will feel pain...if his personal interests in any way contradicted the interests of the collective."[109]

Among Bolsheviks fixated on immortality was Krasin, the 1905-era expert in terror. He predicted in 1920 that the moment "will come when science will become all-powerful, that it will be able to recreate a deceased organism" and even "to resurrect great historical figures." Lenin's death in January 1924 presented "an obvious choice"; in February, Krasin insisted that the significance of Lenin's grave would surpass that of Mecca and Jerusalem and urged the construction of a mausoleum.[110] There the incarnation of Bolshevism would be preserved—we are to assume, until his next earthly life. Lenin left us with little evidence about his attitude towards death, but in an incidental and ostensibly half-conscious statement he expressed a conviction that "those who really merit the name of a political personality do not die in politics when they die physically."[111]

Hazani reflects on the universal "semi-religious quality" of the radicals' desire to regulate the natural laws. Here, again, the Bolsheviks carried on the tradition demarcated by the French Revolution. Politics aside, its visionaries sought to control infinity by defining "September 22, 1792—the beginning of the first year—as the zero point of time." Romme's *decreter l'eternite* aspired "to arrest the temporal flux—i.e. to conquer death."[112] To do so, the person must disappear as a conscious being: "The more perfect individual of the future highly-cultural society will feel like one of the necessary elements" of nature, and himself "will be automatic, like nature."[113]

Victorious Bolshevism, a "self-consciously secular movement" in power, replicates the larger phenomenon of "active apocalyptic millennialism."[114] Illustrative indeed is Trotsky's belief in the impending victory over physical decay in the soon-to-be-built social paradise. He concluded his *Literature and Revolution* (1924) with "a rhapsodic vision of the new man" born in communist revolt: "Man will become immeasurably stronger, wiser and subtler; his body will become more harmonized, his movements more rhythmic, his voice more musical. The forms of life will become dynamically dramatic. The average human type will rise to the heights on an Aristotle, a Goethe, or a Marx. And above this ridge new peaks will rise."[115]

The Communists were proposing no less than "a salvationist religion,"[116] featuring a guarantee of eternal life on earth—the issue of more than cursory preoccupation also for many Nazis, particularly in the SS. Aside from their involvement with occult practices, fascination with black magic, uncanny forms of paganism, and pseudo-scientific experiments with reviving the deceased, the Nazi version of repudiated death presupposed a form of mystic fusion with the racially pure "body of Germany," similarly, the Bolsheviks conceptualized self-negation within the "victorious proletarian class" as secular salvation.

The conquest of death is inseparable from the totalistic mindset, with its distinction between the *faithful*, the potentially immortal true believers, and the *abominable*, the embodiment of a designated evil.[117] Thus, "Islam... is the only Divine way of life which brings out the noblest human characteristics, developing and using them for the construction of human society... Those who deviate from this system and want some other... are truly enemies of mankind!"[118] Against them any means are justified, as they were against enemies of the Bolsheviks, whose totalitarianism represented "the modern secular form of the coercive purity." The existential essence of their project barred a compromise, rendering immaterial any negotiations. Its adherents, the "disappointed secular zealots surpassed even the most terrible forms of religious millennialism" in the destruction they brought upon millions they sought to "save" by way of terror. In the same way, across the globe "Promethean messiahs would *carve* the millennial kingdom onto the body social."[119]

CHAPTER 9

The Culture of Death

> The command of the old despotisms was Thou shalt not. The command of the totalitarians was Thou shalt. Our command is Thou art. . . . Never again will you be capable of ordinary human feeling. Everything will be dead inside you. Never again will you be capable of love, or friendship, or joy of living, or laughter, or curiosity, or courage, or integrity. You will be hollow. We shall squeeze you empty and then we shall fill you with ourselves.
>
> —George Orwell, *1984*

> I believe in death.
>
> —Wafa Samir Ibrahim al-Bas, suicide terrorist, after a failed attempt to blow up the Beersheva Medical Center, Israel

Russian modernist writer Dmitrii Merezhkovskii, fashionable in the early 1900s, liked to say, "Religion, that's revolution, and revolution, that's religion,"[1] a new deity to be idolized and served. The "spirit of a religious order" prevailed among the Russian terrorists,[2] "martyrs of the idea"[3] in the prerevolutionary era, who pursued symbolic immortality by espousing and projecting death. Their death-wishing often took the shape of death- or terror-worship, practiced by members of various terrorist groups, including the SR Combat Organization. Soon after its formation in 1902, it turned into a sect whose members "developed their own values and their own elitist *esprit de corps*,"[4] which presupposed reverence for the "holy terror" as a sacred thing. To take up the mission that the Russian Orthodoxy fell short of fulfilling, "in essence, they wished to set up a church," Camus confirmed; from that church, "a new god would come."[5] Against the background of sectarian mentality, an assortment of Christian and socialist concepts coexisted with self-destructive ideation.

For Mariia Benevskaia, an ardent Christian Orthodox who never parted with the Gospels, preparations for fatal acts were religious rituals. Kaliaev, nicknamed "the poet," composed prayers in verse exalting the glory of the Almighty. Sazonov believed that the terrorists continued the work of Jesus: the socialists "want the kingdom of Christ to come to earth.... When I heard my teacher saying: take up your cross and follow me... I could not abandon my cross."[6] Some noncombatant comrades were astonished by the delusion of "the pseudo-greatness" of a consecrated revolutionary sacrifice,[7] compensating for the terrorists' damaged and homicidal reality.

From childhood Ekaterina Breshkovskaia, perhaps the most honored Russian 20th-century female revolutionary, was mesmerized by "the Life of St. Barbara the Martyr," killed by her father for her refusal to marry. Having thrust the religious concept to the entirely secular realm of radical politics, Breshkovskaia deserted her husband and 16-month old baby for the sake of full-time occupation as a radical.[8] She became one among the "brides of the revolution,"[9] emulating their role models of the numerous female martyrs in the Orthodox tradition, the "brides of Christ." These were, in Savinkov's words, the "monastic" types,[10] ready to consecrate themselves totally for their secular deity, the revolt.

Proclamations written by Breshkovskaia were but religious sermons, promising salvation for the revolutionary sacrifice: "Listen, Brothers! Take up arms and follow the people who summon you to battle. Follow and you will be saved. The wicked will rise against you and will marshal their forces, but be not afraid: you are many, there are hundreds of times more of you than of them, and God will be for you and help you, and those of you who will suffer or die in the struggle for justice and freedom will be called saints, and God will take their souls to himself in Heaven."[11] Historian Daniel Field called Breshkovskaia "a secular prophet" and noted that the "IRA and other modern political movements have sometimes tried to use martyrdom to advance their cause." These terrorist groups resemble religious cults as much as ideological organizations.[12] For many members, "experimentation with the cult is part of the protean search,"[13] permeated with a desire to compensate spiritual emptiness through quasi-religiosity.

The connection between secular and religious faiths is also glaring in a reverse tendency—as demonstrated by the Muslim extremists' propensity to exploit Islam for political benefits. "They *are* religious fanatics, but religious ideology is the medium" by which they express their antimodernist stance of resentment toward "Western domination," as well as their social conservatism, contempt for human rights, and proto-fascist attitudes to power.[14] They also employ the notion of a "hijacked Islam" to attain control over Muslim states.

Russia's "godless radicals" found the language of the Apocalypse exhilarating: "And I looked, and behold a pale horse: and his name that sat on him was Death, and Hell followed with him. And power was given unto them over the fourth part of the earth, to kill with sword, and with hunger, and with death, and with the beasts of the earth." Revelations 6:8 was the epigraph to Savinkov's *Pale Horse*, one of the most famous examples of Russian revolutionary prose. The apocalyptic mentality laid the foundations of a peculiar culture of adulated morbidity, which would fully develop under the Bolsheviks.

When terrorists become national leaders, no longer caged in their clandestine cells, they propagate integral features of their psychology beyond the confines of the underground environment. Essentially, the group culture remains as it was in pre-revolutionary times, still contingent on the members' conflict-ridden, weakened, death-in-life inner states and their urgency to ameliorate existential dread by surrendering the self to the immortality of an aggressive collective whole. Beyond the banality of politics, this underlying motivation was behind the Bolsheviks' collectivist effort, invariably validated in dogmatically correct Marxist idiom.

"If the struggle is seen as hopeless in human terms, it is likely that it may be reconceived on a sacred plane," in which victory is rendered possible, against all odds, by a Higher Will.[15] For all their avowed rationalism, the Communists began almost immediately after their October takeover to design quasi-religious mores and social routines based on familiar attributes of the Russian Orthodox tradition and the Church, supplemented with uncanny ingredients of paganism.[16] Bolsheviks and their supporters also sought to adapt the traditional culture to the new Soviet reality, so as to explain the revolution's messianic goals to the public at large: "The Egypt of our time is capitalism. The Pharaoh of our days is the capital. From this slavery the mankind will be taken out. By whom?" The answer: Karl Marx and the "creators, leaders, heroes, martyrs, fighters of socialism—this is the 'Moses' of our time. He will save the humanity."[17]

After 1924, the Bolsheviks set out to create a cult of the "immortal Lenin," a Communist deity and a holy relic. Stalin supervised the great effort to solidify "Leninism," as he called the new religion after "the official idol."[18] The Soviets placed their holy being in the mausoleum—against Lenin's word as to where he wished to be buried—not to give the deceased a final rest, but to invest him with a semi-divine image. Painter Kazimir Malevich proposed that Lenin's body be housed in a cube, a symbol of the fourth dimension; "every working Leninist should have a cube at home to establish a symbolic material basis for a cult," he said. Malevich "envisioned a complete cult, with music and poetry, and Lenin corners instead of icon corners in Russian homes." The cube would be the Soviet equivalent of "a popular fad based on the mystique of the Great Pyramid at Giza."[19]

The personification of the new religion, its archpriest as well as emblem, Lenin took the place of honor in the "red corner" of every place of employment, of every school and kindergarten, among a motley of other sanctified Soviet objects and symbols—banners, uniforms, red stars, and the obligatory sickle and hammer. Soviet Russia was to become a country-wide temple, in which the Communist clerics perfected new rituals, gradually extending to all aspects of life—from countless marches, demonstrations, and festivities to weddings, births, and deaths. The private sphere was withering away; the environment that sanctified and promoted the sacredness of the collective advanced, most importantly, all-pervasive and belligerent nihilism with regard to the individual. And misanthropy expressed itself in the denial of a basic value and meaning in man's existence separate from the organism of the state.

Hatred had reigned within the underground culture, constructed by radical leaders specifically to sustain their subordinates' aggression and to avert any misgivings about proclaimed goals. "Out there," outside the artificially built and closed group, were only enemies, the conscript was given to understand—anyone and anything in the larger world, in which a revolutionary lived "only for the purpose of bringing about its speedy and total destruction.... He must hate everyone and everything in it with an equal hatred," Nechaev had demanded.[20] But comradely love within the conflicted, crime-ridden, and deeply hostile clandestine milieu was also but a late-day myth, aimed to romanticize violence. While designing for the Bolshevik state the machinery of mass murder, the outcasts projected the accumulated loathing and self-hatred onto a society in which they were finally in the position to build an officially sponsored infrastructure for animosity.

It was to be based on fear, a prerequisite for hatred. Now, it was the imperialists and the international bourgeoisie, represented by a random number of "fourteen hostile states," which were allegedly out to destroy the "young socialist republic." When it turned out that the West was not so determined to do away with Communism on its earliest stages, the Bolsheviks provoked enmity by obsessively instigating revolutionary outbursts—from Germany to China. The West remained as compulsive in its tolerance, with one country after another granting diplomatic recognition to the USSR. In the meantime, the growing propaganda machine taught Soviet citizens to hate foreign and domestic foes, new ones being constantly invented. Against them, only the revolutionary Power came to epitomize deliverance. Truly pathological was the content of a poetic anthology *Cheka Smile*, published in Tiflis, whose author sang hymns to death:

> There is not greater joy, there is no better music
> Than a crushing sound of smashed bones and lives.
> This is why, when our eyes are yearning
> And the passion in our breasts begins to boil violently,
> I wish to scribble on your verdict:
> The intrepid: "To the wall! To be executed![21]

Like a primordial idolatrous cult, the insurgency demanded human sacrifice—the lives of its adversaries, along with those of its zealous adherents, who believed that their offerings were the only way to salvation. "We will go to battle bravely—for the Soviet power; and we will die for it—*every single one of us,*" ran a favorite song of the Red Army soldiers. Red was the color of blood to be spilled for the cause:

> The people's flag is deepest red, It shrouded oft our martyred dead, And ere their limbs grew stiff and cold, Their hearts blood dyed its every fold.
>
> . . .
>
> With heads uncovered swear we all To bear it onward till we fall; Come dungeons dark or gallows grim, This song shall be our parting hymn.[22]

Lenin and other Bolshevik leaders acclaimed the heroes' "sacrificial death,"[23] and Soviet citizens were quick to discern obligatory morbidity as a new party line. Some even found it comical: "Comrades!," a would-be Communist leader opened his speech, in a well-liked joke "Yesterday we stood on the edge of the abyss. But, today we have taken a giant step forward!"

With sacrificial death accentuated as the most precious contribution, the revolution was self-destructive, as well as destructive—suicidal, in the final analysis. It also harbored a deep-seated paradox. Extremists in power sought to reaffirm their flimsy, would-be existence through new collective values and meanings. The cult-like environment sustained this form of symbolic immortality and supplied "a continuous opportunity for the experience of transcendence."[24] At the same time, theirs was an effort to fabricate a sociocultural climate to champion death and undercut life at its very core.

"Allah, deal with the Jews, your enemies and the enemies of Islam. Deal with the Crusaders, and America, and Europe behind them"—this theme has been most common in the Fatah and Hamas sermons since at least September 2000.[25] The militant leaders in the PA today, having not yet succeeded in establishing their state, have managed to institute slaying as a defining societal attribute. Like the Bolsheviks, they are perpetually at work to create the conditions of internal strife, which the extremists exploit to generate hatred and direct the accumulated aggression of the mistreated people at the outside enemy—lest the victims blame the real culprits. Privately, Arab intellectuals admit, "We live in a culture of death."[26] Perhaps nothing is a better symbol of such a culture than a favorite name, "Jihad," for which there was a Bolshevik-era analogy, a list of trendy names for Russian baby girls: "Revoliutsionera," "Ideia," and, of course, "Terrora."[27]

"For the Palestinian people death has become an industry," boast its official managers.[28] The hate speech is an element of the gigantic enterprise of indoctrination, extending from Iran and Saudi Arabia to PA.[29] "O brother believers, the criminals, the terrorists are the Jews... They are the ones who must be butchered and killed," says a preacher, apparently convinced that his audience would not mind his claims' inner contradiction; "Allah will torture them at your hands."[30] This speech followed the October 12, 2000, lynching of two Israeli reservists in Ramallah, when the murderers entertained the crowds by dragging the mutilated bodies around the city chained to a car. The carnage reached a climax when one of the slayers boasted his blood-stained palms to a maddened mob of "engineered haters"—a scene reminiscent of Orwell's macabre festivities during "Hate Weeks."[31]

Since then, the episode has been repeatedly reenacted in Palestinian school plays as part of the campaign to initiate children in death culture early in their lives. A home video shows several children acting out a beheading.[32] Watching, we are left to guess whether in kindergartens and summer camps "educators" smear children's palms with red paint or real blood to represent that of their "dead friends.'"[33] "What is your most lofty aspiration?" six-year-olds in Hamas attire are asked during a kindergarten graduation ceremony; they are trained to scream in unison, "Death for the sake of Allah!"[34]

Enculturation in bloodshed aims to prepare children for martyrdom. "Allah had honored our youth... by choosing you and by choosing from among you the Shahids," Sheikh Mudeiris stated in a sermon on May 2, 2003.[35] A shahid in Jerusalem "is worth 70 Shahids in a place other than this good land," elaborates Sheikh Ibrahim Mudeiris; "blessings to those who wage [jihad] with their body and are killed for the sake of Allah."[36] Preachers tell the youngsters that those who die as martyrs feel no pain and receive rewards in the afterlife; even when a shahid "turns into torn organs that spread all over, in order to meet Allah, Muhammad, and his friends, it would not be a loss," states Sheikh Isma'il Aal Radhwan.[37]

Posters in kindergartens scream, "The children are holy martyrs of tomorrow."[38] Hamas-run TV produces and broadcasts a kids' program in which a Mickey Mouse look-alike character named Farfur teaches the young viewers to pray until "world leadership under Islamic rule" is established. On June 29, 2007, in the final episode of this child drama, Farfur is beaten to death by an Israeli and becomes a shahid, joining the other glorious martyrs.[39] Assaud the Rabbit takes his place on the Al-Aqsa TV in Gaza and promises children to "eat the Jews" and kill the Westerners, "the cowardly infidels... Criminals... Criminals."[40] A puppet character threatens another dummy, which personifies the U.S. president: "I will kill you, Bush, because that is your fate." Then a stub: "Ahhh, I killed him!"[41] Children's books are filled with similar messages.[42] "We don't encourage our children to hate the Jews. We just tell them... that the Jews killed their families, and they reach the conclusion to hate the Jews on their own," explains an unsuccessful suicide terrorist, who, although imprisoned, dreams of having children some day—to bring them up as shahids.[43]

In the PA, an entire communication network exists for the purpose of producing "tragic news events." Raw footage produces "Pallywood"—media manufacturing of bloody incidents, testifying to Israel's intentional targeting of civilians and other "crimes against humanity."[44] A vivid example is the alleged killing of a Palestinian boy, Mohammed al-Dura (a Durah), in September 2000, whose poster and TV image the forgers used to brainwash children across the PA-controlled areas into *shahada*.[45] The Zionist agents are accused of spreading food that contains cancer-causing ingredients and of deliberately poisoning air and water. The Israelis are blamed for selling sports shoes that "cause the wearer to become paralyzed" and perfumes that lead to drug addiction, as well as of distributing AIDS, "sexually stimulating drops and chewing gum," so as to "weaken and destroy" the Palestinian youth. Film clips of official PA TV have been fabricated to show the alleged victims of depleted uranium and nerve gas attacks convulsing and vomiting. Israelis are said to have performed Nazi-like experiments on Palestinian prisoners: "Many of the male and female inmates received injections from needles...which caused their hair and facial hair to fall out permanently...others lost their sanity, or their mental condition is constantly deteriorating...and some are suffering from infertility." Reenacted for the cameras are also scenes of rape by Israeli soldiers.[46]

"Pallywood" turns Israel into a boogeyman: "Then the Israeli officer pounded [3-year old] Muhammad's head with his riffle's stock, and his warm blood was sprinkled upon [his 6-year old brother] Khaled's hands"—so ends a fairytale, a required reading for third-graders in Iran.[47] Outside the PA, the mass-scale vilification campaign produces public outcry and mass support for the Intifada. Another byproduct of the organized deceit is the possibility to attribute to the victim the brutal intentions of the victimizer. Such model projections were broadcast for months from the Iranian television sets, when every Monday millions of Persian- and Arabic-speakers viewed the Sahar 1 TV series *For You, Palestine*, or *Zahra's Blue Eyes*, a graphic story about the Israeli kidnappings of Palestinian children—to be used for body parts.[48] This blood libel, originally intended for Muslim viewers, has recently reached Europe.[49]

The image of a schoolboy waving his revolver and shouting revolutionary slogans left a striking impression on the Russian public around 1905. It entered into popular humor in a morbid anecdote: when a schoolteacher asked his pupils to name the greatest inventor of the century, one boy eagerly volunteered, "Browning!"[50] "I think that soon children will play revolution,"[51] predicted an oppositionist in 1904. To be sure, by 1905, nothing was more fun than to place at the front door of a police officer a "bomb" made from a watermelon painted black and stuffed with garbage.[52] At the time, however, the Russian extremists could only dream of terrorist schools to educate children as future fighters.[53] Presently, in the climate of endless violence in Afghanistan, such schools and camps have been graduating young Tajik refugees, as well as scores of Afghan and Pakistani children, who become suicide bombers sometimes as early as the age of 11.[54] Training is rigorous, as shown on the April 2007 video that captures a 12-year-old on behest of the Talibans practicing beheadings by actually decapitating a Pakistani "traitor."[55] In the PA terrorist instruction is a segment of a regular military summer camp curriculum, in which professional combatants coach boys and girls and indoctrinate them in hatred for Israel, the United States, and the UN.[56]

"The world and its leadership should hear my message," runs an ad in the PA-owned daily, published in honor of the first birthday of a boy named Jihad Al-Aksa Dia Fauzi Maala, also celebrating the first anniversary of the Intifada.

Next to a photograph of a beautiful baby is the suicidal death threat: "we, the Palestinian children, are the timebombs around the neck of the occupation."[57] "Tomorrow's Pioneers' army will redeem the Messenger [Muhammad], with their possessions and their blood," incites a host of the Hamas TV program for the young audience.[58] Such communications are a step forward from the Soviet conditioning of children to emulate the mythologized figure of 14-year-old martyr Pavlik Morozov, who did not spare his father's life, or his own, for the sake of the Marxist ideal. Still, there was an entire tradition of the "young pioneer heroes"—homegrown Russian variants of shahada—with rites and folklore, accentuating especially the graphic details of torture the child-heroes suffered at the hands of the enemy. To be sure, the Communists were not motivated by expectations of otherworldly rewards; while not Jihad-proper, their version of self-sacrifice entailed fascination with agony synonymous to torments described in Lives of Saints. The legacy highlighted all essential attributes of a "culture of martyrdom,"[59] to be concocted by contemporary terrorists in power.

"Until the final issue [between capitalism and communism] is decided, the state of awful war will continue," Lenin had pledged in 1921,[60] and for the sake of acclimating Soviet children to the idea, adult professionals introduced paramilitary uniforms in schools; martial training from grade 6; parades, special greetings, and insignia; as well as endless psychological reprogramming. "Our entire life is struggle" was a refrain of the official song.

The word "struggle" pervaded Soviet routines and lexicon: children were required to struggle for good grades, for exemplary conduct, for neat handwriting, for clean hands and ears, and for the right to call themselves heirs of those who had fallen in the class struggle of the past. "Only through conflict, solely on the blood of the hated class, the luminous communist tomorrow can be erected" was the punch-line of new education.[61] It underscored the totalist belief in a cosmic war.[62]

The Soviet pedagogical manual for librarians working with children, published in 1920, considered the following real-life issue: "A 12-year old girl is afraid of blood...It is necessary to work out a list of books...which would force the girl to give up the instinctual revulsion for the red terror."[63] Communist writers and poets composed a colossal body of brainwashing "children's literature"—of woeful quality, analogous to "A Letter from a Shahid to His Mother" by Abdul Badi Iraq, an imaginary farewell of the suicide bomber:

> My Dear Mother,
>
> ...I wrapped my body with determination, with hopes and with bombs.
> I asked [reaching] towards Allah and the fighting homeland.
> The [explosive] belt makes me fly, strengthens me to make haste.
> I calm it [the explosive], we should stay steadfast, we have not yet reached [our destination].
> I freed/launched myself; I freed/launched myself, [detonated myself] like lava burning old legends and vanity,

> I freed/launched my body, all my pains and oppression, towards the packs of beasts ...
> The wedding is the wedding of the land.
> Sound a cry of joy, O mother, I am the groom.[64]

Official Hamas and Fatah eulogies, television broadcasts, the naming of soccer tournaments after suicide terrorists, monument inaugurations and school ceremonies, the writing of essays and poems in class, and religious sermons have the common denominator of depicting the suicide mission as an act of ultimate virtue. Islamic University in Gaza, *alma mater* of many terrorists, has held a competition for the best martyr's farewell testament.[65] To extol self-sacrifice for Allah and the Palestinian people is the purpose of media interviews with parents of suicide bombers, in which moms and dads "praise their child's act and call for others to follow."[66] In July 2009 the Hamas TV children's program *Tomorrow Pioneers* aired a special broadcast in which the children of Rim Riashi were invited to the studio to watch and comment on a video reenactment of their mother's 2004 suicide bombing.[67] The televised event was in keeping with Sheikh Mudeiris's May 2, 2003, statement: "We have the right to congratulate the Shahids' families, not to extend condolences and sorrow."[68]

In the culture of death, "every Palestinian mother or wife must be proud and lift up her head because Allah chose her husband or her son to be among the Shahids. This is the best thing in this world," said Umm Nidal Farhat, a Palestinian woman who had lost two sons to jihad, in an interview published in the Israeli-Arab *Kul Al-Arab* weekly on February 27, 2004. "I always longed to be the mother of a Shahid," she confessed, the way an ambitious American parent would acknowledge that she always wanted her child to go to Harvard to validate her life. "[As far as I am concerned], let all my sons be Shahids."[69] It is impossible to ascertain how many Arab mothers are indeed proud of their young martyrs, who have become shahids; it is highly doubtful that the majority of parents are so brainwashed as to rejoice about their death. However passionately some express in public the officially required ecstasy on their son's "wedding day," privately they mourn the loss and try to keep their other adolescents from engaging in violence.[70] The bereaved father of a suicide bomber complained in a newspaper interview that ideologists of terror never dispatch their own sons and daughters to death: "Who gave them religious justification to send our children to blow themselves up?," he cried and called the terrorist leaders "snakes."[71] Still, "over time a cult of martyrdom that generated posters, videos, songs, and societal glorification grew up in Palestinian society,"[72] in which children do serve as a means to bring prestige to their parents—in ways concomitant with the values of their sociocultural context, that of obligatory veneration of suicide terrorism.

Their self-sacrifice is rewarded—sometimes in very tangible ways—already in this world, in fact. It is an open secret that families of suicide bombers are paid for their missions, and although many claim to have received no more than a lump sum of $300, some collect up to $25,000 subsidies after a suicide attack.[73] According to Wafa al-Bas, her parents had known of her intention to become a shahida and accepted both her fear of being a burden to the family and her wish to help through "the financial compensation" from Fatah[74]—to supplement the enhanced prestige in the neighborhood and the moral satisfaction of having raised a martyr. "Blessings for whoever has raised his sons on the education of Jihad and Martyrdom" and "put a belt of explosives on his body or on his sons' and plunged into the midst of the Jews," repeatedly preached Sheikh Ibrahim Madhi, one of the most admired imams; "shame and remorse on whoever refrained from raising his children on Jihad."[75] There is no doubt that "these educational methods have influenced many Palestinian children who express their wish to become Shahids."[76]

Polls show that between 72 and 80 percent of children living in the PA yearn to die as martyrs,[77] morbid ideation being an integral component of their worldview. "We don't want this world," affirms Yussra, an 11-year-old victim of indoctrination-in-death: "We want the Afterlife. We benefit not from this life, but from the Afterlife.... Every Palestinian child... says, O Lord, I would like to become a *shahid*."[78]

"Let's play the Shahid Game!" Nada, a seven-year-old girl, says to her friends. The children bring an old sheet, spread it on the ground, and then begin to argue over who will be the shahid. Six-year-old Fa'iz says, "You were the Shahid yesterday, today it's my turn! I'm younger than you. I will be the one to die!"[79]

Psychologists agree that before the assailants are capable of murder, they must undergo the process of dehumanization—"that state of mind where the structural and dynamic features central to being human are seriously interfered with, often to the extent that the individual stops feeling, and behaving, like a human being."[80] In order to achieve this state—a key juncture in forging the terrorists—their dispatches encourage and condition them to dehumanize the enemy, to turn him into "a stereotype of negative qualities," to "satanize" him, or derogate him into the rank of inanimate, subhuman, or nonhuman object of eradication.[81] A preferred technique of death cult ideologists has been to portray terrorist targets as animals.

"Is it wrong to kill a bloodthirsty tiger, who splits chests open with its claws and tears people's heads off with its jaws?" asked anarchist Michele Angiolillo who in 1897 killed Antonio Cánovas del Castillo, a leading Spanish conservative politician and historian; "is it a crime to crush a poisonous reptile?" In line with Nechaev's "Catechism," which referred to "brutes in high positions," animals to "be exploited in every possible way" and "transformed into slaves,"[82] the radical publications in early-20th-century Russia developed a motley of clichés to denigrate the autocracy as a predatory creature, "the rapacious kite that tears to pieces the Russian people" and "drinks their blood." There developed an entire subculture aimed at dehumanizing enemies of the revolution under a collective label of "beasts." A typical example of this genre is a satirical poem, "Two Beasts," whose hero was Baron A. V. Kaul'bars, commander of the Odessa military district, notorious for his repressive measures in the area overrun with anarchy:

> The panther was the jungle's plague.
> Kaul'bars was Odessa's rogue.
> ...
> One shot men, the other ate:
> Why should they have a different fate?
> ...
> You mean the panther is a beast
> And Kaul'bars is a man, at least?
> ...
> Nowadays, it is my stand,
> A general cannot be a man.
> Nowadays, if you insist,
> A general is just a beast....[83]

Dehumanization of the enemy is exonerating; it spares the victimizer feelings of guilt and remorse; it frees him from self-perception as a murderer who must find ethical justification for the legitimacy of his acts. Terrifying monsters are ideal objects of disgust, but even "in a case of a just grievance, our hatred comes less from a wrong done to us than from the consciousness of our helplessness, inadequacy, and cowardice—in other words from self-contempt" and humiliation. Much like homicidal sociopaths, political murderers go to great pains to work out the utmost hatred for victims of their cruelty. Architects of the death culture visualize their victims as "depraved creatures, deserving...extermination"[84] and persistently associate dehumanization with self-defense.

Allah has described Jews as "apes and pigs, the calf-worshipers," Sheikh Madhi has insisted in his sermons and television speeches; "whoever can fight them with a sword or a knife, should go out; whoever can fight them with his hands, should go out" because "the Jews have exposed their fangs."[85] He is one in the army of inciters of violence against "the snakes" and "the rats of the world," who "want to drink the blood of Muslims."[86] "We saw how they...eat life."[87]

On the other hand, to earn a beastly label, the terrorists' enemy does not have to have a distinct national identity: in their licentiousness "the Europeans stand lower than dogs and pigs," has declared a Rotterdam Imam Khalil el-Moumni, who has encouraged physical attacks against homosexuals because "if the sickness of homosexuality spreads itself, everyone can become infected."[88] For his part, Ali Ghufron (better known by his nom-de-guerre, Mukhlas), a perpetrator of the October 12, 2002, Bali bombing, considered all Westerners to be "dirty animals and insects that need to be wiped out."[89]

Various adherents of ideological totalism in the 20th century regarded violence as a "mode of purification,"[90] when the perpetrator "is cured" by sacrificing himself, just as his healthy cleanness is restored through destruction of the enemy.[91] Lenin elucidated the redemptive purpose of cleansing "Russia's soil of all harmful insects, of scoundrel fleas, bedbugs"; Stalin referred to the annihilation of the would-be enemies of the state as a "purge"; the Nazis sought "to clean all impurities" and to decontaminate the body of Germany by making it *judenrein*—literally, "pure of Jews." "Israel . . . is a cancer," preach Hamas religious leaders,[92] and suicide terrorists who follow them view their self-sacrifice as purifying. Paradoxically, both the impure and the pure share fate in death, "the former as contagion-bearing vermin, the latter as saints."[93]

Nechaev maligned the contemporary "filthy social order,"[94] and Ivan Pavlov, a Maximalist theoretician, echoed the theme of contamination in his 1907 publication, *The Purification of Mankind.* Pavlov divided humankind into "ethical races." The race of predators, including the authorities and the capitalists, had acquired so many negative traits that it must be isolated as "morally inferior to our animal predecessors: the vile characteristic of the gorilla and the orangutan progressed and developed in it to proportions unprecedented in the animal world." The superior race was that of the revolutionaries, and especially the terrorists, who fought against these subhumans, in comparison with whom no beasts "appeared to be monsters." The most threatening feature of the predator race, according to Pavlov, was that their vile qualities inevitably transmitted to succeeding generations, so that the children of the oppressors and exploiters were bound "to exhibit the same malice, cruelty, meanness, rapacity, and greed" as their parents. It followed that in order to save, or purify, mankind from the menace of the rapidly multiplying forces of the bestial degenerates, their entire race must be exterminated lest they took over the world.[95] Pavlov's party colleague M. A. Engel'gardt calculated—anticipating Zinov'ev's annihilation proposal quite precisely, a discrepancy in a couple of million notwithstanding—that for socialism to take root in Russia, it would be essential to eliminate no fewer than 12,000,000 counterrevolutionaries.[96] The Nazi lexicon, replete with microbes and bacteria, was, as it turns out, a reinvention of the wheel. To compensate, the Nazis indulged in the opportunity to gas hundreds of thousands with Zyklon B, a widely used decontamination agent.

"Having a human body does not necessarily mean having a human mind," psychologists note specifically with regard to terrorists, whose lack of empathy evinces a salient sign of dehumanization.[97] By continuously habituating those under their control to homicide, militant leaders rob them of their humanity, which presupposes ability to empathize with suffering. Orwell had envisaged children begging to be allowed to watch a public hanging; we recall his forewarning when we see victims of glaring child abuse in Palestinian cities photographed as witnesses and participants in the slaughters of "Zionist collaborators"[98]

The first victims of terrorism then—even before it has a chance to strike against the others—are terrorists themselves, the way the initial victims of Nazism were the Germans, dehumanized and turned into homicidal tools.

Before the SS officers actively involved themselves in the process of torturing and killing children, terrible things had to happen to the torturers, so that, deprived of fundamental empathy, they would not see a toddler as a human child: "It's about experiencing the total freedom of barbarism—freedom even from human nature, which says, Love children, and Love life."[99] The constructors of a murderous culture sustain it with the help of the people they have damaged on the deepest level—killed as individuals and refashioned into instruments of death.

"Our task," outlined Nechaev for the army of militant nihilists, is destruction—"terrible, total, universal."[100] Such passion for apocalyptic annihilation surpasses a specific tradition or time period. "If we analyze the psychic reality of these men," notes Erich Fromm in relation to the Nazis, "we find that they were destroyers and not revolutionaries. They hated not only their enemies, they hated life itself."[101] Hazani includes the alienated, miserable, frustrated, and angry terrorists in Russia and elsewhere in "the Internationale of thanatophiles, of which Nazi Germany was a distinguished member."[102] They are engaged in explicit or implicit death-worship, with "modern secular instances of thanatophilia"—love of mortality and ruin—carrying "religious overtones."[103]

"Those who replace us will have to build on the ruins, amid the deadly silence of a graveyard," promised *Pravda* on July 13, 1921.[104] Moreover, the magnificent necropolis would extend beyond the borders of the isolated state of the former Russian empire. As a religion, the Bolshevik death cult had to be not only eternal, but also ubiquitous—like that of the Nazis, who considered their ideology to be of "universal... everlasting importance," a "sacred foundation," as Hitler wrote in *Mein Kampf*.[105] The Soviets were committed "to the vision of a total salvation in this world"[106] as a result of a worldwide revolution, with terror eradicating every sign of heresy. Their "world revolution" was but an effort to promulgate militant messianism as far and wide as it was allowed to penetrate. Immediate political objectives aside, this was why the Soviet Union sponsored terrorism worldwide.[107]

Worldwide is also radical Islamists' predilection for death. "We tell them," the Jews and the Christians, Mufti Sheikh Ikrimeh Sabri declared at the Al-Aqsa Mosque in Jerusalem, "in as much as you love life, the Muslim loves death and martyrdom."[108] "We desire Death, as you desire Life," affirm extremist politicians in Gaza.[109] "The Americans are fighting so they can live and enjoy the material things of life," said Taliban official Mohammad Hussein Mostassed, "but we are fighting so we can die in the cause of God." Having killed 191 and wounded at least 1,800 in a 10-bomb explosion on four packed morning commuter trains in Madrid on March 11, 2004, the terrorists reiterated, "You love life, but we love death."[110]

Some experts trace the origins of the death cult to 633, just one year following the death of Muhammad, when the Muslim general Khalid ibn al-Walid, nicknamed "Sword of Allah," had entered Persia in the first phase of the great Arab conquests of the 7th century. Writing to the governor of a frontier district, Dast Maysan, Walid demanded: "submit to Islam and be safe... else you will have only yourself to blame for the consequences, for I bring the men who desire death as ardently as you desire life."[111] "Life itself is only a death running its course. A person's clothes are his shroud; his house is his grave, his life his death, and his death his true life...Life is a sickness whose cure is death," wrote the 11th-century nihilist Abul Ala al-Ma'arri.[112] Still, a widespread scholarly opinion holds that whereas death-worship and martyrdom were hardly the highlights of early Islam,[113] they have become "defining features of modern totalitarianism."[114]

Whatever the case, the Ku Klux Klan–like disguise of the Hamas militants during armed rallies indicates cult rituals. Like Hitler's frolics, their tense acting out contributes to the theatricality of "performance violence" we have come to expect in a death culture. Invariably, it strives to hide the triviality of malice behind the hysterical and the pompous—a manufactured grandiosity. The ostentatious spectacle seeks to impress by tasteless exaggeration and special effects, frightening in their blatancy, like the message of the Nazi parades and the September 11 *dance macabre.*

A key attribute of radical Islamism and of other forms of totalism is "the aestheticization of death"[115] The Bolsheviks' compulsiveness about the need to incarcerate the lifeless body of Lenin leaves an eerie feeling that, as far as they were concerned, death as the final phase of living was somehow incomplete and required further structuring. The Soviets thus ventured beyond death, seeking to "kill it," as an integral element in life's course. They detested its spontaneous mobility, "filled with ambiguities," offers Jungian psychologist John Haule; they wanted "a static thing, where every piece of reality is pinned down,"[116] the non-being in its ultimate manifestation. Like other destroyers, they could not suffer the exuberance of unstructured dynamic aliveness—the complex world of colors and sounds, filled with contradictions and ironies—in dissonance with the tedium and single-mindedness of their tomblike selves.[117] "Aestheticization" that "shrouds death in glory" enhanced their effort to overcome anxiety, Hazani suggests.[118]

The aesthetics of their pallid environment stamped by its builders' projected desolate and stale, morbid inner state reflected the wide-ranging entanglement of the dead-in-life. The attempt was to overpower anxiety by regulating the spontaneous and the transient—fleeting time and motion—to gain eternity, even if it had to be the eternity of a graveyard. The stock-still dominated Stalin's and Hitler's visual representations of death, monstrous constructions in the capitals, concrete symbols of the cult. Today such aesthetics are conspicuous in the Hezbollah and Hamas initiation ceremonies, in which the participants are photographed as statues frozen in the Nazi salute.[119]

"Hitler's talents as stage manager reached their summit when the object of celebration was death...he could always invent impressive effects for funeral ceremonies,"[120] marketing the splendor of death's mythology. The terrorists' effort to present their struggle as drama is complicated by the fact that their audiences are desensitized to brutality; a regular act of political murder no longer sells well. Still, there is always room for a creative experiment with theatrical effects of inspired butchery, such as broadcasted beheading rituals. Muslims who have resisted being forged into instruments of murder call videotaped decapitations "real-life theaters of shame."[121]

On stage is a masked terrorist, playing the executioner; around him are several accomplices with guns and knives. He reads a list of demands before a TV camera. The victim is on his knees, weeping and begging for mercy. The viewer sees his agony as the leading actor of the horrid reality show severs his head, while other participants chant "Allahu Akhbar." The slayer displays his bloody trophy, and together the terrorists recite verses from the Qur'an.[122] A crucial selling point is that their bliss in the moment of murder resembles sexual ecstasy, exposing also the megalomania typical for serial killers: the act of turning a "human being into a terrified, helpless victim of violence, physical torture, and mutilation is charged with high sadomasochistic drama."[123]

Camus has noted that "the sinister excites," arousing "a thrill that sometimes takes an overly sexual form."[124] Ideology-loaded brutality may have a particular attraction in revealing the "pornography of torture" and "sexualized joy of humiliating violence,"[125] as it substitutes the coarseness of physical nature with the crudeness of destruction, which is sublimated by association with a lofty cause. With the Red Terror temporarily halted, in the early 1920s Soviet Russia experimented with "sexual communism," which included "nude marches, group sex, and free-love leagues."[126] Equally entrancing must have been a New York newspaper photograph of "women in Madrid parading naked in public, except for skimpy faux suicide-bomb belts worn as bikinis. Such were the titillations of murder and suicide."[127] Girls with guns as "the ultimate desire and fear fantasy of a patriarchal, inhibited society" may at least partially account for the allure of the Baader-Meinhof Gang in Germany.[128]

"Every time I put on my ski mask, I feel the warmth of the proletarian community around me," Professor Negri said, describing his feelings about partaking in terrorist enterprises, side by side with his comrades in the Workers' Autonomy. He said that he was bothered neither by the pain of his adversary nor by his personal risk: "rather, it fills me with feverish excitement, like a man waiting for his lover."[129] Unconsciously, Negri described the tendency for "erotization of death."

"Politicized religions—and the religious warriors in particular—are obsessed with sex," which is related more closely to political violence than is generally recognized. The extremists are "powered by a sexual imaginary"[130] and consistently employ deviant erotica for their objectives. Leaders of the Baader-Meinhof Gang, whose membership was divided evenly between men and women, relied on a unique blend of pornography, group sex, and revolutionary rhetoric to indoctrinate their followers.[131] Dispatchers might have exploited aggressiveness associated with throbbing gender confusion of a young Russian hermaphrodite to recruit him as an assassin.[132] Similarly predisposed to violence could have been the miserable Faiza Amal Jumaa, a 35-year-old woman whose appearance and behavior suggest a woman trapped in a man's body," a volunteer as a Hamas suicide bomber.[133]

The classic case of relying on sex for coercive recruitment involved the quasi-revolutionary Symbionese Liberation Army, which in 1974 made newspaper headlines after kidnapping Patricia (Patty) Hearst, the 19-year-old granddaughter of a newspaper magnate, in California. In compliance with the SLA extortion demands, the Hearst family donated six million dollars worth of food to the poor of the San Francisco Bay Area, but instead of freeing their hostage, the radicals sought to convert the young woman to their cause. They kept Hearst locked and blindfolded in a closet and repeatedly raped her to break her spirit. As a survival technique, she initially pretended to accept their ideology and began to take part in group sex "bonding" routines. Within two months, she was a full-fledged member of the conspiracy and, under the adopted name Tania (a tribute to the wife of Che Guevara), played a role in a San Francisco bank robbery.[134]

Psychologists and philosophers have emphasized the proximity between Eros and Thanatos; Freud employed these concepts as poetic metaphors of the Greek mythology that exist side by side.[135] For those affected by thanatophilia, "Eros is displaced from woman to death," manifesting a fixation on the romanticized and "eroticized death . . . as opposed to the butchery of killing."[136] The individual and even a whole group may seek the legitimacy of death-worship by attaching it to, and rationalizing it with, a particular political idea.

The universality of thanatophilia is evident in suicidal ideation and expression—in words and deeds—by adherents of various epochs and cultures. Whether or not death-worship is the primary drive behind the lofty rhetoric of self-sacrifice must be determined on a case-to-case basis, except when we are dealing with a constructed cult of martyrdom "that trains kindergartners to become bombs, that fetishizes death, that sends people off joyfully to commit mass murder.[137] This cult attaches itself to a political cause but parasitically strangles it," as it strangulates the dream of a Palestinian state. "But that's the idea. Because the death cult is not really about the cause it purports to serve. It's about the sheer pleasure of killing and dying. It's about massacring people while in a state of spiritual loftiness."[138]

Its engineers envisage death as a defining feature of the collective identity, designed to consecrate and augment the status of the deity. It is entitled to perpetual human sacrifice, as clarifies an Islamist leader of Algeria Ali Benhadj: "If a faith, a belief, is not watered and irrigated by blood, it does not grow. It does not live. Principles are reinforced by sacrifices, suicide operations and martyrdom for Allah. Faith is propagated by counting up deaths every day, by adding up massacres and charnel-houses."[139]

"This is not exotic," says Paul Berman. "This is how the leaders of Germany used to speak, sixty years ago. Bolsheviks were not afraid to speak like that. . . . This is the totalitarian cult of death. *This* is a terrible thing that got underway more than eighty years ago."[140] Just over a hundred years ago—to be exact, modern terrorism had turned into thanatophilia, a contemporary form of totalist death-worship.

Epilogue

> How so! I plunge, plunge without fail
> My blood-black sabre into your soul.
> That art God neither wants nor wists,
> It leaps to the brain from Hell's black mists.
>
> Till heart's bewitched, till senses reel:
> With Satan I have struck my deal.
> He chalks the signs, beats time for me,
> I play the death march fast and free.
>
> —Karl Marx, "The Fiddler" (*Wild Songs*, 1837)

> Because ye have said, "We have made a covenant with death, and with hell are we at agreement; when the overflowing scourge shall pass through, it shall not come unto us; for we have made lies our refuge, and under falsehood have we hid ourselves."
>
> —Isaiah 28:15

A heap of bodies on the floor. They are compressed against one another so tightly that no one can move a limb without squashing a neighbor. Some sit literally on top of the others, and their bodies are doubled up, bent, and twisted. Those who have no place to sit stand—for hours. It is difficult to breathe; people gasp for hot air. From time to time, a woman, who has begun to "lose it"—so the others think—stands up and slowly starts to make her way around the bodies, as if in delirium. An armed man points an automatic rifle at her face and yells for her to sit. She flops down without looking, falling on someone, a child.

Small children, who had screamed for hours out of fear, now cry from hunger, older kids try to be brave. But anyone would have given up food for a drop of water; it is just around the corner, but their guards do not permit anyone to bring it. Mothers ask older boys to pee in empty baby bottles and offer their toddlers to try "beer." Most people have almost no clothes on; even teenage girls have stripped to their underpants—the heat is seething; it is like being inside an oven.

When guards get bored, they entertain themselves by mocking their prisoners and by teasing children. They let one drink and refuse water to others; they grab milk bottles as women try to feed their babies; they give children chocolate and say that it was poisoned. The guards laugh and film themselves with their victims.

These are not familiar scenes from the Holocaust. Nor is it a replay of *Sophie's Choice*, when the captors allowed 11 women to leave with their babies but did not permit them to take their other children to safety. This happened only several years ago, when Beslan School No.1 became a mini-replica of a concentration camp. The Nazis, devoted clergymen of a death cult, kept excellent records of their abundant sacrifices—on paper and in photographs. The death-worshippers inside the school shot a video to commemorate death's triumphant entrance into postmodernity.[1]

For a while after all captives had been herded into the gym, the children could not calm down, recalled teacher Alik Tsagolov: "There was horrible screaming and yelling around. The bandits came up to me, pointed an automatic rifle, and threatened to shoot me, if children did not shut up. And thus they repeatedly 'hushed' the kids—by threatening to kill." The older kids soaked their shirts in water in the toilet and wrung a few drops into the small children's open palms. "I will shoot you all with such great pleasure!" screamed one terrorist, as the kids cried, hugged one another, and said their last goodbyes.[2]

They ordered, "Sit down and if you make any noise, we will kill 20 children," 10-year-old Georgy Farniyev later told a BBC correspondent. The journalist noted that the boy kept repeating a phrase that he had said to himself for three days of captivity again and again, like a mantra: "Stay as quiet as a mouse.... As quiet as a mouse."

"Lord, help me!" whispered a 10th-grader, but a terrorist heard him: "The Lord has nothing to do with this. Pray to Allah!" he screamed.[3] Other hostage-holders tore off the children's baptismal crosses and laughed: "Pray to whoever you want. Those who will get out of here alive are beloved by Allah." "I will personally kill you," said a captor to Islam Hadikov, a Muslim boy who thought he would not be harmed by a coreligionist. A witness said that it might have been the same terrorist who shot a 15-year-old in the back as he tried to help a girl wounded in the explosion.

The only terrorist who survived and was captured "was the most sadistic," testified a former hostage, Kazbek Dzarasov. "I saw him come to the gym just to beat children. He punched a 10-year-old in the stomach with a foot;

he broke another boy's collar bone with a rifle butt." Other "bandits made us wipe the blood off the floor with our aprons," recounted 12-year-old survivor Dzerasa Szestelova, after the terrorists had singled out and executed fathers, adult men whom they considered a threat, and then forced older children to drag the bodies across the gym and dump them out a second-story window. Stress and sleep deprivation might have caused the criminals' hysterical outbursts and flare-ups of anger; they "were suffering from withdrawal symptoms which are usually accompanied by aggressiveness and uncontrollable behaviour," deputy prosecutor general of Russia's southern federal district was quoted as explaining by Interfax: "their extreme brutality could...have been spurred on by the fact that some of them had run out of drugs."[4]

We will probably never find out the reason for the first blast inside the school, but in a way, it does not matter: the longer the hostage crisis lasted, the greater was the chance for a catastrophe; one of the explosive devices had to go off sooner or later. A bomb that the terrorists sloppily attached to the basketball hoop did not fall down for two days by sheer miracle. On the third day it did.

Professor Tazret Gatagov was the first doctor to enter the building. In his diary he described what he saw inside:

> The entire floor is covered with burnt bodies, body parts, debris—a meter-and-a-half tall mound. My eyes grasp pictures from hell. Here is a woman in her last convulsion holding onto her toddler...Next to this, a child's hand and leg. There lays on a smoldering board the head of another child...Half of the head of a woman, whose right hand is holding her hair—all black from the ashes....Everywhere there are bits and pieces of children's holiday clothes, kids' shoes, aprons, ribbons, school supplies. Every inch of the gym—fragments of ripped and charred bodies of children and adults...I walked the roads of the Second World War as a reconnaissance unit commander, but never had I seen such a horrifying picture of mass destruction of women and children.[5]

Many Beslan residents blame the Russian security forces for an utter disregard for human cost during the botched rescue effort, when numerous hostages lost their lives in "friendly fire." The federal authorities have never acknowledged that their proverbial incompetence was in part to blame for the Beslan bloodbath, just as they have not recognized that the gas they used against the Chechens during the October 23, 2002, liberation mission at the Dubrovka theater in Moscow "liberated" 130 hostages not only in the literal meaning of the word. Yet whatever the Russians' "ineptitude in responding to the attack, the essential nature of this act was in the act itself"—that "a team of human beings could go into a school, live with hundreds of children for a few days, look them in the eyes and hear their cries, and then blow them up."[6]

In the chaos that followed the explosion, the survivors ran away from the school, while "the combatants fired at hostages, as if they were targets in a shooting gallery." Numerous witnesses report that to the end, the terrorists strove to inflict as much death as possible. To the last moment, they used children as shields not because they had hopes of saving themselves but solely to increase the number of casualties.[7] Death alone was their final end.

On February 3, 2005, the CNN quoted Chechen warlord Basaev: in the future his men were planning to carry out operations similar to the school holdup. Beslan was not "an accident," but a "normal," if imperfectly handled, terrorist project, he said. Nor was it "a tragedy," maintained journalist David Brooks; "it was a carefully planned mass murder operation."[8]

The choice of targets in Beslan could not have been more explicit as the terrorists' message about the profundity of intended destruction, unscrupulous even in comparison to motiveless atrocities committed by terrorists a hundred years ago. To replace "Perovskaia, Sazonov, and Kaliaev who . . . thought about personal responsibility, the victim and the atonement, came individuals who shot without thinking . . . at those who just happened to be at hand . . . in an unlikely hour—a common policemen or a clerk."[9] A glaring point of comparison is a famous story associated with Ivan Kaliaev's initial abortive attempt to assassinate the Grand Duke Sergei. On February 2, 1905, the terrorist waited for the governor general to arrive at the Bolshoi Theater. Kaliaev was about to cast his bomb when he noticed inside the carriage Sergei's wife and his young nephews, children of the Grand Duke Pavel Aleksandrovich, and instantly opted to forsake an opportunity for a sensational act. The story might have been one of the myths created to romanticize political violence in Russia, but even an imaginary tale reveals at least a tenuous adherence to humanism. Though responsible for indiscriminate brutality and terrible loss of life among civilians, early 20th-century terrorists did not intentionally target children.

A century later, the health and safety of children are among the few impervious values in our skeptical postmodern reality. Correspondingly, terrorism as a brutal form of counterculture came to direct itself specifically against that which remains ethically and socially sacred. I would venture even that proponents of thanatophilia inevitably *had* to strike against children—the quintessence of vitality, of sparkling aliveness, the most vibrant and spontaneous of the living, the very symbol of life.

The mass murder in Beslan was not the first time that the terrorists have chosen children as targets. In a cross-border raid from Lebanon on May 15, 1974, gunmen from the Democratic Front for the Liberation of Palestine (DFLP), a faction affiliated with the PLO, took 102 students and their teachers hostage in the northern Israeli town of Ma'alot, which the children from Safed were visiting during a school trip. Some managed to escape by jumping out the windows, but when the IDF special unit assaulted the building, the terrorists detonated hand grenades and sprayed the 14- to 16-year-olds with machine-gun fire, killing 21 and wounding 66. On June 1, 2001, an Arab suicide bomber blasted himself and yet another 21 Israeli teenagers in the "Delphinarium" disco in Tel Aviv. In 2002, the Chechen terrorists chose the Dubrovka theater as their site specifically during the "Nord-Ost" musical based on the novel *The Two Captains* by Veniamin Kaverin, a favorite travel adventure story for the young audience.

What happened in Beslan, however, was essentially different from past terrorist attacks against children; there, the death-worshippers took their sacrificial destruction to a new level. Beslan is a town of relatives; everyone has familial ties to everyone else. Even distant family members are very close, so much more the siblings, little ones are frequently left in the care of their older brothers and sisters. In this traditional community, for decades people live on the same street or in the same house and are more than neighbors: they spend a great deal of time socializing, celebrating birthdays and holidays together; they have common troubles and memories; their children grow up as playmates and "share moms."[10] There are no children of "others," felt the Beslan massacre survivors who risked their lives and evacuated little hostages, hoping that someone else would help their sons and daughters to get away from under the terrorists' fire.[11] Prisoners inside the school constituted approximately 3.3 percent of Beslan's 35,500 inhabitants, but by orchestrating the holdup, the extremists aimed at every household and the *locality as a whole:* by murdering and maiming hundreds of children, they mutilated *the town.*

Psychologists who have been treating victims in Beslan designate it as a "special place," a "death space" or "zone," analogous to "zones of sadness," which instantaneously mushroomed from Ground Zero into areas of Manhattan and Brooklyn, as far as Staten Island and New Jersey on 9/11.[12] In Beslan, one and all have experienced dying and bereavement and are suffering from collective traumatization, as well as individual intense posttraumatic stress and anxiety disorders. Their sense of time is broken into "before" and "after" the violent incident, to which the residents refer as "the event" or simply as "that" (as in "when *that* happened"). Such an attitude "is present in any conversation, regardless of the topic, no matter with whom one starts talking."[13]

"Beslan is a very sick place," confirmed Moscow psychologist Elena Morozova, working with the town children, who require "continued special attention... We are looking at a lost generation."[14] Nearly 90 first-graders were killed in the school holdup; this age group is "the most vulnerable" in Beslan, mental health professionals reported a year after the siege. "I don't want to go to school," says seven-year-old Georgy Sidakov; "I don't want to be dead." For these children "school means death," explains local hospital psychologist Fatima Bagayeva, who has been taking care of the youngest survivors. "They have no other memory of school. They are living with terrible trauma and grief, but when they turn to parents or other relatives, they see that they can't cope, either."[15]

Parents of the children murdered in Ma'alot took their son's and daughter's bodies home for burial in Safed; the "Delphinarium" and Dubrovka carnages horrified yet did not stop the lives of citizens in metropolitan Tel Aviv and Moscow. But Beslan became a closed "infected sphere," explain the locals; it is like living in a cemetery. Psychologists elucidate that in this town people "have no sense of the future," which in most cases is "associated with travel in space," in thoughts about physical relocation to another place, where there is life.[16] Whether or not they have lost loved ones, they are affected for life, the way the Holocaust survivors are, except that terror victims of Beslan have remained among their dead in the "town of angels," as they call their little Auschwitz.[17]

Sderot is the Israeli "trauma zone." With few fatalities, it is not a site to pick up sensational news items; random and inaccurate Qassam fire from Gaza has become almost a regular event. Cries for help from terrorized residents largely fall on deaf ears, despite sympathetic press coverage of special cases, such as that involving two Ethiopian children killed by a rocket outside their home, or a boy whose legs were torn off in a blast. Yet the shelled town is another instance where, overlooked by most observers, modern terrorism has reached a new phase "of singling out children's sites."[18]

There is a "Qassam generation"—kids who over the last eight years have been growing under the rockets, terrorism being the hallmark of their daily life. A Sderot child is aware of the location of every bomb shelter on his way to a local store; some prefer to walk 40 minutes to school every morning instead of 10 because the circuitous route has better protection; others argue that the safest way is to run all the way.[19] During periods of heavy shelling, parents keep them at home for days or entire weeks; even during ceasefire school attendance is sparse, often as low as 60 percent.[20] Like children in Beslan, their peers in Sderot react emotionally to loud noises, such as those of a thunderstorm or even a voice. I was once present at an open lesson in a local school, and a heavy object fell in the yard outside the classroom window: there was instant silence; everyone tensed up; eyes opened and for a second or two became hollow—it was quiet hysteria.

Every playground is equipped with protective shields. Some slides and climbing walls are under metal covers; the make-belief tunnels and labyrinths are made of concrete pipes, so that small children can play inside in relative safety. Each has his own sophisticated routines and safety rituals for performing most ordinary tasks; in this generation, there is no one who has not been deeply traumatized by the habitual threat of violence. The family of almost two-year-old Tair remembers that "red"—for "Red Alert"—was among her first words. After a recorded warning she would add as a matter of course: "threw... fell," explaining what happened. Like "orange" of the old days, Qassam" is the word always in people's minds and on the tip of the tongue: when a science teacher asked her little students why a lizard needs its scales, everyone in class knew: "Against the Qassams!"[21]

In truth, Sderot children know much more about animals than their peers elsewhere. If you see a flock of pigeons go up in the air and fly in the same direction, it is a safe bet that in a few seconds there will be a rocket blast: the birds hear the warning message, understand what this means, dash to safety. The siren sets off the crazy barking of the dogs throughout the town, and when yet another family among the 3,000 evacuees leaves, its home destroyed by a missile, abandoned animals join into packs. Children see dogs who suffer from skin disease caused by depression. Their own pets hide under tables and in dark corners at the first sounds of the siren going off; they cry and refuse to get out for days. A few have died of heart attacks. Dogs have jumped out of the high-floor window once they hear the recorded voice of the "Red Alert."[22]

Many kids like to visit and help at local farms, but after a rocket landed on one of them, several children had to be treated for hysteria. Another blast sent a deaf-mute son of the owner to the hospital for shock-treatment. A 9-year-old was riding when her horse flew into a wild gallop triggered by sudden shelling, and this was the last time the girl's father brought her to the ranch, considered a dangerous "open area."

After a few goats and sheep died in explosions, the rest began to have miscarriages. In their fleece the owners found shrapnel pieces and sold for meat hundreds of anxiety-stricken, self-aborting animals. The children noted that after a Qassam assault, horses looked like people in rocket shelters: paralyzed with aftershock, immobile, eyes filled with tears—exactly like human's.

The "death space" that the terrorists have succeeded in creating in Beslan by way of the massacre of children, "singled out as special targets,"[23] in Sderot has been systematically constructed over the course of eight years. The Qassam rockets are very imprecise and do not inflict great casualties, but as it turns out, not much blood-spilling is necessary to keep the town population in perpetual fear, as long as it is sustained over a long time and reinforced systematically. "A present for the start of the new school year," the Islamic Jihad Web site flaunted the terrorists' September 2007 missile attack, which sent 12 kindergarteners to the hospital for shock treatment.[24] Whether the terrorists purposely schedule the bombardments for the early mornings and late afternoons when the children go to and from school cannot be ascertained, but this is less relevant than the fact: the town residents fear that this was indeed the intent.

In Beslan, children are frightened to enter the new school—a beautiful state-of-the-art facility with a swimming pool, "to replace the 19th-century, red-brick School No. 1, now a debris-strewn shell."[25] In Sderot they hesitate to venture outside their houses, in which one room is always a rocket shelter: "I am going, Mommy; I really have to go...I am already going...I will go," 11-year-old Michele says; she lingers at the door every time she has to leave for her morning classes. In school shelters, children appreciate an improvised "therapeutic workout": together they count from 15 to 1 and then scream as loud as they can to muffle the sound of the explosion. There youngest kids learn a 15-second song they sing to relax during a shelling:

> My heart pounds—bum, bum, bum, but I am not afraid;
> Hands—shake, shake, shake them....
> Boom, it fell.
> Good that it's over.[26]

Sderot is severely damaged with collective anxiety. At present, the full extent of the trauma is known only indirectly; for example, by evidence of symptomatic panic, tenseness, insomnia, nightmares, diminished concentration and ability to perform regular tasks, periodic aggressiveness, depression, as well as high percentage of powerful tranquillizers prescribed to town residents; psychiatrists have classified dozens, if not hundreds as handicapped.[27] Irrational behaviors are widespread, and no one considers odd a woman who protects herself from the rockets by placing a pillow and a tin basin on her head as a helmet when she hears the "Red Alerts."[28] Mass fear is not a cut-rate sacrifice, when the devotees of death are incapable of showing themselves to be as free-handed as they proved to be in the Ossetian town at the other end of the world. And having demonstrated quite a commitment to destruction in the designated "fear zone" of Sderot, the terrorists have also tried their hand at transforming larger communities into similar sectors of terrorization by systematically shelling the cities of Beersheba and Ashkelon.

The extremists' success has been limited thus far: biological, chemical, and radiological strikes, with the potential to deactivate vast regions, although a constant concern for security specialists, are easily put into effect only in the imagination of horror film producers. On the other hand, we have seen the real-life outcome of a doomsday scenario on 9/11. A very serious threat is an "electromagnetic pulse (EMP) attack," which "could wreak havoc on the nation's electronic systems—shutting down power grids, sources, and supply mechanisms." Nuclear or non-nuclear EMP, "a high-intensity burst of electromagnetic energy caused by the rapid acceleration of charged particles," able to send electrical systems into chaos, has been called a "weapon of mass disruption" because of its capability to neutralize an area's electronic infrastructure for communications, transportation, water, food, and medical facilities.[29] A possibility for such "bloodless murder" would be consistent with terror patterns over the past century—from assassinations aimed to punish specific targets to "motiveless terror" against civilians to creation of "death zones," a postmodern trend that represents the most aggressive form of mass counterculture.

In the Americas, across Europe, in Asia, and in the Middle East, for millions of people terrorism has become a personal issue, although it is doubtful that we have fully integrated the global experience of living under the sword of Damocles—a state of affairs unprecedented in human history. Nor has it been easy to accept that the terrorists act irrationally only from our point of view: they follow their own logic of thanatophilia consistently and with precision. As long as we insist on "cognitive egocentrism"[30]—projection of our values onto the terrorists, for whom hostility is a way of life—we are destined not to comprehend. Due to our tacit longing to circumvent violence, we are then fated to feel overwhelmed, traumatized, feeble, and ashamed of our impotency in the face of the threat. The fear begs for lingering ignorance, soothing, if only superficially, yet detrimental in the long run. A vicious circle is thus sustained—such that fellow citizens who live two hours away from the terrorized town of Sderot are barely familiar with the situation there, to say nothing of most people outside of Israel.

"We don't want to stare into this abyss." Since 9/11, "too many people have become experts at averting their eyes"[31]—hostages to the ubiquitous threat, behaving as if victims of the collective Stockholm syndrome. One pitiful victim was a stone-faced British police officer literally looking the other way while a crowd of instigators raved on the streets of London to "behead," "massacre," and "butcher those who mock Islam" in response to the September 2005 publication in the Danish newspaper *Jyllends-Posten* 12 cartoons of the Prophet Muhammad.[32] No action was taken against "incitement to murder—an extremely serious offense." As a reason, a senior Scotland Yard officer cited "fears of a riot."[33]

That liberty in the United States is being sacrificed to fear is glaring in a recent scandal involving Yale University Press, which has removed caricatures of Muhammad from its new book by Brandeis professor Jytte Klausen.[34] The decision rested on the specialists' warning about "a substantial likelihood of violence," the Yale University statement explained. One consultant, Fareed Zakaria, editor of *Newsweek International*, a world affairs columnist, and CNN host, confirmed that Yale's press "was confronted with a clear threat of violence and loss of life." The university's judgment effectively declared: "We do not negotiate with terrorists. We just accede to their anticipated demands," said Cary Nelson, president of the American Association of University Professors. For her part, the author "reluctantly agreed to have the book published without the images" because she believed that no other university press would print them either. Incidentally, her work reveals "a misperception that Muslims spontaneously arose in anger over the cartoons, whereas they were mere symbols manipulated by those *already* involved in violence."[35] Anyone who ever lived under a totalitarian rule could elucidate the process by which "spontaneous events" are organized.

Beslan should have swept away any lingering illusions about modern terrorism—those that even 9/11 had not revoked. Instead, reluctance to see it as a type of totalitarian death order has caused people to engage in a "mental diversion" and "rush off in search of more comprehensible things to hate."[36] This has also contributed to proclivity for self-blame. "Why do they hate us?" a CNN journalist asked while interviewing a Carnegie Foundation–based foreign affairs authority, reiterating a question that has been on Americans' minds since 9/11. "President Bush's explanation is that they hate our freedom. What do you think?" "They don't hate our freedom; they hate our policy,"[37] answered the specialist, insinuating that the U.S. government could solve the problem of political extremism overnight, if only it listened to competent advice—presumably his own, which would lead to a superior strategy. What it would be, he neglected to outline, and little wonder: America has made conciliatory steps (and, to an even greater extent, so did Israel), but it is not easy to find common ground with proponents of death-worshipping terrorism, presupposing no compromise. Islamist position on liberty and our other values which threaten fundamentalism is recapped in the slogan "Freedom Go to Hell!"[38]

Concrete actions may be triggers, but it is "precisely in the vitriol, the desperation, the viciousness of the response that we see evidence of a more profound phenomenon than policy disputes."[39] Time and again the jihadists have declared an all-out war against people of different nationalities and faiths, lumped into one category of the infidels. The "non-believers" are held in contempt, yet feared; they are also envied and hated not for a specific *modus operandi* but—as ordains generic totalitarism—for who they allegedly are. And they have been tipped off as to the magnitude of intended carnage: "Be prepared for the *real* Holocaust!"[40]

"If the Jews left Palestine to us, would we start loving them? Of course not.... They are enemies not because they occupied Palestine. They would have been enemies even if they did not occupy a thing," clerics such as Muhammad Hussein Ya'qoub say, speaking very frankly in Arabic—making statements not intended for those who prefer to deceive themselves: "We will fight, defeat, and annihilate them, until not a single Jew remains on the face of the Earth."[41] It is as if the Biblical Amelek has decided to break portentous silence and finally speak his mind.

Annihilation of Israel is Amalek's raison d'être, and he is prepared to go all the way to achieve his only goal. Traditional Judaism is very clear on this point: the archenemy of the Jews fights them even when the struggle is against his interests. Amalek's hatred is infinite, and he acts on it, consumed by his ferocious passion—literally, until it incinerates him. Gratifying his zest, he self-destroys eagerly.

Alluring as it may be, the analogy is facile. The scholar, after all, "must steadfastly resist the temptation to over-simplify and think conventionally." He must instead "make himself docile to the leadings of mysterious Fact,"[42] which is that Amalek directs his effort against Israel alone, whereas his accomplices, operating all over the world, though not entirely impartial, refrain from discrimination.

Bin Laden called a "personal obligation of every Muslim... to kill Americans and their allies," military and civilian, regardless of where they are,[43] ostensibly in retaliation for Western aggression in the Middle East and elsewhere. But terrorist rhetoric and activities show no correlation to a particular policy. "America, England, and Australia are cited as enemies, but alongside Germany, Canada, Netherlands, Italy, Japan, Russia, China, India, Sweden, Belgium," and the list goes on.[44] "Embrace Islam... stop your oppressions, lies, immorality, and debauchery"; terrorists' demands are ideological declarations, not attempts to start a dialogue.[45] "Europe. You will pay. Your extermination is on its way."[46] Tantamount to voluntary blindness would be to deny that a new "death cult has no reason and is beyond negotiation."[47] When a stated goal is to create an "Islamic state of North America by... 2050,"[48] unawareness of the totalist message would be akin to Orwellian "doublethink."

Terrorists belong to the psychosocial category of the dislocated, the insecure, the angry, and the dehumanized. While many leaders do not live up to "the ascetic ideal," they promulgate the view of "ordinary enjoyment as trivial and even discreditable," synonymous to "a perfidious compromise with the enemy." The rank-and-file practice self-mortification and grow full of self-admiration. They turn into "morose, severe judges of all those that fall short" of their ersatz-holiness,"[49] which is often "accompanied by . . . the sins of pride, envy, chronic anger and an uncharitableness pushed sometimes to the level of active cruelty." Their cheerless "life runs its course against a colorful and dramatic background of collective pageantry" and "serves to accentuate its worthlessness." They look down on those who are not like themselves and are "morally equipped to wish and to be able to do harm on the very largest scale and with a perfectly untroubled conscience."[50]

The inmost purpose of their attacks is to shatter life, to which they cannot belong or relate, and with which they cannot reconcile. For them, it is the source of unremitting pain; much like serial killers, they experience life as "existential isolation that is far beyond human tolerance."[51] For them, love of death is not an allegory. They do aspire to flee from the insufferable confinement among the living, "to escape from the prison-house of this world."[52]

Terrorists' compensatory self-gratification in killing and dying is infused with murky spirituality. Violence is a rite and an amulet to ward off profound anxiety. It is also a path to transcendence in death—their deity, to which they consecrate themselves and their victims. Few clichés have survived as long as the one about history repeating itself, far as we are from being able to resolve a pivotal question of *why* it does. Conspicuous behavior typologies "seem familiar, as if the repertory of human forms were limited. The historian then discovers similarities...only partly concealed beneath the surface of the events themselves"[53]—parallels that imply the need to ask what history is recurrently trying to tell us. At the very least, it eliminates confusion and clarifies our vision; for those who seek them, history offers deeper ethical and spiritual insights. As far as terrorism is concerned, it exposes those of its facets that the perpetrators would rather keep hidden. If we are to believe Lamartine, "history teaches everything, even the future," offering us a chance. Our awareness of a precedent and reflection upon it should help illuminate alternatives to past mistakes.

Organized murder as a modern form of death-worship falls within a long-existing tradition. It shares traits with a line of antecedents, such as the lethal Thug or Thuggee cult in India, which, incidentally, popular opinion has speciously pigeonholed as terrorist.[54] Some link the sect to ancient Sagartians, but more recently, for nearly two centuries until their eradication in the mid-1830s, its Hindu, Sikh, and Muslim members ritually slaughtered tens of thousands of highway travelers in honor of the goddess Kali. "The more terror the victims experienced, the more Kali enjoyed their deaths."[55]

Deification of homicide as part of the Thug doctrine was no more or less crude than the ideological arguments and rituals of their 20th- and 21st-century successors across the globe. "One who is afraid of death will not gain resurrection" was the credo of the Rumanian "Iron Guard"; championing a dogmatic mélange of fascism and religious-nationalist theology, its members, known as Legionnaires, "embraced death," and engaged in terrorism in the in the inter-war period. Among the Guards, a eulogized feat of glory was the

1936 murder of a renegade leader: 10 participants shot and hacked "the traitor" with an axe, smeared his blood on each other's faces, sang and danced around the body in ecstasy, celebrating "the mysticism of blood," and then surrendered themselves to the police. "A legionnaire loves death," was the movement's official motto, and a line from the hymn for the Guard's youth wing might have been adopted *verbatim* for the Islamist folklore: "Death, only death in the Legion / Is the dearest wedding of all."[56]

Regardless of the espoused creed, be it secular, as among the Russian extremists, or religious, such as radical Islam, the terrorist cult practices a *modern type of paganism.* The "gods to whom human sacrifice is offered are personifications, not of Nature, but of man's own home-made political ideals" or, rather, intricate psychological and spiritual workings that take radical political forms. "Fanaticism is idolatry," if only inasmuch as the zealot "worships something which is the creation of his own desire." "Preoccupied with eternity,"[57] he venerates death for the benefit of attaining symbolic immortality.

Like other idolaters, terrorists contrive to manipulate the object of adulation. For them, it is the course and the "will of destruction," which they revere. The thanatophiliac rites reflect attempts to mega-manage murder. The practitioners seek simultaneously to serve and stage-direct extermination, taking for granted that they can always guide its ways.

We can certainly be reassured by history: all past death cults have been destroyed or self-destroyed, claimed and consumed by their own venomous inner void that they are no longer able to propel and impose onto their environment, built to be conducive to suicide. Perhaps this explains the enigmatic tendency of revolutions to devour themselves. It is patent in Stalin's gargantuan guzzle of the Bolshevik party, which in the previous decade had destroyed the entire Russian radical tradition, the socialists and the anarchists, the seasoned experts in demolition.

Death also turned on its servants who had assumed it to be under control when the Nazi regime could not longer project violence. Hitler's behavior in the final phase of the war was shaped by his desperate effort to realize "the strategy of grandiose doom," the ultimate suicidal act of Nazi death cult. As early as the autumn of 1944, with the allied armies at the German border, he had sanctioned the "scorched earth" procedures in the territory of the Reich, insisting that "nothing but a desert should be left to the enemy." At first seemed justifiable by operational considerations, the plan soon developed into "an abstract mania for destruction" without any discernable purpose. As the allies approached Berlin, the Nazi leaders sent 10-year-olds against the Russian tanks and also killed themselves, their spouses, their mistresses, and their pets. The wife of Nazi propaganda minister Joseph Goebbels, who, like Hitler, wished that "they could have smashed everything to pieces,"[58] crushed cyanide capsules in her six children's mouths before she and her husband committed suicide on May 1, 1945. Shoko Asahara contemplated group suicide as "a way out" of perceived government conspiracy against his cult.[59] For these and other thanatophiles death was an insatiable but not fastidious deity; any sacrifice brought to its altar was accepted, as long as deliveries were steady and arrived in increasing quantity.

"And you have taken your sons and your daughters... and these have you sacrificed... to be devoured" (Ezekiel 16:20); "even their sons and their daughters do they burn in the fire to their gods" (Deuteronomy 12:31). The hijackers of Islam offer Muslim children to Moloch by turning them into suicide bombers. They expose them to bullets and use them as human shields to protect adult terrorists. They also murder their children by dehumanization, while indoctrinating them in brutality. Projecting death onto the posterity, they are killing their future.

To be sure, the millennial extremism is also a reaction to the crisis of devaluated meanings in our own past and present. The apocalyptic terrorism this book described "contained a fundamental critique of the world's post-Enlightenment secular culture and politics."[60] Twentieth-century history reveals the terrible cost of an encounter with militant nihilism amid a spiritual vacuum, of being locked in a struggle emasculated by obscurity of purpose beyond survival. Our experience may therefore demand that societies endangered by totalism search for a "third truth"—between and beyond death-worshipping fundamentalism and postmodernity. Challenged with fragmentation of values and ideals, with isolation, self-alienation and inauthenticity, with ethical relativism, with half-hearted "meaculpism," and with faithlessness, we may need to loosen an uptight grip on individualism—an abiding social idol, trivialized and reduced to egocentrism, boundless as it is hollow. Our predicament perhaps presents us with a chance to get out of our own cultural confinement, overloaded with life-undermining attributes. Beyond the walls of "our own box," new solutions and creative opportunities may become apparent.

An alternative to debilitating existence and suicide inherent in thanatophilia is a compound intensity of being alive. It revels itself as animated spontaneity and creativity, as personal integrity, genuine dignity, courage, and empathy. It is present in every manifestation of vitality—our last word in the continuing "dialogue between the spirit and the dust."[61] In the existential dispute between humanity and the dehumanizing terror, nothing is more important than the understanding of our options:

"I have set before thee life and death, the blessing and the curse; therefore choose life" (Deuteronomy 30:19).

Notes

Note that some references provide two dates (e.g., December 10 [23], 1906). The Russian calendar was changed in 1917. The old and new calendars are 13 days apart. Both the old- and the new-style dates have been retained where they appear in the original Russian sources.

INTRODUCTION

1. Cited in Boaz Ganor, "Defining Terrorism—Is One Man's Terrorist Another Man's Freedom Fighter?" 1–3, 13, http://www.ict.org.il/ResearchPublications/tabid/64/Articlsid/432/currentpage/1/Default.aspx.

2. For detailed discussion see Daniel Pipes, "Terrorism: The Syrian Connection," *National Interest* (Spring, 1989), http://www.danielpipes.org/1064/terrorism-the-syrian-connection

3. Ganor, "Defining Terrorism," 4–6.

4. Richard Jackson, "A Defense of the Concept of 'State Terrorism'," unpublished paper to be presented at the International Studies Association (ISA), 51st Annual Convention, February 17–20, 2010, New Orleans, 4.

5. Ganor, "Defining Terrorism," 8.

6. David Brooks, "Cult of Death," *New York Times*, September 7, 2004, http://www.nytimes.com/2004/09/07/opinion/07brooks.html.

7. A typical argument is as follows: "Like many utopian movements, anarchists developed as intolerable social and political conditions led its proponents to imagine and strive for a different, more just, world, in which the beleaguered would at last prevail. This vision transcends national boundaries and cultures" (John Merriman, *The Dynamite Club: How a Bombing in Fin-de-Siècle Paris Ignited the Age of Modern Terror* [New York: Houghton Mifflin Harcourt, 2009], 4).

8. See, for example, Robert Pape, *Dying to Win: The Strategic Logic of Suicide Terrorism* (New York: Random House, 2005); and Noam Chomsky, "War on Terror"

(Amnesty International Annual Lecture hosted by Trinity College, January 18, 2006).

9. Richard Jackson, "In Defense of Terrorism: Finding a Way through a Forest of Misconceptions," *Behavioral Sciences of Terrorism and Political Aggression* (forthcoming 2011).

10. Eric Hoffer, *The True Believer* (New York: Harper & Row, 1951), 15.

11. Robert Jay Lifton, "Cult Formation," *The Harvard Mental Health Letter* 7, no. 8 (February 1981). Thus, I do not devote much space to radical anticolonial struggle, such as in India or Palestine during the British rule, since these national autonomy movements did not strive to remold the world by violent means in accordance with an ideological or religious view. Nor do I focus on cases of violence committed by independent terrorists, such as Timothy McVeigh, who had only one accomplice and later renounced the intent to kill children in the April 19, 1995, Oklahoma City massacre.

12. Robert Jay Lifton, *Thought Reform and the Psychology of Totalism: A Study of "Brainwashing" in China* (Chapel Hill: University of North Carolina Press, 1989), 419.

13. Hoffer, *The True Believer*, 80–81.

14. Michael J. Mazarr, *Unmodern Men in the Modern World: Radical Islam, Terrorism, and the War on Modernity* (New York: Cambridge University Press, 2007), vii.

15. Steven G. Marks, *How Russia Shaped the Modern World* (Princeton, NJ: Princeton University Press, 2003), 37.

16. Anna Geifman, "Terrorism's Cult of Death against Children in Beslan," *Clio's Psyche* 16, no. 2 (September 2009): 184.

17. Ibid.; Murat Kaboev, "Anzhela Ambalova: 'Annushki net uzhe...'" *Golos Beslana* 14 (October 2, 2002): 2.

18. Geifman, "Terrorism's Cult of Death against Children in Beslan," 185.

19. Ibid., 185–86.

20. Personal communication from L. Gatagova, September 11, 2004. Partially published in Anna Geifman, *La mort sera votre dieu!: du nihilisme Russe au terrorisme islamiste* (Paris: Les Editions de La Table Ronde, 2005).

21. These missiles are named after Sheikh Izz ad-Din al-Qassam, an Islamic leader of the Black Hand group that targeted Jews and vandalized rail lines constructed by the British in Mandate Palestine betweem 1930 and 1935. Izz ad-Din al-Qassam Brigades is the military wing of Hamas. Its Arabic acronym stands for *Harakat al-Muqāwamat al-Islāmiyyah*,, the "Islamic Resistance Movement," which came into being in 1988, after the outbreak of the first anti-Israel Intifada (literally "shaking off," uprising or resistance) in December 1987.

22. "Follow up to Operation Cast Lead: A Summary of Statistics," Sderot Media Center, http://sderotmedia.org.il/bin/content.cgi?ID=309&q=6&s=16.

23. "School resumes in Israel despite rocket threat," MSNBC, January 11, 2009, http://www.msnbc.msn.com/id/28605322/.

24. Dalia Harpaz and Ben Kaminsky, "Israel and Gaza—The Civilians' Distress," *The Epoch Times*, January 1, 2009, http://www.theepochtimes.com/n2/content/view/9554/.

25. Interviews with terrorists reveal that in most cases, the intended victims of an attack "are not perceived by the suicide bomber or dispatcher as victims, and therefore human emotions toward them are irrelevant" (Anat Berko, *The Path to Paradise: The Inner World of Suicide Bombers and Their Dispatchers* [Westport, CT: Praeger Security International, 2007], 10).

26. Mazarr, *Unmodern Men in the Modern World*, vii, 38.

27. Mark Juergensmeyer, *Terror in the Mind of God: The Global Rise of Religious Violence* (Berkeley: University of California Press, 2003), 125.

28. See, for example, Clara Beyler, "Messengers of Death: Female Suicide Bombers," 3, http://www.keren-inbar.org.il/INB/cache/pic_22500.pdf; Eli Berman, *Radical, Religious, and Violent: The New Economics of Terrorism* (Cambridge: Massachusetts Institute of Technology Press, 2009), 2; Luca Ricolfi, "Palestinians, 1981–2003," in *Making Sense of Suicide Missions*, ed. Diego Gambetta (Oxford: Oxford University Press, 2005), 81.

29. Donald D. MacRae, "Bolshevik Ideology: The Intellectual and Emotional Factors in Communist Affiliation," cited in Richard Landes, "Totalitarian Millennialism: The Bolshevik Apocalypse," In *Heaven on Earth: The Varieties of the Millennial Experience* (upcoming in Oxford University Press).

30. Article Six of the Hamas Charter (August 18, 1988), http://www.mideastweb.org/hamas.htm

31. Meir Litvak, "The Islamization of the Palestinian-Israeli Conflict: The Case of Hamas," *Middle Eastern Studies* 34, no. 1 (January 1998): 149, 155–56.

32. Dr. Emanuel Tanay, "A German's Point of View on Islam," http://forums.catholic.com/showthread.php?t=302643.

33. Anna Geifman, *Thou Shalt Kill: Revolutionary Terrorism in Russia, 1894–1917* (Princeton, NJ: Princeton University Press, 1993), 17.

CHAPTER 1

1. Mia Bloom, *Dying to Kill: The Allure of Suicide Terror* (New York: Columbia University Press, 2005), 5–7.

2. Franklin L. Ford, "Reflections on Political Murder: Europe in the Nineteenth and Twentieth Centuries," in *Social Protest, Violence and Terror in Nineteenth- and Twentieth-Century Europe*, ed. Wolfgang J. Mommsen and Gerhard Hirschfeld (New York: St. Martins, 1982), 6.

3. Martin A. Miller, "The Intellectual Origins of Modern Terrorism in Europe," in Martha Crenshaw, ed., *Terrorism in Context* (University Park: Pennsylvania State University Press, 1995), 46–47.

4. Norman M. Naimark, "Terrorism and the Fall of Imperial Russia," published lecture, Boston University, April 14, 1986, 4.

5. Edvard Radzinsky, *Alexander II: The Last Great Tsar* (New York: Free Press, 2005), 415.

6. M. Pokrovsky, cited in Marks, *How Russia Shaped the Modern World*, 17.

7. Lokerman, "Po tsarskim tiur'mam," *Krasnyi arkhiv* [cited hereafter as *KA*] 25 (1926): 179.

8. Naimark, "Terrorism and the Fall of Imperial Russia," 6–7.

9. Baron [Bibineishvili], *Za chetvert' veka* (Moscow-Leningrad, 1931), 85.

10. For analysis of terrorist statistics see Geifman, *Thou Shalt Kill*, 21, 264nn57, 58, 59.

11. "25 let nazad. Iz dnevnika L. Tikhomirova," *KA* 4–5, no. 41–42 (1930): 114; Count Witte, cited in Naimark, "Terrorism and the Fall of Imperial Russia," 19.

12. Geifman, *Thou Shalt Kill*, 21, 264n61.

13. N. S. Tagantsev, *Smertnaia kazn'* (St. Petersburg, 1913), 141.

14. Baron [Bibineishvili], *Za chetvert' veka*, 85.

15. Hugh Phillips, "The War against Terrorism in Late Imperial and Early Soviet Russia," in *Enemies of Humanity*, ed. Isaac Land (New York: Palgrave Macmillan, 2008), 214.

16. "Smertnaia kazan' v Rossii ostaetsia?" *Novoe vremia*, January 22, 1910, Arkhiv Partii Sotsialistov-Revoliutsionerov, International Institute of Social History, Amsterdam [cited hereafter as PSR, followed by "box" and "folder" numbers], 4:346; "Iz obshchestvennoi khroniki," *Vestnik Evropy* 12 (1906): 886.

17. "Iz obshchestvennoi khroniki," *Vestnik Evropy* 9 (1906): 422–23.

18. Cited in O. V. Budnitskii, "P. A. Kropotkin i problema revoliutsionnogo terrorizma," *Izvestiia vuzov. Serero-kavkazskii region. Obshchestvennye nauki*, No. 3 (1994), 35.

19. A. V. Gerasimov, *Na lezvii s terroristami* (Paris: YMCA Press, 1985), 92.

20. Contemporary liberal journalist cited in "Iz obshchestvennoi khroniki," *Vestnik Evropy* 8 (1907): 842.

21. Walter Laqueur, *Terrorism* (Boston-Toronto: Little, Brown & Co., 1977), 105; Boris Souvarine, *Stalin: A Critical Study of Bolshevism* (New York: Alliance Group Corporation, Longmans, Green, 1939), 93; *Volia* 89 (December 10 [23], 1906); 26, PSR 7:592.

22. William C. Fuller Jr., *Civil-Military Conflict in Imperial Russia 1881–1914* (Princeton, NJ: Princeton University Press, 1985), 150.

23. Geifman, *Thou Shalt Kill*, 21.

24. A. I. Spiridovich, *Istoriia bol'shevizma v Rossii* (Paris, 1922), 120–21.

25. *Iskry*, 8, PSR 2:132.

26. Spiridovich, *Istoriia bol'shevizma v Rossii*, 120. See also Jonathan W. Daly, *The Watchful State: Security Police and Opposition in Russia, 1906–1917* (DeKalb: Northern Illinois University Press, 2004), 16.

27. V. Kniazev, "1905," *Zvezda* 6 (1930): 230–32, 247.

28. "Aforizy," *Zabiiaka* 3 (January 26, 1906): 7, Boris I. Nicolaevsky Collection, Hoover Institution Archives, Stanford, CA [cited hereafter as Nic.], 436:13.

29. E. Iu. Kuz'mina-Karavaeva cited in W. Bruce Lincoln, *Sunlight at Midnight: St. Petersburg and the Rise of Modern Russia* (New York: Basic Books, 2000), 210.

30. Boris M. Segal, *The Drunken Society: Alcohol Abuse and Alcoholism in the Soviet Union—A Comparative Study* (New York: Hippocrene Books, 1990), 503.

31. "Russian" here refers to any inhabitant of the Russian empire. The processes being described may be applied to representatives of Russian Orthodox, Jewish, or other ethnic and religious groups residing in the country. Third-person masculine is used throughout the book for stylistic purposes when referring to both males and females.

32. For discussion of the cross-cultural approach toward collectivism in reference to Russia, see Daniel Rancour-Laferriere, *The Slave Soul of Russia: Moral Masochism and the Cult of Suffering* (New York: New York University Press, 1995), 202–7, 283n1; and Christine D. Worobec, Peasant Russia: Family and Community in the Post-Emancipation Period (Princeton, NJ: Princeton University Press, 1991), 6.

33. Peter Berger cited in Mazarr, *Unmodern Men in the Modern World*, 41.

34. Eugene M. Kayden, "Leonid Andreyev: 1871–1919," http://worldlibrary.net/eBooks/Wordtheque/en/aaabnxe.txt.

35. Robert J. Lifton, *Boundaries: Psychological Man in Revolution* (New York: Random House, 1970), 43.

36. Andrei Belyi, *Na rubezhe dvukh stoletii* (Chicago: Russian Language Specialties, 1966), 5.

37. Reference to Lifton in Moshe Hazani, "Sacrificial Immortality: Towards a Theory of Suicidal Terrorism and Related Phenomena," in *The Psychoanalytic Study of Society*, vol. 18, ed. L. Bryce Boyer, Alan Dundes, Stephen M. Sonnenberg (Hillsdale, NJ: Analytic Press, 1993), 417.

38. "Between 1850 and 1914, about 1.7 million people were added to the population" of St. Petersburg, "bringing the total to around 2.2 million—but just over one million arrived after 1890 and nearly 350,000 came after 1908. . . . The economic boom of the nineties signaled the onset of growth not before experienced. Between 1890 and 1914 the capital's citizenry grew each year by an average of 50,000 inhabitants." By 1914, nearly three-quarters of the capital's inhabitants were peasants, "as compared with fewer than a third half a century before" (Statistics cited in James H. Bater, "Between Old and New: St. Petersburg in the Late Imperial Era," in *The City in Late Imperial Russia*, ed. Michael F. Hamm [Bloomington: Indiana University Press, 1986], 2–3, 46, 51–52).

39. Lincoln, *Sunlight at Midnight*, 212.

40. Karen Horney, Neurotic Personality of Our Time (New York: W. W. Norton and Company, Inc., 1937), 270, 278–279.

41. Aldous Huxley, The Perennial Philosophy (New York: Harper & Row, 1944), 163.

42. Belyi, *Na rubezhe dvukh stoletii*, 4.

43. Carlton J. H. Hayes, *A Generation of Materialism* (New York: Harper, 1941), 254. Fritz Stern's classic *The Politics of Cultural Despair: A Study in the Rise of the Germanic Ideology* (Berkeley: University of California Press, 1961) analyzes the roots of Hitler's variant of the *völkische* movement in the loss of connection with traditional cultural norms.

44. Cited in Lincoln, *Sunlight at Midnight*, 212.

45. Hoffer, *The True Believer*, 39, 79–81, 21.

46. Iurii Karabchievskii, *Voskresenie Maiakovskogo* (Munich: Strana i mir, 1985), 86.

47. Aleksandr Blok cited in Lincoln, *Sunlight at Midnight*, 210.

48. Belyi, *Na rubezhe dvukh stoletii*, 4.

49. Robert J. Lifton, *The Broken Connection: On Death and the Continuity of Life* (New York: Basic Books, 1979), 17.

50. Paul Avrich, *Russian Anarchists* (Princeton, NJ: Princeton University Press, 1967), 44.

51. Cited in Lincoln, *Sunlight at Midnight*, 212.

52. Aleksei Tolstoi, *Ordeal* (Moscow: Progress Publishers, 1953), 28–29.

53. Miller, "The Intellectual Origins of Modern Terrorism in Europe," 58–59.

54. Archetypal Nihilist Bazarov in Ivan Turgenev's *Fathers and Children* (New York: Dover Publications, 1998), 150.

55. Beyond its narrow aesthetic meaning, in this book "culture" denotes the social, psychological, and ethical values of a society in a given historical phase.

56. "Terrorism Statistics. Terrorist Acts 1968–2006 Incidences (Most Recent) by Country," http://www.nationmaster.com/graph/ter_ter_act_196_inc-terrorist-acts-1968-2006-incidences; and "Terrorism Statistics. Terrorist Acts 2000–2006 Incidences (Most Recent) by Country," http://www.nationmaster.com/graph/ter_ter_act_200_inc-terrorist-acts-2000-2006-incidences.

57. Berman, *Radical, Religious, and Violent*, 1.

58. "Terrorism Deaths in Israel—1920–1999" (Israel Ministry of Foreign Affairs), January 1, 2000, http://www.mfa.gov.il/MFA/Terrorism-+Obstacle+to+Peace/Palestinian+terror+before+2000/Terrorism%20deaths%20in%20Israel%20-%20

1920–1999; and "Victims of Palestinian Violence and Terrorism since September 2000" (Israel Ministry of Foreign Affairs), http://www.mfa.gov.il/MFA/Terrorism+Obstacle+to+Peace/Palestinian+terror+since+2000/Victims+of+Palestinian+Violence+and+Terrorism+sinc.htm.

59. As compared to the ratio of 1.73 in attacks carried out over the same period by various nationalist and separatist organizations (the Irish IRA, Basque ETA, and others) and the much less lethal figure of 0.32 in exploits by Communist and the left socialists groups, such as the Italian Red Brigades, which specialized in hijackings and assaults on state and private property ("Terrorism and Its Increasing Lethality over Time," September 4, 2007, http://ajacksonian.blogspot.com/2007/09/terrorism-and-its-increasing-lethality.html).

60. As compared to the national/separatist 1.86 and the radical left 0.49 deaths/incident ratio. Although in absolute terms the number of people killed in a given attack by religious zealots has declined somewhat due to enhanced security efforts, in the period after 1999, it has nevertheless been twice as great as in the average terrorist occurrence (ibid.).

61. Hoffer, *The True Believer*, 33.

62. Ibid., 45.

63. Mazarr, *Unmodern Men in the Modern World*, 2, 15.

64. Randy Borum, et al., "Psychology of Terrorism." University of South Florida: October 2003. http://www.ncjrs.gov/pdffiles1/nij/grants/208551.pdf.

65. Francis Fukuyama and Nadav Samin, "Can Any Good Come of Radical Islam?" *Commentary* (September 2002), http://www.commentarymagazine.com/viewarticle.cfm/can-any-good-come-of-radical-islam-9498?search=1. As a counter-example, "India—seldom discussed in this context, yet boasting an immense Muslim population of more than 130 million—persists with democratic rule and a generally moderate politics," despite rampant poverty (Mazarr, *Unmodern Men in the Modern World*, 211).

66. Jessica Stern, "The Protean Enemy," *Foreign Affairs* (July/August 2003), http://www.cfr.org/pub6146/jessica_stern/the_protean_enemy.php.

67. Diego Gambetta and Steffen Hertog, "Engineers of Jihad," *Sociology Working Papers*, Paper Number 2007–10, p. 9, Department of Sociology, University of Oxford, http://www.sociology.ox.ac.uk/swp.html.

68. John Dawson, "The Bali Bombers: What Motivates Death Worship?," *Capitalism Magazine* (October 19, 2003), http://www.capmag.com/article.asp?ID=3000.

69. Stephen Holmes, "Al-Qaeda, September 11, 2001," in Gambetta, ed., *Making Sense of Suicide Missions*, 138.

70. Mazarr, *Unmodern Men in the Modern World*, 195.

71. Pipes, "Terrorism: The Syrian Connection," http://www.danielpipes.org/1064/terrorism-the-syrian-connection.

72. David Leppard and Chris Gourlay, "Farouk Abdulmutallab Was Barred from Britain," *The Sunday Times* (December 27, 2009), http://www.timesonline.co.uk/tol/news/uk/crime/article6968539.ece.

73. Hezbollah expert Judith Palmer Harik quoted in Gambetta and Hertog, "Engineers of Jihad," p. 5, www.sociology.ox.ac.uk/swp.html.

74. Shaul Kimhi and Shmuel Even, "Who Are the Palestinian Suicide Terrorists?" JCSS (Jaffee Center for Strategic Studies: Tel Aviv University) 6, no. 2 (September 2003), http://www.isranet.org/Israzine/Israzine_V1N3_WhoareTerrorists.htm.

75. Gambetta and Hertog, "Engineers of Jihad," p. 10, www.sociology.ox.ac.uk/swp.html.

76. Counterterrorist expert at Georgetown University Bruce Hoffman quoted in Bobby Ghosh, "Most Domestic 'Jihadists' Are Educated, Well-Off," *Time* (December 14, 2009), http://www.time.com/time/nation/article/0,8599,1947703,00.html.

77. Sayyid (Syed) Qutb, a leading ideologue of Islamism in the 20th century, cited in Mazarr, *Unmodern Men in the Modern World*, 44.

78. Borum, et al., "Psychology of Terrorism," http://www.ncjrs.gov/pdffiles1/nij/grants/208551.pdf.

79. Mazarr, *Unmodern Men in the Modern World*, 9, 65.

80. Oliver Roy, "Why Do They Hate Us? Not Because of Iraq," *New York Times* (July 22, 2005), http://www.nytimes.com/2005/07/22/opinion/22roy.html?_r=1.

81. Fukuyama and Samin, "Can Any Good Come of Radical Islam?" http://www.commentarymagazine.com/viewarticle.cfm/can-any-good-come-of-radical-islam-9498?search=1.

82. Mazarr, *Unmodern Men in the Modern World*, 17, 9.

83. Ibid., 172, 9, 7.

84. Hoffer, *The True Believer*, 42.

85. Roy, "Why Do They Hate Us? Not Because of Iraq," http://www.nytimes.com/2005/07/22/opinion/22roy.html?_r=1.

86. Hoffer, *The True Believer*, 42.

87. Psychiatrist Hechmi Dhaoui cited in Mazarr, *Unmodern Men in the Modern World*, 27.

88. Ibid., 12.

89. Miller, "The Intellectual Origins of Modern Terrorism in Europe," 59.

90. Salman Akhtar, "Some Reflections on the Nature of Hatred and Its Emergence in the Treatment Process," *The Birth of Hatred*, ed. Salman Akhtar, Selma Kramer, and Henri Parens (Northvale, NJ: Jason Aronson, 1995), 89.

91. Hoffer, *The True Believer*, 92.

92. Lifton, "Cult Formation."

93. Cited in Miller, "The Intellectual Origins of Modern Terrorism in Europe," 59–60.

94. Ibid., 60.

95. Fukuyama and Samin, "Can Any Good Come of Radical Islam?" http://www.commentarymagazine.com/viewarticle.cfm/can-any-good-come-of-radical-islam-9498?search=1.

96. Hoffer, *The True Believer*, 113.

97. Cited in Fukuyama and Samin, "Can Any Good Come of Radical Islam?" http://www.commentarymagazine.com/viewarticle.cfm/can-any-good-come-of-radical-islam-9498?search=1. Charles Watson, and G.-H. Bousquet refer to radical Islam as "a totalitarian system tout court;" Bertrand Russell, Jules Monnerot, and Czeslaw Milosz compare Islamism to communism; among others, Carl Jung, Karl Barth, Said Amir Arjomand, Maxime Rodinson, Manfred Halpern, and even Hitler note its similarities to fascism or Nazism (Ibn Warraq, "Islam is Totalitianism," *New English Review* [January 2009]), http://www.newenglishreview.org/custpage.cfm/frm/30778/sec_id/30778).

98. Fukuyama and Samin, "Can Any Good Come of Radical Islam?" http://www.commentarymagazine.com/viewarticle.cfm/can-any-good-come-of-radical-islam—9498?search=1.

99. Bruce B. Lawrence, *Defenders of God: The Fundamentalist Revolt against the Modern Age* (New York: Harper & Row, 1989), 1, 17.

100. Viktor E. Frankl, *Man's Search for Meaning* (New York: "Pocket Books," 1984), 177.

101. Cited in Juergensmeyer, *Terror in the Mind of God*, 214. Having apprehended a dissident, KGB agents in charge of "terrorization operations" in the USSR in the mid-1980s beat him half-conscious and then released him: "You are an open letter we are sending to your friends," they said (F. Finkel, personal communication, Boston, October 5, 2009).

102. Robert Struble Jr., *Treatise on Twelve Lights*, http://www.tell-usa.org/totl/0-Introduction.htm.

CHAPTER 2

1. Richard Pipes, *Struve: Liberal on the Right, 1905–1944* (Cambridge, MA: Harvard University Press, 1980), 154.

2. Hoffer, *The True Believer*, 48.

3. Bruce Maddy-Weitzman, "Palestinian and Israeli Intellectuals in the Shadow of Oslo and Intifadat al-Aqsa (The Tami Steinmetz Center for Peace Research, Tel Aviv University, 2002), http://www.tau.ac.il/dayancenter/PalestinianandIsraeliIntellectuals-bruce.pdf.

4. "K delu Fomy Kochury," *Byloe* 6 (1906): 102–3.

5. K. V. Gusev, *Partiia eserov: ot melkoburzhuaznogo revoliutsionarizma k kontrrevolutsii* (Moscow, 1975), 75.

6. "Telegrammy," *Ezh* 1 (n.d.): 13, Boris I. Nicolaevsky Collection, Hoover Institution Archives, Stanford, CA [cited hereafter as Nic.], 435:12.

7. Boris Savinkov, *Vospominaniia terrororista* (Khar'kov, 1926), 55–58.

8. Edward H. Judge, *Plehve: Repression and Reform in Imperial Russia, 1902–1904* (Syracuse, NY: Syracuse University Press, 1983), 234.

9. Savinkov, *Vospominaniia terrorista*, 102.

10. Phillips, "The War against Terrorism," 213.

11. *Zerkalo* 1 (1906): 11, Nic. 436:19.

12. *Sprut* 15 (April 26, 1906): 6, Nic. 436:5.

13. "Obvinitel'nyi akt po delu o pisariakh," September 22, 1907, 1–2, 5, Arkhiv Partii Sotsialistov-Revoliutsionerov, International Institute of Social History, Amsterdam [cited hereafter as PSR, followed by "box" and "folder" numbers], 3:170I.

14. Supplement to the journal *Sygnaly*, vyp. 1 (St. Petersburg, January 8, 1906), Nic. 436:3.

15. *Signal*, vyp. 3 (27 November 1905), Nic. 436:3.

16. Tagantsev, *Smertnaia kazn'*, 92. Other sources cite even greater and seemingly exaggerated numbers—almost 4,400 casualties among the officials *killed* in 1905–1906 alone (Phillips, "The War against Terrorism," 214).

17. Geifman, *Thou Shalt Kill*, 21, 264n61.

18. Cited in Naimark, "Terrorism and the Fall of Imperial Russia," 17.

19. Police report from Paris dated September 14, 1906, Arkhiv Zagranichnoi Agentury Departamental Politsii (Okhrana Collection), Hoover Institution Archives, Stanford University, Stanford, CA [cited hereafter as Okhrana, followed by "box" and "folder" numbers], VIj:15C; newspaper clipping from *Tovarishch* 349 (August 19 [September 1], 1907), PSR 8:650; newspaper clipping from *Rus'* 143 (May 25, 1908), PSR

8:653; "Sudebnaia khronika," newspaper clipping from *Kolokol* 852 (January 3, 1909), PSR 7:602.

20. Cited in Budnitskii, "P. A. Kropotkin i problema revoliutsionnogo terrorizma," 37.

21. M. Rakovskii, "Neskol'ko slov o Sikorskom," *Katogra i ssylka* 41 (1928): 147.

22. Jon Elster, "Motivations and Beliefs in Suicide Missions," in *Making Sense of Suicide Missions*, ed. Diego Gambetta, 249; Bloom, *Dying to Kill*, 29–30.

23. "Pribaltiiskii krai," *KA* 4–5, no. 11–12 (1925): 272.

24. S. M. Pozner, ed., *Boevaia gruppa pri TsK RSDRP(b) (1905–1907 g.g.) Stat'i vospominaniia* (Moscow-Leningrad, 1927), 122.

25. For example, references in "Dekabr'skie dni v Donbasse," *KA* 6, no. 73 (1935): 102, 115–16, 121.

26. M. Ivich, ed., "Statistika terroristicheskikh aktov," *Pamiatnaia knizhka sotsiaista-revoliutsionera*, vyp. 2 (n.p., 1914), 8–9; leaflet issued by the Minsk PSR Committee, August 5, 1905, PSR 5:435; A. D. Kirzhnits, ed., *Evreiskoe rabochee dvizhenie* (Moscow, 1928), 174; V. Iakubov, "Aleksandr Dmitrievich Kuznetsov," *KS* 3, no. 112 (1934): 134; March 3, 1905, police report, pp. 5–6, 18, Okhrana XIIIc(2):6A.

27. Cited in Spiridovich, *Istoriia bol'shevizma v Rossii*, 120–21.

28. *Gosudarstvenaia Duma. Stenograficheskie otchety* [cited hereafter as GD] (St. Petersburg, 1906) 23, no. 2: 1128, and 4, no. 1: 232.

29. Cited in Daly, *The Watchful State*, 33–34.

30. Gerasimov, *Na lezvii s terroristami*, 146; June 11 (May 29), 1906, report, Okhrana XIIc(1):1A; January 4 (17), 1907, report, Okhrana, XIIIb(1):1A, outgoing dispatches (1907), doc. 3.

31. P. L'vov-Marsiianin, "Rabochii druzhinnik Nikita Deev," *KS* 8 (1924): 234–35.

32. "Pis'ma E. P. Mednikova,' in *Zubatov i ego korrespondenty*, ed. B. P. Koz'min (Moscow-Leningrad, 1928), 111.

33. "Krovavye itogi," clipping from an unidentified newspaper, PSR 2:137.

34. I. N. Moshinskii (Iuz. Konarskii), "F. E. Dzerzhinskii i vorshavskoe podpol'e 1906 g.," *KS* 50 (1928): 17; Souvarine, *Stalin*, 93.

35. "Krovavye itogi," clipping from an unidentified newspaper, PSR 2:137.

36. See, for example, January 29, 1904, police report, pp. 1–2, Okhrana XIIIc(2):4A; August 4, 1905, police report, p. 23, Okhrana XIIIc(2):6B; police reports dated August 25, 1905, p. 10; September 1, 1905, p. 7; and September 8, 1905, p. 15, Okhrana XIIIc(2):6C; Iurenev, "Rabota R. S.-D. R. P. v Severo-Z apadnom krae," *PR* 8–9, no. 31–32 (1924): 188.

37. Baron [Bibineishvili], *Za chetvert' veka*, 85.

38. Aleksandr Rozhdestvenskii, "Desiat' let sluzhby v Prokurorskom Nadzore na Kavkaze" (Santiago, Chile, 1961), 21b, Alexander Rozhdestvenskii Collection, International Institute of Social History, Amsterdam [cited hereafter as AR].

39. Geifman, *Thou Shalt Kill*, 23.

40. Ia. K. Pal'vadze, *Revoliutsiia 1905–7 gg. v Estonii* (Leningrad, 1932), 69.

41. Tagantssev, *Smertnaia kazn'*, 160–61.

42. Geifman, *Thou Shalt Kill*, 30.

43. *Satiricheskoe obozrenie* 1 (1906): 2, Nic. 436:1.

44. In one striking example, attempts to arrest a Latvian terrorist chief named Epis failed after he had ordered his personal bodyguards to open fire at the police. Having been repeatedly shot at, officers refused to follow orders and instead began to salute the revolutionary hero every time they encountered him, casually strolling in the streets (Geifman, *Thou Shalt Kill*, 40).

45. "Pis'mo V. V. Radko," in *Zubatov i ego korrespondenty*, ed. B. P. Koz'min (Moscow-Leningrad, 1928), 43.

46. Jonathan W. Daly, *Autocracy under Siege: Security Police and Opposition in Russia, 1866–1905* (DeKalb: Northern Illinois University Press, 1998), 177.

47. Naimark, "Terrorism and the Fall of Imperial Russia," 19.

48. Gerasimov, *Na lezvii s terroristami*, 8.

49. For numerous references, see Geifman, *Thou Shalt Kill*, 274n180.

50. "Pis'ma E. P. Mednikova," 112–13; "25 let nazad. Iz dnevnika L. Tikhomirova," *KA* 63; "Iz dnevnika Konstantina Romanova," *KA* 6, no. 43 (1930): 113–15, and *KA* 1, no. 44 (1931): 126; Gerasimov, *Na lezvii s terroristami*, 9, 35.

51. "Iz materialov Departamenta Politsii," PSR 1:26.

52. Fuller, *Civil-Military Conflict*, photograph between pp. 164 and 165.

53. "Slukhi," *Sprut* 13 (March 21, 1906): 4, Nic. 436:5.

54. Examples described in "Krest'ianskoe dvizhenie v Zapadnom Zakavkaz'e," *KA* 2, no. 99 (1940): 111, 115; and Grauzdin, "K istorii revoliutsionnogo dvizheniia v Latvii," *KS* 7, no. 92 (1932): 109.

55. Cited in Phillips, "The War against Terrorism," 214.

56. Count V. N. Kokovtsov, *Iz moego proshlogo. Vospominaniia 1903–1919 gg.*, vol. 1 (Paris, 1933), 230; "Vzryv na Aptekarskom ostrove," *Byloe* 5–6, no. 27–28 (1917): 212.

57. Cited in A. Serebrennikov, ed., *Ubiistvo Stolypina. Svidetel'stva i dokumenty* (New York: Teleks, 1986), 37.

58. Faleev, "Shest' mesiatsev voenno-polevoi iustitsii," *Byloe* 2, no. 14 (1907): 47–50; Richard Pipes, *The Russian Revolution* (New York: Vintage Books, 1990), 170; Fuller, *Civil-Military Conflict*, 174–75.

59. April 5 (18), 1905, report from L. Rataev to the director of the police department, Okhrana XIc(5):1. Examples of such legal malfunctioning are described in "Bor'ba s revoliutsionnym dvizheniem na Kavkaze," *KA* 3, no. 34 (1929): 193, 197; and *Volia* 71 (October 4, 1906): 4, PSR 7:569.

60. M. Spiridonova, "Iz zhizni na Nerchinskoi katorge," *KS* 14 (1925): 192–93.

61. Hugh Phillips, "From a Bolshevik to a British Subject: The Early Years of Maksim M. Litvinov," *Slavic Review* 48, no. 3 (Fall 1989): 390–91.

62. Spiridonova, "Iz zhizni na Nerchinskoi katorge," 192.

63. Pipes, *The Russian Revolution*, 169–70.

64. Cited in Arthur Brice, "Shining Path Rebels Stage Comeback in Peru," http://edition.cnn.com/2009/WORLD/americas/04/21/peru.shining.path/index.html.

65. Ibid.

66. Abraham Ascher, *P. A. Stolypin: The Search for Stability in Late Imperial Russia* (Stanford, CA: Stanford University Press, 2001), 138.

67. Rostov, "S pervoi volnoi," *KA* 20 (1925): 54.

68. Fuller, *Civil-Military Conflict*, 175; Pipes, *The Russian Revolution*, 170; Phillips, "The War against Terrorism," 215.

69. Cited in Phillips, "The War against Terrorism," 215.

70. Ibid., 213, 215.

71. Cited in report dated July 7 (20), 1907, Okhrana, XIIIb[1]:1B, Outgoing Dispatches (1907), doc. 296.

72. Cited in Serebrennikov, ed., *Ubiistvo Stolypina*, 42.

73. V. Maevskii, *Borets za blago Rossii* (Madrid, 1962), 69–70 ; Aleksandr Galias, "'Ne naprasano ty poesh'…'Ocherk istorii odesskoi estrady do 1941 goda," http://www.odessitclub.org/publications/almanac/alm_35/alm_35_231-246.pdf.

74. Discussion and references in Geifman, *Thou Shalt Kill*, 207, 344–45nn2, 3, 4.

75. Ibid., 249.

76. Descriptions of Maximalist attacks on uniform-clad individuals in *Obzor revoliutsionnogo dvizheniia v okruge Irkutskoi sudebnoi palaty za 1908 god*, 19, Nic. 197:2.

77. "Sudebnaia khronika. Delo o predpolagavshmsia vzryve okhrannogo odeleniia," *Tovarishch* (October 19, 1907), PSR 8:650.

78. Phillip Zimbardo, "Vantage Point: Faceless Terrorists Embody 'Creative Evil,'" *Stanford Report*, September 26, 2001, http://news-service.stanford.edu/news/2001/september26/zimbardo-926.html.

79. Juergensmeyer, *Terror in the Mind of God*, 128.

80. Benjamin Netanyahu, *Fighting Terrorism* (New York: Noonday Press, 1995), 94.

81. The name of this group derived from a black day in the history of the al-Fatah movement—September 1970, when King Hussein of Jordan used arms against the rebellious Palestinian militia in his country, killing over 4,000 militants and expelling the rest. According to a close associate of al Rais ("the chief," as Arafat was often called among Palestinians), he and his lieutenants could send the Black September combatants "anywhere to do anything and they were prepared to lay down their lives to do it. No question. No hesitation. They were absolutely dedicated and absolutely ruthless" (Bruce Hoffman, "How the Terrorists Stopped Terrorism. All You Need is Love," *Atlantic Monthly* [December 2001], http://www.theatlantic.com/doc/200112/hoffman).

CHAPTER 3

1. Miller, "The Intellectual Origins of Modern Terrorism in Europe," 58.

2. Geifman, *Thou Shalt Kill*, 21, 264nn57–59, 61.

3. Juergensmeyer, *Terror in the Mind of God*, 121

4. Petr Kropotkin, ed., *Russkaia revoliutsiia i anarkhizm. Doklady chitannye na s'ezde Kommunistov-Anarkhistov v oktiabre 1906 goda* (London, 1907), 3; report of July 11, 1910, Okhrana XVIb(5):5B.

5. P. Katenin, *Ocherki russkikh politicheskikh techenii* (Berlin, 1906), 100.

6. I. Genkin, "Sredi preemnikov Bakunina," *Krasnaia letopis'*, 1, no. 22 (1927): 197; "Sudebnaia khronika," *Russkie vdeomosti* 111 (1908), PSR 2:150; "Anarkhizm i dvizhenie anarkhizma v Rossii," 56, Nic. 80:4.

7. Discussed in Geifman, *Thou Shalt Kill*, 128–29, 132.

8. Naimark, "Terrorism and the Fall of Imperial Russia," 18; Genkin, "Sredi preemnikov Bakunina," 199; "Feodosei Zubar' (Nekrolog)," 2, Okhrana XXIVe:2d.

9. References in Geifman, *Thou Shalt Kill*, 309n58.

10. *GD*, 1907, 9–1:486. For details see Viktor P. Obninskii, ed., *Polgoda russkoi revoliutsii* (Moscow, 1906), 157.

11. Laqueur, *Terrorism*, 42; Gosudarstvennyi Arkhiv Rossiiskoi Federatsii, Moscow [cited hereafter as GARF, followed by "folder" and "case" numbers] f. 102, DPOO, op. 1905, d. 2605: 122.

12. "Obzor revoliutsionnogo dvizheniia v okruge Irkutskoi sudebnoi platy za 1908 god," 33, Nic. 197:3.

13. "Sovremennaia letopis'," *Byloe* 10 (1906): 342.

14. Juergensmeyer, *Terror in the Mind of God*, 103–4, 122–23.

15. See, for example, Anna Politkovskaia, *Putin's Russia: Life in a Failing Democracy* (New York: Metropolitan Books, 2004): 76–77.

16. Brooks, "Cult of Death," http://www.nytimes.com/2004/09/07/opinion/07brooks.html.

17. "Chronicle of the Battle in Beslan," *Kommersant*, September 3, 2004, http://www.kommersant.com/page.asp?id=-1663.

18. Christoph Reuter, *My Life Is a Weapon: A Modern History of Suicide Bombing* (Princeton, NJ: Princeton University Press, 2002), 150.

19. Interview of the Azerbaijan President Heydar Aliyev by Andrey Karaulov, for *The Moment of Truth* TV program, "Heydar Aliyev's Heritage" International Online Library, http://library.aliyev-heritage.org/en/5157806.html; Farhad Mammadov, "Azerbaijani Intelligence Agencies to Strengthen Struggle against Extremist Organizations," http://www.eurasianet.org/resource/azerbaijan/hypermail/200110/0057.html.

20. Paul Quinn, "Inside al-Qaeda's Georgia Refuge," *Time*, October 19, 2002, http://www.time.com/time/world/article/0,8599,366217,00.html. References to other media sources in Dan Darling, "Thoughts on Beslan," September 5, 2004, http://windsofchange.net/archives/005468.html.

21. Sheila MacVicar and Henry Schuster, "European Terror Suspects Got al Qaeda Training, Sources Say," CNN, February 6, 2003, http://www.cnn.com/2003/US/02/06/sprj.irq.alqaeda.links/.

22. Bloom, *Dying to Kill*, 131.

23. Ibid., 140.

24. Cited in Darling, "Thoughts on Beslan," http://windsofchange.net/archives/005468.html. Violence in the region continues, escalating since the summer of 2008, despite the Kremlin declaration of April 16, 2009, about an end to its decade-long "anti-terrorist operation" in the Republic of Chechnya (Sarah E. Mendelson, "Peace in Chechnya?" Center of Strategic and International Studies [CSIS], April 16, 2009, http://www.csis.org/index.php?option=com_csis_pubs&task=view&id=5417).

25. Israel Ministry of Foreign Affairs, http://www.mfa.gov.il/MFA/Terrorism+Obstacle+to+Peace/Palestinian+terror+since+2000/Victims+of+Palestinian+Violence+and+Terrorism+sinc.htm.

26. Ricolfi, "Palestinians, 1981–2003," in Diego Gambetta, ed., *Making Sense of Suicide Missions*, 313n58.

27. Al-Aqsa TV, April 3, 2009, cited in Palestinian Media Watch Bulletin, April 26, 2009, http://pmw.org.il/Bulletins_Apr2009.htm#b190409.

28. "Jihad Against Jews and Crusaders," World Islamic Front Statement (February 23, 1998), http://www.fas.org/irp/world/para/docs/980223-fatwa.htm.

29. Iurenev, "Rabota R. S.-D. R. P. v Severo-Zapadnom krae," 188; Pozner, ed., *Boevaia gruppa pri TsK RSDRP(b)*, 122.

30. Leonard Schapiro, *Russian Studies* (New York: Viking, 1988). 273; V. Shul'gin, *Dni* (N.p. 1925), 53–54.

31. Kirzhnits, *Evreiskoe rabochee dvizhenie*, 258, 297, 355–56; reports of April 28, 1905, p. 9, and of August 4, 1905, pp. 12, 16, Okhrana XIIIc(2):6B.

32. "Pribaltiiskii krai," *KA* 4–5, no. 11–12 (1925): 271–72n.

33. Ibid., 272.

34. A. Lokerman, "Po tsarskim tiur'mam. V Ekaterinoslave," *KS* 25 (1926): 180.

35. "Pribaltiiskii krai," 272; references in Geifman, *Thou Shalt Kill*, 275n201; "Krest'ianskoe dvizhenie v Zapadnom Zakavkaz'e," 114.

36. "Review of D. Beika's *God lesnykh brat'ev*" [undated], 11–12, Nic. 121:5; GARF, f. 102, DPOO, op. 1905, d. 2605: 144–44ob; "Pribaltiiskii krai," 279n.

37. Ibid., 269; Ianis Luter Bobis, *Stranitsy zhizni revoliutsionera-podpol'shchika. Sbornik statei i vospominanii* (Riga, 1962), 132, 167.
38. Geifman, *Thou Shalt Kill*, 23.
39. *Vodovorot* 6 (1906): 12, Nic. 436:11.
40. This figure may include the proceeds of non-political assaults (*Russkoe slovo* 8 [March 1908], PSR 4:346).
41. Lokerman, "Po tsarskim tiur'mam," 180.
42. Sandra Pujals, "The Accidental Revolutionary in the Russian Revolution: Impersonation, Criminal Activity, and Revolutionary Mythology in the Early Soviet Period, 1905–1935" *Revolutionary Russia* 22, no. 2 (2009), 191–92.
43. "Sudebnaia khoronika," *Tovarishch* 375 (September 19, 1907), PSR 8:650.
44. "Sudebnaia khronika," *Russkie vedomosti* 111 (May 13, 1908) and "Iz zala suda," *Russkoe slovo* (May 14, 1908), PSR 2:150; *Al'manakh. Sbornik po istorii anarkhicheskogo dvizheniia v Rossii* (Paris, 1909), 57, 61, 63; Obzor revoliutsionnogo dvizheniia v okruge Irkutskoi sudebnoi palaty za 1908 god, 35, Nic. 197:3.
45. Kantor, "Smertniki v tiur'me," *KS* 6 (1923): 127n.
46. "Iz obshchestvennoi khroniki," *Vestnik Evropy* 8 (1907): 842.
47. Unidentified newspaper clipping, October 17, 1906, PSR 4:346.
48. Vladimir Zhabotinskii, *Piatero* (Jerusalem: Biblioteka-Aliia, 1990), 160–61; P. P. Zavarzin, *Zhandarmy i revoliutsionery* (Paris, 1930), 179.
49. Gershuni, "Ob ekspropriatsiiakh" (undated letter to comrades), 4, Nic. 12:1.
50. "Anarkhizm," 51–52, Okhrana XVIb[5]:5A; *Russkoe slovo* 9 (January 13, 1909), PSR 8:653; *Al'manakh*, 35.
51. "Stolypin's New Policy, Repression and Reform," *New York Times*, September 5, 1906, http://query.nytimes.com/mem/archive-free/pdf?_r=1&res=9C07E7DD143DE433A25755C0A96F9C946797D6CF.
52. Kirzhnits, *Evreiskoe rabochee dvizhenie*, 258; other references in Geifman, *Thou Shalt Kill*, 275n196.
53. *Volia* 69 (September 29, 1906): 3, PSR 7:569.
54. References in GARF, f. 102, op. 1912, d. 88, 1, 7–7ob.
55. "Bor'ba s revoliutsionnym dvizheniem na Kavkaze," 216.
56. Obzor revoliutsionnogo dvizheniia v okruge Irkutskoi sudebnoi platy za 1908 god, 11–13, Nic. 197:3.
57. *Novoe vremia* (May 16, 1907), PSR 4:346; G. Nestroev, *Iz dnevnika Maksimalista* (Paris, 1910), 41.
58. *Russkoe slovo* (June 15, 1908), PSR 8:653.
59. Robert Fulford, "When Palestinians Become Oppressors," *The National Post* (February 2, 2004), http://www.robertfulford.com/2004-02-02-eid.html.
60. Justin Huggler and Sa'id Ghazali, "Palestinian Collaborators Executed," *Independent*, October 24, 2003, http://www.fromoccupiedpalestine.org/node/944.
61. Khaled Abu Toameh, "Hamas Condemns Collaborator to Death," July 20, 2008, http://www.jpost.com/servlet/Satellite?cid=1215331034395&pagename=JPost%2FJPArticle%2FShowFull.
62. See, for example, http://www.youtube.com/watch?v=I1M4eH9Kk7I.
63. Middle East Facts Photo Gallery, http://middleeastfacts.com/Gallery/thumbnails.php?album=11.
64. Private video (graphic images; discretion advised), http://www.metacafe.com/watch/666615/ever_heard_of_the_ramallah_lynching/.

65. Cited in "Widespread Use of Torture by PA, Hamas," *Jerusalem Post*, July 28, 2008, http://www.jpost.com/servlet/Satellite?cid=1215331122903&pagename=JPost%2FJPArticle%2FShowFull.

66. Cited in http://archives.econ.utah.edu/archives/marxism/2007w22/msg00224.htm.

67. Stathis N. Kalyvas and Ignacio Sánchez-Cuenca, "Killing without Dying: The Absence of Suicide Missions," in *Making Sense of Suicide Missions*, ed. Diego Gambetta, 218.

68. B. Raman, "Terrorist Strikes in Istanbul," South Asia Analyst Group, Paper 839, November 17, 2003, http://www.southasiaanalysis.org/%5Cpapers9%5Cpaper839.html.

69. Landes, "Totalitarian Millennialism: The Bolshevik Apocalypse," *Heaven on Earth*.

70. Elster, "Motivations and Beliefs in Suicide Missions," 249.

71. Jessica Stern, "How Terrorists Hijacked Islam," *USA Today*, October 1, 2001, http://www.alhewar.org/SEPTEMBER%2011/how_terrorists_hijacked_islam_by.htm.

72. O. V. Aptekman, "Partiia 'Narodnogo Prava,'" *Byloe* 7, no. 19 (1907): 189; G. Ul'ianov, "Vospominaniia o M. A. Natansone," *KS* 4, no. 89 (1932): 71.

73. "Iz otcheta o perliustratsii dept. politsii za 1908 g.," *KS* 2, no. 27 (1928): 156.

74. Edmund Wilson, *To the Finland Station: A Study in the Writing and Acting of History* (New York: Harcourt Brace, 1940), 272.

75. O. Piatnitskii, *Zapiski bol'shevika* (Moscow, 1956), 65.

76. Zhabotinskii, *Piatero*, 47.

77. See, for example, "Hamas Using Children as Human Shield," http://video.google.com/videosearch?hl=en&source=hp&q=hamas+uses+children+as+shields&um=1&ie=UTF-8&ei=8i7qSoSqAdTklQfutbX_BA&sa=X&oi=video_result_group&ct=title&resnum=1&ved=0CBIQqwQwAA#.

78. See, for example, "Hamas Booby Trapped School and Zoo 11 Jan. 2009," http://www.youtube.com/watch?v=uHhs9ihSmbU&NR=1.

79. Videos in "Hamas Terrorist Hides Behind White Flag Gaza 8 January 2009," http://www.youtube.com/watch?v=YJgfZ9_6miE&eurl=http%3A%2F%2Fwww%2Etheaugeanstables%2Ecom%2Fcategory%2Fpalestinian%2Dculture%2F&feature=player_embedded#t=78.

80. Ben Arnoldy, "In Afghanistan, Taliban Kills More Civilians Than US," *The Christian Science Monitor*, July 31, 2009, http://www.csmonitor.com/2009/0731/p06s15-wosc.html.

81. Psychologist Wolfgang Giegerich cited in Mazarr, *Unmodern Men in the Modern World*, 27–28.

82. Yaakov Katz, "UNRWA Suspends Aid to Gaza After Hamas Again Seizes Supplies," *Jerusalem Post*, February 6, 2009, http://www.jpost.com/servlet/Satellite?cid=1233304705842&pagename=JPost%2FJPArticle%2FShowFull; Brenda Gazzar and Yaakov Katz, "UN: Hamas Stole from Gaza Warehouse," *Jerusalem Post*, February 5, 2009, http://www.jpost.com/servlet/Satellite?cid=1233304681684&pagename=JPost/JPArticle/ShowFull.

83. Katz, "UNRWA Suspends Aid to Gaza."

84. "IDF: Hamas Seized 3 UNRWA Ambulances," August 6, 2009, http://www.jpost.com/servlet/Satellite?cid=1249418530852&pagename=JPost%2FJPArticle%2FShowFull.

85. See photograph in Yaakov Katz, "Hamas Threw 'Medicine Grenades' at IDF," *Jerusalem Post*, February 13, 2009, http://www.jpost.com/servlet/Satellite?cid=1233304770155&pagename=JPost%2FJPArticle%2FShowFull.
86. Bloom, *Dying to Kill*, 42.
87. Cited in Daniel Pipes, "PLO, Inc.," *American Spectator* (February 1991), http://www.danielpipes.org/204/plo-inc.
88. "Financial assets of Arafat, PLO, difficult to determine," Associated Press (November 8, 2004), http://www.billingsgazette.com/news/world/article_f347ce50-8d5d-5b10-aa34-796400a513e7.html; Daniel Pipes, "Arafat's Billions" (December 24, 2006), http://www.danielpipes.org/blog/2003/11/arafats-billions.

CHAPTER 4

1. "Pis'mo S. V. Zubatova A. I. Spiridovichu po povodu vykhoda v svet ego knigi 'Partiia s.-r. i ee predshestvenniki,'" *KA* 2 (1922), 281; Gerasimov, *Na lezvii s terroristami*, 195.
2. "Pamiati S. V. Sikorskogo," *KS* 41 (1928): 147; Nestroev, *Iz dnevnika maksimalista*, 8.
3. Boris Nikolajewski, *Azeff the Spy. Russian Terrorist and Police Stool* (New York, 1934), 54.
4. A. Spiridovich, *Partiia sotsialistov-revoliutsionerov i ee predshestvenniki (1886–1916)* (Petrograd, 1918), 123–24; A. Spiridovich, *Zapiski zhandarma* (Moscow, 1991), 122; Savinkov, *Vospominaniia terrorista*, 22.
5. Gershuni, "Ob ekspropriatsiiakh," 1–2, Nic. 12:1.
6. Pujals, "The Accidental Revolutionary," 184.
7. Norman M. Naimark, *Terrorists and Social Democrats. The Russian Revolutionary Movement under Alexander III* (Cambridge, MA: Harvard University Press, 1983), 241–42.
8. Naimark, "Terrorism and the Fall of Imperial Russia," 5. According to another scholar, workers performed at least 50 percent of all SR attacks (Maureen Perrie, "Political and Economic Terror in the Tactics of the Russian Socialist Revolutionary Party before 1914," in *Social Protest, Violence and Terror*, ed. Wolfgang J. Mommsen and Gerhard Hirschfeld, 68, Table 6.2).
9. Moskovich, "K istorii odnogo pokusheniia," *Byloe* 14 (1912): 38.
10. A. Zonin, "Primechaniia k st. Medvedevoi 'Tovarishch Kamo,'" *Proletarskaia revoliutsiia* [cited hereafter as PR] 8–9, no. 31–32 (1924): 144; I. Dubinskii-Mukhadze, *Kamo* (Moscow, 1974), 186–87.
11. *Al'manakh*, 37.
12. Moskovich, "K istorii odnogo pokusheniia," 39.
13. "Bolkhov. Derevenskie anarkhisty," *Russkoe slovo*, October 23, 1907, PSR 8:650.
14. Cited in Geifman, *Thou Shalt Kill*, 155.
15. V. Ropshin, *Kon' blednyi* (Nice, 1913), 32.
16. Savinkov denied it until 1924 (Richard B. Spence, *Boris Savinkov: Renegade on the Left* [New York, 1991], 92; M. Gorbunov, "Savinkov, kak memuarist," *KS* 3, no. 40 [1928]: 174n–175).
17. Aileen Kelly, "Self-Censorship and the Russian Intelligentsia, 1905–1914," *Slavic Review* 46, no. 2 (Summer 1987): 201–2.
18. http://www.freerepublic.com/focus/news/667398/posts. For his role in the Munich massacre during the 1972 Olympic Games, Salameh was killed by Israeli

security forces in Beirut on January 22, 1979 (James M. Markham, "Life and Death of a Terrorist," *New York Times*, July 10, 1983, http://www.nytimes.com/1983/07/10/books/life-and-death-of-a-terrorist.html).

19. Savinkov, *Vospominannia terrororista*, 50–51.

20. A. Martsinskovskii, "Vospominannia o 1905 g. v.g. Rige," *PR* 12 (1922): 328; Geifman, *Thou Shalt Kill*, 70.

21. Holmes, "Al-Qaeda, September 11, 2001," in Gambetta, ed., *Making Sense of Suicide Missions*, 131, 138.

22. Grigorii Frolov, "Terroristicheskii akt nad samarskim gubernatorom," *Katogra i ssylka* 1, no. 8 (1924), 117.

23. *Al'manakh*, 45.

24. Vitiazev, Isakovich, and Kallistov, "Iz vospominanii o N. D. Shishmareve," *KS* 6 (1923): 261.

25. "Feodosei Zubar' (Nekrolog)," 15, Okhrana XXIVe:2d.

26. V. I. Sukhomlin, "Iz tiuremnykh skitanii," *KS* 55 (1929): 103.

27. *Byvshie liudi. Al'manakh* 1 (n.p., n.d.), 9, Nic. 757:5.

28. Boris Nicolaevsky, introduction to the "Bol'shevistskii Tsentr": "K istorii 'bol'shevistskogo Tsentra,'" 119, Nic. 544–11.

29. Report of December 16 (3), 1907, Okhrana XIc[4]:1; Souvarine, *Stalin*, 126; Geifman, *Thou Shalt Kill*, 301n236.

30. Cited in Chuzhak, "Lenin i 'tekhnika vosstaniia,'" *KS* 12, no. 73 (1931): 111.

31. N. E. Burenin, *Pamiatnye gody Vospominaniia* (Leningrad, 1967), 85.

32. Cited in Geifman, *Thou Shalt Kill*, 88.

33. Baron [Bibineishvili], *Za chetvert' veka*, 145; cited in Geifman, *Thou Shalt Kill*, 141.

34. Pozner, ed., *Boevaia gruppa pri TsK RSDRP(b)*, 180–84; Rostov, "S pervoi volnoi," 52–53.

35. For examples, see Geifman, *Thou Shalt Kill*, 93.

36. Pozner, ed., *Boevaia gruppa pri TsK RSDRP(b)*, 92.

37. Letters from D. Shub to P. A. Garvi dated June 16, November 1, 1947, and December 1, 1947, Nic. 438:19.

38. December 23, 1916, police report, Okhrana XVIIa:4W.

39. A. Sukhov, "Tri mesiatsa raboty v Shendrikovskoi gruppe," PR 10, no. 45 (1925): 118.

40. Aleksandr Rozhdestvenskii, "Desiat' let sluzhby v Prokurorskom Nadzore na Kavkaze" (Santiago, Chile, 1961), 49, AR.

41. S. Maglakelidze and A. Iovidze, eds., *Revoliutsiia 1905–1907 gg. V Gruzii. Sbornik dokumentov* (Tbilisi, 1956), 277–78.

42. Cited in Geifman, *Thou Shalt Kill*, 100.

43. For examples, see Ibid., 103–5.

44. "Obzor partiii, primykaiushchikh k RSDRP," 30, Okhrana XVIb(6):1C; *Ianis Luter Bobis*, 80.

45. Burtsev, *Doloi tsaria!*, 22, PSR 1:19.

46. Savinkov, *Vospominaniia terrorista*, 201.

47. Beloborodov, "Iz istorii partizanskogo dvizheniia na Urale," *Krasnaia letopis'* 1, no. 16 (1926): 93–98.

48. Nestroev, *Iz dnevnika maksimalista*, 112.

49. Emphasis added, "Vzryv na Aptekarskom ostrove," 212.

50. Pozner, ed., Boevaia gruppa pri TsK RSDRP(b), 118; *Leonid Borisovich Krasin ("Nikitich"). Gody podpol'ia* (Moscow, Leningrad, 1928), 232.

51. "Pokushenie na ubiistvo g.-m. Kosheleva," 1, Nic. 199:7.

52. "Obzor partiii, primykaiushchikh k RSDRP," 32–33, Okhrana XVIb(6):1C.

53. "Obzor deiatel'nosti Litovskoi sotsial-demokraticheskoi partii," 1909, 14, Okhrana XXII:2.

54. Pozner, ed., Boevaia gruppa pri TsK RSDRP(b), 79.

55. Juergensmeyer, *Terror in the Mind of God*, 126.

56. Political theorist Yaron Ezrahi cited in Thomas L. Friedman, "Behind the Masks," *The New York Times*, June 20, 2007, http://select.nytimes.com/2007/06/20/opinion/20friedman.html?_r=1.

57. Cited in Dawson, "The Bali Bombers," http://www.capmag.com/article.asp?ID=3000.

58. "Materialy o provokatorakh," PSR 5:518.

59. Hoffer, *The True Believer*, 64.

60. Stephen R. Bowers, Ashley Ann Derrick, and Mousafar Olimov, "Suicide Terrorism in the Former USSR," *Journal of Social, Political, and Economic Studies* 29, no. 3 (Fall 2004): 271.

61. Cited in Landes, "Totalitarian Millennialism: The Bolshevik Apocalypse," *Heaven on Earth*.

62. Ibid; E. H. Carr, Michael Bakunin (New York: Octagon Books, 1975), 24; Mikhail Bakunin, God and the State, http://www.marxists.org/reference/archive/bakunin/works/godstate/index.htm..

63. Cited in Juergensmeyer, *Terror in the Mind of God*, 110, 113.

64. Hoffer, *The True Believer*, 65.

65. Cited in reports of August 9 (22) and May 17 (30), 1907, Okhrana XXIVi:1B.

66. Jan Willen van Henten and Friedrich Avemarie, *Martyrdom and Noble Death* (London and New York: Routledge, 2002), 1.

67. Hoffman, "How the Terrorists Stopped Terrorism," http://www.theatlantic.com/doc/200112/hoffman.

68. Cited in Simon Reeve, "One Day in September," 20–21, http://books.google.co.il/books?id=BcAsBHZ4DLwC&pg=PA20&lpg=PA20&dq=black+september%2Blick&source=bl&ots=vkZJlItF71&sig=s22XTmilgGrP1gZX780eWvFi67M&hl=en&ei=I9JPSoIBoYqdA8aosaAF&sa=X&oi=book_result&ct=result&resnum=1.

69. R. A. Gorodnitskii, *Boevaia organizatsiia partii sotsialistov-revoliutsionerov v 1901-1911 gg.* (Moscow: ROSSPEN, 1998), 80–81.

70. Grigorii Gershuni, *Iz nedavnego proshlogo* (Paris: Tribune russe, 1908), 17.

71. Landes, "Totalitarian Millennialism: The Bolshevik Apocalypse," *Heaven on Earth*.

72. The gas was administered in very high dosage, which left one in seven (possibly up to 200) hostages dead and hundreds hospitalized in critical condition and in some cases caused permanent impairment (Scott Peterson, "Gas Enters Counterterror Arsenal," *Christian Science Monitor*, October 29, 2002, http://www.csmonitor.com/2002/1029/p01s03-woeu.html).

73. Francis Fukuyama and Nadav Samin, "Can Any Good Come of Radical Islam?" http://www.commentarymagazine.com/viewarticle.cfm/can-any-good-come-of-radical-islam-9498?search=1.

74. Jessica Stern, "How Terrorists Hijacked Islam," http://www.alhewar.org/SEPTEMBER%2011/how_terrorists_hijacked_islam_by.htm.

75. Von Hans Magnus Enzensberger, Schreckens Männer: Versuch über den radikalen Verlierer (Frankfurt am Main: Edition Suhrkamp, 2006).

76. Huxley, The Perennial Philosophy, 243; Jonathan Spyer, fellow at the Global Research in International Affairs at the Interdisciplinary Center in Herzliya, interview to the *Jerusalem Post*, cited in http://www.theaugeanstables.com/2007/08/17/how-liberals-unconsciously-pursue-the-politics-of-the-worse/. See also Litvak, "The Islamization of the Palestinian-Israeli conflict," 148.

77. Reuter, *My Life Is a Weapon*, 125.

78. Bernard Lewis, *The Crisis of Islam: Holy War and Unholy Terror* (New York: Modern Library Edition, 2003), 154.

79. Mazarr, *Unmodern Men in the Modern World*, 190.

80. Thomas Friedman cited in Pipes, "Terrorism: The Syrian Connection," http://www.danielpipes.org/1064/terrorism-the-syrian-connection.

81. According to official Israeli sources, "The Palestinian Authority allocated vast sums of money from its budget to pay salaries to Fatah terrorists (45 million dollars a month from Arab countries, 9 million dollars a month from the European Unity)," The Involvement of Arafat, PA Senior Officials and Apparatuses in Terrorism against Israel—Corruption and Crime (May 6, 2002), http://www.mfa.gov.il/MFA/MFAArchive/2000_2009/2002/5/The%20Involvement%20of%20Arafat-%20PA%20Senior%20Officials%20and.

82. Cited in Mazarr, *Unmodern Men in the Modern World*, 190.

83. Ibid.; Berko, *The Path to Paradise*, 6–7.

84. Cited in Dawson, "The Bali Bombers," http://www.capmag.com/article.asp?ID=3000.

85. I. Grossman-Roshchin, "Dumy o bylom," *Byloe* 27–28 (1924): 179.

86. Amy Knight, "Female Terrorists in the Russian Socialist Revolutionary Party," *Russian Review* 38, no. 2 (April 1979): 152.

87. For discussion of al-Qaeda's remarkable "willingness to forge broad—and sometimes unlikely—alliances" within and outside of bin Laden's International Islamic Front for Jihad Against the Jews and Crusaders, see Stern, "The Protean Enemy," http://www.cfr.org/pub6146/jessica_stern/the_protean_enemy.php.

88. B. Raman, "Terrorist Strikes in Istanbul," South Asia Analyst Group, Paper 839, November 17, 2003, http://www.southasiaanalysis.org/%5Cpapers9%5Cpaper839.html.

89. Marks, *How Russia Shaped the Modern World*, 320.

90. Pipes, "Terrorism: The Syrian Connection," http://www.danielpipes.org/1064/terrorism-the-syrian-connection.

91. Elena Ovcharenko and Maksim Chizhikov, "Arabskikh terroristov gotovili v Krymu," *Komsomol'skaia Pravda*, September 28, 2001.

92. Bloom, *Dying to Kill*, 121.

93. For discussion of the clandestine Soviet role in financing and training of the PLO terrorists see Roberta Goren, *The Soviet Union and Terrorism* (London-Boston-Sydney: George Allen & Unwin, 1984), 136–42.

94. Bloom, *Dying to Kill*, 34.

95. Geifman, *Thou Shalt Kill*, 202–6.

96. Cited in Walid Phares, *Future Jihad: Terrorist Strategires against America* (New York: Palgrave Macmillan, 2005), 81.

97. Stern, "The Protean Enemy," http://www.cfr.org/pub6146/jessica_stern/the_protean_enemy.php.

98. Sam Gaines, "The Gun Still Speaks: Interview with Richard Huffman," http://www.baader-meinhof.com/essays/EyeInterview.html.

99. Pipes, "Terrorism: The Syrian Connection," http://www.danielpipes.org/1064/terrorism-the-syrian-connection.

100. Bloom, *Dying to Kill*, 120, 138–39.
101. Pipes, "Terrorism: The Syrian Connection," http://www.danielpipes.org/1064/terrorism-the-syrian-connection.
102. Aaron Clauset and Kristian Skrede Gleditsch, "The developmental dynamics of terrorist organizations," *Physics and Society* (June 2009), http://arxiv.org/abs/0906.3287.
103. Stern, "The Protean Enemy," http://www.cfr.org/pub6146/jessica_stern/the_protean_enemy.php.

CHAPTER 5

1. Cited in Serebrennikiov, ed., *Ubiistvo Stolypina*, 319.
2. Cited in Pujals, "The Accidental Revolutionary," 181.
3. Reference, for example, in "Iz obshchestvennoi khoroniki," *Vestnik Evropy* 8 (1907): 844.
4. Cited in Serebrennikiov, ed., *Ubiistvo Stolypina*, 319.
5. *Al'manakh*, 162–63.
6. Philip Pomper, "Russian Revolutionary Terrorism" in *Terrorism in Context*, ed. Martha Crenshaw (Philadelphia: Penn State Press, 1995), 71.
7. "Sergey Nechayev 1869: The Revolutionary Catechism," http://www.marxists.org/subject/anarchism/nechayev/catechism.htm.
8. Marks, *How Russia Shaped the Modern World*, 13.
9. Pomper, "Russian Revolutionary Terrorism" in *Terrorism in Context*, 73.
10. Petr Struve cited in Serebrennikiov, ed., *Ubiistvo Stolypina*, 319. The appearance of "the new breed of combatants and expropriators" is also noted in Lokerman, "Po tsarskim tiur'mam," 186.
11. Nestroev, *Iz dnevnika maksimalista*, 218.
12. Sukhomlin, "Iz tiuremnykh skitanii," 104.
13. "Ko vsem!" and "Opoveshchenie," undated leaflet issued by the Elizavetgrad PSR Committee, PSR 9:747; GARF, f. 102, 00, op. 1911, d. 302: 20.
14. "In the beginning, when throwing a letter with a threat or pointing a revolver, they would refer to some anonymous 'party,' but soon they discarded even this much and began to just mug, without any veil" (Zhabotinskii, *Piatero*, 160).
15. PSR 5:443.
16. Report 10981 from the governor of Moscow to the police department, dated October 16, 1907, Okhrana XXVd:2D; GARF, f. 102, 00, op. 1911, d. 302: 20.
17. "Anarkhizm," 81–82, Okhrana, XVIb[5]:5A.
18. "Dopros Gerasimova. 26 April 1917 goda," Padenie tsarskogo rezhima, v. 3 (Leningrad, 1925): 3.
19. Zavarzin, *Zhandarmy i revoliutsionery*, 180–81, 185.
20. GARF f. 102, DPOO, op. 1915, d. 12, ch. 6: 1–2.
21. *Sekira* 12 (1906): 7, Nic. 436:2.
22. E. Koval'skaia, "Po povodu stat'i M. P. Orlova 'Ob Akatui vremen Mel'shina,'" *KS* 52 (1929): 164.
23. "The Aftermath of Beslan," Hudson Institute, November 15, 2006, http://www.hudson.org/index.cfm?fuseaction=publication_details&id=4306&pubType=HI_Articles.
24. Gambetta and Hertog, "Engineers of Jihad," p. 24, www.sociology.ox.ac.uk/swp.html.

25. Terrorist expert Ariel Merari cited in Berko, *The Path to Paradise*, 150.
26. Unaddressed letter from G. Gershuni dated February 23, 1906, p. 4, Nic. 12:1.
27. T. S. Krivov, *V leninskom stroui* (Cheboksary 1969), 70–71; *Al'manakh*, 104.
28. See, for example, PSR 2:127.
29. *Al'manakh*, 97, 149.
30. Pozner, ed., *Boevaia gruppa pri TsK RSDRP(b)*, 102–3, and Nicolaevsky, "Bol'shevistskii Tsentr," Notes to Documents, 1–14, 15, n. 32, Nic. 544:11.
31. Gerasimov, *Na lezvii s terroristami*, 87, 91.
32. Nestroev, *Iz dnevnika maksimalista*, 75–76.
33. Zavarzin, *Zhandarmy i revoliutsionery*, 188.
34. Nicolaevsky, introduction to the "Bol'shevistskii Tsentr," 32, Nic. 544:11.
35. Souvarine, *Stalin*, 96; Tat'iana Vulikh, "Osnovnoe iadro kavkazskoi boevoi organizatsii," 3–4, Nic. 207:11; Tat'iana Vulikh, "Vstrecha s gruppoi bol'shevikov-eksistov," 1, Nic. 207:10.
36. Report of August 6 (19), 1912, Okhrana XXVb:1. Details in Geifman, *Thou Shalt Kill*, 158–59.
37. Many examples in Ravich-Cherkasskii, "Moi vospominaniia o 1905 gode," *Letopis' revoliutsii* 5–6, no. 14–15 (1925): 319; Iurenev, "Rabota R. S.-D. R. P. v Severo-Zapadnom krae," 176; Kochetov, "Vologodskaia ssylka 1907–1910 godov," *KS* 4, no. 89 (1932): 87–88; Zavarzin, *Rabota tainoi politsii*, 113; *Al'manakh*, 89, 93–94, 103.
38. Dubinskii-Mukhadze, *Kamo*, 68.
39. Report of January 16 (29), 1909, Okhrana XXVc:1.
40. Report of August 4 (17), 1907, Okhrana XXVc:2M.
41. Pipes, "Terrorism: The Syrian Connection," http://www.danielpipes.org/1064/terrorism-the-syrian-connection.
42. Nestroev, *Iz dneivnika maksimalista*, 221.
43. G. Jefferson Price cited in Pipes, "Terrorism: The Syrian Connection," http://www.danielpipes.org/1064/terrorism-the-syrian-connection.
44. "Anarkhizm," 64, Okhrana, XVIb[5]:5A; "Delo anarkhistov-expropriatorov," *Tovarishch* 379 (September 23, 1907), PSR 8:650; Gershuni, "Ob ekspropriatsiiakh," 2, Nic. 12:1; Komarov, "Ocherki po istorii mestnykh i oblastnykh boevykh organizatsii," *KS* 25 (1926): 79.
45. Petr Kropotkin's letter to Mariia Gol'dsmit, Nic. 81:4.
46. Lokerman, "Po tsarskim tiur'mam," 185.
47. Koval'skaia, "Po povodu stat'i M. P. Orlova," 165; I. V. Shaurov, *1905 god* (Moscow, 1965), 235.
48. Lokerman, "Po tsarskim tiur'mam," 187; Nestroev, *Iz dneivnika maksimalista*, 222.
49. "Sergey Nechayev 1869: The Revolutionary Catechism," http://www.marxists.org/subject/anarchism/nechayev/catechism.htm.
50. Cited in V. Zenzinov, "Stranichka iz istorii rannego bol'shevizma" (n. d.), 11, Nic. 392:4.
51. I. Genkin, "Anarkhisty," *Byloe* 3, no. 31 (1918), 164.
52. Report of April 22, 1904, 4, Okhrana XIIIc(2):4A; Reference 27, Okhrana XVIIn:8; "K tovarishcham anarkhistam-kommunistam," Nic. 3:3.
53. See, for example, Zavarzin, *Zhandarmy i revoliutsionery*, 180, and Al'manakh, 45–46.
54. I. Ivanova, "Sadanul pod serdtse finskii nozh," *Rossiiskaia provintsiia* (4), 1995, http://sergeiesenin.niv.ru/press/sadanul_pod_serdtce_fenskei_nogh.html.

55. Peter B. Neubauer, "Hate and Developmental Sequences and Group Dynamics: Concluding Reflections," in *The Birth of Hatred*, ed. Salman Akhtar, Selma Kramer, and Henri Parens (Northvale, NJ: Jason Aronson, 1995), 159.

56. Ivanova, "Sadanul pod serdtse finskii nozh," http://sergeiesenin.niv.ru/press/sadanul_pod_serdtce_fenskei_nogh.html.

57. Cited in Manfred Hildermeier, *Die Sozialrevolutionäre Partei Russlands: Agrarsozialismus und Modernisierung in Zarenreich (1900–1914)* (Cologne, 1978), 138.

58. Handwritten copy of an article written by Peskel, "S-ry i maksimalisty na Litve," PSR 3:269.

59. GARF, f. 102, DPOO, op. 1912, d. 80, ch. 3: 54–54ob; "Bor'ba s revoliutsionnym dvizhenie na Kavkaze," 195; K. Zakharova-Tsederbaum, "V gody reaktsii," *KS* 60 (1929): 77–78.

60. *Al'manakh*, 104.

61. "Pribaltiiskii krai," 272.

62. "SKP uznal rastsenki boevikov na ubistva prokurorov i militsionerov," Lenta.ru, July 17, 2009, http://lenta.ru:80/news/2009/07/03/pricelist/.

63. 1907 report filed by police agent Krauso, Okhrana XXIVh:4k; "Obvinitel'nyi akt po delu o pisariakh," PSR 170I; "Iz dnevnika A. N. Kuropatkina," *KA* 1, no. 8 (1925): 97.

64. "Dashnaktsutiun. Obvinitel'nyi akt," 248, Nic. 256"5.

65. Report of June 10, 1904, Okhrana XIIIc(2):4B.

66. "Pribaltiiskii krai," 272.

67. For multiple references see Geifman, *Thou Shalt Kill*, 327n159.

68. Berko, *The Path to Paradise*, 150.

69. Maureen Perrie, "Social Composition and Structure of the Socialist Revolutionary Party before 1917," *Soviet Studies* 24 (October 1972): 231.

70. "Obvinitel'nyi akt o meshchanakh Movshe Arone Davidove Zakgeime i Tsirle Khaimovoi Shkol'nik," 1, PSR 9:778.

71. See, for example, Nadel'shtein, "Butyrskie ocherki," *KS* 45–46 (1928): 197; "Pamiati S. V. Sikorskogo," 146; Tashkentets, "Pervaia viselitsa v g. Penze," *KS* 50 (1928): 93; *Russkoe slovo* 21 (October 1907), PSR 8:650.

72. M. Liadov, *Iz zhizni partii v 1903–1907 godakh* (Moscow, 1956), 135.

73. Friedman, "Behind the Masks," http://select.nytimes.com/2007/06/20/opinion/20friedman.html?_r=1.

74. *Russkoe slovo* 129 (June 6, 1907), PSR 8:650.

75. Police Department materials, protocol dated September 17, 1901, St. Petersburg, PSR 8:675; "Vzryv v Znamenskom monastyre v Kurske," PSR 3:293.

76. Kniazev, "1905," 247.

77. "Participation of Children and Teenagers in Terrorist Activity during the Al-Aqsa Intifada," January 30, 2003, http://www.mfa.gov.il/MFA/MFAArchive/2000_2009/2003/1/Participation+of+Children+and+Teenagers+in+Terrori.htm.

78. Sukhomlin, "Iz tiuremnykh skitanii," 103; copy of a letter from Beilin to Musil', Outgoing Dispatches (1907), doc. 450, Okhrana, XIIIb(1):1C.

79. Tagantsev, *Smertnaia kazan'*, 163.

80. Berko, *The Path to Paradise*, 153.

81. "Columbia: Armed Groups Send Children to War." Human Rights Watch (February 21, 2005), http://www.hrw.org/en/news/2005/02/21/colombia-armed-groups-send-children-war.

82. Victoria Garcia, "A Risky Business: U.S. Arms Exports to Countries Where Terror Thrives," Center for Defense Information (November 21, 2001), http://www.cdi.org/terrorism/arms-exports.cfm.

83. Shaul Kimhi and Shemuel Even, "Who Are the Palestinian Suicide Bombers?" *Terrorism and Political Violence* 16, no. 4 (Winter 2004): 826.

84. Berko, *The Path to Paradise*, 130.

85. "The Third Jihad," Part 1, http://www.road90.com/watch.php?id=tAfPJzb7Yc; "Suicide Attacks in Afghanistan (2001–2007)," United Nations Assistance Mission in Afghanistan, 9 September 2007, p. 90, http://www.reliefweb.int/rw/RWFiles2007.nsf/FilesByRWDocUnidFilename/EKOI-76W52H-full_report.pdf/$File/full_report.pdf.

86. Zavarzin, *Rabota tainoi politsii*, 111–12.

87. Iagudin, "Na Chernigovshchine," *KS* 57–58 (1929): 301.

88. Kimhi and Even, "Who Are the Palestinian Suicide Bombers?" 826.

89. Report of February 24 [March 8], 1912, Okhrana, XXIVa:1A.

90. M. Gorbunov, "Savinkov, kak memuarist," *KS* 4, no. 41 (1928): 169–70; report of November 18 (December 1), 1910, Okhrana XXIVi:2P.

91. Geifman, *Thou Shalt Kill*, 316–17n29, 158.

92. Jay Bergman, *Vera Zasulich* (Stanford, CA: Stanford University Press, 1983), 27–28; Deborah Hardy, *Land and Freedom: The Origins of Russian Terrorism, 1876–1879* (New York: Greenwood Press, 1987), 55.

93. For examples, see Arkhiv L. P. Menshchikova, International Institute of Social History, Amsterdam, 0-BB, 1–2; *Parus* 96 (June 7, 1907), PSR 8:653; April 2, 1909, police report, Okhrana XIX:6; Zavarzin, *Rabota tainoi politsii*, 131–36; April 21, 1905, police report, 4, Okhrana XIIIc(2):6B.

94. Dubinskii-Mukhadze, *Kamo*, 156.

95. Maksim Gor'kii cited in Geifman, *Thou Shalt Kill*, 255.

96. E-mail sent Wednesday, June 10, 2009.

97. "Anarkhizm," 51–52, Okhrana, XVIb[5]:5A.

98. "The Proletarian Armed Squads: Or Rather, Prison and Machine Guns," *Gnosis: Italian Intelligence Magazine* 2 (2006), http://www.sisde.it/gnosis/Rivista7.nsf/ServNavigE/21.

99. Stern, "The Protean Enemy," http://www.cfr.org/pub6146/jessica_stern/the_protean_enemy.php; details in "The Third Jihad," Part 1, http://www.road90.com/watch.php?id=tAfPJzb7Yc.

100. "The Aftermath of Beslan," http://www.hudson.org/index.cfm?fuseaction=publication_details&id=4306&pubType=HI_Articles; "Khodov, Vladimir. Uchastnik zakhvata shkoly v Beslane," http://www.lenta.ru/lib/14163039/; "Pozyvnoi 'Abdula,'" Ukraina kriminal'naia, September 7, 2004, http://cripo.com.ua/?sect_id=2&aid=2331.

101. Ibid.

102. Jeremy McDermott, "Farc aura of invincibility shattered," BBC News, March 1, 2008, http://news.bbc.co.uk/2/hi/americas/7273320.stm.

103. Cited in Simon Romero, "Cocaine Trade Helps Rebels Reignite War in Peru," *New York Times*, March 17, 2009, http://www.nytimes.com/2009/03/18/world/americas/18peru.html?_r=2. See also Brice, "Shining Path Rebels Stage Comeback in Peru," http://edition.cnn.com/2009/WORLD/americas/04/21/peru.shining.path/index.html.

104. James Bovard, "The Bush Administration's 'Drugs = Terrorism' Fraud," The Future of Freedom Foundation, April 2002, http://www.fff.org/comment/com0204f.

asp; and "UN Agencies Report Massive Increase in Opium Poppy Production in Afghanistan," http://www.narcoterror.org/afghanistan.htm.

105. Michel Chossudovsky, "Hidden Agenda behind the 'War on Terrorism': US Bombing of Afghanistan Restores Trade in Narcotics," Centre for Research on Globalisation (CRG), May 20, 2002, http://www.globalresearch.ca/articles/CHO205B.html.

106. Bowers, Derrick, and Olimov, "Suicide Terrorism in the Former USSR," 271.

107. Andrew Osborn, "Beslan Hostage-Takers 'Were on Drugs,'" *The Independent*, October 18, 2004, http://www.independent.co.uk/news/world/europe/beslan-hostagetakers-were-on-drugs-535298.html. These claims "were backed up by Alexander Torshin, the chairman of the parliamentary inquiry into the tragedy, who said that many of the witnesses he and his colleagues had interviewed had said the same." On the other hand, a source in the North Ossetian police's forensic services denied that all Beslan terrorists were taking drugs, although admitting that there "may have been some drug addicts among them" ("Drug Addiction among the Beslan Terrorists," *Pravda Online*, November 19, 2004, http://newsfromrussia.com/world/2004/10/19/56680.html).

108. Denis MacEoin, "Suicide Bombing as Worship: Dimensions of Jihad," *Middle East Quarterly* 16, no. 4 (Fall 2009), http://www.meforum.org/2478/suicide-bombing-as-worship.

109. Interview with P. K., U.S. Army intelligence agent, about his service in Iraq in 2003–2004. March 14, 2007, Boston, MA. Name and rank withheld due to his ongoing service in the military.

110. Ibid.

CHAPTER 6

1. Between 2000 and 2007, there were a total of 140 suicide bombings in Israel, which killed 542 individuals ("Victims of Palestinian Violence and Terrorism since September 2000," Israeli Ministry of Foreign Affairs, http://www.mfa.gov.il/MFA/Terrorism-+Obstacle+to+Peace/Palestinian+terror+since+2000/Victims+of+Palestinian+Violence+and+Terrorism+sinc.htm).

2. Mikail Prishvin, "Nachalo veka" (unfinished novella).

3. Zhabotinskii, *Piatero*, 193–99.

4. Robert Tracy, ed., *Osip Mandelstam's Stone* (Princeton, NJ: Princeton University Press, 1981), 131.

5. Richard Stites, cited in Kirk Rodby, The Dark Heart of Utopia: Sexuality, Ideology, and the Totalitarian Movement (New York-Bloomington, IN: iUniverse, Inc. 2009), 216.

6. Laura Engelstein, *The Keys to Happiness: Sex and the Search for Modernity in Fin-de-Siècle Russia* (Ithaca, NY: Cornell University Press, 1992), 216.

7. Andrei Belyi, *Petersburg* (Bloomington: Indiana University Press, 1978), 9.

8. Bernice Glatzer Rosenthal, ed., *The Occult in Russian and Soviet Culture* (Cornell University Press, 1997), 1. Most luminous representatives of the literary elite, such as writers Viacheslav Ivanov, Aleksei Remizov, Nikolai Berdiaev, Vasilii Rozanov, Fedor Sologub, and many others, took part in "pseudo-pagan gatherings." One typical "spiritual séance" is sufficient as an illustration. It entailed "crucifying" a sacrifice-volunteer (a handsome Jew), whose wrists and feet were "symbolically nailed." Ivanov and his wife cut an artery below his hand, close to the pulse, so that blood would drop into a special cup. Then they mixed blood with wine and drank it, passing the cup around the circle, and concluded the "mystic rite" with "brotherly kissing." For discussion see

A. Etkin, *Khlyst (Sekty, literature i revoliutsiia)* (Moscow: Novoe literaturnoe obozrenie, 1998), 8–9. Rituals of imitative worship varied, but sacraments of blood, preferably that of a Jew or a "Jewish virgin," was one constant element (ibid., 10).

9. Term coined in Paul Zweig, *The Heresy of Self-Love: A Study of Subversive Individualism* (New York-London: Basic Books, 1968), vi.

10. "Materialy o provokatorakh," PSR 5:518.

11. Cited in Nestroev, *Iz dnevnika maksimalista*, 218.

12. Report of June 28 (July 11), 1913, Okhrana XXII:1B.

13. Cited in Nathan Leites, *A Study of Bolshevism* (Glencoe, IL: The Free Press Publishers, 1953), 345.

14. V. M. Chernov, *Pered burei* (New York: Izdatel'stvo imeni Chekhova, 1953), 169.

15. Stern, "The Protean Enemy," http://www.cfr.org/pub6146/jessica_stern/the_protean_enemy.php.

16. Dmitrii Merezhkovskii, "Revoliutsiia i religiia," *Russkaia mysl'* 2–3 (1907).

17. Andrei Belyi, *Nachalo veka* (Moscow-Leningrad: Gosudarstvennoe izdatel'stvo khudozhestvennoi literatury, 1933), 3; Belyi, *Na rubezhe dvukh stoletii*, 3.

18. Tolstoi, *Ordeal*, 29.

19. Vladimir Chizh cited in Laura Goering, " 'Russian Nervousness': Neurasthenia and National Identity in Nineteenth-Century Russia," *Medical History* 47 (2003): 45.

20. Belyi, *Nachalo veka*, 3.

21. Tolstoi, *Ordeal*, 30.

22. Alexander Blok, "The People and the Intelligentsia," in *Russian Intellectual History: An Anthology*, ed. Marc Raeff (New York: Humanity Books, 1978), 362.

23. Historians of the Middle Ages and the antiquity are familiar with periods of similar spiritual turmoil, as described, for example, in Zweig, *The Heresy of Self-Love*, 4–9.

24. Hazani, "Sacrificial Immortality," 425.

25. Cited in Venozhinskii, *Smertnaia kazn' i terror* (St. Petersburg, 1908), 28.

26. Eugene Kayden, "Leonid Andreyev: 1871–1919," http://worldlibrary.net/eBooks/Wordtheque/en/aaabnxe.txt.

27. Laqueur, *Terrorism*, 130, 127.

28. Kayden, "Leonid Andreyev," http://worldlibrary.net/eBooks/Wordtheque/en/aaabnxe.txt.

29. Cited in Susan K. Morrissey, *Heralds of Revolution*, 185.

30. Ibid.

31. Roberta Ann Kaplan, " 'A Total Negation of Russia': Russian Intellectual Perception of Suicide, 1900–1914" (unpublished paper, Harvard University, 1988), 32.

32. Susan K. Morrissey, *Suicide and Body Politic in Imperial Russia* (New York: Cambridge University Press, 2006), 315.

33. "Land and Sea in the Traditional Russian World View," http://enspire.syr.edu/nevaproject/river&city/land&sea.html.

34. Lincoln, *Sunlight at Midnight*, 212.

35. George Reavey, "Foreword," in Andrey Biely, *St. Petersburg* (New York: Grove Press, 1959), vii.

36. Aleksei Nikolaevich Tolstoi, "khozhdenie po mukam," http://kulichki.com/moshkow/TOLSTOJA/hozhdenie1.txt.

37. Morrissey, *Suicide and Body Politic*, 316.

38. Morrissey, *Heralds of Revolution*, 197.

39. Laqueur, *Terrorism*, 130.

40. "Sergey Nechayev 1869: The Revolutionary Catechism," http://www.marxists.org/subject/anarchism/nechayev/catechism.htm.

41. Lev Tikhomirov cited in Richard Pipes, *The Degaev Affair. Terror and Treason in Tsarist Russia* (New Haven, CT: Yale University Press, 2003), 17–18.

42. Emad Salib, "Suicide Terrorism: A Case of Folie *à* Plusieurs?" *British Journal of Psychiatry* 182 (2003): 476.

43. Knight, "Female Terrorists," 152.

44. Savinkov, *Vospominaniia terrorista*, 40.

45. Huxley, The Perennial Philosophy, 163.

46. Semen Frank, *Sochinenia* (Moscow: Pravda, 1990), 153.

47. Mark Aldanov, "Azef," *Poslednie novosti* (1924), Nic. 205:19.

48. Atmosphere of acrimony and disparagement among the terrorists, prototypes of the SR Combat Organization, is depicted in Ropshin's *Kon' blednyi.*

49. Savinkov, *Vospominaniia terrorista*, 40, 117.

50. Naimark, "Terrorism and the Fall of Imperial Russia," 5; Laqueur, *Terrorism*, 121.

51. Daniel Field, "Ekaterina Breshkovskaia" (unpublished manuscript).

52. Anne Speckhard and Khapta Akhmedova, "Black Widows: The Chechen Female Suicide Terrorists," in *Female Suicide Bombers: Dying for Equality?* ed. Yoram Schweitzer (Tel Aviv: Jaffee Center for Strategic Studies [JCSS], 2006), 76.

53. Field, "Ekaterina Breshkovskaia" (unpublished manuscript).

54. Letter from Lidia Pavlovna Ezerskaia, PSR 1:2.

55. Knight, "Female Terrorists," 151, 153.

56. A strikingly similar case involved a 21-year-old Wafa Samir Ibrahim al-Bas from the northern Gaza Strip, who carried 10 kilograms of explosives hidden in her underclothes to blow herself up in the Soroka Medical Center in Beersheva on June 20, 2005. Al-Bas had been badly burned in an accident in late 2004, seriously injured, physically and cosmetically deformed. After being apprehended, she initially denied that her volunteering for the suicide act "had been connected with her difficult external appearance caused by the many burns and scars on her body." Subsequently, however, Al-Bas admitted that her handlers had "exploited her disability and resulting poor mental state" and ordered her to carry out a suicide attack in the Israeli hospital where she was being treated (Yoram Schweitzer, "Palestinian Female Suicide Bombers: Reality vs. Myth" in *Female Suicide Bomber*, ed. Schweitzer, 36–38).

57. Undated letter from M. A. Spiridonova, PSR 4:351.

58. Oliver Radkey cited in Knight, "Female Terrorists," 159.

59. An undated letter and a letter dated March 6 [1906] from Spiridonova, PSR 4:351.

60. For example, Sheikh Isma'il Aal Radhwan cited in "Blessings for Whoever Has Saved a Bullet in Order to Stick It in a Jew's Head," Jihad Watch, December 27, 2003, http://www.jihadwatch.org/archives/000501.php.

61. "The Role of Palestinian Women in Suicide Terrorism," Israel Ministry of Foreign Affairs, January 30, 2003, http://www.mfa.gov.il/MFA/MFAArchive/2000_2009/2003/1/The%20Role%20of%20Palestinian%20Women%20in%20Suicide%20Terrorism.

62. Yoram Schweitzer, "Palestinian Female Suicide Bombers: Virtuous Heroines or Damaged Goods?" 16, http://www.labat.co.il/articles/palestinian%20female%20suicide%20bombers.pdf. (Originally published in Cindy Ness, ed., *Female Terrorism and Militancy: Agency, Utility, and Organization* [Routledge, 2008].)

63. Bowers, Derrick, and Olimov, "Suicide Terrorism in the Former USSR," 269.

64. Schweitzer, "Palestinian Female Suicide Bombers," 39–40. See also Berko, *The Path to Paradise*, 5–7, 96.

65. Lewis, *The Crisis of Islam*, 153.

66. Kimhi and Even, "Who Are the Palestinian Suicide Bombers?" 827.

67. Bloom, *Dying to Kill*, 163.

68. MacEoin, "Suicide Bombing as Worship," http://www.meforum.org/2478/suicide-bombing-as-worship. A male variant "might be a homosexual who has gotten a threat that if he does not enlist, his sexual deviance will be publicized," bringing disgrace to his family (Kimhi and Even, "Who Are the Palestinian Suicide Bombers?," 825–26; Berko, *The Path to Paradise*, 2).

69. For examples and discussion, see Schweitzer, "Palestinian Female Suicide Bombers," 5, 29, 32, 38.

70. Bloom, *Dying to Kill*, 163.

71. Schweitzer, "Palestinian Female Suicide Bombers," 3, 31, 33.

72. In February 1986 Hindawi received a first payment of $12,000 from his Syrian bosses, he admitted after he was apprehended; the full amount for a successful operation was to be $250,000. On the other hand, treason would be punished by the next-day elimination of a quarter of his 500 family members living in Syria. Had the London airport security been less vigilant, 375 passengers would have been killed on April 17, 1986—the date possibly chosen "because of its proximity to Passover and the greater likelihood of a full flight" (Pipes, "Terrorism: The Syrian Connection," http://www.danielpipes.org/1064/terrorism-the-syrian-connection).

73. Rim Riashi (Reem Riyashi) cited in Itamar Marcus and Barbara Crook, "Kill a Jew—Go to Heaven. A Study of the Palestinian Authority's Promotion of Genocide," Palestinian Media Watch, http://palwatch.org/STORAGE/special%20reports/Kill_Jew_go_to_heaven.pdf.

74. MacEoin, "Suicide Bombing as Worship," http://www.meforum.org/2478/suicide-bombing-as-worship.

75. Pipes, "Terrorism: The Syrian Connection," http://www.danielpipes.org/1064/terrorism-the-syrian-connection; L. G. Praisman, *Terroristy i revoliutsionery, okhranniki i provokatory* (Moscow: ROSSPEN, 2001), 32–33.

76. Geifman, *Thou Shalt Kill*, 308.

77. Cited in ibid., 49, 93, 101, 111.

78. Cited in Ivan Bunin, *Okaiannye dni* (Leningrad, 1991): 65.

79. Spiridonova, "Iz zhizni na Nerchinskoi katorge," 192–93.

80. Phillips, "From a Bolshevik to a British Subject," 390.

81. Savinkov, *Vospominaniia terrorista*, 61.

82. Ascherson, "A Terror Campaign of Love and Hate," http://www.guardian.co.uk/world/2008/sep/28/germany.terrorism.

83. Medvedeva Ter-Petrosian, "Tovarishch Kamo," *PR* 8–9, no. 31–32 (1924): 141.

84. Undated letter from P. Polivanov to his comrades, PSR 1:63.

85. Knight, "Female Terrorists," 149–50; Savinkov, *Vospominaniia terrorista*, 186.

86. O. H. Radkey, *The Agrarian Foes of Bolshevism: Promise and Default of the Russian Socialist Revolutionaries, February–October 1917* (New York, 1958), 70.

87. Cited in O. V. Budnitskii, "'Krov' po sovesti': terrorizm v Rossii (vtoraia polovina XIX-nachalov XX v.," *Otechestvennaia istoriia*, 6 (1994), 205.

88. "So many times in my youth I thought of killing myself," wrote Boris Vnorovskii to his parents before his attack against Dubasov, but "I continued living…for

you" (cited in Savinkov, *Vospominaniia terrorista*, 218). By joining the Combat Organization, Vnorovskii gave himself a mandate to die.

89. Bloom, *Dying to Kill*, 163.

90. Cited in Berko, *The Path to Paradise*, 1.

91. Schweitzer, "Palestinian Female Suicide Bombers," 28.

92. Moshe Hazani, "Red Carpet, White Lilies: Love of Death in the Poetry of the Jewish Underground Leader Avraham Stern," *The Psychoanalytic Review* 89 (2002): 32.

93. Schweitzer, "Palestinian Female Suicide Bombers," 31–32.

94. Cited in Berko, *The Path to Paradise*, 1.

95. Cited in Geifman, *Thou Shalt Kill*, 164.

96. GARF, f. 102, DPOO, op. 1912, d. 13, ch. 60B; V. O. Levitskii, "A.D. Pokotilov," *KS* 3 (1922): 159, 171; Savinkov, *Vospominaniia terrorista*, 26–27; Spence, *Savinkov*, 47. On March 31, 1904, an enormous blast shook the Northern Hotel in St. Petersburg. The suite where the bomb laboratory was located and the adjacent rooms were demolished. The police identified the mangled corpse of Pokotilov only by his unusually small hands. The constantly trembling hands of an alcoholic might have caused the explosion while he was assembling the bomb that finally took away his life (Geifman, *Thou Shalt Kill*, 53).

97. Knight, "Female Terrorists," 150.

98. Kaplan, "A Total Negation of Russia," 42.

99. Report of December 22, 1901, Okhrana, XVIIIb[1]:1, Outgoing dispatches [1901], doc. 11.

100. I. Zhukovskii-Zhuk, "Pamiati Lidii Petrovny Sture," *KS* 19 (1925): 253.

101. Report of December 4 [17], 1904, Okhrana XVIIh:2G.

102. Ami Pedahzur, *Suicide Terrorism* (Cambridge, UK: Polity Press, 2005), 141.

103. Cesare Lombroso, *Les anarchistes* (Paris: Flammarion, n.d.), 93–99.

104. Hazani, "Red Carpet, White Lilies," 35.

105. Ariel Merari, "The Readiness to Kill and Die: Suicidal Terrorism in the Middle East," in *Origins of Terrorism*, ed. Walter Reich (Cambridge, England, 1990), 193.

106. Copy of March 14, 1907, letter from a revolutionary from St. Petersburg to Dmitriev in Geneva, Okhrana, XXIVi:1B.

107. Jon Gambrell, "Web posts suggest lonely, depressed terror suspect," *Associated Press* (December 29, 2009) , http://news.yahoo.com/s/ap/20091229/ap_on_re_af/af_airliner_attack_internet_postings;_ylt=ArRqKgX8u5GwQHYJBBT9EhhvaA8F;_ylu=X3oDMTM1cWZkN3ZwBGFzc2V0A2FwLzIwMDkxMjI5L2FmX2Fpcmx-pbmVyX2F0dGFja19pbnRlcm5ldF9wb3N0aW5ncwRjcG9zAzEEcG9zAzIEc2VjA3luX3RvcF9zdG9yeQRzbGsDd2VicG9zdHNzdWdn.

108. Without those "wonderful... few years, my life would have had no real meaning," affirmed Ezerskaia, decades after the terrorist leaders had provided her and other broken men and women with justification for their otherwise empty lives (cited in Geifman, *Thou Shalt Kill*, 316n15).

109. Juergensmeyer, *Terror in the Mind of God*, 191, 193.

110. Cited in Serebrennikov, ed., *Ubiistvo Stolypina*, 79, 84, 105, 130, 139.

111. Ibid., 146–47.

112. Moshe Hazani, "The Breakdown of Meaning and Adolescent Problem Behavior," *International Journal of Adolescent Medical Health* 15, no. 3 (2003): 207–18.

113. Cited in James Frank McDaniel, "Political Assassination and Mass Execution: Terrorism in Revolutionary Russia, 1878–1938" (PhD dissertation, University of Michigan, 1976), 97.

114. Nestroev, *Iz dnevnika Maksimalista*, 78.
115. Ibid.
116. G. Novopolin, "Delo ob ubiistve general-gubernatora V. P. Zheltonovskogo," *KS* 31 (1927): 26–39.
117. Zavarzin, *Zhandarmy i revoliutsionery*, 145.
118. Pozner, ed., *Boevaia gruppa pri TsK RSDRP(b)*, 33.
119. Cited in Kimhi and Even, "Who Are the Palestinian Suicide Bombers?" 826. See also Beyler, "Messengers of Death," 19, http://www.keren-inbar.org.il/INB/cache/pic_22500.pdf. In "our society, the... grief for the loss of ten daughters will not match the grief of the loss of one boy," said in an interview Amjad Ubeidi, an Islamic Jihad senior operative, who on October 4, 2003, had sent female bomber Nihadi Jardat to explode in the Maxim restaurant in Haifa, which killed21 people and wounded 50 (cited in Schweitzer, "Palestinian Female Suicide Bombers," 30).
120. See, for example, http://www.mfa.gov.il/MFA/MFAArchive/2000_2009/2002/8/Answers+to+Frequently+Asked+Questions-+Palestinian.htm.
121. Hoffer, *The True Believer*, ii.
122. For discussion see Juergensmeyer, *Terror in the Mind of God*, 12.
123. Cited in Neal Ascherson, "A Terror Campaign of Love and Hate," *The Observer*, September 28, 2008, http://www.guardian.co.uk/world/2008/sep/28/germany.terrorism.
124. Sam Vaknin, *Malignant Self Love*, http://samvak.tripod.com/msla2.html.
125. Copy of a letter with illegible signature written in Paris to Lala Rabinovitch in Genera, June 9, 1906, Okhrana, XVIIn:5A.
126. Kropotkin, ed., *Russaia revoliutsiia i anarkhizm*, 51; GARF, f. 102, DPOO, op. 1902, d. 500, 86; Police department materials, protocol dated September 17, 1901, PSR 8:675.
127. Hannah Arendt cited in Miller, "The Intellectual Origins of Modern Terrorism in Europe," 60.
128. "Avtobiografiia V. Bushueva," PSR 1:28.
129. Moshe Hazani, "Apocaliptism, Symbolic Breakdown and Paranoia: An Application of Lifton's Model to the Death-Rebirth Fantasy," in *Apocalyptic Time*, ed. Albert I. Baumgarten (Brill, 2000), 16.
130. Thomas Friedman cited in Bloom, *Dying to Kill*, 89.
131. Vamik Volkan, *The Need to Have Enemies and Allies: From Clinical Practice to International Relationships* (Northvale, NJ: Jason Aronson, 1988), 33.
132. Jerrold Post, "Terrorist Psycho-Logic: Terrorist Behavior as a Product of Psychological Forces," in *Origins of Terrorism*, ed. Reich, 31.
133. J. S. Piven, "Narcissism, Sexuality, and Psyche in Terrorist Theology," 247, http://www.atypon-link.com/GPI/doi/pdf/10.1521/prev.2006.93.2.231.
134. W. W. Meissner cited in Hazani, "Red Carpet, White Lilies," 32. Similar argument in R. D. Laing, *Self and Others* (New York: Routledge, 1969), 31.
135. Cited in Geifman, *Thou Shalt Kill*, 64.
136. Cited in Knight, "Female Terrorists," 150.
137. Berko, *The Path to Paradise*, 10; Hazani, "Sacrificial Immortality," 436.
138. Aleksandr Blok, "Pliaska smerti," *Poeziia, dramy, proza*, http://books.google.co.il/books?id=OlW26d2gYVAC&hl=en&source=gbs_navlinks_s.

CHAPTER 7

1. V. Dal'nii, "Terror i delo Azeva," *Izvestiia Oblastnogo Zagranichnogo Komiteta* 9 (1909): 10, PSR 1:88.

2. Cited in Ivanova, "Sadanul pod serdtse finskii nozh," http://sergeiesenin.niv.ru/press/sadanul_pod_serdtce_fenskei_nogh.html.

3. Miriam Beard cited in Hoffer, *The True Believer,* 54–55.

4. M. Barsukov, "Kommunist-bundar,'" 202–3, Nic. 747:10; *G. I. Kotovskii. Dokumenty i materially* (Kishinev, 1956), 12, 29–30; "Vospominaniia byvsh. Okhrannika," *Bessarabskoe slovo,* 1930, Nic. 203:25.

5. Ivan Turgenev, "Porog," *Novyi sbornik revoliutsionnykh poem i stikhotvorenii* (Paris, 1899), 61–62.

6. Philip Pomper, "From Russian Revolutionary Terrorism to Soviet State Terror" (unpublished paper, Wesleyan University, 2003), 11.

7. P. Miliukov, *God bor'by* (St. Petersburg, 1907), 118.

8. Grigorii Aronson, *Rossiia nakanune revoliutsii* (Madrid, 1986), 144.

9. V. A. Maklakov, *Iz vospominanii* (New York, 1954), 351.

10. Cited in Thomas Riha, *The Russian European: Paul Miliukov in Russian Politics* (London, 1969), 78, 83.

11. Cited in Shmuel Galai, *Liberation Movement in Russia 1900–1905* (Cambridge, England, 1973), 220.

12. A. A. Kizevetter, *Napadki na partiiu Narodnoi Svobody (vospominaniia 1881–1914)* (Prague, 1929), 53.

13. See V. V. *Leontovich, Istoriia liberalizma v Rossii 1762–1914* (Paris, 1980), 478; and *GD,* 1906, 4, 1: 138.

14. *GD,* 1907, 9, 1: 445, 477.

15. For multiple references to Kadet press releases, see Geifman, *Thou Shalt Kill,* 341nn85–86.

16. *GD,* 1907, 9, 1: 479, and 8, 1: 392.

17. References in Geifman, *Thou Shalt Kill,* 342nn90–91.

18. *Rech'* 81 (April 19, 1907): 1; Pipes, *Struve,* 56.

19. Pipes, *Struve,* 56.

20. Cited in V. V. Shelokhaev, *Kadety—glavnaia partiia liberal'noi burzhuazii v bor'be s revoliutsiei 1905–1907* gg. (Moscow, 83), 160.

21. "Klub Partii Narodnoi svobody (iz neizdannykh vospominanii kn. D. I. Bebutova)," undated manuscript, pp. 15–16, Nic. 779:2.

22. June 9 (22), 1906, report to DPD, Okhrana XVIIg:2D.

23. May 11, 1906, report from a police agent in Paris, Okhrana VIj:15C. Many SRs, too, argued for the advantageous temporary alliance with the liberals: "For the present, the Kadets are not our enemies and are no threat to us...There is no need to fight against them" (cited in B. V. Levanov, *Iz istorii bor'by bol'shevistskoi partii protiv eserov v gody pervoi russkoi revoliutsii* [Leningrad, 1974], 117).

24. *GD,* 1906, 4, 1: 231.

25. Cited in Riha, *The Russian European,* 83.

26. F. Shatsillo, *Russkii liberalism nakanune revoliutsii 1905–1907 gg.* (Moscow, 1985), 300.

27. February 7 (20), 1906, report to DPD, Okhrana XXVa:1.

28. *GD,* 1906, 29, 2: 1496.

29. *GD,* 1906, 15, 1: 642; Miliukov, *God bor'by,* 353.

30. *GD,* 1906, 29, 2: 1496.

31. Miliukov, *God bor'by,* 354; *Rech'* 77 (June 1, 1906): 1; I. Kizevetter, *Napadki na partiiu Narodnoi Svobody,* 54.

32. *GD,* 1906, 29, 2: 1496. Similar statements in Obninskii, *Polgoda russkoi revoliutsii,* 153.

33. *GD*, 1906, 29, 2: 1487.
34. *GD*, 1906, 11, 1: 442.
35. *GD*, 1906, 29, 2: 1495–96.
36. *Rech'* 18 (March 25, 1906): 2.
37. Paul Berman, *Terror and Liberalism* (New York: Norton, 2003), 130–31.
38. Kayden, "Leonid Andreyev," http://worldlibrary.net/eBooks/Wordtheque/en/aaabnxe.txt.
39. Marks, *How Russia Shaped the Modern World*, 34.
40. Geifman, *Thou Shalt Kill*, 274n190.
41. For multiple examples, see ibid., 274–75n190 and 338n22.
42. *Leonid Borisovich Krasin ("Nikitich"). Gody podpol'ia* (Moscow-Leningrad, 1928), 142.
43. Zalezhskii, "V gody reaktsii," *PR* 2, no. 14 (1923): 338.
44. Cited in Kaplan, "Total Negation of Russia," 39. Spiridonova became an object of infatuation and in prison received love letters from many admirers; this was a popular craze indeed (see undated letter from Spiridonova, no. 11, PSR 4:351).
45. Excerpt from an unsigned letter from Kiev dated March 2, 1904, to N. Shpitsman in Berlin, Okhrana XXIVI:1.
46. Zavarzin, *Zhandarmy i revoliutsionery*, 149.
47. Cited in Geifman's interview with Iulia Segal', July 17, 2009, Jerusalem, Israel. "There is perhaps no more reliable indicator of a society's ripeness for a mass movement than the prevalence of unrelieved boredom," the ennui; in the early stages, "the bored "are more likely to join as sympathizers and supporters than" the exploited and oppressed" (Hoffer, *The True Believer*, 53–54).
48. *Sprut* 13 (March 21, 1906): 6, Nic. 436:5.
49. Tambov PSR Committee leaflet dated May 15, 1906, PSR 4:351; *Volia* 7 (May 9, 1906): 3, PSR 7:569.
50. A. Tyrkova-Vil'iams, *Na putiakh k svobode* (New York, 1952), 298, 300.
51. Ibid., 345.
52. The revolutionaries acknowledged their debt in a leaflet issued by the Nizhnii Novgorod SR Committee, May 1905, PSR 4:320.
53. Manfred Hildermeier, "The Terrorist Strategies of the Socialist-Revolutionary Party in Russia 1900–1914," in *Social Protest, Violence and Terror*, ed. Wolfgang J. Mommsen and Gerhard Hirschfeld (New York: 1982), 84.
54. Marks, *How Russia Shaped the Modern World*, 20.
55. Cited in Ibid., 20–21.
56. Ibid., 34.
57. "The Proletarian Armed Squads," *Gnosis: Italian Intelligence Magazine* 2 (2006), http://www.sisde.it/gnosis/Rivista7.nsf/ServNavigE/21. Fanon's famous *Wretched of the Earth*, was originally published in French as *Les Damnés de la Terre*. This title is taken from the first line of *The Internationale (L'Internationale)*, a worldwide communist and anarchist anthem.
58. Johann Hari, "Red Alert? An Interview with Antonio Negri," http://www.johannhari.com/archive/article.php?id=435.
59. http://www.normanfinkelstein.com/in-defense-of-hezbollah/.
60. Excerpt from April 2004 speech broadcast in "The Third Jihad," Part 1, http://www.road90.com/watch.php?id=tAfPJzb7Yc.
61. Cited in Maddy-Weitzman, "Palestinian and Israeli Intellectuals in the Shadow of Oslo and Intifadat al-Aqsa," http://www.tau.ac.il/dayancenter/PalestinianandIsraeliIntellectuals-bruce.pdf.

62. Miller, "The Intellectual Origins of Modern Terrorism in Europe," 61.

63. Huxley, The Perennial Philosophy, 91.

64. Ismail Haniya, Hamas PM, Al-Aqsa TV, Gaza, October 15, 2008, "Hamas in Their Own Voices," http://mignews.co.il/news/politic/world/170109_134656_15869.html.

65. Speech by Hamas leader Khaled Mash'al, Al-Jazeera TV, Qatar, February 3, 2006. "Hamas in Their Own Voices," http://mignews.co.il/news/politic/world/170109_134656_15869.html.

66. Yunis Al-Astal, Hamas MP and cleric, Al-Aqsa TV, Gaza, April 13, 2008, http://mignews.co.il/news/politic/world/170109_134656_15869.html.

67. Berman, *Terror and Liberalism*, 134–35.

68. Avi Erlich, *Ancient Zionism: The Biblical Origins of the National Idea* (New York: Free Press, 1995).

69. Cited in Berman, *Terror and Liberalism*, 135–36, 138–39.

70. I. V. Gessen, "V dvukh vekakh," *Arkhiv russkoi revoliutsii* 22 (1937): 226; "Denvnik A. A. Polovtseva," *KA* 4 (1923): 104.

71. Berman, *Terror and Liberalism*, 130–31.

72. Bloom, *Dying to Kill*, 40.

73. Article Twenty of the Hamas Charter (August 18, 1988), http://www.mideastweb.org/hamas.htm.

74. David Remnick, "Amos Oz Writes the Story of Israel," *The New Yorker* (November 8, 2004), http://www.pierretristam.com/Bobst/library/wf-269.htm.

75. Huxley, The Perennial Philosophy, 109.

76. See, for example, Alan M. Dershowitz, *The Case against Israel's Enemies: Exposing Jimmy Carter and Others Who Stand in the Way of Peace* (Hoboken, NJ: John Wiley & Sons, 2008), 80–83,119, and Oren Gross, "CUPE Ontario's proposed boycott of Israeli academics is just plain anti-Semitic," *The Globe and Mail*, January 13, 2009, http://www.theglobeandmail.com/news/opinions/article965181.ece.

77. "The Sixth Annual Israeli Apartheid Week 2010," http://apartheidweek.org/; "Noam Chomsky Rails Against Israel, Again," *BU Today* (March 3, 2010), http://www.bu.edu/today/node/10533.

78. Danny Rubinstein and Joseph Agassi cited in Kenneth Levin, *The Oslo Syndrome: Delusions of a People under Siege* (Smith & Kraus: 2005), 367, 377.

79. Ilan Pappe cited in *Monthly Magazine*, January 1999, http://www.middleeast.org/archives/1999_01_29.htm.

80. Ran HaCohen, "Fascism Needs an Enemy," July 20, 2009, http://original.antiwar.com:80/hacohen/2009/07/19/fascism-needs-an-enemy/.

81. Radio Islam, http://radioislam.org/historia/zionism/quotes.html. It is interesting that Muslim women, specifically female inmates in Israeli prisons, find these accusations outrageous and insulting (Khaled Abu Toameh, "Anti-Israel TV Show Angers Palestinians," The Jerusalem Post (April 4, 2010), http://www.jpost.com/JewishWorld/JewishNews/Article.aspx?id=172472.

82. Cited in Levin, *The Oslo Syndrome*, 435.

83. For thesis abstract in English and chapter on "dehumanization," see http://storage.wirade.ru/files/TalNitzan-englishabstract%2Bdewomanizationpart.pdf?attredirects=0. For full text see http://storage.wirade.ru/files/TalNitzan-fulltext.pdf/.

84. Netta Cohen Dor-Shav, "The Ultimate Enemy—Jews Against Jew," http://www.radiobergen.eu/essays/pathologyc.htm.

85. Levin, *The Oslo Syndrome*, 366–67.

86. Cited in Jonny Paul, "TAU historian accused of anti-Semitism," *Jerusalem Post* (November 16, 2009); Sand's *Invention of the Jewish People* (Brooklyn, NY: Verso, 2009) was lauded in *Haaretz* as "one of the most fascinating and challenging books published here in a long time" (Tom Segev, "An Invention called 'The Jewish people'" July 23, 2009, http://www.haaretz.com/hasen/spages/959229.html), yet slammed by specialists as incompetent. Nonetheless, the French version *Comment le peuple juif fut inventé* (Paris: Fayard, 2008) received the "Aujourd'hui Award" for best nonfiction political or historical work and was on Israel's best-seller list for months.

87. Cited in Joel S. Fishman, "The Cold-War Origins of Contemporary Anti-Semitic Terminology," *Jerusalem Viewpoints* 517 (May 2–16, 2004), http://www.jcpa.org/jl/vp517.htm.

88. "'Russikii' professor trebuet unichtozhit' vse poseleniia," July 24, 2009, http://izrus.co.il/obshina/article/2009-07-24/5545.html; Faycal Falaky, G21 Interview: Dr. Yuri Pines, Hebrew University, http://www.g21.net/midE2.htm.

89. Fathi Hammad, Hamas MP, Al-Aqsa TV, Gaza, September 29, 2008; Wael Al-Zarad, Hamas cleric, Al-Aqsa TV, Gaza, March 25, 2008; and Muhsen Abu 'Ita, Hamas cleric, Al-Aqsa TV, Gaza, October 15, 2008, "Hamas in Their Own Voices," http://mignews.co.il/news/politic/world/170109_134656_15869.html.

90. Sudan TV, Channel 4 (Iran), June 15, 2007, "Hamas in Their Own Voices," http://mignews.co.il/news/politic/world/170109_134656_15869.html.

91. Faycal Falaky, G21 Interview: Dr. Yuri Pines, Hebrew University, http://www.g21.net/midE2.htm.

92. *Haaretz*, May 15, 2001; *Davar*, April 5, 1988.

93. Gideon Levy, "Heads to the Right," *Haaretz*, http://www.haaretz.com/hasen/spages/962041.html.

94. Fishman, "The Cold-War Origins of Contemporary Anti-Semitic Terminology," http://www.jcpa.org/jl/vp517.htm; Yeshayahu Leibowitz cited in *Haaretz*, September 27, 1985; see also Cohen Dor-Shav, "The Ultimate Enemy," http://www.radiobergen.eu/essays/pathologyc.htm.

95. Sander L. Gilman, *Jewish Self-Hatred: Anti-Semitism and the Hidden Language of the Jews* (John Hopkins University Press, 1986); Cohen Dor-Shav, "The Ultimate Enemy," http://www.radiobergen.eu/essays/pathologyc.htm.

96. Amos Oz cited in Yoram Hazony, *The Jewish State: The Struggle for Israel's Soul* (New York: Basic/New Republic Books, 2000), 319.

97. Says Israeli writer Efraim Kishon, "Behind the chase after ratings, lurks no small measure of self-hatred, the sad legacy of a people which...has clothed itself in the vile accusations of its persecutors" (cited in Cohen Dor-Shav, "The Ultimate Enemy," http://www.radiobergen.eu/essays/pathologyc.htm).

98. Philip Weiss, "At NYU, Devilish Shlomo Sand Predicts the Jewish Past and Pastes the Zionists," *Mondoweiss*, October 17, 2009, http://mondoweiss.net/2009/10/at-nyu-devilish-shlomo-sand-predicts-the-jewish-past-and-pastes-the-zionists.html.

99. Levin, *The Oslo Syndrome;* see section 2. Anna Freud first described the mental process of identification with the aggressor to ameliorate anxiety in *The Ego and the Mechanisms of Defense* (1936). Coined by psychiatrist and criminologist Nils Bejerot, the term "Stockholm syndrome" refers to the Norrmalmstorg bank robbery in Stockholm. During the six days after the assailants took bank employees hostage on August 23, 1973, the victims became emotionally attached to their captors and defended them even after they had been liberated.

100. Israel Shahak, *Jewish History, Jewish Religion: The Weight of Three Thousand Years* (London: Pluto Press, 2002), 34; Interview of Israel Shahak to Anne Joyce, editor of *American-Arab Affairs* (June 12, 1989), http://www.mepc.org/journal_shahak/shahak29.asp.

101. Cited in Dershowitz, *The Case against Israel's Enemies*, 112.

102. Juergensmeyer, *Terror in the Mind of God*, 126.

103. Isaeli writer and politician Yossi Beilin cited in Ari Shavit, "Mister Nice Guy," *Haaretz Magazine*, June 14, 2001.

104. Richard Falk, "International Law and the al-Aqsa Intifada," *The Middle East Report* 217 (Winter 2000), http://www.merip.org/mer/mer217/217_falk.html.

105. Cited in Tammi Rossman-Benjamin, "Anti-Zionism and the Abuse of Academic Freedom: A Case Study at the University of California, Santa Cruz," *Jerusalem Center for Public Affairs*, 77 (February 1, 2009), http://www.jcpa.org/JCPA/Templates/ShowPage.asp?DBID=1&TMID=111&LNGID=1&FID=381&PID=0&IID=2812.

106. Discussed in Berman, *Terror and Liberalism*, 151.

107. Richard A. Posner, Public Intellectuals: A Study of Decline (Cambridge, MA: Harvard University Press, 2001); Arthur Schlesinger and Leopold Labedz cited in Paul Bogdanor, "The Top 200 Chomsky Lies," http://www.paulbogdanor.com/chomsky/200chomskylies.pdf.

108. An alternative defense mechanism against fear is laughter, as analyzed by Mikhail Bakhtin. It is employed in various "special cultural forms of diminishing the frightening, presented as a 'funny monster'" (discussed in O. S. Nikol'skaia, "Affektivnaia sfera cheloveka: vzgliad skvoz' prizmu detskogo autizma," http://www.autism.ru/read.asp?id=56&vol=103). This option is not available to hostages and thus cannot be an alternative to the Stockholm syndrome.

109. Ralph Schoenman, *The Hidden History of Zionism* (Santa Barbara, CA: Veritas Press, 1988).

110. For example, cited in Levin, *The Oslo Syndrome*, 279.

111. Report of "Galei-TsAHAL" of July 27, 2009, cited in http://cursorinfo.co.il:80/news/novosti/2009/07/27/rogatka-madim-zahal/.

112. As in, for instance, the description of a database, set up to afford researchers "the unique opportunity to begin developing concrete theory about why and how terrorism events emerge from the bottom-up." Network data "describe the relations that individuals shared in select attack networks. The codebooks (available below) describe the nature of the data in detail, distinguishing between the operational status of network members (the role in an attack of individual 'nodes') and the social ties between them. Social ties are the 'edges' or lines in network graphs that convey the mediums of social exchange for material resources and social influence" (http://doitapps.jjay.cuny.edu/jjatt/data.php).

113. Audrey Kurth Cronin, "Behind the Curve: Globalization and International Terrorism," *International Security* 27 no. 3 (Winter 2002–3): 34.

114. "Terrorism: from Samson to Atta (Part II: Myths: Framing the Problem)," *Arab Studies Quarterly* (ASQ) (January 2003), http://www.encyclopedia.com/Arab Studies Quarterly (ASQ)/publications.aspx?pageNumber 1; and Tessa Daley, "Milton's Samson as a Terrorist," http://www.english.sbc.edu/Journal/Archive/05-06/Daley.htm.

115. *Spiegel* interview with Homeland Security Secretary Janet Napolitano, March 16, 2009, http://www.spiegel.de/international/world/0,1518,613330,00.html.

116. See, for example, Arnon Groiss and Nethanel (Navid) Toobian, eds., *The War Curriculum in Iranian Schoolbooks* (New York: American Jewish Committtee and the Center for Monitoring the Impact of Peace, 2007), 38–45; and Arnon Groiss, ed., *The West, Christians, and Jews in Saudi Arabian Schoolbooks* (New York: Center for Monitoring the Impact of Peace and the American Jewish Committee, 2003), 118.

117. Bill Ashcroft and Pal Ahluwalia, *Edward Said* (Routledge, 2001), 133.

118. Jamie Glazov, "From Russia with Terror," *FrontPageMagazine.com*, March 1, 2004, http://www.frontpagemag.com/readArticle.aspx?ARTID=13975.

119. "Taking Aim Radio" with Ralph Schoenman and Mya Shone, http://takingaimradio.com/.

120. Elias Davidsson, "Terrorism Deaths in Western Europe 2001–2006. Statistics Show That the EU and NATO Are Deceiving the Public," March 28, 2007, http://911truth.eu/en/index.php?id=1,60,0,0,1,0.

121. Dvoikh, "Pogibshie 17 oktiabria 1905 g.—17 oktiabria 1906 g," *Vestnik Partii Narodnoi Svobody* 33–35 (Moscow, 1906): 1808–15, 1725–36.

122. Berman, *Radical, Religious, and Violent*, 1.

123. Cited in Berman, *Terror and Liberalism*, 159.

124. Frank Lentricchia notes "a paranoid fantasy," essential "to the sustaining, in ostensibly democratic contexts, of the illusion of totalitarianism" (cited in John Brannigan, *New Historicism and Cultural Materialism* [New York: St. Martin's Press, 1998], 78).

125. Tyrkova-Vil'iams, *Na putiakh k svobode*, 166.

126. "This 'hurray' in the language of the samurais...the most popular clamor among the educated opposition in Russia, was worth an entire confession (Zhabotinskii, *Piatero*, 133).

127. Levin, *The Oslo Syndrome*, 388–390.

128. Gil Ronen, "Hebrew Univ. to Readmit Convicted Terrorist to Chemistry Lab," http://www.isracampus.org.il/third%20level%20pages/HebrewU%20-%20Amiram%20Goldblum%20-%20terroist%20fellow.htm.

129. Among other observers, Israeli novelist Aharon Megged noted that some steps toward "peaceful collaboration" with the terrorists "seem animated by a subconscious suicidal drive" (cited in Levin, *The Oslo Syndrome*, 370).

CHAPTER 8

1. Maximilien Robespierre, "Sur les principes de morale politique," Discours devant la Convention le 17 pluviôse an II (5 février 1794), http://www.royet.org/nea1789-1794/archives/discours/robespierre_principes_morale_politique_05_02_94.htm.

2. Berman, *Radical, Religious, and Violent*, 2–3.

3. Jackson, "A Defense of the Concept of 'State Terrorism,'" 7, 13.

4. Lenin, *Polnoe sobranie sochinenii*, vol. 5, (Moscow, 1959), 7.

5. Ibid., vol. 11, 340–43; Chuzhak, "Lenin i 'tekhnika' vosstaniia," *KS* 12, no. 73 (1931): 77.

6. Discussed in Geifman, *Thou Shalt Kill*, 92–96.

7. Trotsky cited in Laqueur, *Terrorism*, 68.

8. Cited in Phillips, "The War against Terrorism," 219.

9. Cited in V. A. Posse, *Moi zhiznennyi put'* (Moscow-Leningrad, 1929), 321.

10. Cited in Pipes, *The Russian Revolution*, 791–92.

11. Cited in Leites, *A Study of Bolshevism*, 355.

12. Cited in Robert Conquest, *Reflections on a Ravaged Century* (New York: Norton, 1999), 98.

13. On the general history of the Cheka, see Leonard D. Gerson, *The Secret Police in Lenin's Russia* (Philadelphia: Temple University Press, 1976), and George Leggett, *The Cheka: Lenin's Political Police* (Oxford: Clarendon Press, 1986).

14. Cited in Leites, *A Study of Bolshevism*, 353.

15. Cited in Pipes, *The Russian Revolution*, 805, 790.

16. Cited in Robert D. Warth, "Cheka," *The Modern Encyclopedia of Russian and Soviet History* (MERSH), vol. 6 (Academic International Press), 218.

17. James Bunyan and H. H. Fisher, *The Bolshevik Revolution, 1917–1918: Documents and Materials* (Stanford: Stanford University Press, 1934), 297–98.

18. Cited in Pipes, *The Russian Revolution*, 800–801, 804–5.

19. Richard Sakwa, *The Rise and Fall of the Soviet Union, 1917–1991* (New York: Routledge, 1999), 75.

20. Cited in Pipes, *The Russian Revolution*, 800–801, 804–80.

21. Ibid., 787.

22. Ibid., 820.

23. Cited in Yevgenia Albats and Catherine A. Fitzpatrick, *The State within a State: The KGB and Its Hold on Russia—Past, Present, and Future* (New York: Farrar Straus & Giroux, 1994).

24. Noi [Noah] Zhordaniia, *Moia zhzn'* (Stanford, CA: Stanford University Press, 1968), 80; Zeev Ivianski, "The Terrorist Revolution: Roots of Modern Terrorism," *Inside Terrorist Organizations*, ed. David C. Rapoport (London, 1988), 133.

25. "Kronika vooruzhenoi bor'by," *KA* 4–5, no. 11–12 (1925): 170.

26. V. Bonch-Bruevich, "Moi vospominaniia o P. A. Kropotkine," *Zvezda* 6 (1930): 196.

27. Report of May 26 (June 8), 1906, Okhrana XIX:13; Zavarzin, *Rabota tainoi politsii*, 128.

28. Warth, "Cheka," 218.

29. See, for example, Mikhail Osorgin, *Vremena* (Ekaterinburg: Sredne-Ural'skoe knizhnoe izd-vo, 1992), 577. Numerous cases of execution of family members are cited in Mark Kramer, ed., *The Black Book of Communism: Crimes, Terror, Repression* (Cambridge, MA: Harvard University Press, 1999).

30. Orlando Figes, *A People's Tragedy: The Russian Revolution: 1891–1924* (New York: Penguin, 1998), 647.

31. Robert Gellately, *Lenin, Stalin, and Hitler: The Age of Social Catastrophe* (New York: Knopf, 2007), 58–59; cited in Viktor Aksiuch, "Infernal'nost' leninizma," *Regnum* (April 22, 2010), http://www.regnum.ru/

32. Sergei Mel'gunov, *"Krasnyi terror" v Rossii, 1918–1923* (Moscow: PUICO, 1990), 108.

33. See numerous examples in Ibid., 50–51, 96–106; Nicholas Werth cited in Mark Kramer, ed., The Black Book of Communism, 78; see also 86–88.

34. Budnitskii, "'Krov' po sovesti'," 204.

35. Leites, *A Study of Bolshevism*, 406; "Haunted, above all, by the specter of a fierce backlash of the sort that had struck Russia after 1905, the Bolsheviks had few qualms about using terror to thwart this historical possibility, nay probability. This fear and resolve became obsessive once the socialist revolution miscarried in central and western Europe" (Arno J. Mayer, *The Furies: Violence and Terror in the French and Russian Revolutions* [Princeton, NJ: Princeton University Press, 2001], 255). Immediately after the Bolshevik takeover, Lenin's associates, who had provided for the party

by expropriations, began making financial preparation for the time when they would again be forced underground (see Geifman, *Thou Shalt Kill*, 256).

36. Cited in "Story of the Red Flag," http://revcom.us/a/045/story-red-flag.html; cited in Isaac Deutscher, The Prophet Armed: Trotsky, 1879–1921 (New York-London: Verso, 2003), 378–79; cited in Leites, *A Study of Bolshevism*, 406–7, 414.

37. Horney, *Neurotic Personality of Our Time*, 166.

38. James M. Glass, *Psychosis and Power. Threats to Democracy in the Self and the Group* (Ithaca, NY: Cornell University Press, 1995), 129.

39. V. I. Lenin, "Speech Delivered at an All-Russia Conference of Political Education Workers of Gubernia and Uyezd Education Departments," November 3, 1920, *Collected Works*, 4th English ed., vol. 31 (Moscow: Progress Publishers, 1965), 340–61.

40. Discussed in Leites, *A Study of Bolshevism*, 43–44, 360, 387.

41. Cited in Pipes, *The Russian Revolution*, 792n.

42. Olga Chernov-Andreyev, *Cold Spring in Russia* (Ann Arbor, MI: Ardis, 1978), 209–30.

43. Analysis of the Bolshevik–Left SR breakup in Lutz Hafner, "The Assassination of Count Mirbach and the 'July Uprising" of the Left Socialist Revolutionaries in Moscow, 1918," *Russian Review* 50, no. 3 (July 1991): 324–44.

44. http://www.youtube.com/watch?v=DnuDg2316dk.

45. Itamar Marcus and Barbara Crook, "Fatah Broadcasts Graphic Images of Hamas Torture," June 18, 2009, http://newsblaze.com/story/20090618155831zzzz.nb/topstory.html.

46. See Bruce Hoffman's analysis of his interview with a senior Fatah representative in Hoffman, "How the Terrorists Stopped Terrorism," http://www.theatlantic.com/doc/200112/hoffman.

47. Pujals, "The Accidental Revolutionary," 184.

48. Pipes, *The Russian Revolution*, 792.

49. See, for example, M. G. Nechaev, *Krasnyi terror i tserkov' na Urale* (Perm: Izd-vo Permskogo gosudarstvennogo pedagogicheskogo institutta, 1992).

50. Mel'gunov, *"Krasnyi terror" v Rossii*, 46.

51. Pipes, *The Russian Revolution*, 838, 792.

52. Pujals, "The Accidental Revolutionary," 181.

53. In a random sample of personal files of self-proclaimed revolutionaries, rejected from membership in the Society of Former Political Prisoners and Exiles of the Soviet Union, approximately 80 percent mentioned common criminal activity before and/or after the revolution (ibid, 1, 3–4, 9).

54. Cited in Warth, "Cheka," 218.

55. In a different context, philosopher Ernest Gellner would summarize the recruiters' logic as follows: "you are safe with us; we like you the better because the filthier your record the more we have a hold on you" (1991 interview with Ernest Gellner conducted by John Davis of Oxford University for *Current Anthropology* 32, no. 1 [February 1991], http://www.lse.ac.uk/collections/gellner/InterGellner.html).

56. See, for example, V. I. Shishkin, "Krasnyi banditizm v sovetskoi Sibiri," *Sovetskaia istoriia: problemy i uroki* (Novosibirsk, 1992); Mel'gunov, *"Krasnyi terror" v Rossii*, 139–44.

57. Examples in ibid., 115.

58. Cited in Pipes, *The Russian Revolution*, 798–99, 826.

59. Knight, "Female Terrorists," 149–50.

60. See, for example, Roizman, "Vospominaniia o Frumkinoi," *KS* 28–29 (1926): 383.

61. Kniazev, "1905," 235, 241, 243.

62. Cited in Geifman, *Thou Shalt Kill*, 170, 323, 325, 209.

63. Ibid., 168.

64. "Down Syndrome Bombers Kill 99 in Iraq," *Jerusalem Post*, February 1, 2008, http://www.jpost.com/servlet/Satellite?cid=1201523808635&pagename=JPost%2FJPArticle%2FShowFull.

65. *Rech'* 149 (September 9, 1906): 2.

66. G. A. Aleksinskii, "Vospominaniia, "15, Nic. 302:3.

67. See, for example, Chernov-Andreyev, *Cold Spring in Russia*, 215.

68. Osorgin, *Vremena*, 575.

69. "Primechniia k st. Medvedeva 'Tovarishch Kamo,'" 146.

70. Dubinskii-Mukhadze, *Kamo*, 5, 195–96; Medvedeva-Ter-Petrosian, "Tovarishch Kamo," 141–42.

71. Cited in Pipes, *The Russian Revolution*, 823. For examples of "executioners' illness," see Mel'gunov, *"Krasnyi terror" v Rossii*, 143–44.

72. Albats and Fitzpatrick, *The State within a State*, 95. Cheka tortures described in Mel'gunov, *"Krasnyi terror" v Rossii*, 120–30.

73. Research by Dane Archer cited in Zimbardo, "Vantage Point: Faceless Terrorists Embody 'Creative Evil,'" *Stanford Report*, http://news-service.stanford.edu/news/2001/september26/zimbardo-926.html.

74. Osorgin, *Vremena*, 586.

75. See, for example, Keiron Walsh, "Genetic Factors in Aggression" (October 30, 2009), http://alevelpsychology.co.uk/aggression/biological-factors/genetic-factors-in-aggression.html. I am grateful to Dr. Tatyana Leonova at the Rockefeller University for acquainting me with scientific research on this topic.

76. Mayer, *The Furies*, 235.

77. For example, Dzerzhinskii, a Pole, in his youth wanted to "exterminate all Muscovites" (cited in Pipes, *The Russian Revolution*, 802).

78. "Sergey Nechayev 1869: The Revolutionary Catechism," http://www.marxists.org/subject/anarchism/nechayev/catechism.htm.

79. For numerous examples, see T. I. Vulikh, "Osnovnoe iadro kavkazskoi boevoi organizatsii," 7, Nic. 207:11; Pozner, ed., *Boevaia gruppa pri TsK RSDRP(b)*, 170n; Aleksandr Sokolov-Novoselov, *Vooruzhennoe podpol'e* (Ufa, 1958), 39n; Kh. I. Muratov and A. G. Lipkina, *Timofei Stepanovich Krivov* (Ufa, 1968), 111; *Soldaty leninskoi gvardii* (Gor'kii, 1974), 201, 204; *Soldaty leninskoi gvardii (kniga vtoraia)* (Gor'kii, 1977), 310, 313, 316–17; V. Iakubov, "Aleksandr Dmitrievich Kuznetsov," *KS* 3, no. 112 (1934): 134, 138; G. Shidlovskii, "O. G. Ellek (Pamiati starogo bol'shevika)," *KS* 9, no. 106 (1933): 143–44.

80. Leggett, *The Cheka*, 269.

81. T. S. Krivov, *V leninskom stroiu* (Cheboksary, 1969), 110–12, 128; Ivan Myzgin, *So vzvedennym kurkom* (Moscow, 1964), 21; G. Z. Ioffe, *Krakh rossiiskoi monarkhicheskoi kontrrevoliutsii* (Moscow, 1977), 149–51; Nikolai Ross, ed., *Gibel' tsarskoi sem'i. Materialy sledstviia ob ubiistve tsarskoi sem'i (avgust 1918-fevral'; 1920)* (Frankfurt, 1987), 586; Richard Haliburton, *Seven League Boots* (Indianapolis, IN, 1935), 120, 140; "Kommentarii V. I. Nikolaevskogo k knige L Shapiro," *The Communist Party of the Soviet Union* (1958 manuscript), p. 4, Nic. 519:30B; letter from B. I. Nicolaevsky to T. I. Vulikh dated May 25, 1956, Nic. 207:16.

82. For examples of former terrorists of various ideological trends using their past experience for the benefit of Soviet organs of repression, see William J. Fishman, *East End Jewish Radicals, 1875–1914* (London, 1975), 291; Henry J. Tobias, *The Jewish Bund in Russia from Its Origins to 1905* (Stanford, 1972), 348; R. M. Aslamova-Gol'tsman, "Svetloi pamiati I. Ia. Bartkovskogo," *KS* 48 (1928): 158–59; Zavarzin, *Rabota tainoi politsii,* 157; "Vospominaniia byvsh. okhrannika," *Bessarabskoe slovo* (1930), Nic. 203:25.

83. Hoffer, *The True Believer,* 83.

84. Vladimir Brovkin, *Behind the Front Lines of the Civil War* (Princeton, NJ: Princeton University Press, 1994), 408–9.

85. Cited in Mel'gunov, *"Krasnyi terror" v Rossii,* 32.

86. Cited in Pipes, *The Russian Revolution,* 793.

87. Leites, *A Study of Bolshevism,* 384.

88. Osorgin, *Vremena,* 575, 578.

89. Mel'gunov, *"Krasnyi terror" v Rossii,* 188.

90. Pipes, *The Russian Revolution,* 822.

91. Cited in Budnitskii, "'Krov' po sovesti'," 209n.

92. Cited in Leggett, *The Cheka,* 114.

93. Iu. M. Steklov cited in Budnitskii, "'Krov' po sovesti'," 207.

94. Pipes, *The Russian Revolution,* 829, 832, 836, 790.

95. Unnamed author of memoirs "The Death Boat," cited in Mel'gunov, *"Krasnyi terror" v Rossii,* 190.

96. Landes, "Totalitarian Millennialism: The Bolshevik Apocalypse," in *Heaven on Earth.*

97. Introduction in Lion Feuchtwanger, *Moscow 1937. My Visit Described for My Friends* (New York: Viking Press, 1937).

98. Chomsky, cited in Paul Hollander, *Political Pilgrims: Western Intellectuals in Search of the Good Society* (New Brunswick, NJ: Transaction Publishers, 1998), xxxviii.

99. Sartre cited in Landes, "Totalitarian Millennialism: The Bolshevik Apocalypse," in *Heaven on Earth;* Dmitrii Radyshevskii, "Liberaly za dzhikhad," http://www.jerusalem-korczak-home.com/np/rad/09/np167.html.

100. Michail Ryklin, "On the Trail of Red Pilgrims," interview to Caspar Melville, *New Humanist,* http://newhumanist.org.uk/1995.

101. Michael J. Thompson's review of Foucault and the Iranian Revolution: Gender and the Seductions of Islamism by Janet Afary and Kevin B. Anderson (Chicago: University of Chicago Press, 2005), Democratiya 1 (Summer, 2005), http://www.dissentmagazine.org/democratiya/article_pdfs/d1Thompson.pdf.

102. Radyshevskii, "Liberaly za dzhikhad," http://www.jerusalem-korczak-home.com/np/rad/09/np167.html. Individually, each also fears "exile from the community of true believers that had given his life so much purpose," the fate of writer André Gide, a renegade Soviet sympathizer, who dared make public his disillusionment with Communism in *Retour de L'U.R.S.S.* in 1936 (Landes, "Totalitarian Millennialism: The Bolshevik Apocalypse," in *Heaven on Earth*).

103. Title of the French philosopher Raymond Aron's 1955 masterpiece, *L'Opium des intellectuels*—an inversion of Marx's denigration of religion as "the opium of the people." (Cited in Roger Kimball, "Raymond Aron and the Power of Ideas," *New Criterion* (May 2001), http://findarticles.com/p/articles/mi_hb3345/is_9_19/ai_n28839622/.

104. Detailed discussion in Mikhail Ryklin, *Kommunizm kak religiia. Intellektualy i Oktiabr'skaia revoliutsiia* (Moscow: "Novoe literaturnoe obozrenie," 2009).

105. Leites, *A Study of Bolshevism*, 351.
106. Reich, ed., *Origins of Terrorism*, 31, 33.
107. Karabcheevskii, *Voskresenie Maiakovskogo*, 183–84.
108. Cited in Eliot Borenstein, *Man without Women: Masculinity and Revolution in Russian Fiction, 1917–1929* (Chapel Hill, NC: Duke University Press, 2001), 29–30.
109. Cited in Rodby, *The Dark Heart of Utopia*, 203.
110. Bernice Glatzer Rosenthal, *New Myth, New World: from Nietzsche to Stalinism* (Pennsylvania State University Press, 2002), 188.
111. Cited in Leites, *A Study of Bolshevism*, 137.
112. "Ce Romme est un métaphysicien obscur," remarked perceptively a contemporary opponent of this effort to rule over time by "un alchemiste politique" (Edmond Biré, *Journal d'un bourgeois de Paris pendant la Terreur*, vol. 4 (Perrin: Paris, 1794), 51.
113. E. Poletaev, N. Punin, *Protiv tsivilizatsii* (Petrograd, 1923), 22.
114. Landes, "Totalitarian Millennialism: The Bolshevik Apocalypse," in *Heaven on Earth*.
115. Leon Trotsky, *Literature and Revolution* (New York: Russell & Russell, 1957), 256.
116. Donald D. MacRae, "Bolshevik Ideology: The Intellectual and Emotional Factors in Communist Affiliation," *Cambridge Journal* 5 (1951): 167.
117. Hazani, "Apocaliptism, Symbolic Breakdown and Paranoia," 29.
118. Syed Qutb, "The Characteristics of the Islamic Society and the Correct Method for its Formation," Milestones, http://evans-experientialism.freewebspace.com/qutb.htm.
119. Landes, "Totalitarian Millennialism: The Bolshevik Apocalypse," in *Heaven on Earth*.

CHAPTER 9

1. Etkind, *Klyst*, 203.
2. Martha Crenshaw, "Theories of Terrorism: Instrumental and Organizational Approaches," in *Inside Terrorist Organizations*, ed. David C. Rapoport (London: Powell's Books, 1988), 20.
3. P. A. Kropotkin cited in Budnitskii, "P. A. Kropotkin i problema revoliutsionnogo terrorizma," 36.
4. Knight, "Female Terrorists," 147.
5. Cited in Budnitskii, "'Krov' po sovesti'," 208n.
6. Savinkov, *Vospominaniia terrorista*, 194–96; GARF, f. 5831 (B. V. Savinkov), op. 1, d. 559: 5; "Iz pisem E. Sazonova," letter dated May 1906, pp. 4–5, Nic. 12:1.
7. "Materialy o provokatsiiakh," PSR 5:518; Knight, "Female Terrorists," 147.
8. So would other women-extremists in the following century, including Ulrike Meinhof, who left her husband, dumped her two small daughters in a hippie commune in Sicily to take up a gun, and, as a member of the Red Army Faction, then participated in series of spectacular bank raids, clashes with the Berlin police, lethal bombings of American army bases in Germany, and attacks on right-wing newspapers. *Spiegel* journalist Stefan Aust, author of *The Baader Meinhof Complex* (Random House, 2008), who had met several gang members before they went underground, arranged the "benevolent kidnap" of Meinhof's daughters to save them from being sent to a Palestinian orphanage, as per the RAF decision (Neal Ascherson, "A Terror Campaign of Love and Hate," *The Observer*, September 28, 2008, http://www.guardian.co.uk/world/2008/sep/28/germany.terrorism).

9. "Marriage of love" to the revolution entailed the bliss of fading away or "dying in it," akin to a noxious enchantment with the non-being, imbuing many romantic texts: "In truth I am in love with death; no maiden ever took more pleasure in the contemplation of her bridal attire than I in fancying my limbs already enwrapt in their shroud: is it not my marriage dress?" Mary Shelley, *Mathilda*, cited in Anne Kostelanetz Mellor, *Mary Shelley: Her Life, Her Fiction, Her Monsters* (New York: Methuen, 1988), 195.

10. Savinkov, *Vospominaniia terrorista*, 117. Notably, in her youth Meinhof wished to become a nun (Aleksandr Tarasov, "V'etnam blizko, ili Partizanskaia voina na beregakh Reina," http://scepsis.ru/library/print/id_658.html). One veteran of the SR combat unit Viacheslav Malyshev in fact made an impressive ecclesiastical career. He left Russia after the Civil War, in which he had fought against the Reds. Eventually, he found himself in Jerusalem and became a monk. In 1949, already an archimandrite and dean of St. Nicholas Russian Orthodox Church in Teheran, he wrote to former SR leader Chernov, then residing in New York, proposing, "with God's help," to resume direct action against the Bolsheviks, perhaps via the Soviet-Iranian border (Geifman, *Thou Shalt Kill*, 253–54).

11. Cited in Field, "Ekaterina Breshkovskaia," (unpublished manuscript). I am grateful to Professor Daniel Field for the text of this proclamation, quoted in the original Russian in Anna Geifman, *Na sluzhbe u smerti* (New York: Liberty, 2006), 212.

12. Crenshaw, "Theories of Terrorism," 20; Zeev Ivianski, "Fathers and Sons: A Study of Jewish Involvement in the Revolutionary Movement and Terrorism in Tsarist Russia," *Terrorism and Political Violence* 2, no. 2 (1989): 154.

13. Lifton, "Cult Formation."

14. Richard J. Rubenstein cited in Mazarr, *Unmodern Men in the Modern World*, 30.

15. Juergensmeyer, *Terror in the Mind of God*, 165.

16. Bolshevik state religiosity analyzed in Nina Tumarkin, *Lenin Lives!: The Lenin Cult in Soviet Russia* (Cambridge, MA: Harvard University Press, 1983), 65ff.

17. Cited in Mikhail Vaiskopf, *Pisatel' Stalin* (Moscow: Novoe literaturnoe obozrenie, 2002), 151n176. In 1918, official party poet Dem'ian Bednyi published in *Pravda* his own version of the Bolshevik Exodus, a poem "Promised Land," depicting Lenin and Trotsky as Moses and Aaron and the Mensheviks as the disbelieving, pagan-worshipping, rebellious Jews (ibid., 150).

18. Ibid., 159.

19. Rosenthal, *New Myth, New World*, 188.

20. "Sergey Nechayev 1869: The Revolutionary Catechism," http://www.marxists.org/subject/anarchism/nechayev/catechism.htm.

21. Cited in Mel'gunov, *"Krasnyi terror" v Rossii*, 175.

22. Jim Connell, "The Red Flag," http://webpages.dcu.ie/~sheehanh/rf-lyrics.htm.

23. Cited in Leites, *A Study of Bolshevism*, 137.

24. Lifton, "Cult Formation."

25. Sermon by Dr. Ahmad Abu Halabiya, former Rector of the Islamic University in Gaza and member of the PA-appointed "Futwa Council," at the Sheikh Zayed bin Sultan Al-Nahyan mosque on October 13, 2000, broadcast live on the official PA television, http://www.aish.com/jw/me/48882612.html.

26. Reuter, *My Life as a Weapon*, 93.

27. Phillips, "The War against Terrorism," 218.

28. Public speech of Member of the Palestinian Legislative Council member Fathi Hamad, Al-Aqsa TV, February 29, 2008, http://www.youtube.com/watch?v=RTu-AU-E9ycs.

29. Arnon Groiss, ed., *The West, Christians, and Jews in Saudi Arabian Schoolbooks*, 151–59.

30. Ibid.

31. Private video (graphic images; discretion advised), http://www.metacafe.com/watch/666615/ever_heard_of_the_ramallah_lynching/. For a full story see Israel's Media Watch, http://www.geocities.com/CapitolHill/2527/press104.htm.

32. "The Third Jihad," Part 1, http://www.road90.com/watch.php?id=tAfPJzb7Yc.

33. "Finish Celebration of a Summer Camp," http://www.israel-wat.com/pics1_eng.htm#a5.

34. "Muslim Kindergarten Graduation Ceremony," Al-Aqsa TV, May 31, 2007, http://www.youtube.com/watch?v=6WHdWgES-Uw&NR=1&feature=fvwp.

35. Steven Stalinsky, "Palestinian Authority Sermons 2000–2003," MEMRI, December 26, 2003, http://www.memri.org/bin/articles.cgi?Area=sr&ID=SR2403.

36. Sermon by Sheikh Ibrahim Mudeiris at Sheikh Ijlin Mosque, Gaza City, August 15, 2003, and August 22, 2003, Broadcasts on Palestinian Television, Palestinian Authority Friday Sermons, MEMRI, September 16, 2003, http://www.memri.org/bin/articles.cgi?Page=archives&Area=sd&ID=SP57403.

37. August 17, 2001, sermon broadcast live on Palestinian TV from the Sheik 'Ijlin mosque in Gaza, "PA TV Friday Sermon Calls for Jihad and Martyrdom," MEMRI, August 24, 2001, http://www.memri.org/bin/articles.cgi?Page=subjects&Area=conflict&ID=SP26101.

38. Berman, *Terror and Liberalism*, 112.

39. "Behind the Headlines: Hamas' Mickey Mouse Teaches Children to Hate and Kill," Israel Ministry of Foreign Affairs, http://www.mfa.gov.il/MFA/About+the+Ministry/Behind+the+Headlines/Hamas+Mickey+Mouse+teaches+children+to+hate+and+kill+10-May-2007.htm.

40. Hamas children's TV: "Rabbit Puppet Vows to Eat the Jews" (February 8, 2009) and "Rabbit Puppet Vows to Kill and Eat the Danes" (February 22, 2008), Palestinian Media Watch, http://www.palwatch.org/main.aspx?fi=455#470.

41. "Hamas in Their Own Voices," http://mignews.co.il/news/politic/world/170109_134656_15869.html.

42. For examples of textbooks and children's readings filled with incitement for violence, see http://www.mfa.gov.il/MFA/MFAArchive/2000_2009/2001/11/SPOTLIGHT-+Incitement-+Antisemitism+and+Hatred+of.htm.

43. Cited in Berko, *The Path to Paradise*, 110–12.

44. "Palliwood Staging Area? You Decide for Yourself," http://video.google.com/videoplay?docid=7332726655958371305. See also "Pallywood Introduction," http://seconddraft.org/index.php?option=com_content&view=article&id=59&Itemid=199.

45. For complete analysis of the story, see "Al Durah Affair: The Dossier,"http://www.theaugeanstables.com/al-durah-affair-the-dossier/.

46. Robert S. Wistrich, *Muslim Anti-Semitism: A Clear and Present Danger* (The American Jewish Committee, 2002), 34, http://www.ajc.org/atf/cf/%7B42D75369-D582-4380-8395-D25925B85EAF%7D/WistrichAntisemitism.pdf; Palestinian news agency FPNP cited in Itamar Marcus and Barbara Crook, "Hamas police official: Israel smuggles 'sexual stimulants' to destroy Palestinian youth" (Bulletin July 17, 2009), PMW, http://co117w.col117.mail.live.com/default.aspx?n=1309909505; and Al-Hayat Al-Jadida, July 4, 2008, "Canada and the Palestinian Authority" (Special Report, March 25, 2009), PMW, http://pmw.org.il/Bulletins_Apr2009.htm#b050409.

47. Cited in Groiss and Toobian, eds., *The War Curriculum in Iranian Schoolbooks*, 109.

48. MEMRI TV Project Special Report: Iranian TV Drama Series about Israeli Government Stealing Palestinian Children's Eyes, December 22, 2004, http://www.memri.org/bin/latestnews.cgi?ID=SD83304.

49. Morten Berthelsen and Barak Ravid, "Top Sweden Newspaper Says IDF Kills Palestinians for Their Organs," *Haaretz*, August 22, 2009, http://www.haaretz.com/hasen/spages/1108384.html. Original publication in Sweden's largest daily newspaper, *Aftonbladet*, http://www.aftonbladet.se/kultur/article5652583.ab.

50. *Sekira* 12 (1906): 7, Nic. 436:2.

51. Excerpt from an unsigned letter from Kiev dated March 2, 1904, to N. Shpitsman in Berlin, Okhrana XXIVI:1.

52. *Volia* 71 (October 4, 1906): 4, PSR 7:569.

53. Kropotkin, *Russkaia revoliutsiia i anarkhizm*, 3; "Anarkhizm," 1, Okhrana XVIb[5]:5A.

54. "Suicide Attacks in Afghanistan (2001–2007)," 90, http://www.reliefweb.int/rw/RWFiles2007.nsf/FilesByRWDocUnidFilename/EKOI-76W52H-full_report.pdf/$File/full_report.pdf.

55. "The Third Jihad," Part 1, http://www.road90.com/watch.php?id=tAfPJzb7Yc.

56. See, for example, "Pictures from the Children of Jihad (Holy War) Summer Camp," http://www.israel-wat.com/q6_eng.htm#a1; http://www.mfa.gov.il/MFA/MFAArchive/2000_2009/2002/8/Answers+to+Frequently+Asked+Questions-+Palestinian.htm; "Participation of Children and Teenagers in Terrorist Activity during the Al-Aqsa Intifada," January 30, 2003, http://www.mfa.gov.il/MFA/MFAArchive/2000_2009/2003/1/Participation+of+Children+and+Teenagers+in+Terrori.htm; and "Hitlerjugend," http://somebodyhelpme.info/palikids/palikids.html (graphic images; discretion required).

57. *Al-Hayat Al-Jadida*, October 6, 2001, ed. Itamar Marcus, Palestinian Media Watch: A Self Portrait of Palestinian Society, http://www.pmw.org.il/murder.htm#murder9.

58. Hamas children's TV: "Rabbit Puppet Vows to Kill and Eat the Danes," Palestinian Media Watch, February 22, 2008, http://www.palwatch.org/main.aspx?fi=455#470.

59. Kimhi and Even, "Who Are the Palestinian Suicide Bombers?" 828.

60. Cited in Leites, *A Study of Bolshevism*, 347.

61. A. G. Asmolov, *Naperekor oppozitsii dushi* (Moscow: Nachala-press, 1994), 28.

62. Juergensmeyer, *Terror in the Mind of God*, 166.

63. Cited in Mel'gunov, *"Krasnyi terror" v Rossii*, 187–88nn.

64. *Al-Hayat Al-Jadida*, February 27, 2003, ed. Itamar Marcus, Palestinian Media Watch: A Self Portrait of Palestinian Society, http://www.pmw.org.il/murder.htm#murder9.

65. Reuter, *My Life Is a Weapon*, 89–90.

66. Kimhi and Even, "Who Are the Palestinian Suicide Bombers?" 829.

67. Hamas TV: "Kids Shown Video of Their Mother's Suicide Bombing Death" [Al Aqsa TV, 3 July 2009], Palestinian Media Watch, http://www.palwatch.org/main.aspx?fi=157&doc_id=1001.

68. Stalinsky, "Palestinian Authority Sermons 2000–2003," http://www.memri.org/bin/articles.cgi?Area=sr&ID=SR2403.

69. Cited in "Umm Nidal: Mother of the Murderers," March 3, 2004, Jihad Watch, http://www.jihadwatch.org/archives/001047.php.

70. Valid Shebat, "Iz Palestinskogo terrorista v plamennogo sionista," speech March 7, 2004, *Spektr*, 7 (073), http://www.spectr.org/2004/073/shebat.htm.

71. Cited in Berko, *The Path to Paradise*, 97.

72. Speckhard and Akhmedova, "Black Widows: The Chechen Female Suicide Terrorists," 75.

73. Reuter, *My Life Is a Weapon*, 87; Bloom, *Dying to Kill*, 236n88; Joyce M. Davis, *Martyrs: Innocence, Vengeance, and Despair in the Middle East* (New York: Palgrave Macmillan, 2003), 124; "Participation of Children and Teenagers in Terrorist Activity during the Al-Aqsa Intifada," January 30, 2003, http://www.mfa.gov.il/MFA/MFAArchive/2000_2009/2003/1/Participation+of+Children+and+Teenagers+in+Terrori.htm; Merle Miyasato, *Suicide Bombers. Profiles, Methods and Techniques*, http://fmso.leavenworth.army.mil/documents/Suicide-Bombers.pdf. For copies of correspondence translated from the Arabic, see "Documents Seized During Operation Defensive Shield Linking Arafat to Terrorism," April 15, 2002, http://www.mfa.gov.il/MFA/MFAArchive/2000_2009/2002/4/Documents%20seized%20during%20Operation%20Defensive%20Shield.

74. Schweitzer, "Palestinian Female Suicide Bombers," 38.

75. Cited in "Blessings for Whoever Has Saved a Bullet in Order to Stick It in a Jew's Head," December 27, 2003, Jihad Watch, http://www.jihadwatch.org/archives/000501.php.

76. Kimhi and Even, "Who Are the Palestinian Suicide Bombers?" 829.

77. U.S. Senate Committee Hearing on Palestinian Education (2003), http://www.teachkidspeace.org/doc105.php.

78. Cited in "Young Children Convinced of Death as a *Shahid* as Ideal" [PA TV June 2002], TV Archives—Video Library, http://www.pmw.org.il/tv%20part1.html.

79. Reported in the PA official daily *Al-Hayat Al-Jadida* on December 26, 2001, cited in Arab Indoctrination for Suicide, http://www.freeman.org/m_online/nov03/indoctrination.htm.

80. Salman Akhtar, "Dehumanization: Origins, Manifestations, and Remedies," in *Violence or Dialogue? Psychoanalytic Insights on Terror and Terrorism*, ed. Sverre Varvin and Vamik D. Volkan (New York: The International Psychoanalytical Association, 2003), 132.

81. Volkan, *The Need to Have Enemies and Allies*, 120; Juergensmeyer, *Terror in the Mind of God*, 186.

82. "Sergey Nechayev 1869: The Revolutionary Catechism," http://www.marxists.org/subject/anarchism/nechayev/catechism.htm.

83. PSR 3:216.

84. Hoffer, *The True Believer*, 88. Albert Bandura's experiment showed that students could be extremely aggressive toward a group of their peers only because they were assigned the dehumanizing label of being just "like animals" (Phillip Zimbardo, "Vantage Point: Faceless terrorists embody 'creative evil,'" Stanford Report, September 26, 2001, http://news-service.stanford.edu/news/2001/september26/zimbardo-926.html.

85. Cited in Friday sermon on PA TV: "Blessings to Whoever Saved a Bullet to Stick It in a Jew's Head," MEMRI, August 8, 2001, http://www.memri.org/bin/articles.cgi?Page=archives&Area=sd&ID=SP25201.

86. Cited in Arnon Groiss, ed., *Palestinian Textbooks: From Arafat to Abbas and Hamas* (New York: The Center for Monitoring the Impact of Peace and American Jewish Committee, 2008), 15; in Aluma Solnick, "Based on Koranic Verses, Interpretations, and Traditions, Muslim Clerics State: The Jews Are the Descendants of Apes, Pigs, and Other Animals," MEMRI, November 1, 2002, http://www.memri.org/bin/articles.cgi?Area=sr&ID=SR01102; and in Itamar Marcus and Barbara Crook, "Hamas Blood Libel: Jews Drink Muslim blood," April 5, 2009, http://

pmw.org.il/Bulletins_Apr2009.htm#b190409. A three-year-old girl's interview (live), "Arabs Brainwashed Little Girls to Hate Jews," http://www.youtube.com/watch?v=ZL0C2QvqIlo&NR=1.

87. PA TV, March 4, 2008, cited in Itamar Marcus, "The Genocide Mechanism," Palestinian Media Watch, Bulletin, April 26, 2009, http://pmw.org.il/Bulletins_Apr2009.htm#b190409.

88. Cited in Philip Jenkins, *God's Continent: Christianity, Islam, and Europe's Religious Crisis* (Oxford University Press, 2009), 188. "Europe Is the Cancer. Islam Is the Answer," screamed one placard at a 2006 Islamist rally in London ("Muslim Demonstration" photographs, http://www.snopes.com/photos/politics/muslimprotest.asp).

89. Cited in Dawson, "The Bali Bombers," http://www.capmag.com/article.asp?ID=3000.

90. Hazani, "Red Carpet, White Lilies," 25.

91. Robert J. Lifton, *The Nazi Doctors* (New York: Basic Books, 1986), 488.

92. Cited in Pipes, *The Russian Revolution*, 790; cited in Itamar Marcus and Barbara Crook, "Imam Who Participated in 'Congress of Imams and Rabbis for Peace' Calls for Extermination of Jews," April 19, 2009, http://pmw.org.il/Bulletins_Apr2009.htm#b190409.

93. Hazani, "Red Carpet, White Lilies," 25.

94. "Sergey Nechayev 1869: The Revolutionary Catechism," http://www.marxists.org/subject/anarchism/nechayev/catechism.htm.

95. I. Pavlov, *Ochistka chelovechestva* (Moscow, 1907), 9, 14–15, 17–18, 23, 30.

96. Posse, *Moi ziznennyi put'*, 407.

97. Akhtar, "Dehumanization," 135, 132.

98. Middle East Facts Photo Gallery, http://middleeastfacts.com/Gallery/thumbnails.php?album=11.

99. Brooks, "Cult of Death," http://www.nytimes.com/2004/09/07/opinion/07brooks.html.

100. "Sergey Nechayev 1869: The Revolutionary Catechism," http://www.marxists.org/subject/anarchism/nechayev/catechism.htm.

101. Erich Fromm, *The Anatomy of Human Destructiveness* (New York: Holt, Rinehart, and Winston, 1973), 279.

102. Hazani, "Red Carpet, White Lilies," 45.

103. Ibid., 43.

104. Cited in Mel'gunov, *"Krasnyi terror" v Rossii*, 190.

105. Cited in Mariia Tendriakova, *Okhota na ved'm. Istoricheskii opy intolerantnosti* (Moscow: Smysl, 2006), 110.

106. Landes, "Totalitarian Millennialism: The Bolshevik Apocalypse," in *Heaven on Earth*.

107. See discussion in Pipes, "Terrorism: The Syrian Connection," http://www.danielpipes.org/1064/terrorism-the-syrian-connection. See also Riad El-Rayyes and Dunia Mahas, *Guerrillas for Palestine* (London: Portico Publications, 1976): 131. According to a former colonel at the Main Intelligence Directorate of the Soviet army, which oversaw the process of manufacturing terrorist cadres in the East-bloc countries during the Cold War, "the methods and ideology of training terrorists…have remained substantially unchanged [over the century]" (cited in Marks, *How Russia Shaped the Modern World*, 37).

108. Cited in Steven Stalinsky, "Dealing in Death," *National Review*, May 24, 2004, http://www.nationalreview.com/comment/stalinsky200405240846.asp.

109. Fathi Hamad, Al-Aqsa TV, February 29, 2008, http://www.youtube.com/watch?v=RTu-AUE9ycs.

110. Dawson, "The Bali Bombers," http://www.capmag.com/article.asp?ID=3000.

111. Denis MacEoin, "Suicide Bombing as Worship," *Middle East Quarterly* 16, no. 4 (Fall 2009), http://www.meforum.org/2478/suicide-bombing-as-worship.

112. Cited in Catherine Cobbam, trans., *An Introduction to Arab Poetics: Translation of Literary History and Criticism by Adonis* (London: Saqi Books, 1990), 65.

113. Keith Lewinstein, "The Revaluation of Martyrdom in Early Islam," in *Sacrificing the Self: Perspectives on Martyrdom and Religion*, ed. Margaret Cormack, (New York: Oxford University Press, 2002), 79, 86–87.

114. Fukuyama and Samin, "Can Any Good Come of Radical Islam?" http://www.commentarymagazine.com/viewarticle.cfm/can-any-good-come-of-radical-islam-9498?search=1.

115. Ibid.

116. Author's personal communication with Dr. John Haule (Summer 2005).

117. Hitler loathed the "brilliant, charming, cosmopolitan Vienna" for its "Semitism," preferring the "homogeneous Munich" ("Adolf Hitler, Time Magazines's [sic.] 1938 Man of the Year," http://www.scrapbookpages.com/DachauMemorial/TimeCover.html).

118. Hazani, "Red Carpet, White Lilies," 43.

119. "Hitlerjugend," http://somebodyhelpme.info/palikids/palikids.html (graphic images; discretion required).

120. "As Adorno said of Richard Wagner's music: 'Magnificence is used to sell death'.... Though such rituals were supposed to be highly positive and inspirational, in fact they struck another note, stirring apocalyptic associations and awakening a fear of universal conflagrations or dooms" (Joachim C. Fest, *Hitler* [Harcourt, 1974], 513).

121. Cited in Stalinsky, "Dealing in Death," http://www.nationalreview.com/comment/stalinsky200405240846.asp.

122. Extremely graphic beheading images; discretion advised: http://www.google.com/search?hl=en&source=hp&q=beheading+video&aq=0&oq=beheading.

123. Akhtar, "Dehumanization," 138.

124. Cited in Berman, *Terror and Liberalism*, 143. Sexual characeristics of terrorism has been a theme in fiction, most recently in Aleks Tarn's *Kvazimodo* ("Mosty kul'tury" (Jerusalem: "Gesharim," 2004).

125. Jerry S. Piven, "Ambivalence and Apathy Regarding Post 9/11Torture," *Clio's Psyche*16, no. 2 (September 2009), 166.

126. Rodby, The Dark Heart of Utopia, 229.

127. Berman, *Terror and Liberalism*, 131, 143.

128. Ascherson, "A Terror Campaign of Love and Hate," http://www.guardian.co.uk/world/2008/sep/28/germany.terrorism.

129. Johann Hari, "Red Alert? An interview with Antonio Negri," http://www.johannhari.com/archive/article.php?id=435.

130. Roger Friedland, "Religious Terror and the Erotics of Exceptional Violence," *Anthropological Journal on European Cultures* (forthcoming), http://www.ideologiesofwar.com/docs/FriedlandReligiousTerror.pdf.

131. Sam Gaines, "The Gun Still Speaks," http://www.baader-meinhof.com/essays/EyeInterview.html. While training in a Palestinian camp in Jordan, the German female terrorists would sunbathe naked on the roofs of their living quarters in full sight of their Muslim comrades, disrespectful of their feelings about modesty and obviously provocative. Appositely, the 2008 film about "The Baader Meinhof Complex" shows Gudrun Ensslin, Baader's girlfriend and accomplice, "strutting naked in the Lebanese sun, jeering at shocked Palestinian recruits. 'What's the matter? F-cking [sic] and shooting; it's the same thing!' " (Ascherson, "A Terror Campaign of Love and Hate," http://www.guardian.co.uk/world/2008/sep/28/germany.terrorism).

132. E. D. Nikitina, "Nash pobeg," *KS* 56 (1929), 124, 127n.

133. Schweitzer, "Palestinian Female Suicide Bombers: Virtuous Heroines or Damaged Goods?" 15, http://www.labat.co.il/articles/palestinian%20female%20suicide%20bombers.pdf.

134. "Patricia Campbell Hearst (1954–)," *Guerrilla*, http://www.pbs.org/wgbh/amex/guerrilla/peopleevents/p_p_hearst.html; Patty Hearst Profile, http://www.cnn.com/CNN/Programs/people/shows/hearst/profile.html; Amy Zalman, "Patty Hearst (SLA)," http://terrorism.about.com/od/groupsleader1/p/PattyHearst.htm.

135. Adrian N. Carr and Cheryl A. Lapp, *Leadership is a Matter of Life and Death: The Psychodynamics of Eros and Thanatos Working in Organisations* (New York: Palgrave Macmillan, 2006), 9, 58–59.

136. Hazani, "Red Carpet, White Lilies," 44.

137. Hazani illuminates thanatophilia via a case study of Avraham Stern (*nom-de-plume* and *nom-de-guerre* "Yair"), a leader of paramilitary Lehi and hero of the Jewish anti-British uprising. "I despise myself with all my soul," he confesses, and "lonely, unneeded, and pitiful . . . miserable, corrupted, angry," he wishes "to give life to the fullest, so as to disappear tranquilly into the eternity." A decadent and aesthete, Yair "reifies, regifies, glorifies, and deifies death"; and writes inter alia:

To the devil with life, leprous and lice-infested It is long overdue that against the wall I smashed my head, mockingly, Sneering at myself, scornful.

(Yair's poetry in the Russian original, the Central Zionist Archive, A 549/28. I am grateful to Moshe Goncharok for introducing me to these materials.)

Although Yair created "a deity of war and death" and endowed "weapons, death, and killing with a quasi-sacred status," his thanatophilia was strictly a personal matter. (Hazani, "Red Carpet, White Lilies," 3, 14) Lehi, though an extremist national liberation organization, was not a death-endorsing, totalistic ideological movement; nor was it founded on the cult of martyrdom or sought promote a messianic consciousness. Moreover, it took no part in building the Jewish state after it had acquired independence.

Among several lone perpetrators of violence in Israel, in 1994 Doctor Baruch Goldstein shot 29 Arab worshippers in the Tomb of the Patriarchs in Hebron, allegedly as a reaction to overheard calls to "kill the Jews." The act "was immediately condemned in the most damning terms by all Israeli parties and virtually entire Jewish population." Goldstein's apologists "did not number more than a few hundred at most" and hardly represent "death culture" (Levin, *The Oslo Syndrome*, 363).

138. Brooks, "Cult of Death," http://www.nytimes.com/2004/09/07/opinion/07brooks.html.

139. Cited in Berman, *Terror and Liberalism*, 119–20.

140. Ibid., 120.

EPILOGUE

1. Fatima Tebieva, "Pobyvali v adu," *Golos Beslana* 60 (December 4, 2004): 1; Yana Voitova, "Beslan Children Testify," *The St. Petersburg Times* (August 26, 2005), http://www.sptimes.ru/index.php?action_id=2&story_id=15341. Parts of the video may be seen in "The Third Jihad," http://www.thethirdjihad.com/911stream/911stream.php.

2. Treatment of hostages described in Alena Tedeeva-Bagaeva, "Radovalas', chto budet samoi krasivoi," *Golos Beslana* 57 (May 17, 2005): 2; and in Tamila Sautieva, "Krasavitsa Dzerassa," *Golos Beslana* 94 (September 3, 2005): 2.

3. Tebieva, "Pobyvali v adu," 1.

4. "Drug Addiction among the Beslan Terrorists," *Pravda Online*, http://newsfromrussia.com/world/2004/10/19/5680.html.

5. Original partially published in Tazret Gatagov, "Ia uvidel v sportzale to, chto ne videl na fronte," *Golos Beslana* 24 (October 14, 2004): 2.

6. Brooks, "Cult of Death," http://www.nytimes.com/2004/09/07/opinion/07brooks.html.

7. Ego vzorvali vmeste s terroristom," *Golos Beslana* 77 (July 21, 2005): 2.

8. Brooks, "Cult of Death," http://www.nytimes.com/2004/09/07/opinion/07brooks.html.

9. Budnitskii, "'Krov' po sovesti'," 207–8.

10. Natal'ia Ambalova, "Rebiata s nashego dvora," *Golos Beslana* 68 (December 22, 2004): 1.

11. Marina Tsagaraeva, "Chuzhikh detei ne byvaet," *Golos Beslana* 31 (October 22, 2004): 1.

12. Charles B. Strozier and Katie Gentile, "Responses of the Mental Health Community to the World Trade Center Disaster," in *Living with Terror, Working with Trauma*, ed. Danielle Knafo (Lanham, MD: Rowman and Littlefeld Publishers, 2004), 416.

13. B. M. Masterov, "Khronotop travmy i puti sotsial'no-psikhologicheskoi reabilitatsii," in A. L. Venger and E. I. Morozova, eds., *Beslan, 5 let vmeste. Sbornik materialov spetsialistov, rabotaiushchikh v Beslane* ("Agava:" Moscow, upcoming in 2010).

14. Cited in Peter Finn, "School Is Symbol of Death for Haunted Children of Beslan," *Washington Post*, August 28, 2005, http://www.washingtonpost.com/wp-dyn/content/article/2005/08/27/AR2005082701157_pf.html.

15. Ibid.

16. Masterov, "Khronotop travmy."

17. Lidiia Grafova, "Ne zabyvaite: vy zhivete v gorode angelov!" *Golos Beslana* 73 (December 29, 2004): 1.

18. Berman, *Terror and Liberalism*, 112.

19. Interview with Oshrat Panaitova, teacher, March 14, 2008, Sderot, Israel.

20. "School Resumes in Israel Despite Rocket Threat," http://www.msnbc.msn.com/id/28605322/.

21. Interview with Lior Sh'itrit, coordinator of after-school children programs, February 17, 2008, Sderot, Israel.

22. Anna Geifman, "Terrorism and Shared Death Anxiety," *Clio's Psyche* 15, no. 3 (December 2008): 141–43; see also Anna Geifman, "Animal Farm in Sderot," *The Jerusalem Post*, August 5, 2008, http://www.jpost.com/servlet/Satellite?pagename=JPost/Page/IndexParMult&cid=1123495333264.

23. Brooks, "Cult of Death," http://www.nytimes.com/2004/09/07/opinion/07brooks.html.

24. Cited in Anav Silverman, "Living with Rockets: Sderot students ready for school bells and rocket sirens," *Jerusalem Post*, September 3, 2009, http://cgis.jpost.com/Blogs/rocketlife/entry/sderot_students_ready_for_school.

25. Finn, "School Is Symbol of Death for Haunted Children of Beslan," http://www.washingtonpost.com/wp-dyn/content/article/2005/08/27/AR2005082701157_pf.html.

26. Interview with Oshrat Panaitova, March 14, 2008 interview with Natal'ia Rakhman, preschool music teacher, February 12, 2008, Sderot, Israel.

27. Evgeniia Kravchik, "Gorod na trankvilizatorakh," February 25, 2008, http://www.zman.com/news/2008/02/25/4004.html; Grigorii Bado, "Posttravmaticheskii sindrom v Sderote," April 1, 2008, http://www.zman.com/news/2008/04/01/7586.html.

28. Interview with Oshrat Panaitova, 18 March 2009.

29. Discussed in Jena Baker McNeill and Richard Weitz, "Electromagnetic Pulse (EMP) Attack: A Preventable Homeland Security Catastrophe," October 20, 2008, The Heritage Foundation, http://www.heritage.org/Research/HomelandSecurity/bg2199.cfm; see also Jack Spencer, "The Electromagnetic Pulse Commission Warns of an Old Threat with a New Face," August 3, 2004, The Heritage Foundation, http://www.heritage.org/research/nationalsecurity/bg1784.cfm.

30. Richard Landes develops this concept in "Cognitive Egocentrism,"http://www.theaugeanstables.com/reflections-from-second-draft/cognitive-egocentrism/.

31. Brooks, "Cult of Death," http://www.nytimes.com/2004/09/07/opinion/07brooks.html.

32. "Muslim Demonstration" photographs, http://www.snopes.com/photos/politics/muslimprotest.asp.

33. Cited in Ibid.

34. Jytte Klausen, *The Cartoons That Shook the World* (New Haven, CT: Yale University Press, 2009).

35. "Yale Slammed for Nixing Muslim Cartoons," *The Jerusalem Post*, September 8, 2009, http://www.jpost.com/servlet/Satellite?cid=1251804517402&pagename=JPost%2FJPArticle%2FShowFull.

36. Brooks, "Cult of Death," http://www.nytimes.com/2004/09/07/opinion/07brooks.html.

37. CNN evening program, November 24, 2004.

38. Poster in "Muslim Demonstration" photographs, http://www.snopes.com/photos/politics/muslimprotest.asp.

39. Mazarr, *Unmodern Men in the Modern World*, 31.

40. "Muslim Demonstration" photographs, http://www.snopes.com/photos/politics/muslimprotest.asp.

41. Al-Rahma TV (Egypt), January 17, 2009, cited in Itamar Marcus and Barbara Crook, "When Hatemongering Is Common Currency," *Ottawa Citizen*, April 24, 2009, http://pmw.org.il/Bulletins_Apr2009.htm#b050409.

42. Huxley, The Perennial Philosophy, 108.

43. Cited in the *Washington Post*, September 16, 2001.

44. Dawson, "The Bali Bombers," http://www.capmag.com/article.asp?ID=3000.

45. November 2002 "Letter to America" attributed to bin Laden, cited in Lewis, *The Crisis of Islam*, 157.

46. Poster in "Muslim Demonstration" photographs, http://www.snopes.com/photos/politics/muslimprotest.asp.
47. Brooks, "Cult of Death," http://www.nytimes.com/2004/09/07/opinion/07brooks.html.
48. "The Third Jihad," Part 1, http://www.road90.com/watch.php?id=tAfPJzb7Yc; also in Hoffer, *The True Believer*, 66; "Invitation to Movement," http://www.sabiqun.net/join.html.
49. William Law cited in Huxley, The Perennial Philosophy, 97.
50. Ibid., 98–99; Hoffer, *The True Believer*, 67.
51. Akhtar, "Dehumanization," 138.
52. Shankara cited in Huxley, The Perennial Philosophy, 7.
53. Zweig, *The Heresy of Self-Love*, 3.
54. Cronin, "Behind the Curve: Globalization and International Terrorism," 34.
55. Bloom, *Dying to Kill*, 5.
56. Viacheslav Likhachev, "Sakral'nyi kosmos iudenfrai: Mircha Eliade i 'evreiskii vopros'," http://eliade.upelsinka.com/cr2.htm; Radu Ioanid, "Rumania: Extract from 'Characteristics of Rumanian Fascism,'" in *Fascism: Critical Concepts in Political Science*, ed. Roger Griffin with Matthew Feldman, (New York: Routledge, 2004), 135.
57. Huxley, The Perennial Philosophy, 192, 252, 243.
58. Joachim C. Fest, *Hitler*, (New York: Harcourt Brace & Co., 1973), 725.
59. Juergensmeyer, *Terror in the Mind of God*, 236.
60. Ibid., 232.
61. Emily Dickinson, "Part Four: Time and Eternity," *Complete Poems* (1924), http://www.bartleby.com/113/4031.html.

Selected Bibliography

PRINTED ENGLISH-LANGUAGE SOURCES

Adonis. *An Introduction to Arab Poetics.* New York: Saqi Books, 2003.

Akhtar, Salman, Selma Kramer, and Henri Parens, eds. *The Birth of Hatred.* Northvale, NJ: Jason Aronson, 1995.

Albats, Yevgenia, and Catherine A. Fitzpatrick. *The State within a State: The KGB and Its Hold on Russia—Past, Present, and Future.* New York: Farrar Straus Giroux, 1994.

Al-Rayyis, Riyad Najib. *Guerrillas for Palestine.* New York: Palgrave Macmillan, 1976.

Andreyev, Olga Chernov. *Cold Spring in Russia.* Ann Arbor, MI: Ardis, 1978.

Ascher, Abraham. *P. A. Stolypin: The Search for Stability in Late Imperial Russia.* New York: Stanford University Press, 2001.

Ashcroft, Bill, and Pal Ahluwalia. *Edward Said.* New York: Routledge, 2001.

Avrich, Paul. *Russian Anarchists.* Princeton, NJ: Princeton University Press, 1967.

Belyi, Andrei. *Petersburg.* New York: Indiana University Press, 1979.

Bergman, Jay. *Vera Zasulich: A Biography.* Stanford, CA: Stanford University Press, 1983.

Berko, Anat. *The Path to Paradise: The Inner World of Suicide Bombers and Their Dispatchers.* Dulles, VA: Potomac Books, 2009.

Berman, Eli. *Radical, Religious, and Violent: The New Economics of Terrorism.* Cambridge, MA: Massachusetts Institute of Technology Press, 2009.

Berman, Paul. *Terror and Liberalism.* New York: Norton, 2003.

Blok, Alexander. "The People and the Intelligentsia." In *Russian Intellectual History: An Anthology,* ed. Mark Raeff. New York: Humanity Books, 1999.

Bloom, Mia. *Dying to Kill: The Allure of Suicide Terror.* New York: Columbia University Press, 2005.

Borenstein, Eliot. *Men without Women: Masculinity and Revolution in Russian Fiction, 1917–1929.* Chapel Hill, NC: Duke University Press, 2001.

Brooks, David. "Cult of Death." *The New York Times,* September 7, 2004.

Brovkin, Vladimir N. *Behind the Front Lines of the Civil War: Political Parties and Social Movements in Russia, 1918–1922.* Princeton, NJ: Princeton University Press, 1994.

Bunyan, James, and H. H. Fisher. *Bolshevik Revolution, 1917–1918: Documents & Materials.* Stanford, CA: Stanford University Press, 1934.

Carr, Adrian N., and Cheryl A. Lapp. *Leadership is a Matter of Life and Death: The Psychodynamics of Eros and Thanatos Working in Organisations.* New York: Palgrave Macmillan, 2006.

Carr, E. H. Michael Bakunin. New York: Octagon Books, 1975.

Robert. *Reflections on a Ravaged Century.* New York: Norton, 1999.

Cramer, Mark, ed. *Black Book of Communism: Crimes, Terror, Repression.* Cambridge, MA: Harvard University Press, 1999.

Cronin, Audrey Kurth. "Behind the Curve: Globalization and International Terrorism," *International Security* 27, no. 3 (Winter 2002–3).

Daly, Jonathan W. *Autocracy under Siege: Security Police and Opposition in Russia, 1866–1905.* DeKalb: Northern Illinois University Press, 1998.

Daly, Jonathan W. *Watchful State: Security Police and Opposition in Russia, 1906–1917.* DeKalb: Northern Illinois University Press, 2004.

Davis, Joyce M. *Martyrs: Innocence, Vengeance, and Despair in the Middle East.* New York: Palgrave Macmillan, 2003.

Dershowitz, Alan M. *The Case against Israel's Enemies: Exposing Jimmy Carter and Others Who Stand in the Way of Peace.* Hoboken, NJ: John Wiley & Sons, 2008.

Deutscher, Isaac. The Prophet Armed: Trotsky, 1879–1921. New York-London: Verso, 2003.

Engelstein, Laura. The Keys to Happiness: Sex and the Search for Modernity in Fin-de-Siècle Russia. Ithaca, NY: Cornell University Press, 1992.

Erlich, Avi. *Ancient Zionism: The Biblical Origins of the National Idea.* New York: Free Press, 1995.

Fest, Joachim C. *Hitler.* New York: Harcourt Brace & Co., 1973.

Figes, Orlando. *People's Tragedy: The Russian Revolution, 1891–1924.* New York: Penguin Books, 1998.

Fishman, William J. *East End Jewish Radicals, 1875–1914.* London: Duckworth, 1975.

Frankl, Viktor E. *Man's Search for Meaning.* New York: Pocket Books, 1984.

Fromm, Erich. *Anatomy of Human Destructiveness.* New York: Holt, Rinehart, and Winston, 1973.

Fuller, William C. *Civil-Military Conflict in Imperial Russia, 1881–1914.* Princeton, NJ: Princeton University Press, 1985.

Galai, Shmuel. *The Liberation Movement in Russia 1900–1905 (Cambridge Russian, Soviet and Post-Soviet Studies).* Cambridge: Cambridge University Press, 1973.

Gambetta, Diego, ed. *Making Sense of Suicide Missions.* New York: Oxford University Press, 2006.

Geifman, Anna. *La mort sera votre dieu!: du nihilisme Russe au terrorisme islamiste.* Paris: Les Editions de La Table Ronde, 2005.

Geifman, Anna. "Terrorism and Shared Death Anxiety." *Clio's Psyche* 15, no. 3 (2008).

Geifman, Anna. "Terrorism's Cult of Death against Children in Beslan." *Clio's Psyche* 16, no. 2 (2009).

Geifman, Anna. *Thou Shalt Kill: Revolutionary Terrorism in Russia, 1894–1917.* Princeton, NJ: Princeton University Press, 1995.

Gellately, Robert. *Lenin, Stalin, and Hitler: The Age of Social Catastrophe.* New York: Knopf, 2007.

Gerson, Lennard D. *Secret Police in Lenin's Russia.* Philadelphia: Temple University Press, 1976.

Gilman, Sander L. *Jewish Self-Hatred: Anti-Semitism and the Hidden Language of the Jews.* New York: Johns Hopkins University Press, 1990.

Goering, Laura. "Russian Nervousness?: Neurasthenia and National Identity in Nineteenth-Century Russia." *Medical History* 47, no. 45 (2003).

Goren, Roberta. *The Soviet Union and Terrorism.* London-Boston-Sydney: George Allen & Unwin, 1984.

Groiss, Arnon, ed. *Palestinian Textbooks: From Arafat to Abbas and Hamas.* The Center for Monitoring the Impact of Peace and American Jewish Committee, New York, 2008.

Groiss, Arnon, ed. *The War Curriculum in Iranian Schoolbooks.* The Center for Monitoring the Impact of Peace and American Jewish Committee, New York, 2007.

Groiss, Arnon, ed. *The West, Christians, and Jews in Saudi Arabian Schoolbooks.* The Center for Monitoring the Impact of Peace and American Jewish Committee, New York, 2003.

Hafner, Lutz. "The Assassination of Count Mirbach and the 'July Uprising' of the Left Socialist Revolutionaries in Moscow, 1918." *Russian Review* 50, no. 3 (1991).

Hamm, Michael F., ed. *City in Late Imperial Russia.* Bloomington: Indiana University Press, 1986.

Hardy, Deborah. *Land and Freedom the Origins of Russian Terrorism, 1876–1879.* New York: Greenwood, 1987.

Harpaz, Dalia, and Ben Kaminsky. "Israel And Gaza? The Civilians' Distress." *The Epoch Times*, January 1, 2009.

Hayes, Carlton Joseph Huntley. *Generation of Materialism, 1871–1900.* Westport, CT: Greenwood, 1983.

Hazani, Moshe. "Apocaliptism, Symbolic Breakdown and Paranoia: An Application of Lifton's Model to the Death-Rebirth Fantasy." In *Apocalyptic Time*, ed. Albert I. Baumgarten (Leiden-Boston-Koln: Brill, 2000).

Hazani, Moshe. "Red Carpet, White Lilies: Love of Death in the Poetry of the Jewish Underground Leader Avraham Stern?" *The Psychoanalytic Review* 89, no. 32 (2002).

Hazani, Moshe. "Sacrificial Immortality: Toward a Theory of Suicidal Terrorism and Related Phenomena." Ed. L. Bryce Boyer, Alan Dundes, and Stephen M. Sonnenberg. *The Psychoanalytic Study of Society* 18, no. 417 (1993).

Hazani, Moshe. "The Breakdown of Meaning and Adolescent Problem Behavior." *International Journal of Adolescent Medical Health* 15, no. 3 (2003): 207–18.

Hazony, Yoram. *The Jewish State: The Struggle for Israel's Soul.* New York: Basic Books, 2001.

Hochschild, Adam. *The Unquiet Ghost Russians Remember Stalin.* New York: Mariner Books, 2003.

Hoffer, Eric. *The True Believer.* New York: Harper & Row, 1951.

Hollander, Paul. *Political Pilgrims: Western Intellectuals in Search of the Good Society.* New Brunswick, NJ: Transaction Publishers, 1998.

Horney, Karen. *The Neurotic Personality of Our Time.* Boston: Norton, 1994.

Huxley, Aldous. The Perennial Philosophy. New York: Harper & Row, 1944.

Ioanid, Radu. "Rumania: Extract from 'Characteristics of Rumanian Fascism'," In *Fascism: Critical Concepts in Political Science*, ed. Matthew Feldman with Roger Griffin. New York: Routledge, 2004.

Ivianski, Zeev. "The Terrorist Revolution: Roots of Modern Terrorism." In *Inside Terrorist Organizations*, ed. David C. Rapport. New York: Columbia University Press, 1988.

Jackson, Richard. "In Defense of "Terrorism: Finding a Way through a Forest of Misconceptions," *Behavioral Sciences of Terrorism and Political Aggression* (forthcoming 2011).

Jenkins, Philip. *God's Continent: Christianity, Islam, and Europe's Religious Crisis.* Oxford: Oxford University Press, 2009.

Juergensmeyer, Mark. *Terror in the Mind of God: The Global Rise of Religious Violence.* Berkeley: University of California Press, 2001.

Kelly, Aileen. "Self-Censorship and the Russian Intelligentsia, 1905–1914." *Slavic Review* 46, no. 2 (Summer 1987).

Klausen, Jytte. *The Cartoons That Shook the World.* New Haven, CT: Yale University Press, 2009.

Knafo, Danielle, ed. *Living with Terror, Working with Trauma.* Lanham, MD: Rowman and Littlefeld Publishers, 2004.

Knight, Amy. "Female Terrorists in the Russian Socialist Revolutionary Party." *Russian Review* 38, no. 2 (1979).

Laing, R. D. *Self and Others.* New York: Routledge, 1969.

Landes, Richard. "Totalitarian Millennialism: The Bolshevik Apocalypse." In *Heaven on Earth: The Varieties of the Millennial Experience.* Oxford University Press, forthcoming.

Laqueur, Walter. *Terrorism.* Boston-Toronto: Little, Brown & Co., 1977.

Lawrence, Bruce B. *Defenders of God: The Fundamentalist Revolt against the Modern Age.* New York: Harper and Row, 1989.

Leggett, George. *The Cheka: Lenin's Political Police.* New York: Oxford University Press, 1987.

Leites, Nathan. *A Study of Bolshevism.* Glencoe, IL: The Free Press Publishers, 1953.

Levin, Kenneth. *The Oslo Syndrome: Delusions of a People Under Siege.* Lyme, NH: Smith & Kraus, 2005.

Lewinstein, Keith. "The Revaluation of Martyrdom in Early Islam." In *Sacrificing the Self: Perspectives on Martyrdom and Religion,* ed. Margaret Cormack. New York: Oxford University Press, 2002.

Lewis, Bernard. *The Crisis of Islam: Holy War and Unholy Terror.* New York: Modern Library Edition, 2003.

Lifton, Robert J. *Boundaries: Psychological Man in Revolution.* New York: Random House, 1969.

Lifton, Robert Jay. *Broken Connection: On Death and the Continuity of Life.* New York: Basic Books, 1979.

Lifton, Robert Jay. *Nazi Doctors: Medical Killing and the Psychology of Genocide.* New York: Basic Books, 2000.

Lifton, Robert Jay. *Thought Reform and the Psychology of Totalism: A Study of "Brainwashing" in China.* Chapel Hill: University of North Carolina, 1989.

Lincoln, Bruce. *Sunlight at Midnight: St. Petersburg and the Rise of Modern Russia.* New York: Basic Books, 2002.

Litvak, Meir. "The Islamization of the Palestinian-Israeli Conflict: The Case of Hamas." *Middle Eastern Studies* 34, no. 1 (1998).

MacRae, Donald D. "Bolshevik Ideology: The Intellectual and Emotional Factors in Communist Affiliation." *Cambridge Journal* 5, no. 167 (1951).

Marks, Steven G. *How Russia Shaped the Modern World: From Art to Anti-Semitism, Ballet to Bolshevism.* Princeton, NJ: Princeton University Press, 2003.

Mazarr, Michael J. *Unmodern Men in the Modern World: Radical Islam, Terrorism, and the War on Modernity.* New York: Cambridge University Press, 2007.

McDaniel, James Frank. "Political Assassination and Mass Execution: Terrorism in Revolutionary Russia, 1878–1938." PhD diss., University of Michigan, 1976.

Mellor, Anne Kostelanetz. *Mary Shelley: Her Life, Her Fiction, Her Monsters.* New York: Routledge, 1989.

Merriman, John. *The Dynamite Club: How a Bombing in Fin-de-Siècle Paris Ignited the Age of Modern Terror.* New York: Houghton Mifflin Harcourt, 2009.

Mommsen, Wolfgang J., and Gerhard Hirshfeld, eds. *Social Protest, Violence, and Terror in Nineteenth- and Twentieth-Century Europe.* New York: St. Martin's Press, 1982.

Morrissey, Susan K. *Heralds of Revolution: Russian Students and the Mythologies of Radicalism.* New York: Oxford University Press, 1998.

Morrissey, Susan K. *Suicide and Body Politic in Imperial Russia.* New York: Cambridge University Press, 2006.

Naimark, Norman M. "Terrorism and the Fall of Imperial Russia." Published lecture, Boston University, Boston, April 12, 1986.

Naimark, Norman M. *Terrorists and Social Democrats. The Russian Revolutionary Movement under Alexander III.* Cambridge, MA: Harvard University Press, 1983.

Napolitano, Janet. "Away from the Politics of Fear." *Spiegel,* March 16, 2009.

Netanyahu, Binyamin. *Fighting Terrorism: How Democracies Can Defeat the International Terrorist Network.* New York: Farrar, Straus and Giroux, 2001.

Nikolajewski, Boris. *Azeff the Spy. Russian Terrorist and Police Stool.* New York, 1934.

Pape, Robert. *Dying to Win: The Strategic Logic of Suicide Terrorism.* New York: Random House, 2005.

Pedahzur, Ami. *Suicide Terrorism.* Cambridge, UK: Polity Press, 2005.

Perrie, Maureen. "Social Composition and Structure of the Socialist Revolutionary Party before 1917." *Soviet Studies* 24, no. 231 (1972).

Phares, Walid. *Future Jihad: Terrorist Strategies against America.* New York: Palgrave Macmillan, 2005.

Phillips, Hugh. "From a Bolshevik to a British Subject: The Early Years of Maksim M. Litvinov." *Slavic Review* 48, no. 3 (1989).

Phillips, Hugh. "The War against Terrorism in Late Imperial and Early Soviet Russia." *Enemies of Humanity: The Nineteenth-Century War on Terrorism,* ed. Isaac Land. New York: Palgrave Macmillan, 2008.

Pipes, Richard. *Degaev Affair: Terror and Treason in Tsarist Russia.* New Haven, CT: Yale University Press, 2003.

Pipes, Richard. *Struve: Liberal on the Right.* Cambridge, MA: Harvard University Press, 1980.

Politkovskaia, Anna. *Putin's Russia: Life in a Failing Democracy.* New York: Metropolitan Books, 2005.

Pomper, Philip. "Russian Revolutionary Terrorism." *Terrorism in Context.* University Park: Pennsylvania State University Press, 1995.

Posner, Richard A. Public Intellectuals: A Study of Decline. Cambridge, MA: Harvard University Press, 2001.

Pujals, Sandra. "The Accidental Revolutionary in the Russian Revolution: Impersonation, Criminal Activity, and Revolutionary Mythology in the Early Soviet Period, 1905–1935." *Revolutionary Russia* 22, no. 2 (2009).

Radzinskii, Edvard. *Alexander II: The Last Great Tsar.* New York: Free Press, 2005.

Rancour-Laferriere, Daniel. *The Slave Soul of Russia: Moral Masochism and the Cult of Suffering.* New York: New York University Press, 1996.

Rapoport, David C. ed. *Inside Terrorist Organizations.* London: Powell's Books, 1988.

Reich, Walter, ed. *Origins of Terrorism: Psychologies, Ideologies, Theologies, States of Mind.* Washington, DC: Johns Hopkins University Press, 1998.

Reuter, Christoph. *My Life Is a Weapon.* Princeton, NJ: Princeton University Press, 2002.

Riha, Thomas. *The Russian European: Paul Miliukov in Russian Politics.* Notre Dame, IN: University of Notre Dame Press, 1969.

Rodby, Kirk. *The Dark Heart of Utopia: Sexuality, Ideology, and the Totalitarian Movement.* New York-Bloomington, IN: iUniverse, Inc., 2009.

Rosenthal, Bernice Glatzer. *New Myth, New World: From Nietzsche to Stalinism*. University Park: Pennsylvania State University Press, 2002.
Rosenthal, Bernice Glatzer, ed. *The Occult in Russian and Soviet Culture*. Ithaca, NY: Cornell University Press, 1997.
Ryan, Kiernan. *New Historicism and Cultural Materialism: A Reader*. New York: Hodder Arnold, 1996.
Sakwa, Richard. *The Rise and Fall of the Soviet Union, 1917–1991*. New York: Routledge, 1999.
Salib, Emad. "Suicide Terrorism: A Case of Folie à Plusieurs?" *British Journal of Psychiatry* 182 (2003).
Schapiro, Leonard. *Russian Studies*. New York: Viking, 1987.
Schoenman, Ralph. *The Hidden History of Zionism*. Santa Barbara, CA: Veritas Press: 1988.
Schweitzer, Yoram, ed. *Female Suicide Bombers: Dying for Equality?* The Jaffee Center for Strategic Studies (JCSS). Tel Aviv: Tel Aviv University, 2006.
Segal, B. M. *Drunken Society Alcohol Abuse and Alcoholism in the Soviet Union: A Comparative Study*. New York: Hippocrene Books, 1990.
Shahak, Israel. *Jewish History, Jewish Religion: The Weight of Three Thousand Years*. London: Pluto Press, 2002.
Shavit, Ari. "Mister Nice Guy." *Haarets Magazine*, June 14, 2001.
Souvarine, Boris. *Stalin: A Critical Study of Bolshevism*. New York, 1939.
Spence, Richard B. *Boris Savinkov: Renegade on the Left*. Boulder, CO: Columbia University Press, 1991.
Stern, Fritz Richard. *Politics of Cultural Despair: A Study in the Rise of the Germanic Ideology*. Berkeley: University of California, 1974.
Tobias, Henry Jack. *Jewish Bund in Russia from Its Origins to 1905*. Stanford, CA: Stanford University Press, 1972.
Tolstoi, Aleksei. *Ordeal*. Moscow: Progress, 1953.
Tracy, Robert, ed. *Osip Mandelstam's Stone*. Princeton, NJ: Princeton University Press, 1981.
Trotsky, Leon. *Literature and Revolution*. New York: Russell & Russell, 1957.
Tumarkin, Nina. *Lenin Lives! The Lenin Cult in Soviet Russia*. Cambridge, MA: Harvard University Press, 1997.
Turgenev, Ivan. *Fathers and Children*. New York: Dover Publications, 1998.
van Henten, Jan Willen, and Friedrich Avemarie. *Martyrdom and Noble Death*. London and New York: Routledge, 2002.
Varvin, Sverre, and Vamik D. Volkan, eds., *Violence or Dialogue? Psychoanalytic Insights on Terror and Terrorism*. New York: The International Psychoanalytical Association, 2003.
Volkan, Vamik D. *Need to Have Enemies and Allies: From Clinical Practice to International Relationships*. Northvale, New Jersey-London: Jason Aronson, 1988.
Warth, Robert D. "Cheka." *The Modern Encyclopedia of Russian and Soviet History* (MERSH), vol. 6., ed. Joseph L. Wieczynski, et al. Academic International Press, 1996–2003, 218.
Wilson, Edmund. *To the Finland Station: A Study in the Writing and Acting of History*. New York: Harcourt Brace, 1940.
Wolfgang, J. Mommsen, and Gerhard Hirshfeld, eds. *Social Protest, Violence, and Terror in Nineteenth- and Twentieth-Century Europe*. New York: St. Martin's, 1982.
Worobec, Christine D. Peasant Russia: Family and Community in the Post-Emancipation Period. Princeton, NJ: Princeton University Press, 1991.
Zweig, Paul. *The Heresy of Self-Love: A Study of Subversive Individualism*. New York-London: Basic Books, 1968.

Index

About the Author

ANNA GEIFMAN (Ph.D., Harvard University) has written *Thou Shalt Kill: Revolutionary Terrorism in Russia, 1894-1917* (Princeton University Press, 1993) and *Entangled in Terror: The Azef Affair and the Russian Revolution* (Rowman & Littlefeld Publishers, Inc., 2000). She is the editor of *Russia under the Last Tsar: Opposition and Subversion, 1894–1917* (Blackwell, 1999) and the author of a psychohistorical essay, *La mort sera votre dieu: du nihilisme russe au terrorisme islamiste* («La Table Ronde:» Paris, 2005). Geifman is Professor of History at Boston University, where she teaches undergraduate and graduate classes on imperial Russia, the USSR, psychohistory, and modern terrorism. She is also a Research Associate in the Political Science Department at the University of Bar-Ilan, Israel.